The Mobilization and Demobilization of Middle-Class Revolt

Adopting Argentina's popular uprisings against neoliberalism including the 2001–02 rebellion and subsequent mass protests as a case study, *The Mobilization and Demobilization of Middle-Class Revolt* analyzes two decades of longitudinal research (1995–2018), including World Bank and *Latinobarómeter* household survey data, along with participant interviews, to explore why nonpolitically active middle-class citizens engage in radical protest movements, and why they eventually demobilize. In particular it asks, how do they become politicized and resist economic and political crises, along with their own hardship?

Theoretically informed by Gramsci's notions of hegemony, ideology and class consciousness, Ozarow posits that to affect profound and lasting social change, multisectoral alliances and sustainable mobilizing vehicles are required to maintain radical progressive movements beyond periods of crisis. With the Argentinian revolt understood to be the ideological forbearer to the autonomist-inspired uprisings which later emerged, comparisons are drawn with experiences in the USA, Spain, Greece UK, Iceland and the Middle East, as well as 1990s contexts in South Africa and Russia. Such a comparative analysis helps understand how contextual factors shape distinctive struggling middle-class citizen responses to external shocks.

This book will be of immense value to students, activists and theorists of social change in North America, in Europe and globally.

Daniel Ozarow is a Senior Lecturer at Middlesex University, London. He is Chair of the Argentina Research Network and Co-editor of two books: *Argentina since the 2001 Crisis: Recovering Reclaiming the Future* (2014) and *De la Crisis de 2001 al Kirchnerismo: Cambios y Continuidades* (2016). He researches on comparative citizen responses to financial crises in Europe and Latin America, workers' self-management, cooperatives, alternative postcrisis production models, transnational labor movements, and how both personal and national debt is resisted. Daniel has recently been published in academic journals, such as *Economy and Society, Sociology, Labor History* and *Latin American Research Review*. He blends his academic research with political activism and is Chair of Jubilee Debt Campaign's Academic Advisory Network and a member of Action for Argentina UK. He regularly features as a political commentator on British and Argentinian affairs and has appeared on television, radio and newspapers, including *Telesur, C5N, Al Jazeera, TN, Radio Nacional Argentina, The Conversation, Labour Briefing, Telám* and *Open Democracy*.

Routledge Studies in Latin American Politics

https://www.routledge.com/Routledge-Studies-in-Latin-American-Politics/book-series/RSLAP

The Mobilization and Demobilization of Middle-Class Revolt

Comparative Insights from Argentina

Daniel Ozarow

Routledge
Taylor & Francis Group
New York London

First published 2019
by Routledge
52 Vanderbilt Avenue, New York, NY 10017

and by Routledge
2 Park Square, Milton Park, Abingdon, Oxon, OX14 4RN

First issued in paperback 2020

Routledge is an imprint of the Taylor & Francis Group, an informa business

© 2019 Taylor & Francis

Library of Congress Cataloging-in-Publication Data
Names: Ozarow, Daniel, author.
Title: The mobilization and demobilization of middle-class revolt : comparative insights from Argentina / Daniel Ozarow.
Description: New York, NY : Routledge, 2019. |
Series: Routledge studies in Latin American politics ; 28 |
Includes bibliographical references and index.
Identifiers: LCCN 2018054411 (print) |
LCCN 2019003444 (ebook) | ISBN 9781351123068 (Master) |
ISBN 9781351123051 (Adobe) | ISBN 9781351123044 (ePub) |
ISBN 9781351123037 (Mobi) | ISBN 9780815358183 (hbk) |
ISBN 9781351123068 (ebk)
Subjects: LCSH: Middle class—Political activity—Argentina. |
Argentina—Politics and government—2002– | Social change—Argentina—History—21st century.
Classification: LCC HT690.A7 (ebook) |
LCC HT690.A7 .O93 2019 (print) | DDC 305.5/50982—dc23
LC record available at https://lccn.loc.gov/2018054411

ISBN 13: 978-0-367-67166-2 (pbk)
ISBN 13: 978-0-8153-5818-3 (hbk)

Typeset in Times New Roman
by codeMantra

Contents

Lists of Figures

List of Tables

List of Abbreviations

ABAE	Argentinian Association of Defrauded Bank Depositors
ARI	Support for an Egalitarian Republic
ATE	State Workers' Association
AUH	Universal Child Benefit
CABA	Autonomous City of Buenos Aires
CAME	Argentinian Federation of Medium-Sized Companies
CC	Civic Coalition
CEPAL	Economic Commission for Latin America and the Caribbean
CGT	General Confederation of Labour
COINAGRO	Inter-Cooperative Agricultural Federation of Argentina
CRA	Rural Confederation of Argentina
CTA-A	Autonomous Argentine Workers' Central
CTA-T	Argentine Workers' Central
CTD	Unemployed Workers' Collective
CTEP	Confederation of Popular Economy Workers
ECB	European Central Bank
ENARSA	Argentina Energy Plc
EU	European Union
EPH	Permanent Household Survey
FAA	Agrarian Federation of Argentina
FIT	Frente de Izquierda y de los Trabajadores
FPDS	Darío Santillán Popular Front
FRENAPO	National Coalition Against Poverty
FREPASO	Front for a Country in Solidarity
GDP	Gross Domestic Product
ILO	International Labour Organization
IMF	International Monetary Fund
INDEC	National Institute for Statistics and Census
ISCA	Social Impact of the Crisis in Argentina
ISI	Import-Substitution Industrialisation
MTD	Movement of Unemployed Workers

MERCOSUR	Southern Common Market
NSMT	New Social Movement Theory
OECD	Organisation of Economic Cooperation and Development
ODSA	Observatory for Argentina's Social Debt
OPSM	Public Opinion, Services and Markets
PAAA	The Peoples' Assembly Against Austerity
PPT	Political Process Theory
PRO	Republican Proposal
RCT	Rational Choice Theory
RDT	Relative Deprivation Theory
RMT	Resource Mobilization Theory
SIDE	State Secretariat of Intelligence
SRA	Rural Society of Argentina
SUTEBA	United Education Workers Union
TUC	Trade Union Congress
UCA	Catholic University of Argentina
UCR	Radical Civic Union
YPF	Fiscal Oilfields

Acknowledgments

I first stepped foot in Argentina in 2003 when I traveled from London to Buenos Aires and Mendoza as a volunteer aid worker with the British NGO, WJR and our local partner, the American Joint Distribution Committee. The challenge was a difficult one. To work with structurally impoverished communities in the Villa 31 shantytown, as well as to provide medical, emotional and educational support to the recently pauperized middle class, and assist them to reconstruct their lives in the wake of one of the worst economic and political crises in world history, which Argentinians faced in 2001–02. During those six months, I fell in love with the country. Most of all with the warmth with which I was welcomed by the people and the resilience, solidarity and creativity that they demonstrated in confronting their situations to emerge from the abyss. I was also captivated by how, during December 2001 and throughout 2002, people united in their millions on the streets regardless of their background or class to rise up against the neoliberal economic model and the corruption-ridden political representatives who had failed them, to demand *¡que se vayan todos!* – that they should all go. But many of them also came together to imagine then construct a new, more democratic and egalitarian society via the neighborhood assemblies, worker-recovered companies, barter clubs, participatory budgets and other experiments in participatory democracy and alternative economic models they were involved in. I was hooked and have realized over the years that as British people and Argentinians, we have far more in common than that which divides us. I also met my Argentinian wife, Tamy during my first visit there. Argentina became a source of intrigue and a passion. Two Masters theses, a PhD (upon which parts of this book are based), and two edited books dedicated to Argentina later, here I am with this monograph.

There are innumerable people whom I have met during the 12-year project that this book has entailed and unfortunately I cannot thank all of them here. First and foremost to my wife and my young son Lennon, for their love, patience and support. I also owe my mum and dad a great deal as they have always been there for me and taught me the values of learning from others and to possess an inquisitive mind. My mother-in-law's hospitality and the support of my father-in-law during visits to Buenos Aires were invaluable to me. I would like to thank Natalja Mortensen, Commissioning Editor at Routledge, for being a wonderful person to work with during the publication process, to Charlie Baker her Editorial Assistant, and to Hannah Brown for reading and commenting on my drafts. I owe a debt of gratitude to my PhD supervisors at Middlesex University, London; Professor Richard Croucher, Dr. Leandro Sepulveda and Dr. Sarah Bradshaw and to the University in general for my PhD studentship and fieldwork visits. Feedback from my PhD external examiners Professor Miguel Martinez Lucio and Professor Patrick Paul Walsh was also invaluable. Thank you to Professor Maxine Molyneux was an early source of inspiration and continues to support me over the years. I must also acknowledge the financial support of the European Commission which funded my final fieldwork visit under the International EU-Latin American Network for Comparative Analysis of Social Inequalities (INCASI) project no. GA-691004 and its Horizon 2020-Marie Curie-Research and Innovation Staff Exchange (RISE) program. I should also mention two marvelous organizations here in the UK which have demonstrated enthusiasm for my work, Action for Argentina UK and the Argentina Research Network.

I truly value the guidance that the following people have provided me in writing this book. Dr. Ezequiel Adamovsky, Dr. Gabriel Kessler and Dr. Maristella Svampa have been academic mentors to me in terms of understanding Argentina's middle class. To Isidro Aduríz for his advice on working with the ISCA database and to Maria Mazzoni, Jorge Rabey, Juliana Di Tullio, Dr. Fabian Triskier, Alejandra Goldschmidt, Sergio Postel, Sergio Widder and Viviana Bendersky for allowing me to conduct key informant interviews with them. The research conducted in this book would not have been possible if the dozens of interviewees I spoke to around the country had not invited me into their homes and shared their experiences with me, so to them I am truly grateful.

Finally, I would like to dedicate this book to my late grandmother Sybil, who sadly passed away during my most recent visit to Argentina when writing up the final manuscript and also to the memory of the 39 fallen victims of the December 2001 uprisings.

¡Venceremos!
Daniel Ozarow,
London, October 2018

1 Middle-Class Resistance to Proletarianization and Neoliberal Crisis from Buenos Aires to Wall Street

'Why is it always us who have to suffer?' She yelled indignantly. 'The common people, the lower middle class I mean. If war is declared, if the Franc is devalued, if there is unemployment or a revolution or any type of crisis, everyone else is able to work things out so that they land on their feet. *We* are the ones who end up getting crushed! We always pay for everyone else's mistakes.' Enraged, she continued; 'Of course they don't fear us. The workers fight back, the rich are powerful. We are the lambs to the slaughter.

Irène Némirovsky, *French Suite*, 2007

We are living through extraordinary political times. In the aftermath of what the IMF (2009) described as the deepest global depression since the Great Depression of the 1930s, millions of "ordinary people" from the squeezed middle class[1] are taking to the streets to engage in rebellion against acute declines in their material conditions and to demand greater democratic accountability. While set in Nazi-occupied France in the 1940s, the quote from Némirovsky's novel above expresses not only many of the frustrations of those in the middle class at the time, but also reflects the myth of middle-class docility in the face of adversity – that had become internalized among such citizens over decades and which continued to exist until her book's year of publication (2007). This was also the eve of an internationalized middle-class revolt when from North America to Europe, to Australasia and Latin America to the Middle East, they started to fight back collectively against the seemingly perpetual "age of austerity," shrinking public-sector spending and fundamental welfare state reform. These characteristics combined and were linked to processes of neoliberal globalization such as outsourcing, labor flexibilization, deskilling, the replacement of highly qualified jobs with technology and social costs, including rising divorce rates that left the middle-class facing an existential crisis. The revolt ended this myth of docility, but these processes have seen middle-class citizens experience eroding household incomes and real-terms salaries, decimated pensions, unemployment, declining social mobility and increasing job insecurity. For a decade, politicians, economists and sociologists have evoked the specter of the disappearance of the middle class. This possibility has intensified since the 2007 subprime mortgage crash and credit crunch in North America (Warren, 2007). While in July 2016, the UK Institute for Fiscal Studies reported that "middle income families with children now more closely resemble the poor than in the past." In the global north, many – especially the young – have had enough of the broken promises that obtaining a degree and working hard will land them a prosperous future. For instance, in 2013 unemployment rates peaked at 64% and 53% in Greece and Spain, respectively, according to Eurostat (2018). Meanwhile in the global south, the contradiction between growing choices as *consumers* in the free market and limited political freedoms as *citizens* has become increasingly stark. In both cases, it has unleashed rebellion and sometimes even revolution (Mason, 2012).

While accompanied by traditional industrial unrest in several national contexts, it has been the highly educated, yet unemployed or low-income earning "squeezed" urban middle-class citizens who have participated and often spearheaded these movements. Among these global uprisings are the *Indignados* protest camps in Spain, the *Kínima Aganaktisménon-Politón* demonstrations in Syntagma Square and across Greece, the *Occupy Wall Street* movement in the USA (all since 2011), the Gezi Park occupation and protests in Turkey in 2013, mass strikes and demonstrations in France, Hungary, Romania, Bulgaria and Russia (2011–18), and, most remarkably, the Arab Spring (2011) which actually toppled governments in Tunisia, Egypt and Libya.[2] Each national movement has manifested a number of characteristics that involve the resurgence and renewal of historic collective repertoires of action in contemporary form, including the occupation of "public space" as a protest method, innovative, nonhierarchical, horizontal organizing structures and direct democracy. The "assembly" and consensus-building have become the key decision-making mechanisms and the initial rejection of interference by political parties or other forms of institutionalization is a further cross-national feature (Parkinson, 2012).

Once these movements have won initial concessions from political elites or it has been repressed or defeated, their subsequent trajectories usually involved demobilization, morphing into small-scale community projects or political fragmentation in the longer term. Their lack of a sustainable mobilizing vehicle after mass, multisectoral collective actions following periods of political or economic crisis is a key factor in this demobilization, with the possible exception of Spain, where *Podemos* became the home of many participants in the *Indignados* protests (2011) and has become part of today's political landscape. In Iceland, participants in the *Kitchenware Revolution* which overthrew the Geir Haarde government in early 2009 following its political and financial crisis, were central to rewriting the national constitution which was voted on by the population.

These demands were soon institutionalized and established the blueprint for the country's social, political and economic renaissance.

Meanwhile, the limitations and dangers faced by such movements in terms of their impact on high politics are demonstrated by the capitulation of the Syriza government in Greece which began as a "movement of the squares" but whose hopes following the extraordinarily brave "Oxi" referendum vote (which rejected the bailout conditions as a solution to the government's debt crisis) were eventually crushed by the European Commission, International Monetary Fund (IMF) and the European Central Bank (ECB). Meanwhile in the USA, the initial excitement generated by *Occupy Wall Street* genuinely helped to reshape political discourse in terms of the need to drastically reduce acute social inequality, the power of the corporations over citizens lives' and for urgent environmental action. This was encapsulated in the election campaign of Bernie Sanders, which eventually petered out with the election of President Donald Trump and the return of right-wing populism. Nevertheless, some of the economic demands were translated (or perhaps co-opted) onto the new administration's anti-neoliberal, protectionist and counter-political establishment agenda.

While numerous texts have analyzed the mobilization and demobilization of these cross-national movements (Chomsky, 2012; Della Porta *et al.*, 2017; Weiner and López, 2018), this book is different. It focuses specifically on the question of how middle-class citizens deal with dramatic and sudden declines in material well-being and the threat of proletarianization following either external economic or internal financial shocks. It then asks why, under such circumstances, some become politicized and resist by joining social movements and collective actions while others confine their responses to individual coping strategies.

Based upon analysis of survey data of those who were originally pauperized during its political and economic crisis in 2001–02, embeddedness in middle-class communities, observation and interviews with non-activist middle-class citizens during a field study in 2007, 2011 and 2016, Argentina is adopted as a case study. Its citizens' rebellion during 2001–02 becomes the focus and the book adopts a Gramscian approach, using his theories of hegemony, ideology and false consciousness, to detail the results of this mixed-methods sociological study into proletarianized or struggling middle-class participation in contemporary protest movements. This 12-year project charts the trajectories of a group of what the literature calls "new urban poor," or struggling middle-class citizens. It explores the political, economic and cultural decisions they took along with their social attitudes and political involvement and how they fluctuated over time. Interview participants also reflect on their memories of the social uprisings of the time and their own involvement. While avoiding the pitfalls of methodological individualism, it also draws upon other elements of social movement theory to analyze the in-group responses of this stratum and the diachronic patterns of behavior they have pursued in Argentina. It seeks to understand how participants made sense of their own pauperization and downward social mobility, how aspects of their "rights" that this citizenship bestowed were being violated and how this affected their social attitudes, opinions, own position vis-à-vis other social sectors and ultimately their political activism. It also seeks their reflections upon the 2001–02 revolt so as to identify whether the radical ideals it espoused were still advocated by participants many years later, or if they draw more critical understandings of them.

It is clear is that those at the forefront of political resistance against the worst excesses of the financial crisis in recent years are no longer simply the organized labor movement or the socially disenfranchised. Although examples such as the wave of industrial unrest in China (the country with the world's largest working class) since 2010 and the UK riots by marginalized sectors in 2011 demonstrate that both these socio-economic groups remain important respective actors in terms of social contention, it is those from the middle class who have either recently become poor or who are currently unemployed or underemployed form a significant and growing political force on the streets and in public space.

The Struggling Middle Class as Political Agents

New urban poor citizens have not traditionally been understood as political agents, nor have they been studied in terms of their political radicalization or collective identity as a social stratum. Indeed, ever since its conceptualization as an area of academic research three decades ago, studies have focused almost entirely on their individual self-improvement strategies (Katzman, 1989, Minujín *et al.*, 1993). A range of disciplinary approaches have been employed to understand how middle-class individuals cope with impoverishment and proletarianization. Work has assessed the psychological (Masseroni and Sauane, 2002), cultural, civic (Minujín, 2007; Adamovsky, 2009) and, above all, economic behavior they exhibit. For instance, Dagdeviren, Donoghue and Meier (2017) noted that in the aftermath of the 2008 crisis in Europe, the "new poor" were poorly equipped to cope with their newfound pauperization and rapid social descent relative to traditionally impoverished communities. They were often more stigmatized and hid their difficulties due to the sense of shame.

"Economic" responses themselves may take one of two forms, either as "adaptive" responses – for example, how consumer behavior is modified to cope with macroeconomic meltdown (Feijóo, 2003; Zurawicki and Braidot, 2005) – or "active" strategies by which human, social and cultural capitals accumulated during their nonpoor pasts are utilized to either explore self-employment opportunities (Feijóo, 2003; Kessler and Di Virgilio, 2008) or utilize social networks to gain labor market advantages

(Lokshin and Yemtsov, 2004). Some work has found that those with the strongest qualifications, networks, communication skills and money often enjoy *least* success in refashioning their lives after pauperization and unemployment (Gabriel, Gray and Goregaokar, 2013), especially if they accept dominant discourses about age and "irreversible decline" (Ainsworth and Hardy, 2009). Meanwhile, Mandemakers and Monden (2013:73) found that losing a high-status job may restrict the practical value of the resources one possesses due to the stress incurred.

Kessler and Di Virgilio's (2008) eminent study of the extent to which newly impoverished middle-class citizens are able to utilize their superior social and cultural capitals (that were accumulated during their nonpoor pasts) to recover their socioeconomic status once they have become pauperized helped to frame understanding about how these differ to those of the long-term poor. Later, Ozarow (2015) found that these capitals may actually act as "poisoned chalices" in terms of recovering upward mobility and financial recovery.

However, these studies have neglected to examine how and why poverty and proletarianization is also resisted through engagement in collective and protest responses, especially during periods of economic crisis (Richards and Gelleny, 2006:777). Indeed, the postcrisis milieu suggests that protest responses are actually widely practiced as a reaction against social descent and pauperization. Therefore, instead of focusing exclusively on their *economic* self-improvement responses, this book seeks to understand why citizens do not merely react to their deteriorating personal circumstances that financial shocks cause by acting solely as economic agents and rational decision-makers who carry out private and *economic* responses, as neoliberal advocates assume.

The focus here is on the domestic agitation (collective protest) that such crises provoke, and on asking why and how newly impoverished or proletarianized people decide to join protest movements to confront their descent.

Myths of Domination

Until the 2008 global crisis, the prevalence of two myths has meant that the potential for protest responses from the middle class against their hardship was rendered unnecessary and irrelevant for so-called Western societies. Equally, these myths were propagated by politicians, mass media and other cultural institutions and so served to limit the possibilities for affected citizens themselves to protest their deteriorating economic conditions. This resulted in collective responses faded from the sociological imagination.

The first myth was that of the "eternal economic boom." It was declared that in the advanced capitalist economies, major macroeconomic shocks had become a thing of the past. If there were, therefore, no grounds to suppose that sudden and widespread outbreaks of impoverishment could occur, nor could mass political resistance to capitalism. For example, following 16 successive years of annual growth in the USA and the UK between 1993 and 2008, it was widely believed among politicians, academics and economists that the US-led housing market bubble and deficit-led boom would continue unabated in the West (Wade, 2009b). When the subprime mortgage crisis began to hit the financial sector, Alan Greenspan, Head of the Federal Reserve, admitted that he "really didn't get it until late in 2005." While on the other side of the Atlantic, between the two of them alone, former British Prime Minister Tony Blair and then Chancellor of the Exchequer Gordon Brown publicly made no less than 16 separate references to the fact that the Labour government had "ended the cycle of boom and bust" between 1997 and 2007 (HM Treasury Records; House of Commons Hansard Archive and Labour Party Annual Conference Archive).

However, the credibility of this myth disintegrated during the current global economic crisis. Moreover, based on the premises that (i) the impact of the crisis is expected to endure for a generation, in the form of low growth in Western societies according to the IMF (2015) and (ii) soaring national debt will lead public spending cuts in the long term, it is almost certain that conspicuous consumption – a key tenet of middle-class identity construction – will be significantly curtailed for a generation. According to a recent Eurostat report (2018), 24% of the European Union's (EU) nonpoor population (or 122 million citizens) are currently at risk of poverty or social exclusion, in addition to the 9% who are already materially deprived.

The second myth was that of middle-class political docility. It was believed that even if something were to go "terribly wrong" and the middle class were to experience mass pauperization or downward mobility, they would "go quietly" unlike the organized working class, confining themselves to private and passive response measures. Extra-parliamentary middle-class discontent would be channeled through campaigning structures such as established nongovernmental organizations (NGOs) or would be reduced to protest voting at elections. For example, the June 2008 *Euromonitor International* Report (Eghbal, 2008) on how Western Europe's middle class has been squeezed by inflation, stagnant wages and the credit crunch concluded that because "middle-class workers" are less likely to be trade union members, they "are most likely to express their frustration through the ballot box."

Neoliberalism and its advocates understand humans as exclusively rational economic agents and thus they tend to ignore or dismiss the social and political impacts of economic shocks by focusing purely on economic coping strategies at individual or household level. Arguments by those such as Phelps Brown (1990) who has suggested that there has been a shift away from the principles of collectivism toward acquisitive individualism in terms of how people defend themselves against attacks on their material conditions need to be scrutinized. First, due to their selectivity in national examples that they refer to in reaching such a conclusion.

Cross-national contextual differences can help explain whether pauperized middle-class citizens display a tendency to respond to their circumstances in terms of either self-improvement or protest actions. This can depend upon the extent to which the respective ruling elites are able to enact defensive strategies of control in order to maintain consent to rule from the population. To use Hirschman's (1970) terminology, it must be noted that the preference for the struggling middle class enact "loyalty actions" (those that support the existing regime by seeking to preserve the status quo) or "exit actions" (whereby citizens merely adapt to the changing situation in a politically "passive" way), rather than "voice responses" – by which they actively speak out against the policy of the ruling regime, or oppose it through protest – can largely be explained by the mitigating power structures and political processes that are specific to national context in question.

Cross-National Middle-Class Resistance

Certainly, national cases exist whereby the mass pauperization of the middle class *has* been met with political docility. For example, in South Africa in the post-Apartheid era and in particular in light of the 1998 Employment Equity Act. The hundreds of thousands of white "new urban poor" citizens who lost their jobs as a result of this "affirmative action" legislation which imposed a legal obligation upon companies to favor black job applicants, were paradoxically greeted with "anticipatory compliance," despite causing great anxiety and resentment (Kanya, 1997:32). Far from outwardly protesting their anger, the overwhelming response from highly skilled white professional South Africans came in the form of "exit strategies," namely, emigration or early retirement. Between 1995 and 2005, according to a survey by the South African Institute of Race Relations (2006), more than one million South Africans emigrated, citing the lack of employment opportunities for whites as a key reason. However, this lack of political resistance to confront their collective downward social mobility needs to be contextualized in a society where these policies were universally comprehended and respected as a remedial strategy to address the legal and historical exclusion of the black majority.

Meanwhile in Russia, both following the fall of the Berlin Wall and transition to capitalism after 1991 and in the wake of its 1998 financial crisis, a significant part of the middle class was afflicted by the painful experience of proletarianization. Yet, the defensive strategies which were enacted by the ruling elite (to break the public-sector strikes and roadblocks by teachers, doctors, scientists and other professionals) included a combination of physical coercion and appeasement. Compromise figure,

Yevgeny Primakov was appointed Prime Minister in 1998 in order to unite the country's political elites and weaken resistance during the latter period. In addition, the fundamentally minimalist form of democracy that evolved during the transition from state communism to capitalism in Russia has resulted in a weak civil society emerging and acute lack of available opportunities for the struggling middle class to manifest their political discontent. A lack of credible alternatives to capitalism – given the discrediting of communism – and an overriding sense of powerlessness (due to the geographical vastness of the country, a lack of suitable mobilizing vehicles and the relative popularity of President Putin, who was initially appointed Prime Minister in 1999) led to widespread alienation among the country's new urban poor and struggling middle class. Many of those in these ranks had held middle- or high-ranking Communist Party positions (effectively the social elite under the USSR) or roles in public-sector professions who had been made redundant after 1991. Rather than fueling action, discontent with their own quality of life after the 1998 crisis translated into either self-blame or political apathy among Russian citizens who principally sought and continue to seek private solutions to collective problems. It was found that only 3% were prepared to join a protest march at the time and just 8% would sign a petition. Where "voice" was expressed, it was manifest "silently," through the ballot box by 25% of those surveyed (Willie, 2001:222).

However, evidence from numerous other countries in recent years demonstrates that impoverished middle-class citizens *do* engage in political protest actions alongside simply pursuing economic self-improvement strategies. These multiple instances of mass protest place Phelps Brown's argument into doubt. For example, Iceland was the most developed country in the world in 2007 (UN Human Development Index) and its people were the happiest (World Values Survey, 2006). Median household income was almost US$70,000 – 1.6 times that in the USA – and there was a weak political culture of large-scale protest movements, other than overcontingent issues such as the 1975 women's strike. Largely due to its sheer affluence, it seemed like the last place in the world to expect a middle-class uprising. Yet in late 2008, plagued by economic meltdown, and collapse of its three major banks, tens of thousands lost their savings, became unemployed or plunged into poverty as salaries plummeted, the currency devalued and an IMF stabilization plan was implemented. Yet under the umbrella campaign group "Voices of the People," 10,000 largely impoverished middle-class people regularly took to streets during late 2008 and 2009, and this culturally placid people overthrew the government. In a country of just 315,000 people, this size of protest is the equivalent of 2 million in the UK and of 10 million in the USA. These protests became known as the Kitchenware Revolution because of the symbolic banging of saucepans, a practice adopted from Argentina which has become a symbol of middle-class resistance to impoverishment (Wade, 2009a). The rebellion in Iceland also shocked Europe's ruling elites who finally started to realize that they couldn't take struggling middle-class docility for granted, prompting France's then President Nicolas Sarkozy to exclaim, "we can't have a European May '68 for Christmas!" (Phillips, 2008).

The *Indignados* movement made up of largely white-collar, young and highly qualified people who occupied city squares throughout Spain in 2011 and 2012, and the rebellion against austerity and pauperization in Greece, are other cases in point that have laid this second myth of middle-class docility to rest. The cases of Argentina, Iceland, Spain and Greece indicate that as Galbraith warned in *The Culture of Contentment* (1992), the middle class in industrialized societies will only continue to tolerate gross income inequality and the prolonged destitution of what he called "the functional underclass" for as long as it was in their self-interests to do so.

Further, Latin America's recent history demonstrates that struggling middle-class citizens do not simply resign themselves to their deteriorating economic circumstances by seeking self-improvement measures, but join collective protest movements too. For example, Venezuela experienced its own episode of new poor radicalism. When the neoliberal reforms that were implemented by President Carlos Andrés Pérez in the 1990s pushed hundreds of thousands into poverty, the limited availability of self-help opportunities, including employment, increased the relative attractiveness of protest as a response for its pauperized and jobless middle class. Many of the middle class frequently participated in roadblocks, building occupations and other collective protest actions.

This situation has repeated itself during the severe economic crisis and hyperinflation to hit Venezuela under President Nicolas Maduro's governments since 2013, with thousands of struggling middle-class citizens joining mass anti-government protests, including the sporadic use of violence. Meanwhile in Uruguay's own economic crisis in 2002/03, the new poor, especially those who lost savings, were also at the forefront of its protest movement. In Brazil, the large-scale protests against the Confederation Cup in 2013 (sparked by an increase in bus fares) then broadened in their demands in subsequent years to target the public money spent on the Rio Olympics, alleged corruption former President "Lula" Da Silva and President Dilma Rousseff against whom impeachment charges were sought. Amid an economic crisis, the millions who took part included a significant proportion of middle-class protestors who were struggling to make ends meet.

Why Argentina?

In January 2002, signs mysteriously began to appear in the *Villa 31* shanty town in Buenos Aires, ironically proclaiming "welcome middle class!"

During its 2001 economic crisis, the largest ever national debt default in history occurred when unemployment reached 25%, gross domestic product (GDP) fell by one-fifth and poverty soared to 54% (INDEC, 2018). Millions of mainly highly educated citizens became impoverished and the middle class was virtually extinguished overnight. Yet, the economic crisis was accompanied by a crisis of political representation. Many of the struggling middle class participated in the enormous popular revolt and protest movement in the year that followed, and Argentina became the ideological forbearer of all these multisectoral but struggling middle class led counter-neoliberal resistance movements. The country soon became an incubator for radical experiments in direct democracy, horizontal decision-making, the occupation of public space and citizens' self-management in what was known as the *que se vayan todos* (Get rid of the lot of them) revolt. This was named after the popular cry during the birth of the movement on the streets of Argentina's urban centers on 19 and 20 December 2001 which removed four presidents in two weeks. Amid the chaos and trauma, there lay hope.

There was widespread recognition that the neoliberal model of President Carlos Menem (1989–99) and then Fernando de la Rúa's (1999–2001) governments had been a disaster given the misery and inequality they had generated. The corruption-ridden, representative democratic system had been exhausted as a project, and the bourgeoning protest movements sought to replace this model with a fairer, more participatory society based around social solidarity (Adamovsky, 2009). Intriguingly, the organizing strategies, tactics and symbolic middle-class tools of protest that came to life during those days were subsequently adopted in the autonomist-inspired uprisings which later emerged in Wall Street, Greece, Spain, Iceland, Turkey and elsewhere.

In Argentina's urban centers, narratives of contention and the performance of class among impoverished middle class citizens were represented in popular chants, *cacerolazos* (pots-and-pans protests), and in the neighborhood assemblies' discourse. These focused around solidarity with "the other"; in particular, between progressive elements of the middle-class and structurally poor and working-class movements, including the *piqueteros* (unemployed workers movement) (Svampa and Corral, 2006).

As shall be elaborated upon later, what made Argentina's revolt unique was how the scale of economic misery and collapse of political legitimacy generated widespread solidarity between millions of previously unpoliticized, struggling middle-class citizens with blue-collar workers, unemployed and long-term impoverished sectors. It was arguably the closest instance of a bottom-up, leaderless attempt at revolution in modern times. As a heterogeneous actor both socioeconomically and politically, there were of course many within the middle class who took part in the collective actions of the 1990s, 2001–02, and the major protests of 2003–18 and others who didn't at all. However, some generalizations can be inferred.

Although many among the struggling middle-class ranks (particularly, teachers, civil servants and small and medium-sized business owners) had participated in protest movements against IMF-imposed conditionality that entailed structural adjustment in return for loans during the 1990s (Adamovsky, 2009), the turning point that transformed many non-activists to join the protests came when President de la Rúa declared a State of Siege on 19 December 2001 in response to widespread lootings and food riots, especially in Greater Buenos Aires. However, his decision merely served to evoke memories of the despised civil-military dictatorship (1976–83), prompting hundreds of thousands of citizens (including many pauperized middle-class citizens) to spill out onto the streets to express their fury as the economic crisis descended into a crisis of political legitimacy. Demanding the overthrow of the entire political establishment, the following two days marked the first major *Cacerolazo* protests, which were neither preplanned nor organized by any particular political party or trade union.[3] Despite the brutal reaction of the state and the murder of 39 protestors by the riot police and shop owners, as portrayed in the moving documentary *39 El Documental, Las Víctimas de 2001* (Dir. Velázquez, 2017), it was during these events that many Argentinians experienced an epiphany about the power of collective action. De la Rúa was infamously forced to flee the demonstrators in a helicopter from the roof of the *Casa Rosada* (Presidential Palace) and promptly resigned from office the following day.

These protests helped to spark many cross-class, grassroots forms of community organization throughout 2002 as the collapse in confidence of the country's political system led to the establishment of hundreds of neighborhood assemblies in Argentina's main cities (Nueva Mayoría, 2006), in which citizens actively participated in horizontal, political decision-making at a local level and discussed solutions to the local and national problems that their politicians could not resolve. Ongoing street protests, community kitchens, participation in countercultural movements as well as a surge in the level of participation in barter clubs were witnessed. 5,356 such clubs were formed around the country and were used by three millions citizens in 2002 alone (Gomez and Helmsing, 2008:2496) as the post-default nation faced an acute liquidity crisis. Argentinians didn't just protest against a government or a system, but they lived out the changes they wanted to see through their participation in solidarity economy actions and acts of direct democracy. Meanwhile, just weeks earlier, millions had also demonstrated their indignation at the ballot box with half of voters either spoiling their ballot papers, abstaining completely (in a country where voting is obligatory) or voting for revolutionary left-wing parties during the legislative elections of October 2001. The protest movements were characterized by an expansive political edge and were inspired by an exceptional atmosphere of political discord and the ideas of autonomy, removal of hierarchy and the promotion of horizontal decision-making rather than solely economic need. As scores of bankrupt factories and workplaces were taken over by their employees and "recovered" under worker's control and *piqueteros* blocked roads and bridges daily around the country, the insurrectionary mood that permeated society led the ruling elites to take fright that the country was on the verge of revolution. In this book, I stop short of arguing that Argentina's 2001–02 uprisings represented a revolutionary situation. No situation of dual-power existed at the time (Astarita, 2008), despite attempts to construct an Inter-Neighborhood Assembly in order to coordinate the local-level assemblies and expand its territorialized presence.

However, in subsequent years through a blend of initial repression (2001–02), protest fatigue, implosion of certain movements, state co-optation by the left-wing governments of Néstor Kirchner (2003–07) and Cristina Fernández de Kirchner (2008–15) and a rapid improvement in the macroeconomic and political climate, the resistance melted away. While many in the struggling middle class supported Néstor and early stages of Cristina's governments, a gradual shift in political tectonic plates led lower middle-class sectors to mobilize in enormous numbers in a series of protests in 2004 and 2006 (the anti-crime *Blumberg* protests), the countryside crisis protests of 2008 and then the mass anti-government protests of 2012 and 2013.

In contrast to the 2001 uprisings, the latter abandoned the hope of achieving a wide-ranging societal transformation. The movement goals of solidarity and the construction of new democratic, participatory and horizontal economic and political structures were replaced by a narrower focus on indicting reformist-Peronist President Cristina Kirchner who they accused of corruption and authoritarianism. Internal enemies such as "the poor" were blamed for the nation's problems, replacing the entire political establishment, globalization and the IMF that were deemed to be the culprits in 2001–02. Materialistic concerns, such as ending inflation and currency controls, became key demands in 2012, reflective of the higher presence of *upper* middle-class citizens in 2012 compared to 2001. As with 2001, the protests themselves remained nonparty political, self-organized and centered on the *cacerolazos*. However, this time they occurred during a period of comparative economic stability, low unemployment and acute political polarization. Although the objectives were very different, the protests symbolized that many of the preoccupations of 2001, such as a perceived lack of democratic accountability, corruption and lack of faith in the political establishment, had remained unresolved (Svampa, 2012).

The book, therefore, explains how the widespread and progressive insurrectionary movements of 2001 and 2002 (led by the struggling middle class) were eventually tamed and why the class solidarity that permeated society at the time disintegrated and was actually followed by the proliferation of reactionary politics among a significant part of Argentina's middle sectors. This tendency increased under the three Kirchner governments (2003–15) until, eventually, as a culmination of this gradual retreat toward conservatism, millionaire businessman, Mauricio Macri was parachuted to the Presidency in December 2015 on a neoliberal and conservative ticket. The epitome of everything that the "losers" of 1990s neoliberalism and the 2001 economic crisis had opposed a decade and a half earlier, many of those who voted for him had been sympathetic to or even actively participated in the *Argentinazo*.[4] Argentina, therefore, allows us to examine the full cycle of contentious politics and to explore how and why citizens supported seemingly contrasting political and economic projects at different times.

The Argentinian social and economic crisis of 2001–02 has, therefore, been chosen as the principal case study country to explain both how middle-class citizens resist proletarianization for a variety of reasons. First of all, the scale of its mass pauperization is unparalleled in a capitalist liberal democracy in recent times (Grimson and Kessler, 2005:87). In all, 7.3 million well-educated, often affluent small business owners, public-sector workers, professionals and other highly skilled workers fell below the poverty line and entered unemployment or low-skilled work in the space of a year (INDEC, 2018).

Second, in terms of its relevance for the study of new urban poverty in the global north and thus responses to it, Argentina shares many contextual, historical and institutional features with other advanced capitalist economies. To start with, as mentioned earlier the characteristics of the protest movements that its impoverished middle class citizens participated in closely match those of post-2008 crisis Europe and North America. Many of the repertoires of collective action that have been proliferated or revived, including the occupation of "public space," involvement in innovative, nonhierarchical, horizontal organizing structures, the general assembly and consensus-building as key decision-making mechanisms along with the rejection of interference by political parties or other forms of institutionalization (Parkinson, 2012), have been adapted from those created in Argentina a decade ago. The country became the first in recent times where these repertoires were practiced on a mass scale as Argentina became a laboratory for a range of social economy experiments during what sociologist Maristella Svampa (2005) describes as the "extraordinary year" of 2002.

The performance of middle-class discontent in 2001–02, often in the form of *cacerolazos*, was depicted by the media and academic studies as "spontaneous," "autonomous" of political parties, "peaceful," and territorialized in the neighborhood vicinity. Thus, the pots-and-pans protests soon came to also symbolize middle-class resistance during subsequent protests in Argentina, as they did in Iceland (2008–09), Spain (2011–15) and Greece (2011–12) in their respective middle-class–led uprisings. Carrying saucepans during protests allowed citizens to express their anger with the government, while saving face regarding any personal financial difficulties they were experiencing. Through the *cacerolazos* they could enunciate their individual middle-class identity through a distinct protest repertoire which distinguished them from trade union, blue-collar or unemployed citizens' groups.

Like Argentina, new urban impoverishment in Western Europe and North America occurred not only within the context of economic crisis but also one of political legitimacy. Their deteriorating living conditions, concern for their future occupational prospects, sense of having been abandoned by their political representatives and by the failure of representative democracy to respond to their preoccupations. This perceived growing schism between the demands of the people and the actions of their national governments and political institutions – which are increasingly believed to be acting in the interests of multinational corporations, wealthy elites and global capital instead of the citizens who elect them, is made explicit in the 2011 Manifesto of the *Real Democracy Now!* Movement in Spain[5] and the Declaration of the Occupation of New York City by *Occupy Wall Street,*[6] for instance. The consequence of three decades of neoliberalism has been to generate a market-driven society whereby cultural and social production is increasingly subject to the process of commodification.

Yet, despite modern capitalism's ever-expanding obsession with being able to offer greater choices *economically* (increasingly differentiated goods and services available for consumers), *socially* (greater tolerance of one's religion or sexuality) and *culturally* (a wider variety of options for educating one's children etc.), citizens are also confronted with a stark contradiction in terms of their narrowing *political* choices. Narratives and proposed solutions offered by political parties, and presidential and parliamentary candidates from different political traditions, have interestingly coalesced around a neoliberal consensus that only seems to be concerned with the "1%." Thus, the growth of these movements has been borne out of this contradiction and rapidly developed into a crisis of political legitimacy among increasing sectors of the population in countries such as Italy, Greece and Spain, most similar to that which Argentina experienced a decade earlier. Argentina thus provides clues about what could happen to the same movements in countries in the global north and the political and financial trajectories of their struggling middle-class citizenry, albeit that they occurred within a specific national context and in a country in a different part of the global production chain.

Third, like North America and most of Europe, Argentina is a G20 member-state that boasts a deeply entrenched welfare state tradition and is one of the few nations in the southern hemisphere that (even today) has a significant middle-class population. The impact that the retreat of the state has had in terms of the consequent downward social mobility of part of a once-thriving middle class draws many parallels with the experience of Organisation of Economic Cooperation and Development (OECD) economies (membership of which Argentina formally requested in June 2018).

Fourth, Argentina's political and industrial relations structures also have much in common with those in the Old Continent. These enable or constrain spaces for its people to respond to pauperization both politically and in terms of self-improvement mechanisms in comparative ways. The Peronist blueprint for the country's hegemonic corporatist mediating relationship between labor, business and state institutions that prevails today was based on the Italian and German corporatism that preceded it in the 1930s and persists today as an industrial relations model. In particular, the historic alignment between the *Confederación General de Trabajo* (CGT) union confederation[7] and the *Justicialista* (Peronist) Party purposely replicates the British Labour Party's relationship with the Trade Union Congress (TUC) (Rock, 1991:69).

Further, Argentina's profound political and economic crisis occurred in 2001 and was followed by a decade of almost uninterrupted high growth (2003–13) before flattening out (2014–17). The depth of the initial crisis is similar to Spain and Greece's; however, the strength of the subsequent recovery makes Argentina an interesting case for longitudinal analysis. The three sets of in-depth interviews conducted over a decade with the sample group provide us a seldom-available opportunity to examine the attitudes, political opinions and actions of citizens at different stages in the economic cycle. Such data are not yet possible to obtain in post-2008 crisis-affected countries.

Finally, the participation of the Argentina's struggling middle class in protest movements in 2001–02 took place in relative international isolation compared to the more recent episodes of new urban poor rebellion in Europe and North America. This makes it an especially useful case study because political mobilization under pauperization was not influenced by a global contagion of resistance, as more recent movements are (Mason, 2012). In the absence of exogenous contributing factors such as these, the findings may be more generalizable to different country contexts.

The Importance of this Book

In the wake of the worldwide economic and political crisis since 2008, there has been a recent upsurge in scholarly interest not only in financial crises but also in the citizen revolts which accompany them during crises of political representation. As discussed earlier, these rebellions have often been led by struggling middle-class sectors and characterized by horizontal models of organizing, self-management and autonomous movements which have sought to avoid co-optation by political parties, trade unions and state institutions. These strategies were copied and later featured in a range of national cases that have been described earlier.

Argentina – whose political and economic context is a decade further on from the post-2008 global crisis uprisings – arouses considerable interest among the broader academic and activist community that wish to draw upon comparative research that provides lessons from that experience of citizen mobilization and then demobilization.

While Latin American students and those interested in Argentina's society are the prime intended readership, this book is targeted beyond either such specialists or academia per se. The monograph draws upon and compares several other national examples from the past two decades to understand how contextual factors shape distinctive struggling middle-class citizen responses to external shocks. It will, therefore, also be highly relevant to readerships across Europe, North America and internationally.

Further, the book is targeted toward both professional and lay readerships and will appeal to postgraduate students and researchers of social change across a wide range of disciplines. It will also be of interest to social movement researchers, Marxists and other theorists of radical social change and those involved in grassroots organizing and labor activists. It contributes toward understanding how grievances that result from proletarianization following economic shocks can become politicized. It asks how such citizens make decisions are made about whether to participate in economic self-improvement and political protest actions in response to such circumstances. The lack of research in this area can be explained by a range of factors. Principally, the nationally representative annual household survey data that are presently available in different countries concentrate almost entirely on financial, consumer, employment and, to a lesser extent, social activities by household units, without asking participants about their participation in protest actions or being able to analyze what the generative factors are that impact on their decision to join them. The University of North Carolina's *Longitudinal Monitoring Survey* in Russia and the American Community Survey in the USA are cases in point. Therefore, a quantitative measurement of how citizens respond to economic shocks in terms of collective actions has proven difficult.

Second, the theoretical complexities involved in demarcating those households that one can classify as belonging to a "new urban poor" social stratum within large and nationally representative survey datasets have militated against any quantitative studies of this nature having been conducted before. Indeed, the qualitative characteristics that conceptually distinguish "new urban poor" households from the "structural poor" (who have unmet basic needs) are often so profoundly obscured within the core data, that this fact alone has proven sufficient to deter analyzes that are of a statistical complexion.

An additional reason why the Argentinian case is especially useful to examine is that the World Bank's *Social Impact of the Crisis in Argentina* (ISCA) Survey (2002) is one of the few available national household surveys that incorporates data on both self-help *and* protest actions in a postcrisis situation. This makes it a hugely valuable resource in terms of observing the full range of possible responses to pauperization.

Third, a study that contains a significant quantitative component in terms of explaining behavioral patterns of those who become impoverished, including their participation in protest actions, is also needed to consolidate upon and frame the qualitative research that has been conducted in a variety of disciplines that *have* explored individual responses to the crisis in terms of their "coping strategies."

Fourth, while the overwhelming majority of *qualitative* studies that have been conducted into how households and citizens cope with internal or external economic shocks focus on the structurally poor (usually in the least developed countries in the world), the few that have turned their attention to non-structural "new" poverty have tended to treat the sample of their study as a homogenous social group, which is usually referred to rather blandly as "the middle class," regardless of whether they actually experienced severe declines in living standards during these economic crises. Scant attention is paid to the diversity within this "class" that makes the nuanced responses of its members to such shocks so intriguing. This includes how hardship or a loss of status affects subjectivities and how this sometimes induces politicized responses or collective forms of action from affected citizens. Yet, it is precisely "this newly impoverished" stratum of the middle class whose collective responses should be of most interest to theorists of social change and thus merit closer analysis. The experience of recent years since the global crisis suggests that it is when such citizens become proletarianized and construct alliances with the traditional poor and working class then take action alongside them within popular movements that their potential to change governments, influence policy changes or draw global media attention is strongest.

In any case, the precise meaning of "the middle class" is so vague that just who constitutes part of it has been highly contested. In Argentina itself, this has been the case ever since Gino Germani conducted the first large-scale study of social class in the country –*Estructura Social en la Argentina* – in 1955 which inflated the size of the "middle class" as it included many working-class occupations (Adamovsky, 2009), while the IMF's own US$10 per day baseline for inclusion is derided by most sociologists. The polemic about its definition has also prevented a sizable number of studies about the middle class from being conducted, especially in recent years. Notable exceptions to this tendency to homogenize middle-class responses in Argentina include work by Aguirre on new urban poor reticence toward enrolment in assistentialist[8] aid programs (2008), Mazzoni's publications on how a limited understanding of citizenship rights restricted new urban poor political activism in the postcrisis period (2007, 2008), and Kessler and Di Virgilio's paper on how the new urban poor utilize their social, cultural and human capital in different ways to the structural poor when faced with material hardship (2008).

It should be noted that each of these contributions, although valuable in its own academic discipline, make few connections between households' economic coping strategies and how they interplay with the decision to engage in political protest as an alternative response. Mazzoni's (2007) discussion of the impact that impoverishment had on beliefs about politics among the new urban poor during Argentina's postcrisis period is an exception. Yet, while insightful, she neither focuses on the process of their politicization, nor the empirical link between the self-improvement and protest actions that they took in response.

The prime focus of research into struggling or impoverished middle-class behavior until now has been how they take financial, employment, entrepreneurial and lifestyle decisions, as opposed to protest actions in response. This has been driven by the valid concern that national governments, international financial institutions and NGOs have neglected policy initiatives that are specifically designed to support those who have recently become (or are vulnerable to becoming) poor (Kessler and Di Virgilio, 2008) and have instead dedicated their efforts to confronting structural poverty. However, although this preoccupation is valid in itself, it has tended to result in newly poor citizens being understood as economic, benefit-maximizing actors in terms of how they resist their hardship, discounting the possibility that such citizens may develop a shared sense of identity and forge collective grievances with them. Typically, the subsequent articulation of their political demands is expressed through collective protest actions which target the government, judicial and financial authorities. Thus, it is necessary to recognize that economic processes cannot be divorced from the social and political consequences that they generate. Coping strategies of "economic" resistance must be analyzed together with "political" resistance and protest.

This study's perspective follows approaches that have previously documented the intrinsic relationship between self-help and protest actions, for example, in the UK (Croucher, 1987) and Soviet Union (Moskoff, 1993). In Argentina itself, Nancy Powers (1999) discussed how material concerns become understood as a "political" problem when personal tolerance of impoverishment declines. This may happen when citizens are either unable to find sufficient economic coping mechanisms to maintain a desired level of needs satisfaction (i.e., if these strategies are undermined or unsuccessful), if one's poverty is experienced more intensely (which invokes greater anger), or when economic and political contexts shape citizens' evaluation of their material interests.

Further, when economic aspirations are frustrated and prolonged, or lifestyle sacrifices become intolerable, citizens begin to examine the structural reasons for their descent, exorcize themselves of culpability for their hardship and protest their condition instead. However, Powers' research is more relevant to the contexts of gradual and atomized pauperization, as her study of Argentina's neoliberal reforms in the 1990s was. In contrast, the sudden mass pauperization like that which exploded in 2001–02 was quite a different circumstance. Further, like Mazzoni, Powers' research is limited in scope to how impoverishment impacts upon "political interests" rather than involvement in collective and protest action itself.

Finally, while the research focus in this book centers on the "new urban poor," rural responses to middle-class impoverishment in Argentina are investigated here for comparative purposes. This comparison of rural-dwelling citizens' collective action responses with those in the urban centers has never been conducted before.

As the first English-language book that examines the waves of mobilization and demobilization of Argentina's struggling middle class, the results are based on the triangulation of data analysis from quantitative surveys and fieldwork interviews with non-activist "average citizens," academic experts, NGOs and social movement organizers reflecting back on their different degrees of participation (or non-participation) in the uprising of 15 years ago. It is perhaps methodologically even rarer to capture and analyze longitudinal data of both a quantitative and qualitative nature over such a long time period, as the book seeks to do.

The December 2001 revolt in Argentina captured the imaginations of sociologists and political scientists both inside the country and internationally. It led to a flurry of scholarship (including in English-language journals and volumes) which sought to explain the uprising and understand the motivations for participation in a range of its nascent movements by certain sectors of society, for instance, on the neighborhood assemblies (Dinerstein, 2003; Svampa and Corral, 2006). Others focused specifically on the motivations of middle-class citizens' protest and solidarity actions with working-class and unemployed workers movements (Barbetta and Bidaseca, 2004) and Briones and Mendoza's (2003) work on women's participation. Meanwhile, Armony and Armony's (2005) analyzed various political and economic factors which explain why citizens engaged in mass mobilizations at the time, especially due to the collapse of the national myths of grandeur and middle-class identity. However, all of these sources only concentrate on the height of the uprising and soon after, without exploring how demobilization occurred or why this solidarity largely eroded under the post-2003 milieu of economic and political "normalization."

Those that do seek to do the latter are either confined to short survey reports (Centro de Estudios Nueva Mayoría's, 2006), or were written in the immediate aftermath of the election of the Néstor Kirchner government (Petras, 2005). However, these only explain the short-term mobilization and demobilization phenomenon, rather than providing a longitudinal study from the vantage point of 15 years after the rebellion, which is one of the key objectives of this book.

Among the English-speaking literature, several works were produced to explain the exciting, organizing models being used by social movements which originated from Argentina's uprising (Lopez-Levy, 2003; Sitrin, 2012). These focus on the structures and evolution of the organizing practices of the movements themselves without individuals' political and financial trajectories or oscillating degrees of participation in such movements being discussed. Later monographs by those such as Olga Onuch (2014) specifically engaged with the question of what prompts "ordinary citizens" to engage in mass uprisings, but is limited to qualitative interviews and focus groups and focuses only on the moment of initial rebellion in 2001–02, without framing the question within a broader quantitative analysis to establish contextual and longitudinal trends.

Yet amid this body of work, the political dimension of pauperization or proletarianization and how it is resisted by middle-class citizens through collective behavior and protest actions (during economic crises and otherwise) has been largely neglected, despite calls to bestow it greater attention (Richards and Gelleny, 2006). A plethora of studies on the *Indignado* uprisings in Spain, the protests in Greece and other rebellions have been conducted in recent years, but few have concentrated on how citizens who face sudden downward mobility or impoverishment develop political agency or how their change in material conditions influenced their responses. In the Argentina context, Mazzoni (2007) provides a rare and valuable exception. This monograph seeks to build on Mazzoni's research by exploring not just how impoverishment affected political attitudes but also the collective and private behaviors that those in this proletarianized middle-class stratum enacted in response. Indeed, there are no studies that have sought to do this in Argentina or otherwise which utilize empirical, mixed-methods longitudinal research that traces the trajectories of citizens over two decades so as to understand these cycles of contention.

Internationally, the post-2008 global crisis milieu presents a context of austerity, falling living standards, a hollowing out of the middle class, stagnant social mobility and declining confidence in political establishment. How citizens – especially the struggling middle class – *are* responding and *will* react in future is a key contemporary social problem which requires such a study.

Methodology

A Qualitative-Dominant, Quantitative Less-Dominant, sequential design is adopted in two phases: drawing upon analysis of World Bank (2002) and *Latinobarómetro* (1995, 2002 and 2005) longitudinal household survey data along with participant interviews (at three points in 2007, 2011 and 2016). In Phase 1, research draws upon evidence from two secondary sources. The first, the World Bank–commissioned ISCA is a nationally representative household survey of 9,209 individuals in 2,800 households. It was conducted by *Public Opinion, Services and Markets* (OPSM; an Argentinian marketing consultancy) in 2002. The survey's aim was to understand how households survived the country's economic crisis and how it affected well-being.

However, for the purposes of this book, the core data were used specifically to (a) identify what forms of resistance Argentinians who became poor during the crisis took; (b) examine how decisions about whether to engage in collective action was affected by differences in their experiences of poverty, biographical histories and labor market position; and (c) understand how social attitudes and political perspectives informed their decision to adopt the actions identified in the 2002 ISCA Survey. These data were triangulated with that of a second, public opinion survey from that same year, IPSOS-MORI's *Latinobarómetro*. This allowed the impact of the following subjectivities on response to be determined (i) how the impoverished urban and rural middle class felt about their own hardship, (ii) the extent to which they were prepared to politically tolerate it and (iii) to what degree they felt that self-help opportunities existed that they could exploit so as to overcome their poverty. 1995 *Latinobarómetro* Survey results were also consulted to observe how newly poor Argentinians' opinions changed between the 1990s and the post-*Argentinazo* period in 2002, then in 2005, thus helping underpin how responses changed over time. (iv) How and why middle-class characteristics, values, habitus and notions of identity affected response.

The participants in the ISCA survey completed a closed questionnaire; once during May/June 2002 and then again during October/November the same year. Its two data collection rounds enabled a "new poor" or impoverished middle-class stratified sample to be obtained from within the core data. This was accomplished by first shortlisting all those individuals who lived in households that had officially become "income poor" (whose monthly per capita income fell below $232 pesos or US$2 per day – the 2002 national poverty line figure) during the five months between each data collection round. Then, only those who also possessed the qualitative characteristics that Minujín (1993) described in his conceptualization of new poverty (see Chapter 2) were selected in the final sample, including "basic needs coverage." In this way, the face validity of the "new poor" concept was preserved, and "the impact of impoverishment" upon action could be determined by comparing pre- and post-pauperization responses during respective periods.

The said characteristics included are as follows: (a) They held a professional qualification, owned a small business and had a university degree (or were currently studying for one); (b) they were homeowners (or were their adult children); and (c) they had worked in a middle-class job or ran a business but had fallen below the income poverty line during the 2001–02 crisis (or were adult children of those who did). These criteria were verified during an initial visit to the residential address and the background pre-interview questionnaire information they supplied. This left 314 cases in the final sample.

Two important data limitations exist. First, the size of the "new poor" sample raised the methodological problem that the results were susceptible to type II errors (by which a null hypothesis is falsely accepted). This may have created an underreporting of statistically significant results. While this important data limitation is acknowledged, attempts were made to mitigate it by measuring the outcome of test results at the 90% (rather than 95%) confidence level. Second, the ISCA survey only recorded *formal* ways of organizing. Therefore, important but often illegal or informal activities such as looting, criminal activity or graffiti were omitted, as were common "legal" individual protest actions like signing petitions or letter writing, or untraceable activities such as absenteeism.

In terms of the *Latinobarómetro* survey, its participants also completed closed questionnaires and were asked to reflect upon the extent to which they were in agreement with a series of statements about politics, institutions, economic models and so on. It is important to highlight that this survey does not record income data. Therefore, only participants whose subjective perception of their circumstances was one of economic descent (and who possessed the three characteristics stipulated above) were included in its new poor/impoverished middle-class sample. Thus, the opinions of those in this sample represent only an *approximation* of those of the "poverty-line defined" new poor sample that resulted from the ISCA survey. Of the 1,200 adults in the original *Latinobarómetro* survey, the new poor stratified sample obtained included 124 cases in 1995 (10% of the sample universe) and 202 cases in 2002 (17%).

How responses were classified requires some elaboration. Households participate in any particular action for a range of motivations. For instance, some may have joined a barter club as part of an idealistic project to help the *community* or even as a "protest" in itself, whereas others may have done so purely due to *individual* survival needs. However, in this book, the responses have been categorized in accordance with how they were clustered as variables by the ISCA survey's designers (OPSM) in the original core data (see *Table 1.1*). The initial experience of pauperization during the start of the 2001 economic crisis destroyed the self-esteem of many newly poor people as they lost the jobs that defined their sense of identity. Many abandoned hope of a brighter future during the descent from a comfortable lifestyle to one of economic hardship, often for the first time in their lives. The desire "to belong" and have their talents

Table 1.1 Classification of Different Response Actions in Argentina during 2002

Response Category	Indicators of Action in This Book
Individual self-improvement	Work, self-employment, rent/dividends, receipt of gifts, redundancy pay, pension, charitable aid, exchanging goods, buying on trust, loan from friends/family, bank loan, savings, credit, sale/pawn of assets, becoming a *cartonero* (waste collector), state aid, non-state aid, other
Collective self-improvement	School soup kitchen, public soup kitchen, communal purchasing, barter clubs, bric-a-bracs, cooperative business, neighborhood job center, community fundraising, babysitting, public welfare lobbying, public works, communal squatting, communal security, other
Individual protest	Voting
Collective protest	*Cacerolazos*, strikes, neighborhood assemblies, pickets, demonstrations, public meetings, church/social group protests, other

Source: Ozarow (2014:190).

recognized by others again, on the one hand, and the need to gain solace, on the other, was what moved many to participate in collectivist actions like the *cacerolazos,* barter clubs, assemblies, worker-"recovered" factories and group therapy sessions (Svampa and Corral, 2006:138). Often, involvement in these actions also helped them to restore confidence in their own abilities and the solidarity that the struggling middle class encountered in these forums helped them to "feel euphoric to be part of a larger social movement in which they could establish new friendships and become part of a 'collective'."

Data on voting behavior were the exception because they were not recorded by ISCA, but obtained separately from *Latinobarómetro*. Thus, actions are regarded as "collective" if they involved a "joint commitment" to a single outcome for multiple households, but whereby each played their part in making it happen. In other words, they are actions which are not reducible to individual intentionality. For instance, the goal of a "barter club" is for multiple households to gain from it because each relies on the production of goods and services by another, in order for the exchange to take place. In cases in which individual households pursue their particular goals independently (such as in the receipt of state aid), they are deemed to be "individual" responses. These usually occurred in physical isolation (like an office or voting booth) and could be performed regardless of others' involvement. While protest usually established some kind of "self-improvement" as its goal, responses are classified in the latter way here only if they sought *immediate* material enrichment. If the desired improvements had to traverse a political stage through the process of "demand-making" to some kind of authority, then they were categorized as "protests."

In addition, self-improvement actions are categorized here as only those that encompass "proactive" strategies, in the sense that they either create additional resources for the household or make increased use of their available physical, financial and human assets. "Reactive" strategies, in which households respond by simply reducing consumption (Lokshin and Yemtsov, 2004), are not considered in this research because, on the one hand, passively reducing one's spending does not constitute "self-improvement" and, on the other, from a policy perspective, what is of interest is to observe how the new poor and middle class utilize their superior capital assets relative to the structural poor – to enact strategies that enable them to escape poverty.

This is not to say that pursuing economic coping strategies (self-improvement) or protest actions are mutually exclusive. Clearly, citizens may participate in both simultaneously. Nor are frustrated attempts to achieve self-help the only reason that middle-class citizens confront impoverishment and downward social mobility through protest mobilizations. Actors may instead cross the thresholds of social convention to openly defy the existing political authorities due to a shared anticipation of either real or imagined losses or gains, compared to their current conditions. As Armony and Armony (2005) assert, citizens may act rationally, but their reference points for responding to crisis are influenced by psychologically and culturally framed cognitive patterns, not only to deficits of political representation, weak institutionalization or a dramatic economic downturn but also to a crisis of national identity conceptions (these will be explained later).

A further linkage between the self-improvement and protest responses that will be analyzed in this book is that under liberal-democratic regimes like Argentina, protest will only ever achieve *limited* material enrichment. The realm of legitimate political contestation is limited to the existing boundaries that are established and reproduced through the system's representative structures, such as parliament, trade unions and lobby groups. Politics is deemed to "happen" only in these spaces, and citizens are socialized into conforming to the status quo as liberal-democratic power relations become naturalized in citizens' minds (Williams, 1977:100). Therefore, after a certain period of protest and when concessions are gained (or the movement is defeated or dies away), the expectation is to resort to "self-improvement strategies" in order to achieve further material gain. For these reasons, neither protest nor self-improvement actions are usually sufficient to satisfy material wants *on their own*. The decision to participate in either one or the other can be dependent on how effective involvement in the alternative has been.

Phase 2 consisted of three periods of fieldwork in Argentina. These were performed in 2007, 2011 and 2016. Several research methods were triangulated. The author conducted participant observation through embeddedness in middle-class citizens' local communities, working and social lives. Systems of meanings participants attached to a variety of research themes mentioned earlier were noted and interpreted.

Concurrently, interviews were conducted in Spanish with 31 middle-class citizens (13 men and 18 women) from households that had become impoverished during the 2002 crisis. Permission was granted to access the anonymized ISCA database. Those initially selected for interview were contacted by OPSM to request permission to disclose their details. Seven were aged 20–29, six 30–39, four 40–49, ten 50–59 and four 60+. Only three were political activists. These were voice-recorded and responses and observations were then thematically analyzed. Respondents were sampled purposively to ensure participation from middle-class people of different ages, genders, locations and situations. All but one of the interview participants had white, European ancestry. This is unsurprising. Two-thirds of Argentinians possess such ethnic origins (Avena *et al.*, 2012), but the proportion within the middle class is higher still (Adamovsky, 2009). Self-selection problems were avoided as only one qualifying participant declined to be interviewed. Interviewees were given pseudonyms to protect their anonymity. Respondent details are given in Appendix.

The same households were returned to each time (where possible, as some limited attrition occurred). Most of those respondents who were not formally interviewed in the third round due to resource constraints corresponded with me through e-mail. Expert interviews were also conducted with ten academics, politicians and NGO coordinators (which provided welfare and employment services to jobless professionals). Home visits were made to gentrified districts of five large cities – Buenos Aires, La Plata, Rosario, Santa Fe and Posadas – and Piedras Blancas, a rural village in Entre Rios Province. Interviews were usually conducted at participants' homes to minimize potential anxiety and embarrassment given the sensitive subject matter. No financial incentive was offered, although a small gift was offered after interviews. The 31 semi-structured interviews each lasted approximately 90 min.

Interviewing vulnerable individuals may encourage them to underplay or exaggerate problems to elicit sympathy. Measures were taken up to manage these possibilities. Advice about interviewing Argentinians in this situation was kindly provided by Isidro Adúriz, ex-Director of OPSM. I told interview participants about my own Argentinian relations who had experienced the 2001 crisis to make them aware that I had some prior knowledge of the situation's realities. As a non-Argentinian, I was surprised at participants' frankness, but discerned through a range of explicit and implicit indications that being viewed as "an outsider" was useful in this regard.

Organization of this Book and Its Main Arguments

This book is composed in the following way: Chapter 1 has provided a background into the global economic crisis, the growing crisis of political representation and how broad sectors of the middle class, especially in North America and Europe, have become subject to downward social mobility, proletarianization and mass pauperization. How such citizens should be understood as political agents who have resisted their condition through demand-making and collective protest in several national contexts since the 2008 global crisis has also been discussed. They do not behave as purely rational economic actors. The economic and political crisis in Argentina in 2001/02 as a paradigmatic case study for analyzing middle-class resistance was introduced, and the study's methodology was outlined.

In Chapter 2, some of the key concepts in the monograph are developed. The origins of new urban poverty (middle-class impoverishment) and their downward mobility as a consequence of neoliberalism and processes of structural adjustment of its "losers," following the Washington Consensus Reforms in the 1990s are explained with reference to European and North America, as well as Latin American and Argentina. Other manifestations of it, either following the 2008 global crises, as a characteristic of the transition economies from communism to capitalism, or in post-Apartheid societies are also observed.

Cross-national comparisons are made between the how the middle class resisted crisis and hardship in Russia (1990s transition to capitalism and 1998 financial crisis), South Africa (post-Apartheid), Argentina (post-2001 crisis), Iceland, Greece and Spain (post-2008 crisis) during the past three decades, and whether citizens coped privately or participated in collective protests as a consequence are examined. The chapter ends by articulating the book's Gramscian theoretical framework and how his concepts of "hegemony," "ideology" and "false consciousness" will be adopted to help to account for how proletarianized citizens responded to their social descent in Argentina since the 1990s.

Chapter 3 is dedicated entirely to our Argentina case study and the research findings. It is divided into two parts. The first section covers the period 1989–2000, incorporating the literature and *Latinobarómetro* data analysis. It argues that the incremental nature of pauperization, relatively stable macroeconomic environment and dominant discourses which atomized and individualized one's personal financial circumstances meant that impoverishment was experienced more in isolation. The result was a tendency to seek self-help solutions to their circumstances and principally private ones at that. While labor and social protests were regular, the involvement of the struggling middle class tended to be organized "from above" and "formally," principally via white-collar trade unions or the representative organizations of small businesses.

The second part is based upon an examination of World Bank and *Latinobarómetro* survey data and covers the period 2001–02. The generative factors that explain why citizens mobilized to join the revolt and how questions of a growing collective identity, grievance forming and the loss of hegemonic consent to rule by the dominant class contributed to this tendency are outlined.

How changes in citizens' attitudes and subjectivities induced a shift in the tendency from "self-blame under Menemismo" in the 1990s to "system attribution" for their circumstances in 2001–02 helps to explain how hegemonic control crumbled are described, such that the neoliberal economic and liberal-democratic order faced a severe challenge from the bourgeoning multisectoral protest movement in 2001. Within the struggling middle class, we then examine which biographical characteristics help explain the tendency for some citizens to join protest movements, while others desist from doing so.

In Chapter 4, results are triangulated from *Latinobarómetro* survey data (2005) and three sets of in-depth interviews (2007, 2011 and 2016) to explore the demobilization and remobilization of Argentina's struggling middle class between 2003 and 2018. Four separate periods are identified: First, the post-2001 crisis appeasement and demobilization of the first two years of Néstor Kirchner's government (2003–05). Second, the sporadic outbursts of rebellion that characterized the latter half of Néstor's government and the first term of Cristina's following the Blumberg protests and Countryside Conflict (2006–11). Third, that of Cristina's second term, when the middle class commenced a series of mass mobilizations against her government (2012–15). Then fourth, the first two years of Mauricio Macri's government (2016–18) which sparked the largest, most multisectoral protests since 2001.

Finally, based upon the findings of our Argentina case study, we draw tentative conclusions about why struggling middle-class citizens are mobilized and demobilized, and what lessons may be provided for and from other national contexts. A theoretical framework is offered to try to explain how struggling middle-class citizens take decisions about whether to engage in protest or self-improvement actions when faced with hardship, and whether these actions are conducted collectively or privately. Suggestions are made as to how it could be adapted and applied in other national contexts. We posit that to effect profound and lasting social change, the middle class must enter into multisectoral alliances and that sustainable mobilizing vehicles must be created, so as to maintain radical action beyond periods of crisis.

Notes

1 In this book, the term "middle class" is largely analyzed subjectively as a political identity, rather than an objectively defined social class with established

boundaries. However, in terms of the empirical work referred to later, it is deemed to consist of highly educated professionals, middle managers, small business owners or skilled white-collar workers, or who are home owners. It is proposed later that while many of those who suffered downward mobility during the 2001–02 economic crisis rejoined the middle class during the post-2003 economic recovery, a significant proportion was also permanently proletarianized.

2 The Arab Spring protests principally demanded political freedoms and end to dictatorship rather than being a reaction against austerity measures. However, they did include a significant "squeezed" middle-class presence, especially well-educated young adults who, analysts claim, were inspired to revolt by their limited prospects for upward social mobility (Mason, 2012).

3 The two trade union confederations, the CGT and rival *Central de Trabajadores de la Argentina* (CTA), organized a general strike on 13 December 2001 but were not formally involved in coordinating the *cacerolazos*, which occurred without any formal degree of organization.

4 Often used to describe the social uprisings that occurred during 19 and 20 December 2001. However, it should be noted that the term is often deliberately avoided by left-wing scholars for its exaggerated and misleading revolutionary and spontaneous signifiers. The uprisings had their roots in a series of territorialized protests against neoliberalism in Argentina in the 1980s and 1990s so were part of the cycle of contentious politics rather than a one-off, spontaneous event.

5 www.democraciarealya.es/manifiesto-comun/manifesto-english/.

6 www.nycga.net/resources/documents/declaration/.

7 The CGT is the largest trade union confederation in Argentina. Its three factions provisionally reunified in July 2016. The CTA itself split into two factions, *CTA de los Trabajadores* and the *CTA Autónoma*.

8 From the Spanish *asistencialismo*. Describes paternalistic, passive forms of aid.

References

Adamovsky, Ezequiel (2009) *Historia de la Clase Media Argentina*. Buenos Aires, Planeta.

Aguirre, Patricia (2008) 'Social Assistance as Seen by the Buenos Aires Poor and New Urban Poor during Convertibility' *Anthropology of Food* [Online] S4, 4 May 2008.

Ainsworth, Susan and Hardy, Cynthia (2009) 'Mind over Body: Physical and Psychotherapeutic Discourses and the Regulation of the Older Worker' *Human Relations*, Vol. 62 (8), pp. 1199–1229.

Armony, Ariel C. and Armony, Victor (2005) 'Indictments, Myths, and Citizen Mobilization in Argentina: A Discourse Analysis,' *Latin American Politics and Society*, Vol. 47 (4), pp. 27–54Astarita, Ronaldo (2008) *La peligrosa ilusión del poder dual en la actual situación política*, Buenos Aires. www.rolandoastarita. com Last accessed January 18th 2019.

Avena, Sergio, Via, Marc, Ziv, Elad, Pérez-Stable, Eliseo J., Gignoux, Christopher R., Dejean, Cristina (2012) 'Heterogeneity in Genetic Admixture across Different Regions of Argentina' *PLoS ONE*, Vol. 7 (4), p. e34695.

Barbetta, Pablo and Bidaseca, Karina (2004) 'Reflexiones sobre el 19 y el 20 de Diciembre de 2001 '¿Piquete y cacerola, la lucha es una sola': Emergencia discursiva o nueva subjetividad?', *Revista Argentina de Sociología*, May-June 2002, Vol. 2, Buenos Aires, Consejo de Profesionales en Sociología pp. 67–88

Chomsky, Noam (2012) *Occupy*. London, Penguin.

Croucher, Richard (1987) *We Refuse to Starve in Silence: A History of the National Unemployed Workers' Movement, 1920–46*. London, Lawrence & Wishart Ltd.

Dagdeviren, Hulya, Donoghue, Matthew, and Meier, Lars (2017) 'The Narratives of Hardship: The New and the Old Poor in the Aftermath of the 2008 Crisis in Europe' *Sociological Review*, Vol. 65 (2), pp. 369–385.

Davies, James C. (1962) 'Toward a Theory of Revolution' *American Sociological Review*, Vol. 27 (1), pp. 5–19.

Della Porta, Donnatella; Andretta, Massimiliano; Fernandes, Tiago; Romanos, Eduardo; O'Connor, Francis and Vogiatzoglou, Markos (eds.) (2017) *Late Neoliberalism and Its Discontents in the Economic Crisis Comparing Social Movements in the European Periphery*. New York, Palgrave Macmillan.

Dinerstein, Ana (2003) '¡Qué se vayan todos! Popular Insurrection and the Asambleas Barriales in Argentina' *Bulletin of Latin American Research*, Vol. 22 (2), pp. 187–200.

Eghbal, Media (2008) 'Inflation and Stagnant Wages Squeeze Western Europe's Middle Class' *Euromonitor International*, 23rd June 2008.

Eurostat (2018) *People at Risk of Poverty or Social Exclusion*. Luxembourg, European Commission.

Feijóo, del Carmen, M. (2003) *Nuevo País, Nueva Pobreza*. Buenos Aires, Fondo de Cultura Económica.

Gabriel, Yiannis, Gray, David and Goregaokar, Harshita (2013) 'Job Loss and Its Aftermath among Managers and Professionals Wounded, Fragmented and Flexible' *Work, Employment and Society*, Vol. 27 (1), pp. 56–72.

Galbraith, John K. (1992) *The Culture of Contentment*. New York, Houghton Mifflin.

Gomez, Georgina and Helmsing, Bert. (2008) 'Selective Spatial Closure and Local Economic Development: What do we Learn from the Argentine Local Currency Systems?' *World Development*, Vol. 36 (11), pp. 2489–2511.

Grimson, Alejandro and Kessler, Gabriel (2005) *On Argentina and the Southern Cone: Neoliberalism and National Imaginations*. Abingdon, Routledge.

Hirschman, Albert (1970) *Exit, Voice, and Loyalty: Responses to Decline in Firms, Organizations and States*. Cambridge, MA, Harvard University Press.

INDEC (2018) *Instituto Nacional de Estadística y Censos*. Buenos Aires. www.indec.gov.ar.

International Monetary Fund (2009) *World Economic Outlook - Crisis and Recovery*, Washington DC, IMF.

———— (2015) *IMF Survey: Lower Potential Growth: A New Reality*. Washington DC, IMF.

Kanya, Adam (1997) 'The Politics of Redress: South African Style Affirmative Action' *The Journal of Modern African Studies*, Vol. 35 (2), pp. 231–249.

Katzman, Ruben (1989) 'La heterogeneidad de la pobreza. El caso de Montevideo' *Revista de la CEPAL*, Vol. 37, pp. 141–152, Santiago de Chile.

Kessler, Gabriel, and Di Virgilio, María (2008) 'La nueva pobreza urbana: dinámica global, regional y argentina en las últimas dos décadas', *Revista de la CEPAL*, Vol. 95, pp. 31–50.

Lokshin, Michael and Yemtsov, Ruslan (2004) 'Household Strategies of Coping with Shocks in Post-crisis *Russia' Review of Development Economics*, Vol. 8 (1), pp. 15–32.

López-Levy, Marcela (2004) *We Are Millions: Neoliberalism and New Forms of Political Action in Argentina.* London, Latin American Bureau.

Mandemakers, Jornt and Monden, Christiaan (2013) 'Does the Effect of Job Loss on Psychological Distress Differ by Educational Level?' *Work, Employment and Society*, Vol. 27 (1), pp. 73–93.

Mason, Paul (2012) *Why it's Kicking Off Everywhere: The New Global Revolutions.* London, Verso.

Masseroni, Susana and Sauane, Susana (2002) 'Psychic and Somatic Vulnerability among Professional Middle-Class Women in Argentina' *Journal of Developing Societies*, Vol. 18 (2–3), pp. 59–80.

Mazzoni, Maria (2007) 'Política y Empobrecimiento' *Revista de la Facultad*, Vol. 13, pp. 185–211, Argentina, Universidad Nacional de Comahue.

——— (2008) 'Ciudadanos de bajo impacto,' *Revista de la Facultad*, Vol. 14, pp. 211–225, Argentina, Universidad Nacional de Comahue.

Minujín, Alberto (2007) *Vulnerabilidad y resiliencia de la clase media en América Latina.* New York, The New School.

Minujín, Alberto, Beccaria, Luis and Bustelo, Eduardo (1993) *Cuesta abajo: Los nuevos pobres: efectos de la crisis en la sociedad argentina.* Buenos Aires, UNICEF/Losada.

Moskoff, William (1993) *Impoverishment and Protest in the Perestroika Years.* Washington, DC, NCSEER.

Némirovsky, Irène (2007) *French Suite.* New York, Vintage Books.

Nueva Mayoría (2006) *La desaparición de los cacerolazos, las asambleas populares, y el fenómeno del trueque, tras la salida de la crisis 2001–02.* Buenos Aires, Centro de Estudios Nueva Mayoría.

Onuch, Olga (2014) "It's the Economy, Stupid,' or Is It? The Role of Political Crisis in Mass Mobilization: The Case of Argentina in 2001' in D. Ozarow, C. Levey, and C. Wylde (eds.), *Argentina Since the 2001 Crisis: Recovering the Past, Reclaiming the Future.* London, Palgrave Macmillan. pp. 89–113.

Ozarow, Daniel (2014) 'When all they Thought was Solid Melted into Air: Resisting pauperisation in Argentina during the 2002 economic crisis' *Latin American Research Review*, Vol. 49 (1), pp. 178–202.

——— (2015) 'Joblessness and Underemployment among the Middle Class in Post-crisis Argentina: Superior Capital Possession as a Poisoned Chalice' *Latin American Studies Association XXXIII International Congress*, Puerto Rico, 28th May 2015.

Parkinson, John R. (2012) *Democracy and Public Space: The Physical Sites of Democratic Performance.* Oxford, Oxford University Press.

Petras, James (2005) 'Argentina: From Popular Rebellion to 'Normal Capitalism,' in J. Petras and H. Veltmeyer eds. *Social Movements and State Power: Argentina, Brazil, Bolivia, Ecuador.* London, Pluto Press.

Phelps Brown, Henry (1990) 'The Counter-Revolution of Our Time' *Industrial Relations: A Journal of Economy and Society*, Vol. 29 (1), pp. 1–14.

Phillips, Leigh (2008) 'Sarkozy Fears Spectre of 1968 Haunting Europe' *EUobserver*, 23rd December 2008.

Powers, Nancy (1999) 'Coping with Economic Hardship in Argentina: How Material Interests Affect Individuals' Political Interests' *Canadian Journal of Political Science*, Vol. 32, pp. 521–549.

Richards, David and Gelleny, Richard (2006) 'Banking Crises, Collective Protest and Rebellion' *Canadian Journal of Political Science*, Vol. 39 (4), pp. 777–801.

Rock, David (1991) 'Argentina 1930–46' in L. Bethell (ed.), *The Cambridge History of Latin America*. Cambridge, Cambridge University Press, Vol. 8, p. 69.

Sitrin, Marina (2012) *Everyday Revolutions: Horizontalism and Autonomy in Argentina*. New York and London, Zed Books.

South African Institute of Race Relations (2006) *White Emigration from South Africa 1995–2005*. 77th Annual Report. Johannesburg.

Svampa, Maristella (2005) *La Sociedad excluyente. La Argentina bajo el signo del neoliberalismo*. Buenos Aires, Taurus.

———— (2012) 'Negro sobre blanco' *Perfil*, 16th September 2012.

Svampa, Maristella and Corral, Damian (2006) 'Political Mobilization in Neighborhood Assemblies' in E. Epstein and D. Pion-Berlin (eds.), *Broken Promises? The Argentinean Crisis and Argentinean Democracy*. New York, Lexington Books, pp. 117–141.

Velázquez, Ayelén (Dir.) (2017) *39 El Documental, Las Victimas de 2001*. 95 mins.

Wade, Robert (2009a) 'Iceland as Icarus' *Challenge Magazine*, Vol. 52 (3), pp. 5–33.

———— (2009b) 'From Global Imbalances to Global Reorganizations', *Cambridge Journal of Economics*, Vol. 33 (4), pp. 539–562.

Warren, Elizabeth (2007) *The Coming Collapse of the Middle Class*. Berkeley, The Graduate Council, California, University of California.

Weiner, Richard R. and López, Ivan (2018) *Los Indignados: Tides of Social Insertion in Spain*. Winchester, Zero Books.

Williams, Raymond (1977) *Marxism and Literature*. Oxford, Oxford University Press.

Willie, Anchrit (2001) 'Political Responses to Dissatisfaction in Russia' *Journal of Happiness Studies*, Vol. 2 (2), pp. 205–235, Springer.

World Bank (2002) 'Impact of the Social Crisis on Argentina Survey (ISCA)' http://go.worldbank.org/D78TBTCP80. Last accessed 12th October 2018.

World Values Survey (2006) Stockholm, *World Values Survey Association,* http://www.worldvaluessurvey.org/ Last Accessed January 18th 2019.

Zurawicki, Leon and Braidot, Nestor (2005) 'Consumers during Crisis: Responses from the Middle Class in Argentina' *Journal of Business Research*, Vol. 58 (8), pp. 1100–1109, Elsevier.

2 That Sinking Feeling

The Experience of Mass Pauperization in Argentina, Hegemony, Control and Contentious Politics

> Then perhaps this misery of class-prejudice will fade away, and we of the sinking middle class may sink without further struggles into the working class where we belong. Probably when we get there it will not be so dreadful as we feared. For after all, we have nothing to lose but our aitches.
>
> George Orwell, The Road to Wigan Pier, 1937

The main actor in this book is the struggling middle class or the "new urban poor" as it is known by sociologists. The mobilization and demobilization of this sector in Argentina, and which class alliances they have made over the past three decades, will be explored in different stages. Collective, class-based responses are closely associated with what Orwell depicted as the fear of "the fall," or of losing their economic and social status tied to their middle-class identity. This has influenced whether the poor or blue-collar working class have been identified as allies, with shared class interests against ruling-class domination with whom to collectively mobilize, or whether they have been viewed as a potential threat to their class position "from below," at moments when they believe their interests and destiny to be shared with the ruling class, while the class "below" them are understood as violent, lazy, uncultured and nothing less than their nemesis. However, first it is necessary to explore the international history of how neoliberal economic and social processes contributed to mass pauperization and to the creation of this social strata, before going on to define who our subject group are and how different theoretical perspectives account for patterns of collective action.

The International Origins of New Urban Poverty under Neoliberalism

Concerns about the emerging phenomenon of new urban poverty and impoverished sections of the middle class were originally discussed in Western Europe in the 1980s as a consequence of the end of welfare capitalism and the goal of "full employment." As economies in North America and what was then the European Community experienced structural adjustment, marketization and transitioned toward neoliberalism, unemployment rose substantially in the latter from 2.4% in 1973 to 11% in 1989. The European Community's 12 member-states also soon experienced a combined increase in poverty from 38.6 million in 1975 to 49.3 million citizens in 1985 (Eurostat Database, 2018). As widespread structural unemployment became a permanent feature of the social landscape due to deindustrialization, the existing welfare state was reconfigured in tandem with the ideological turn away from state interventionism toward the neoliberal model. Welfare coverage was thus transformed from being universalist to targeting beneficiaries. As many people lost traditional social protections or their household's main source of income, it became clear that poverty was no longer simply a problem for the same vulnerable groups that had always received social protection, such as the fractionally unemployed, the elderly or families with large numbers of children. Instead, poverty and precariousness were now affecting much broader sectors for the first time, including people of working age, single-parent families and middle-class households with high levels of personal debt (Kessler and Di Virgilio, 2008:33).

By the late 1980s, the consequences of a decade of neoliberal reforms in Western Europe and North America had led many economists and sociologists to conclude that poverty was becoming a more fluid condition that households could slip in and out of (Katzman, 1989). While marketization sometimes created upward social mobility, the combination of external shocks (continued cycles of economic crisis that were triggered by events such as the 1973 oil shock or Europe's 1992 Exchange Rate Mechanism crisis) and internal household shocks (due to the loss of work, erosion of welfare benefits, divorce etc.) meant that periods of upward mobility were sometimes followed by episodes of acute decline in living standards and even pauperization.

Meanwhile, across the global north, governments were elected that pursued Thatcherite and Reganist agendas to varying degrees during the 1980s and 1990s. Structural adjustment and the policies of economic "liberalization" created unprecedented aggregate wealth in these societies and a flourishing, but relatively small, "new middle class." However, for many others, including the middle sectors, these policies of privatizing state industries, reducing public spending and attacking the power of trade unions resulted in rising vulnerability and pauperization. In addition, the primary institutions of socialization – such as the family and community – deteriorated, and social problems such as crime, rising divorce rates, domestic violence and mental health problems logically followed (Filgueira, 1999; Kliksberg, 2000). Pensions shrank, and social security eroded as universal welfare was withdrawn and societies experienced long-term unemployment (Pressman, 2007).

The first attempts to conceptualize new urban poverty were made in response to an appeal from Ruben Katzman (1989) at the UN Economic

Commission for Latin America and the Caribbean (CEPAL). He argued for the development of a conceptual model that could encapsulate the differential impact of neoliberal economic reforms on those households that had recently been pauperized, but which distinguished them from the structural or long-term poor. This call was answered by the Argentinian sociologist Alberto Minujín and his colleagues in *Cuesta Abajo* (Going Downhill) in 1993. In this groundbreaking work, the authors profiled a sociodemographic group (whom they christened the "new urban poor"). They described how this group had fallen into income poverty from the middle class, during the early 1990s global recession, and how they had begun to share a number of the same social problems experienced by the structural and long-term poor due to their recent hardship (low incomes, unemployment etc.). However, it was found that despite this, they possessed distinct personal characteristics from their nonpoor *pasts* and comparatively superior social, cultural and physical capital possession. These traits impacted heavily on their behavior when adjusting to their new social reality. Accordingly, and influenced by these distinct life experiences and their middle-class *habitus* (Bourdieu, 1977) that shaped their cultural values, attitudes and beliefs, it was found that they responded to financial hardship in a different way to the long-term poor in terms of their consumer responses, labor trajectories and lifestyle choices.

These distinct qualitative features of new urban poor or impoverished middle-class citizens include the fact that they have their basic needs satisfied and enjoy adequate housing conditions, high nutritional standards as well as access to water, gas and an electricity supply. Further, they possess superior levels of education and employment experience (often in a managerial or professional capacity) and are accustomed to *conspicuous* rather than *subsistence* consumption habits (Minujín, 1995:159; Kliksberg, 2000). A preference for proactive responses to dealing with their hardship (especially entrepreneurial strategies, sending additional household members into the labor market or working longer hours) has been detected rather than immediate, adaptive, consumer-orientated measures, which tend to be favored by the structurally poor (Fiszbein, Giovagnoli and Aduriz, 2003; Lokshin and Yemtsov, 2004).

Those in the middle class who enjoyed comfortable lifestyles, yet had been subject to serious financial shocks, had often become so accustomed to their luxury consumption patterns that they found it difficult to reduce their expenditure in accordance with their recently decimated household incomes once impoverished. This "cultural lag" is described by Pierre Bourdieu who in critiquing the notion of the *homo economicus*, explains that economic rationality is often abandoned during severe impoverishment or downward mobility. This continues until such time that they find the "mental peace" required to arrange their lives in "rational terms" and conceive a "plan for life" (Bourdieu *et al.*, 1963:307–308).

Similar patterns were repeated globally after the 2008 crisis. Although such individuals convince themselves that they are being frugal, in reality they become increasingly "poor" as they feel that they have to maintain their dignity and social standing, so for instance continue to take overseas holidays rather than cancelling them, travel around in their car as opposed to cheaper public transport, or dine out with friends in restaurants instead of saving money by cooking at home. Dorling (2010:120) also explained that indebtedness can thus perpetuate itself and intensify the impoverishment process for affected middle-class sectors, as households descend into ever-decreasing standards of social existence, as savings erode and as they assume greater indebtedness. He describes this as the process of moving from being comfortably off to "vulnerable" to "poor," then transitioning from "poor" to "core poor." Other sources suggest that newly impoverished citizens tend to try to retain elements of symbolic cultural capital, such as private education or membership of an exclusive country club, even to the detriment of more immediate health needs in order to maintain a presence that "all is well" to their peers (Kessler and Di Virgilio, 2008:41). They often reject charitable or state aid, despite having fallen below the breadline, because they do not want to be seen as "good for nothings" (Aguirre, 2008:49–54).

Minujín's model thus provided a welcome effort to construct a more comprehensive analysis of the increasingly complex nature of poverty. Although designed initially as a means by which the impact of Washington Consensus policies upon the middle-class sectors in Latin America could be scrutinized, its application was also useful for societies that had undergone similar restructuring in the global north.

The conceptual map in Figure 2.1 illustrates how impoverishment becomes more demographically heterogeneous in societies that either suffer from macroeconomic shocks, experience a retreat of the welfare state, encounter reduced public spending or face significant increases in non-fractional unemployment. It also depicts what has happened in Argentinian society since the 2001 crisis with regard to its poverty map. Area A represents the size of the structural poor (who live below the poverty line and also have unsatisfied basic needs). They are joined below the (diagonal) income poverty line by those in Area C – who despite being income impoverished have their basic needs satisfied. Area B represents the non-poor (usually the majority of the population). The main transformation between time period 1 (pre-shock) and time period 2 (post-shock) is that Area C increases in size (C1 to C2) as those who "have their basic needs satisfied" and are often (but not always) middle class, swell the ranks of the poor. This increase in the size of Area C from C1 to C2, therefore, represents those who have become "new poor" as a result.

Another reason that social scientists identified to explain the growth in new urban poverty was that from North America and Western Europe to Latin America, anti-poverty initiatives in the neoliberal age had consistently and explicitly targeted the structural poor but neglected the vulnerable non-poor. Minujín's (1993) conceptualization of the new urban poor social stratum within the middle class, therefore, served as

Homogeneity of poverty in time period 2

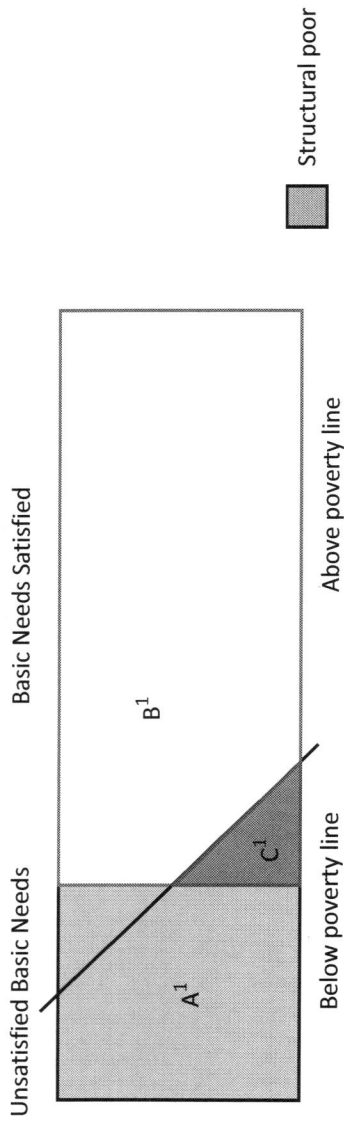

Unsatisfied Basic Needs   Basic Needs Satisfied

A^1

B^1

C^1

Below poverty line   Above poverty line

Heterogeneity of poverty in time period 2

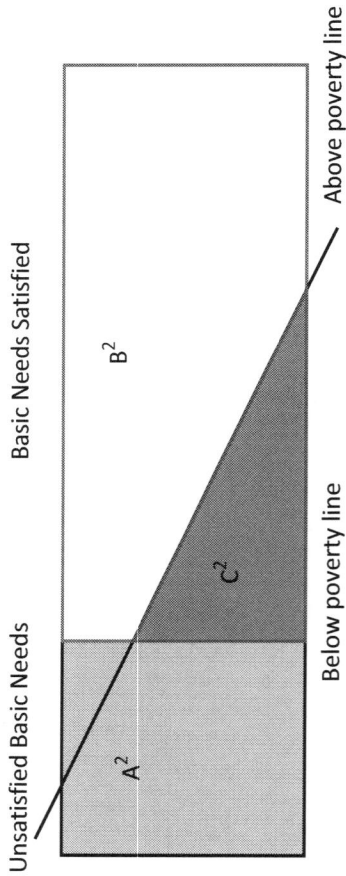

Unsatisfied Basic Needs   Basic Needs Satisfied

A^2

B^2

C^2

Below poverty line   Above poverty line

Structural poor

Non-poor

New poor

Figure 2.1 Growth of New Urban [Middle-Class] Impoverishment after Economic Shocks.
Source: Author, based on Minujin (1995:160).

a plea to policymakers to also consider the qualitative characteristics of both the *non-poor* who were vulnerable to impoverishment or proletarianization and the *recently* pauperized when designing social policy. Enacting new policies that utilize the sophisticated human, cultural, social and economic capital assets that the struggling middle-class possess in abundance would aid their recuperation more effectively than existing policies. Governments, NGOs, welfare agencies and intergovernmental organizations often failed to distinguish between whether the targeted "poor" household members lived on a council estate/in a shanty town and were long-term unemployed or low-skilled workers, or if they were highly educated homeowners who had recently lost their business and resided in a gentrified neighborhood.

In the early 1990s, it was easy to see why the early new urban poverty theorists were optimistic that the impoverished middle class would soon recover their prior socioeconomic status (Silverman and Yanowitch, 2000). Among transition economy theorists, the chaos that was unfolding in Eastern Europe during the change from command economy to capitalism had sparked mass impoverishment and great preoccupation, but this was expected to dissipate once "inefficiencies" had been cleared from the system. Meanwhile, in capitalist societies, it was also anticipated that new urban poverty and middle-class impoverishment would be temporary because it was felt that those affected by it would be able to use their superior capital assets (business and professional contacts, employment experience, sophisticated cultural practices etc.) to quickly recover livelihoods and jobs once economic growth was restored (Minujín, 1995).

Yet, sadly nearly three decades later, the appeals that were made at the time for revised policy initiatives to support such sectors have remained largely unheeded due to the fact that during growth periods, it is neglected as a policy concern yet under recession more universalist welfare is abandoned with support targeted to the most vulnerable. Consequently, while some programs have been effective in lifting large numbers of people out of poverty, an equally sizable proportion of vulnerable, nonpoor citizens have become pauperized according to the UN Development Programme (2004). Many of the impoverished middle class do, of course, emerge from poverty and soon retrieve their previous financial and employment status, but others fail to do so and become increasingly marginalized in the longer term, as Tikhonova (2004:142) found in post-communist Russia, for instance.

Middle-Class Impoverishment in Argentina 1980–2018

In the mid-1970s, Argentina boasted the largest and most influential middle class in Latin America. Yet having prospered under the Import-Substitution Industrialization (ISI) development model[1] since the 1930s, the fortunes of those in this class began to dwindle during the late 1970s and early 1980s when the military junta, which seized power in a coup in 1976, initiated neo-liberal reforms that led to the first of four such waves of new urban poverty in the country. Each of these waves corresponded to either the introduction or deepening of the neoliberal model and are outlined below.

Wave 1 (1976–89)

This wave included the replacement of ISI with early neoliberalism. The military junta (1976–83) sought to control rising inflation and economic instability by liberalizing the economy, freezing public-sector wages, criminalizing much trade union activity and shrinking public spending. The first "wave" of new poverty was unleashed and reached 35% of the population by the time the dictatorship fell in 1983 (INDEC, 2018). When Raúl Alfonsín was elected President soon after, he restored many political and social freedoms (including trade union activity) but regulated wage increases, especially under the Austral Plan from 1985 which also entailed spending cuts. The eventual consequences were so severe that real-terms salaries plummeted by 40% between the 1980s and 1990s (Kessler and Di Virgilio, 2008), and which fell especially acutely during the hyperinflation of 1989, prompting poverty to soar until it reached over half of Argentinians that year.

Wave 2 (1990–2000)

This wave occurred during the 1990s following the implementation of the Washington Consensus. This three-phase process was replicated across Latin America (Bulmer-Thomas, 1996:1).

- An initial period of macroeconomic stabilization through the reduction of public deficits.
- A second stage involving the enactment of structural adjustment reforms so as to open the economy up to trade, privatization and financial liberalization.
- A third and final stage seeking to attract overseas investment and increase productivity.

Argentina had amassed huge external debt in order to fund the civil-military regime (1976–83), having initially borrowed at low interest rates to do so. These soon became unserviceable once world interest rates began to soar in the mid- to late 1970s following the oil crisis. Similar patterns were repeated in other parts of Latin America, leading to a fully-fledged debt crisis in the 1980s. The Washington Consensus was notionally "agreed" between the World Bank, IMF and the region's respective national political leaderships. New loans were approved to Argentina and other Latin American governments so that they could repay the mounting external debts. They were provided on the condition that these governments introduced structural adjustment policies that would save their volatile economies. However, many commentators contest that national governments were subject to enormous external pressure to accept such agreements so had little choice but to accept the terms (Green, 2003). They also argue that the rescue plans were politically and ideologically motivated so as to impose neoliberalism on the region, rather than established as an *economic* but politically "neutral" project.

The second wave of pauperization thus followed in the 1990s, as a consequence of President Menem's neoliberal economic reforms and structural adjustment that "squeezed" the middle class during that decade. Initially, the Convertibility Plan was very successful in terms of both ending hyperinflation and controlling poverty, the latter which was brought back down to 20% by 1993 from its peak of 52% in 1989. However, the privatizations, concentration of industry, large-scale public-sector redundancies and wage freezes led many in the middle class to either lose their jobs or slip into financial hardship and poverty gradually crept up again to 32% by 1999 (Grimson and Kessler, 2005:37).

Wave 3 (2001–03)

During the severe economic crisis of this period, a more sudden and profound third wave of mass impoverishment was sparked by capital flight, sovereign debt default and currency devaluation as GDP plummeted by 20% in three years (INDEC, 2018). It was during this period that the *Corralito*[2] emergency decree was implemented by the government. Under this policy, Argentina's banks temporarily restricted the amount of their savings that depositors could withdraw in order to prevent a bank-run, a measure which lasted a year. Similar measures were taken in Cyprus in 2013 and Greece in 2015. Given that this happened at the height of a deep recession, the impact was exacerbated further as the principal safety net that many middle-class citizens would have otherwise relied upon to avert impoverishment was denied to them.

Unemployment soared to 21.5% in May 2002 (Argentinian Ministry of Labor), thousands of businesses closed and, in the urban centers, poverty rose from 38.3% in October 2001 to 53% in May 2002 (INDEC, 2018). The monumental scale and profundity of the economic crisis in 2001–02 was unprecedented in Argentinian history. However, unlike the North American impoverished middle class of the 1980s and 1990s, who had their parents' or grandparents' experiences of the 1930s Great Depression to draw upon to help them to cope psychologically with such sudden impoverishment, the Argentinian middle class (who had enjoyed two or three generations of upward mobility since arriving as immigrants from Europe) knew nothing other than the greater prosperity that their parents experienced (Kessler and Di Virgilio, 2008:40). As Schutz describes, with no "stock of knowledge" (1987) about how to deal with impoverishment, unlike the traditional poor, the pauperized middle class suffered not only economic poverty but also the painful psychological effects of their newfound situations.

During the peak of Argentina's economic crisis, the opportunities available to engage in income-generating activities were severely restricted, not just because of the scarcity of work available work, but also because of the acute shortage of currency in circulation following the debt default. Further, in the lead up to the government suspending payments on its US$132 billion debt, President de la Rúa enacted the *Corralito*. Because there was scarce flow of liquidity from which to actually earn or spend "money," this arguably prompted households to move beyond the traditional parameters of self-contained survival strategies, toward cooperation with others in the community to achieve self-improvement through participating in barter clubs or other collective activities.

Concurrently, a series of high-profile corruption cases stirred up a cauldron of distrust in the political establishment, sparking a crisis of legitimacy in the political class which was viewed as incompetent and self-serving and had already hemorrhaged support through its mismanagement of the economy. Argentina's traditional "delegative democracy" model of political participation (O'Donnell, 1994:55–69) was also strongly criticized by political scientists at the time due to the fact that it offered little accountability and few mechanisms for active citizen involvement in the democratic process between elections. These all became key grievances of the 2001–02 protest movement that exploded onto the streets.

While it must be recognized that many citizens did not take part in any collective actions at all, a significant proportion of the impoverished middle class became protagonists in both its protest and self-improvement movements, including the protests which overthrew four presidents in two weeks in late 2001 and early 2002. Their participation in *cacerolazos*, *escraches* (pickets of banks and judicial institutions by savers who had their money confiscated in the *Corralito*) and neighborhood assemblies are just some examples of the collective actions that erupted around the country during this period, which was notable for the appearance of struggling middle-class office workers, "still in their suits and ties, joining the protests alongside the long-term poor" (Barbetta and Bidaseca, 2004:82).

In fact, in terms of how income level correlated with protest participation, Fiszbein, Giovagnoli and Aduriz (2003) observe that, interestingly, among the *general* Argentinian population, involvement actually *increased* with household income during the crisis. Among the lowest income quintile, 11.4% of citizens engaged in social protests in 2002. This proportion increased steadily until reaching 17.5% in the second highest income quintile and 22% in the highest (Fiszbein, Giovagnoli and Aduriz, 2003). This suggests that it was the middle class rather than the long-term and structural poor who were most likely to join protests.

This phenomenon may be due to the fact that those on higher incomes were more motivated to take remedial action to the more sudden and unacceptable changes to their way of life than the long-term poor (see discussion of J-curve theory later), as well as in specific protests like the savers' *escraches* outside the banks (which only those who earned enough to have savings accounts in dollars took part in because it was they who would lose their deposits in the corralito), or that those higher up the pre-crisis earnings scale had a greater sense of political citizenship (Mazzoni, 2008), so were more angered by and thus moved to protest during the crisis of political legitimacy of those days. The lower protest participation rate of the poorest in society may also highlight the political alienation, powerlessness and isolation that such citizens often feel.

The extent to which Argentinians were subject to proletarianization and social descent into the working class[3] during the two-decade shift toward neoliberalism is conveyed in the following figures. It is estimated that the size of the country's middle class (using occupational criteria) peaked at 47.4% of the population in 1980, but slumped to 32% by 1991 during the "Lost Decade" (when economic growth in Latin America stagnated), before dipping further to just 21% by 2001 (Torrado, 2005:1085).

Figure 2.2 illustrates how "new poverty" became a prominent feature of the Argentinian socioeconomic landscape under neoliberalism. It conveys a transformation in the country's poverty map, with its "poor" population no longer being restricted to those with unsatisfied basic needs. From 1993 onward – and especially after the 2001–02 crisis – not only it included a large number who were income poor, but also who had their basic needs fulfilled.[4] The space above the "Unsatisfied Basic Needs line" on the graph (but below the "under the poverty line" one) represents the "new poor" (impoverished middle class) population. Although "new poverty" remains a largely temporary and cyclical phenomenon from which citizens tend to eventually be re-absorbed into the labor market, one-third of middle-class workers remained in or close to poverty by 2011, according to Consultora W.[5]

Wave 4 (2015–)

From its peak of 53% in 2002, poverty then fell acutely to about 25% by 2008 as the economy boomed under the initial years of the Kirchner governments. At this point, economic indicators vary widely between Argentina's state statistics agency INDEC and many "independent" consultants. While according to INDEC, poverty continued to fall to 12% by 2015, figures from the Catholic University of Argentina (UCA), for instance, suggest that poverty stabilized at around 25% until that year. When *Cambiemos* (Let's Change) and President Mauricio Macri took office in December 2015 and began to implement austerity measures, the cost of living increased by 54% in a year, as inflation increased further (partly due to several large currency devaluations). Moreover, the Energy

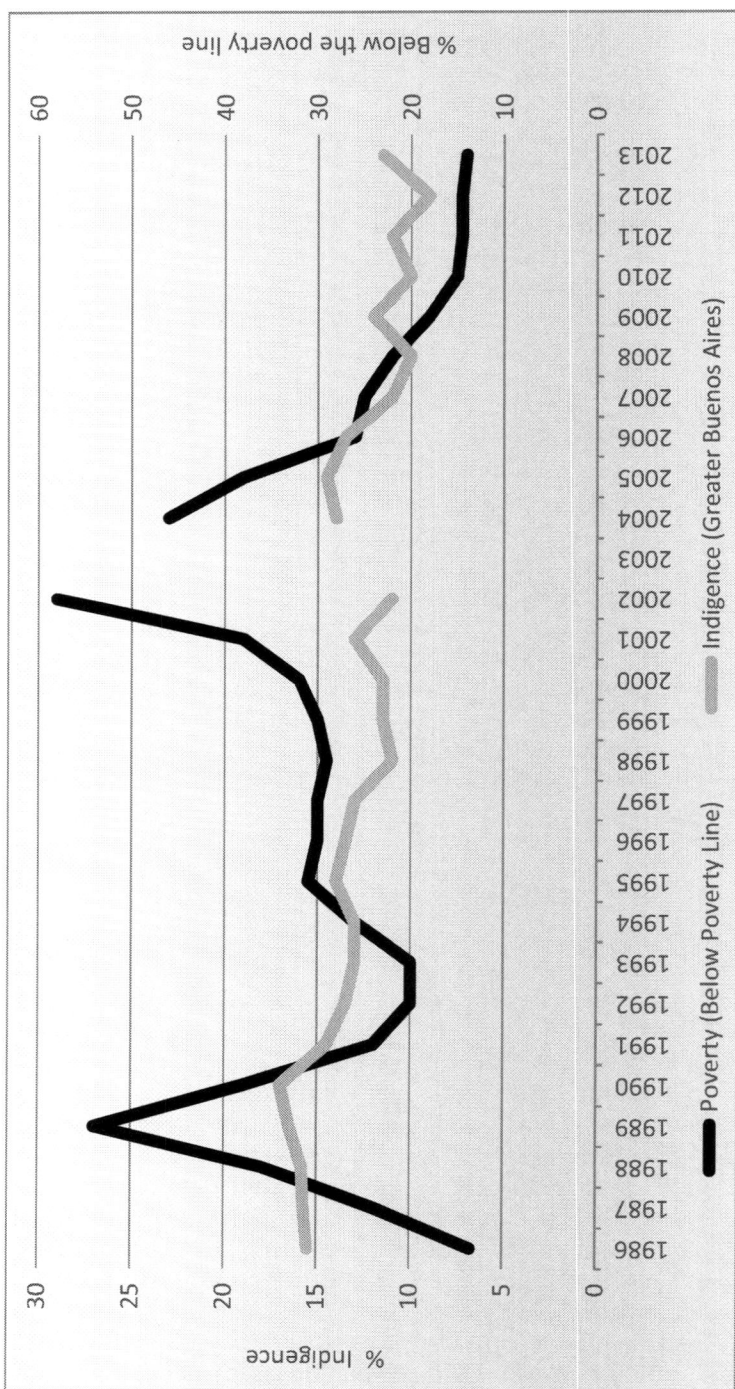

Figure 2.2 Proportion of Argentina's Population Living in Poverty or Indigence: 1986–2013.
Source: Arakaki (2016:287) using INDEC data.

Minister Juan José Aranguren announced that he would halve the US$16 billion subsidy bill. Gas tariffs quadrupled for most consumers, while those for electricity increased six-fold in what soon became known as the *Tarifazo*.

According to the UCA, a further 1.4 million Argentinians became impoverished in the first year of Macri's government alone (*El Pais*, 2017), sparking the fourth wave of new poverty. Small business owners and public-sector workers from the middle-class sectors were among the hardest hit, approximately 200,000 redundancies took place, principally among state workers and struggling small businesses and some fell into poverty themselves. In June 2018, Macri signed a "standby agreement" with the IMF following its currency crisis. It lent Argentina US$50 billion, but among the conditions it imposed were further public spending cuts in the order of US$20 billion by 2020: 74% of financing to the country's provinces, 48% in state subsidies and 81% in capital expenditures. These measures were expected to aggravate poverty and potentially pauperize hundreds of thousands more, including those in the middle class yet again.

Impoverished Middle-Class Mobilization and Social Movement Theory

Given that we have seen how economic crisis, mass pauperization and political rebellions led by the struggling middle class are all political realities both in Argentina and globally, struggling middle-class political mobilization and demobilization must be explained, guided by the different social movement theories. These will be discussed and applied to the context of Argentina's middle class under the neoliberal era.

Rational Choice Theory

Rational choice theory (RCT) argues that human behavior is determined by individuals choosing the actions that they think are best to maximize their own well-being. They choose from a given set of feasible options, and these actions occur *independently* of others. However, a key critique of this is that it is more appropriate to understand that structural forces shape the spaces available for individual agents to perform actions, and as such, individuals are never truly "free" to make their own decisions as utility-maximizing agents. Instead, they are subject to the logic and constraints of the capitalist system. Therefore, the action that they eventually decide upon equates to the outcome of a balance of forces between opposing pressures that create and constrain opportunities to act in different ways – including of interest to us – how they respond to downward mobility and financial shocks.

Rational choice assumptions have also been criticized as atomistic and over-individualistic (Kelly and Breinlinger, 1996). Such an approach assumes that citizens exist in a social vacuum and discounts the possibility that they may develop a sense of shared identity, forge collective grievances with others (in this case, with other middle-class citizens who have also become poor) or recognize the power that solidarity and collective action could have in resisting their social descent (Tajfel and Turner, 1986). Opponents of RCT also claim that under such circumstances, citizens then seek to advance their interests by using both collective economic and collective political channels (McCoy, 1980). The subsequent articulation of political demands is typically expressed through collective protests to government, judicial and financial authorities. Therefore, in order to fully understand the impact of economic crisis and subsequent impoverishment, it is necessary to acknowledge that economic processes cannot be divorced from the social and political consequences that they reap. It is for this reason that this book seeks to analyze economic and political resistance actions together.

Relative Deprivation Theory

This theory explains that citizens are motivated to join protest movements because they feel deprived or due to the perception of their own unequal position. This may occur either in relation to other social groups that have more power, status or economic resources (so they seek to attain this themselves by collectively demanding it), or in relation to what their expectations are (citizens will rebel when they achieve upward mobility or financial enrichment over time but then this suddenly stops or reverses). This may be because a country's economy suffers an economic crisis, for instance.

Their expectations of improvement thus become frustrated, given their declining material position. This is explained in James Davies' fascinating work *When Men Revolt and Why* (1971) and Ted Gurr's *Why Men Rebel* (1970). These two theorists attempted to explain political revolutions and why people overcome different barriers to engage in such protests in order to achieve social change. The *J-Curve model* that Davies developed apportions collective responses to a sudden reversal in fortunes after a long period of economic growth, or what he called "relative deprivation." The association between relative deprivation and the domestic incidence of collective protests was reaffirmed more recently in Richards and Gelleny's (2006:795) cross-national empirical study of crises and domestic agitation in 125 countries between 1981 and 2000. When expectations grow but are left unfulfilled, then a violent or politically radical response is likely. Middle-class radicalization might thus be explained by the desire of those within it to avoid being identified with the lower class at a particular moment of downward mobility. It may also occur due to its failure to become the dominant class when they become conscious of their economic, social and political powerlessness while developing a particularly potent willingness to try to change it (Eder, 1993:163–164).

The "Misery Matters Most" school (whereby a strong association between levels of poverty and prospects for political resistance to pauperization is assumed) is associated with authors such as Goldstone, Gurr and Moshiri (1991) but is refuted here both as a viable basis for developing a theory of revolution and also empirically in our Argentina case study as an explanation for the 2001 uprisings. No association was found between participation in protest actions in Argentina and the level of poverty experienced in the population (see Figure 3.1 in Chapter 3). Instead, drawing upon Melucci's (1989) ideas that bridge the gap between collective action theories and individual motivation to participate in them, the recognition of collective identity and grievance-forming becomes the basis upon which citizens decide to act together.

In the context of our book's topic, it is proposed that through daily interaction with other "newly impoverished" people who experienced the same declining living standards, members of this sector identified common interests and under certain conditions, engaged in collective social, economic and political initiatives to resist their descent in response. Their experience of hardship as an "economic" one can, therefore, not be divorced from actions that took place in the social and political realms and the decisions that newly impoverished households made in response to such shocks. These sometimes extend beyond merely economic self-improvement strategies. Through the recognition that they have become subject to a common injustice (Mansbridge, 2001), shared grievances may be presented in the form of demand-making to a third party through collective protest.

Resource Mobilization Theory

This theory, first discussed by McCarthy and Zald (1977), focuses on the way that social movements mobilize finance and elite support. It explains how shared grievances are not sufficient to explain creation of social movements. Instead, access to and control over resources is the crucial factor, above all else because movements require organizations to acquire and then make resources available to achieve their objectives. These resources may consist of material (financial and physical capital), moral (solidarity and other support), social (networks, strategies, capacity to recruit), human (volunteers, leaders, staff) and cultural (level of experience among activists, knowledge of collective action and understanding of the issues among the movement itself).

Political Process Theory

This set of theories looks at the way that movements and activists use political opportunities in their interaction with established political institutions (Tilly, 1978; McAdam, 1982). For instance, when political contexts change, they can foster or limit social movement activity depending on the circumstance. These act as signals to potential activists to either engage in or increase their participation in a particular protest movement (or withdraw or reduce commitment) because possibilities for success rise (or fall), respectively. Opportunities include: the declining ability or desire by the state to repress dissent, when the ruling elite is divided; if access to elites improves (which can aid the movement achieve its goals) or if the movement gains access to political decision-making power.

Aside from these opportunities available in the political structure, citizens must first also realize that their grievance is shared by a significant number of other citizens, then understand that they are subject to an "injustice" which is not of their own making (Mansbridge, 2001), before thirdly, feeling optimistic enough about their ability to change their circumstances by acting collectively. McAdam (1982) describes this "cognitive liberation" as a prerequisite for protest so that the sociopsychological dynamics of collective attribution and social construction – the framing process (Snow and Benford, 1988) – are satisfied. Lacking any one of these factors, prospects for mobilization will be stifled. The importance of "ideas" and how they are understood (or "framed"), therefore, makes up an essential pillar of collective action.

Clearly, the kind of "cognitive liberation" that is of interest in this book is that which liberates newly impoverished citizens from hegemonic domination. What are the processes that militate toward their passive acceptance of their social descent or which encourage them to solely play out their resistance through economic self-help strategies rather than collective protest actions?

New Social Movement Theory

A group of theories emerged in the 1980s in order to analyze the social movements that organized around race, sexuality, environmentalism, pacifism, human rights and so on from the 1960s onward. These "new" movements are understood to deviate from the "old" working-class movement which Marxists identified as the only one that could challenge the capitalist system for improved material gain. In contrast, those involved in these new movements were seen as having post-materialist motivations. Rather than class conflict, social and political conflicts were key, with social changes in identity, lifestyle and culture emphasized over public policy initiatives as the goal.

New social movement theory emphasizes culture as the main arena and means of protest. Contesting meanings, identities and symbols in cultural spaces is paramount, and activists are less concerned with material enrichment and more interested in promoting expressive, identity-oriented actions whose very form challenges the instrumental rationality of political elites (Touraine, 1981; Melucci, 1989). In his discussion of "middle-class radicalism," Parkin (1968) argued that these movements' key actors often derive from the new middle class and also organize themselves more loosely into informal networks rather than formal organization with membership structures more typical of more traditional labor unions and working-class movements. They combine elements of the new middle class, old middle class and peripheral groups outside the labor market (students, pensioners, housewives, the unemployed etc.). Their high levels of education and their access to information and resources lead to the questioning of the way society is valued and seek to change this rather than necessarily gain materially.

Marxism, Hegemony, Ideology and False Consciousness

The process of middle-class impoverishment has been experienced by millions globally under neoliberalism since the 1990s, including during the current global crisis. Marx and Luxemburg (1906) would argue that this is an inevitable consequence of the logic of capitalist development. The advance of capitalism leads to a hollowing out of the middle class, resulting in proletarianization for many, especially during times of severe economic crisis. However, as this occurs, polarization develops between the proletariat and the bourgeoisie in terms of their class "position." It was Laclau and Mouffe (1985:12), in *Hegemony and Socialist Strategy,* who highlighted the limitations of Rosa Luxemburg's "Sponteneism" (the unity of economic and political struggle), by explaining that although one may experience proletarianization in terms of objective class "position," the development of a corresponding proletarianized political subjectivity and class consciousness cannot be assumed. This is because the material and institutional processes in capitalist societies mask the true relations of forces between the classes.

Thus, citizens who experience proletarianization and slip into the working class in terms of their relation to the production process, often adopt a "false consciousness" due to the ideological control to which they are subjected by the dominant class. That is to say, they believe they still belong to the middle class and also believe that they share class interests or even with the dominant class, thus granting these elites consent to rule over them despite being subjugated by them. Thus, rule by these elites become "hegemonic" because as Gramsci describes (1998 [1929–1935]), it comes to be seen as "common sense" to pursue the interests of the dominant class among broad layers of society.

As a result of not identifying that they have become subject to this process, the economic hardship and social descent of the middle class does not necessarily turn into a political struggle and a direct confrontation between the bourgeoisie and the proletariat, as Luxemburg implied. The logic of "spontaneity" is, therefore, limited, and the prospects for revolution are frustrated. Luxemburg predicted that "revolutionary" social change in modern societies depended on the spontaneous awakening of critical class consciousness, but in contrast, Laclau and Mouffe argue that this change is dependent upon the prior formation of a new alliance of interests and the existence of an alternative hegemony that has already developed a cohesive worldview of its own. They claim that the new revolutionary agent in this case is not only the existing working class but also the unemployed and "proletarianized" middle class. In later chapters, the extent to which an alternative hegemony and class alliances existed in Argentina post-2001 will be explored.

Marxists claim that through their underemployment, unemployment, and loss of workplace autonomy or ability to control the means of production, many of the struggling middle class have become "working class" (Wright, 1978:63) or proletarianized, even if it is psychologically too painful for them to accept. For instance, it is typical for newly poor citizens to seek justifications for why they can still claim to hold a "middle-class identity" in spite of their objectively working-class circumstances.

The Marxist theorist Georg Lukács (1920), contends that the cognitive movement away from this false consciousness toward a true awareness of one's conditions of exploitation by the capitalist class is aided by both the experience of economic crisis and an understanding of Marxist theory, because together these enable workers to develop a clearer understanding of the social totality. It is this totality, he argues, that reproduces the underlying structural reasons for their exploitation or in the case of our subject, their social descent or impoverishment. Capitalism as a system should thus be the target of their struggle, rather than particular isolated issues (racial discrimination, sexism etc.), because ultimately capital seeks to atomize these struggles so as to divert attention away from the systemic cause of the exploitation of the entire working class.

However, Lukács also argues that there is a need for the presence of a revolutionary party to organize the struggle against the capitalist class and to ensure that both bourgeois and working-class reformism are avoided in order to achieve social transformation (Eyerman, 1981:49). However, both the post-2008 global uprisings and Argentina in 2001–02 can largely be understood to have occurred without having an operational Marxist-Leninist revolutionary vanguard party that traditional Marxists argue is essential. Instead, less authoritarian and top-down heuristic politicizing vehicles were drawn upon, which aided the process of an emerging class consciousness through fostering involvement in practical social projects. These were grounded in the labor or social experience and also helped struggling middle-class citizens to understand their own situation as part of an exploited class alongside other groups. This conglomeration of groups that moves beyond the traditional working class are framed as the "decent people" by Podemos in Spain for instance, standing in contrast to "the cast" or political and economic elites. Once they have undergone this transformation in their own subjectivity and recognized the injustice to which they are subject, they are more likely to participate in more radical action to confront the systemic reasons for their pauperization. These processes will be explained later.

Within Marxism, different schools propose a range of mobilizing strategies. Marxist-Leninism posits that the movement necessarily requires the leadership of a workers' vanguard party, whereby an elite group of holders of knowledge must disseminate their revolutionary wisdom by organizing "the masses." In contrast, Hardt and Negri (2004) argue that the twenty-first century is an age in which the masses have themselves become the producers of knowledge due to popular Internet access and mass availability of the media and communications. Thus, "the multitude" can themselves be the revolutionaries via alternative autonomist mobilizing vehicles whereby hierarchical organization is not seen as necessary to achieve these ends. During Argentina's 2001–02 uprisings, such an approach was favored by the struggling middle class and almost all the social movements that came to the fore at that time, during a crisis of political legitimacy in which left-wing parties were also often derided and the objects of suspicion. One question that will be analyzed in Chapter 4 is why these movements dissipated once Argentina's economic recovery began, even though the core ideas remained held by many of the individuals who were involved in them as well as in wider society. How Argentina's middle class were demobilized due to the lack of a sufficient mobilizing vehicle (as Resource Mobilization Theory assumes), and what lessons can be learned for other middle-class–led movements will be discussed later.

Marxism can also help to account for "new poor" political mobilization in terms of who citizens blame for their material loss and social descent. Dialectical materialist thought explains that human history develops as the result of an outcome of forces: the current state of affairs (thesis), which gives rise to its reaction (antithesis), which contradicts or negates the thesis. The tension between the two is resolved by means of a synthesis. In the instance of personal downward mobility like that experienced by the struggling sectors within Argentina's middle class, and as stated by Hegel (in Guess, 1981), indignation at their abasement is

> driven by the contradiction between their human nature ['the thesis' by which they enjoy a comfortable way of life which they have become used to] and their new conditions of life ['the antithesis' which here is manifest as downward mobility and a struggle to make ends meet], which is an outright, resolute and comprehensive negation of that nature.

The reaction from struggling middle-class citizens is to wish to annihilate "the negation/antithesis." In this case, the "antithesis" is their impoverishment or proletarianization and their response is to protest against its perceived cause.

In other words, if such citizens see themselves as "the cause" of their own pauperization during the economic crisis and they accept the dominant class' ideology that such cycles of crisis are "the natural order of things," then they are likely to internalize the reasons for their social descent and act against their own class interests, with potentially dangerous consequences for their own physical and mental well-being as they engage in self-blame. However, if the cause is seen as "external" – due to some kind of institution or process which they do not see as inevitable or disempowered to change – then this opposition to the "antithesis" may manifest itself as collective actions and rebellion.

A further criticism of RCT and the idea that citizen responses to downward mobility will effectively be restricted to economic self-improvement actions that can be found in Marxism is the following. In *The Holy Family* (1844), Marx and Engels explain that when human agents are forced into recognizing that the potential for their capacities to flourish has been constrained and they are less able to maintain the living standards to which they are accustomed, rather than developing new, more sophisticated needs, they instead experience a deteriorating quality of life and so downwardly reconfigure what their needs are. In effect, they employ "adaptive coping strategies." This reevaluation of one's needs is something that is acutely painful to accept. It can generate demoralization, as well as feelings of anger and the desire for resistance. However, actually performing the latter depends upon the political, economic and social contexts in which their circumstances have occurred. This context informs the extent to which they understand themselves to be at fault for their own impoverishment or whether others are deemed to be responsible for it. If the latter is decided upon, then citizens observe to what extent they might undertake specifically *noneconomic* (political) responses to their *economic* decline. Such processes are observed *en masse* in several of the countries discussed so far.

Hegemony and Spaces for the Emergence of Social Movements

Holistic approaches to social movement participation understand that the possibilities for individual citizens to resist impoverishment are not created in a vacuum but are shaped by the pressures that create and constrain opportunities for them to act in other ways. Similarly, the ways in which grassroots movements emerge and conduct their actions are shaped not simply by members' own experiences but also by those of their opponents and the structures and institutions to which they are subject.

Antonio Gramsci's (1998 [1929–1935]) theory of cultural hegemony describes how dominant social groups maintain their position in society and are able to manage the antagonistic class relationships that develop as a result of capitalist production. These antagonisms would otherwise form the basis for resistance from what he calls "the working class" and other exploited social groups, but by exercising hegemonic dominance at all levels of society – backed up by the threat of coercion (through violence and judicial punishment) by the state – the dominant class is able to achieve consent from the masses to govern society in its own interests. Often, workers and our stratum of interest in this book – the proletarianized middle class and other groups – will come to believe that they share interests with those of the ruling class. They develop a "false consciousness" without the latter even having to resort to physical repression. Instead, Gramsci explains how this ability to achieve consent derives partly from the capacity of ruling elites to promulgate ideologies of dominance through a variety of channels. He describes how "cognitive horizons" (belief systems) operate, whereby the existing order is represented as "natural" and purposive and therefore legitimate. The majority thus work to defend the interests of capital, which manages to preserve its domination over the masses, who themselves reproduce and consolidate the hegemony of elite interests without even realizing it. Hegemony, however, is not unidirectional, understood as the imposition of government logic from above. Instead, it is better understood as a reciprocal process between unequal sides in which the popular classes may either support, reshape or even resist the ruling class' attempt to impose hegemony (Balsa, 2006).

Gramsci built on many of the early ideas of Marx and Engels, who in their theories of "ideology" and "false consciousness" – which are described perhaps most clearly in the *German Ideology* (1845) – identified how the actions of capitalists and intellectuals create a distortion between workers' social reality (their objective class interests) and their social consciousness (what they subjectively believe those interests to be).

The application of these concepts then evolved in three stages. For Marx and Engels, the problems of false consciousness and ideology are limited entirely to the realm of the *superstructure* (which includes a society's culture, institutions, political power structures, roles, rituals and the state) that are the outcome of the interaction of social relations at the *base* (that is to say, the forces and relations of production such as employer–employee work conditions, the technical division of labor and property relations). In particular, the two concepts can only be applied to the elite producers of ideas, as under capitalism they delude the working class into believing that they (as these elite idea-formers) are the only ones who can make history. Thus, because the working class are excluded from the superstructure, they are also unable to be "the producers of knowledge," and so their own actions in this regard are confined to the base (Eyerman, 1981:45).

Lenin then developed these concepts in *What is to be Done* (1902), by applying them more closely to the working class whom, he claimed, *could* directly experience false consciousness too. He explained how the strain of being subjected to daily exploitation during their working lives under capitalism generates short-term goals in workers' minds, so they therefore try to "get the best out of a bad situation" in the workplace, whether individually or collectively. For this reason, they tend toward seeking immediate material gain and so develop a "trade unionist" or reformist consciousness rather than a revolutionary one. Solutions which could produce their emancipation from exploitation under capitalism are, therefore, abandoned. For Lenin, this "false consciousness" posed a huge danger, as it represented a political strategy that brought the working class into the superstructure of capitalist society through parliamentary politics and reformist policies and thus further submission to the ideology of the bourgeoisie.

Gramsci then advanced these notions further still. Unlike Marx, not only did he add a new dimension to the analysis by applying the concept of false consciousness directly to the working class (like Lenin), but he was also concerned with how the superstructure – into which the working class were now embedded, along with religion and culture – impacted upon working-class consciousness. He was also more precise than Marx and Engels in terms of describing the methods that the bourgeoise uses to ideologically dominate the working class, explaining that they either use "force" or "hegemony." He sought to map out how strategies to change society could be achieved under different political circumstances (Eyerman, 1981) taking these processes into consideration.

But first, it is important to ask what strategies do the dominant social group use to maintain elite control and prevent resistance from below? It must be remembered that the hegemony of the elites does not exist as a permanent form of dominance but is subject to resistance and so must be constantly defended, renewed and modified in order to guarantee stability and reproduce hegemonic control. The right-hand side of Figure 2.3 illustrates how the dominant class usually uses a combination of "defensive" strategies of accommodation (concessions) and repression or "offensive" strategies of repression via the state, which are delivered in varying doses depending on the political system in place at the time. The state is their principal medium through which these strategies are applied when faced with challenges from below.

Crucially, the significance of the left-hand side of the diagram is emphasized especially strongly by Gramsci. It illustrates how "civil society" institutions are used to instill the culturally dominant ideology. For him, extra-economic models of domination work to reduce the disruption caused by the antagonistic tendencies between capital and labor (particularly during times of economic crises), but these are not confined purely to those of the bourgeois state, but also extend to the institutions of civil society.

Unlike Marx, Gramsci did not locate civil society at the socioeconomic "base," where productive forces and social relations take place. Instead, he described it as constituting part of the political superstructure and the loci from where ideological capital emanates. The latter is required to generate the consensual practices that are needed to fortify the state and protect the elites from subversive challenges. It is within this realm

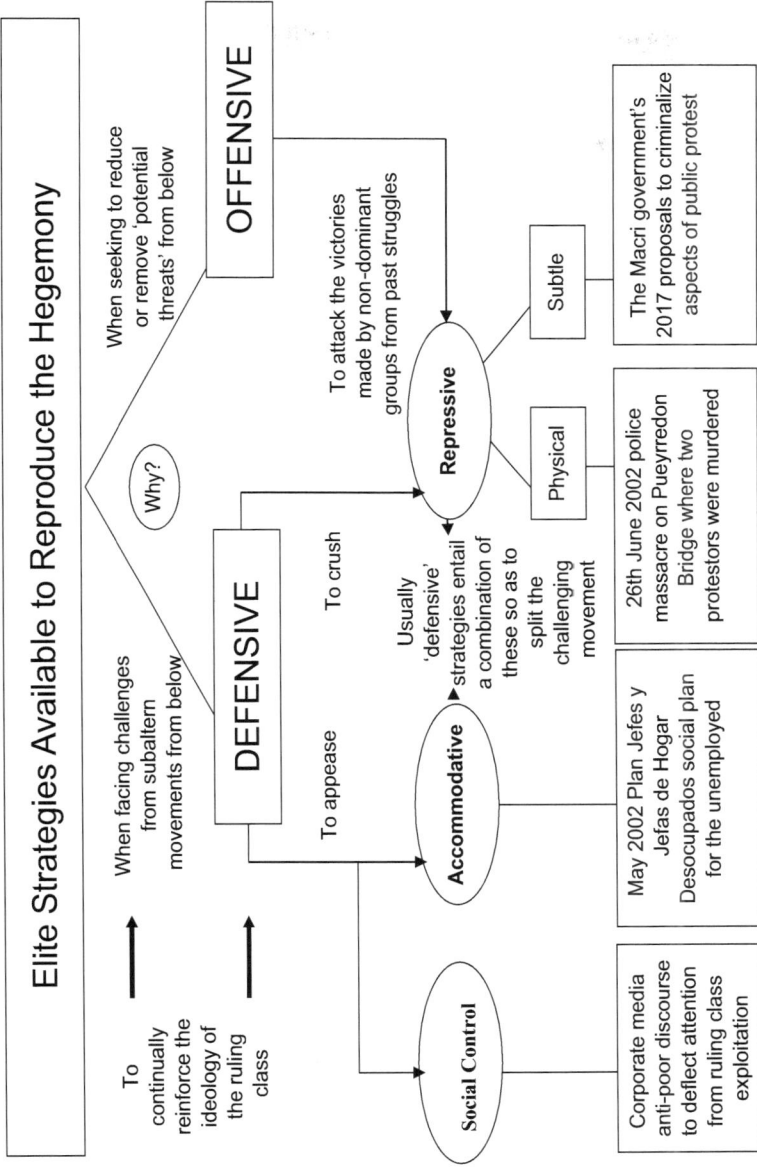

Elite Strategies Available to Reproduce the Hegemony

OFFENSIVE — When seeking to reduce or remove 'potential threats' from below

DEFENSIVE — When facing challenges from subaltern movements from below

To continually reinforce the ideology of the ruling class

Why?

To appease — To crush

To attack the victories made by non-dominant groups from past struggles

Usually 'defensive' strategies entail a combination of these so as to split the challenging movement

Social Control
Corporate media anti-poor discourse to deflect attention from ruling class exploitation

Accommodative
May 2002 Plan Jefes y Jefas de Hogar Desocupados social plan for the unemployed

Repressive
- Physical — 26th June 2002 police massacre on Pueyrredon Bridge where two protestors were murdered
- Subtle — The Macri government's 2017 proposals to criminalize aspects of public protest

Figure 2.3 Defensive and Offensive Strategies used by Elite Groups to Preserve Hegemony.
Source: Author, based upon ideas in Nilsen (2009).

of civil society that the reproduction of capitalist hegemony is integral and, so by implication, is the understanding of what creates and prevents revolution (Burawoy, 2008:23).

A range of authors have expanded on Gramsci's work by examining how hegemony is reproduced through these institutions of civil society. These include the mass media which in *Manufacturing Consent* (1988), Herman and Chomsky explain the need to capture advertising revenue from big business, which inevitably shapes an editorial bias in favor of the ruling class in terms of what they feature and how they report news stories. The media also constantly resort to forms of symbolic violence, such as ridicule, in order to delegitimize counterhegemonic ideas (Bourdieu, 1998). Meanwhile, social theorists such as Nye (1958) focus on the role of the family as a means of achieving social control, and Marx himself (1844) famously declared religion to be the "opium of the people" in his critique of Hegel's idealism and overtures toward the Church, because he argued it was an obvious diversion from the "class struggle."

Certainly, the state also plays an important role in guaranteeing the consent of the people to be governed by those with contrasting interests to their own. In particular, the existence of the welfare state reinforces the idea that citizens should remain loyal to their country, because it seemingly "protects" them (Miliband, 1969). The state is also necessary for the reproduction of capitalism and the preservation of elite interests, because it actually helps to reproduce the exploitation of workers and the poor by protecting property rights as the foundation of the legal system, and the capitalist processes which create the conditions of their hardship in the first place (Gough, 1979). State schools prepare and educate the future workforce to contribute to the production process (and the creation of surplus for owners and managers) and state health systems enable workers to remain productive and overcome illness to be able to work. Indeed during the 2007–08 financial crisis, it was the state itself that effectively saved financial capitalism. As mortgages failed following the subprime crash, the largest banks in the USA, the UK, Belgium, Iceland, Spain, Russia, Ireland and Ukraine were saved through nationalizations or bailouts costing trillions of dollars in total. Through the support of the state, elite interests come to be seen as the "general interest" of all social groups, including by their use of nationalism, which has traditionally been applied by the ruling class to proliferate the idea that the working class' interests should be aligned with the domestic bourgeoisie against a foreign enemy.

In *Pedagogy of the Oppressed*, Paulo Freire (1970) discusses how the state education system and the classroom are used to instill subordination and discipline from an early age. Education is used as a means to consciously shape children into subordination to capitalist authority and can only become part of an emancipatory process through the development of a critical awareness of one's social reality through reflection and action.

However, authors such as Anderson (1976) have criticized Gramsci for exaggerating the importance of ideological hegemony and underplaying the role of the threat of state violence in securing consent, because of his insistence that it is "culture" which is the preferred mechanism through which bourgeois power is asserted. However, Gramsci understood that ultimately the threat of state coercion will always be executed when consensual hegemonic practices fail. His own experience of incarceration in Italy when in a situation of hegemonic crisis during the 1920s made him well aware of this. At that time, the ruling elite was struggling to maintain ideological domination through many of the subjugation and accommodation processes described, so resorted to force to subdue challenges from below.

Anderson mistakenly suggests that the consensual nature of bourgeois authority resides in the state alone, because it is the only locus where the public interest is seen to be represented and where legitimacy is constructed. However, given that Anderson was writing in the mid-1970s, it is likely that his views were influenced by contemporary currents of thought and the social and political events of the time. During an era that represented the "golden age" of welfare capitalism, state interventionism and redistribution of income, it is easy to understand why he may have attributed an elevated level of importance to the state as a medium for reproducing the hegemony of the dominant class. Today, as a result of the neoliberal project in contrast, one can observe how many state functions have been devolved to private enterprise, civil society organizations and NGOs to deliver and how these are becoming increasingly important tools to reproduce hegemony.

Cultural Framing

In order to account for collective action of the struggling middle class, one final element that must be considered is the presence and utilization of "framing processes" and "mediating frames" (Snow *et al.*, 1986). That is to say, it is the shared meanings and definitions that people apply to their situations that are what actually mobilize those who are aggrieved about their circumstances to act.

Ryan (2005:133) suggests that justice frames are best presented as a counternarrative which proposes a counterhegemonic view, in which participants are invited to imagine a better world through the frame that is presented to them. By enabling citizens to confront the contradictions between their present existence and their imagined better situation, it brings these contradictions to the fore and exposes them. Applied to the context of this book, newly pauperized citizens in Argentina in 2001–02 started to understand this and resisted their pauperization collectively not just through protest but also politically, through participation in working models of collective self-help that established a bridge between their present existence (whereby the capitalist system of accumulation had become naturalized and accepted as "the norm") and this imagined better society that normally seems so remote and impossible to achieve.

Becoming aware or participating in collective self-help actions demonstrates how in real life, alternative social systems that are based upon solidarity can move from the sociological imagination to function in reality, especially if a justice frame is found that helps struggling middle-class citizens to recognize the injustice they have suffered themselves alongside others who have undergone the same experience (Mansbridge, 2001). In such cases, they might begin to feel a sense of solidarity with the injustices experienced by the indigent poor, who they would then recognize had been victims in the same way as them, but long *before* the crisis, as opposed to after it in the case of Argentina. The likelihood that proletarianized urban middle-class citizens will come to realize that they have a common political cause to rally around together with the long-term poor, unemployed and those who made up the bulk of working class – instead of each fighting disparate and lonely struggles against them – increases if the "sites" of social integration, like those mentioned here, are replicated and connected.

The frame can then be grounded in "rituals of solidarity" (McAdam, McCarthy and Zald, 1996) through these initiatives in a way that pure "imagining" fails to do. Promoting involvement in small-scale, practical collective actions thus makes the achievement of a more solidaristic society more believable and attainable in the minds of the middle-class citizens who become involved in them. For this sector, it also helps to raise awareness of the contrast between the lived experience of poorly remunerated, low-skilled, weakly autonomous and often barely appreciated effort that their individually performed daily work entails, in contrast to the positive experiences that collective self-help projects generate in terms of utilizing skills, building self-esteem, solidarity and more profound personal relationships with others. Consequently, political engagement can be understood as a combination of having found a practical channel through which they can explore and understand the contradictions in their own lives by proposing an alternative to their current realities (framing), together with involvement in a practical experience to help them believe that achieving this alternative is possible. The extent to which this recipe applied within our case study sample will be investigated.

Legacy of Exclusionary Corporatism on the 2001–02 Rebellion

In Argentina, the elites have historically found it difficult to perpetuate their ideological domination over the subaltern classes. This has been a consequence of the country's unusual pattern of capitalist development and class relations and, in particular, the arrested political development of its liberal bourgeoisie. These features combine to having made it susceptible to periods of military dictatorship and state use of violence to assert authority. It is in this context that the crisis of neoliberal hegemony – which arose during the 2001–02 uprisings and opened spaces for different forms of resistance – can be better understood. First, the country's economic and political history will be examined, so as to place these uprisings into historical context.

In the 1930s, Argentina adopted an ISI model of state-centered development to protect the economy against its foreign dependency in the wake of the Great Depression. One of the main impacts of this was that it led to a rapidly expanding, powerful and potentially revolutionary urban working class in the emerging industrial centers. The labor force was heavily influenced ideologically by exiled Spanish, Italian and Russian immigrant workers – many of whom were communists or anarchists (Munck, 1987). Following a series of unsuccessful uprisings (which were supported by the Radical Civic Union [UCR] Party) against the military or Conservative governments, the organized labor movement became perceived as a serious threat to the capitalist order at the time. Due to its size and militancy, it was impossible to crush, so the ruling class realized that its political power to overthrow the state via revolution could only be contained through the establishment of corporatist state apparatus to appease and co-opt the labor movement into retreat. This was the role that General Juan Perón and Peronism came to play.

Under Perón's time in office as Labor Minister and Vice President (1943–45), employers were forced to improve working conditions and workers were given greater protections against dismissal with the establishment of labor courts to handle their grievances. The working day was also reduced in several industries, and paid holidays/vacations were granted to the entire workforce. Minimum wages, maximum hours and holidays for rural workers were all granted by Perón, who became enormously popular among much of the labor movement. At the same time, he was despised by the conservative establishment, including sectors of the ruling military.

On 17 October 1945, massive trade union demonstrations in Buenos Aires forced the ruling military to release Perón from arrest following a public speech he had made in favor of social reforms. These protests marked the birth of the Peronist movement in Argentina and the date was later commemorated as Loyalty Day.[6] One of the main effects of the protests and the affirmation of his popularity among the population was that it persuaded sections of the ruling class that the only way to prevent a revolutionary challenge and to consolidate their power was to compromise. Thus when Perón became president a few months later in February 1946, henceforth a corporatist alliance was established between the bulk of the labor movement (CGT union federation), the military, the domestic industrial bourgeoisie and (initially) the Church. This created a model of class relations that endured long throughout his two governments (1946–55), long after Perón was exiled in 1955 following the *Revolución Libertadora* and which continues to this day. While Argentinian corporatism traces its roots back to military leader, President Uriburu's government from 1930, it was under Perón that the model became more deeply woven into Argentina's social fabric, especially in terms of the incorporation of the labor unions.

However, an important consequence of establishing corporatist class relations at a relatively early stage in the country's industrial development was that its liberal bourgeoisie was unable to secure political superiority or implement a liberal-democratic program. To some degree, this explains why Argentina's modern history has been littered with dictatorships – fascist or otherwise – and why only quasi-democratic institutions have developed since (Levitsky and Murillo, 2005). For example, its trade union movement has failed to gain "independence" from Peronist domination. Only the Peronist union Confederation, the CGT, has full legal recognition to collectively bargain nationally (other confederations like the *CTA Autónoma* and the *CTA de los Trabajadores* are denied this right despite it being in contravention of ILO Convention 87 on free and democratic trade union organization and also a Supreme Court ruling). Further, the loyalty of its urban poor has been assured through the cynical use of informal clientelist electoral practices by Peronist and other political parties (Auyero, 2001). It is the presence of such class relations at the base that has meant that at the level of the superstructure, the mediating civil society institutions (unions, political parties etc.) and those of the state (judiciary, police etc.) have been weak. Consequently, liberal democracy has never fully developed or been institutionally embedded to the same extent as it has in Western Europe, for example.

As Guillermo O'Donnell (1994) explains, the kind of democracy that was established during the country's political transition in the 1980s was "delegative," in the sense that only minimalist notions of political participation were expected of citizens or even permitted. The electorate was supposed to subordinate itself to locally elected politicians or presidential decisions in between elections. Yet this system failed to provide accountability or opportunities for direct participation in the decision-making process. Under President Menem's government in the 1990s, such practices were reinforced when provincial caudillos were effectively financed via the federal government to bolster subnational authoritarianisms as well as their corruptive practices (Armony and Armony, 2005:30).

The other effect of October 1945 was that it led to Perón's democratic election in February 1946. At a time of immense political polarization, middle- and upper-class anti-Peronists of European descent viewed the ascendency of the largely working-class, dispossessed and often darker-skinned Peronists[7] to power with horror (Adamovsky, 2009). Although racial and class identities had been conflated in Argentina ever since President Sarmiento first outlined his national vision, the Peronist victory in 1946 seemed to confirm it.

The tangible unity of struggling middle class with unemployed and blue-collar workers on the streets during the 2001–02 revolt was one of the most fascinating characteristics of the rebellion. One of the most popular chants of those days was "[middle-class] pot-banger and [unemployed] piquetero, the struggle is one and the same!" Yet, this unity was a temporary phenomenon. The historical tendency to associate one's class identity and interests with one's racial background contributed to the reinvigoration of false consciousness that many newly impoverished middle-class Argentinians possessed soon after the 2001–02 crisis ended and political normality was restored. Due to racial stigmatization, many failed to realize their shared class interests with *Mestizo* workers in the longer term, meaning that these deep-seated racial divisions could be exploited by the dominant class once again as they sought to reestablish control after 2003 by demonizing and scapegoating the structural poor.

In Argentina, consent for rule by the ruling class has historically been secured through the implementation of this corporatist model. This has proved to be highly exclusionary in social and political terms. In demobilizing and asserting control over potential challenges from below (by effectively granting privileges and material gains to or co-opting the support of parts of the labor movement or other civil society groups that have been most open to accepting it), traditionally corporatism has led to periods of "bureaucratic authoritarian" regimes. Even more recently under democracy, it has prevented significant parts of organized labor, social organizations and social sectors from being able to present a united and sustained movement to further their political and economic goals. The legacy is a highly polarized society where the political stakes of being excluded from the government of the day are enormous.[8] This is because the fortunes of interest groups within subaltern sectors are heavily dependent on whether their respective corporatist ally is in power locally (via its governors and municipal councils) or nationally. Another effect of this was that Argentina's political legitimacy had been in free fall for decades, spurring the growth or autonomism as a political philosophy, given that the state was deemed to have been complicit in the endemic political corruption, clientelism (vote-buying or political participation in exchange for welfare and the erosion of social protections) and loss of labor rights. However, its political institutions suffered a significant collapse of confidence as resistance from below exploded during the uprisings. The economic crisis thus acted as a "tipping point" 2001–02 for many "ordinary citizens" to join the protests who did not previously see themselves as activists (Onuch, 2014).

Tolerance of Hardship Before, During and Since the 2001 Legitimacy Crisis

This book helps to understand why Argentina's middle-class radicalism was ignited during the 2001 uprisings (having been more individualized, more disparate and less numerous during the 1990s), then remained potent throughout much of 2002, yet died away toward 2003. It also examines the period of relative demobilization (with sporadic bouts of rebellion) under the Kirchner governments (2003–15), culminating in the election of President Mauricio Macri (2015–). In doing so, the question of why other social movements that achieved prominence during this period – especially Argentina's unemployed workers movement (known as the piqueteros) – managed to remain active and maintain an important role on Argentina's political stage while simultaneously movements of the struggling middle class effectively withdrew, is examined.

Social scientists have drawn heavily upon structuralist critiques to suggest that in general, the decision to become involved in collective forms of action was due to the spaces that were opened for them to do so during the "crisis of legitimacy" in the political and legislative institutions, which occurred during late 2001 and early 2002 (Palomino, 2005:19). The struggling middle class, alongside other sectors throughout the country, began to organize collectively to improve their own economic circumstances because, in Weberian terms, the governing polity could no longer secure consent to rule from its people. Indeed, the government was widely believed to be incompetent in both its economic management and political leadership – a view that fostered both economic and political self-organization from below.

Opposition to neoliberalism in the late 1990s was being mobilized on the streets by organizations such as the CTA union confederation and CAME (Argentinian Federation of Medium-Sized Companies). However, opponents to the government were suddenly dealt a dramatic opportunity when the popular Vice President "Chacho" Álvarez resigned in late 2000, citing President de la Rúa's inability to tackle corruption. This led to an outbreak of infighting among the President's cabinet and opened up fissures in the ruling *Alianza* governing coalition. To a large extent, Álverez himself had been credited with holding this fragile alliance together himself, so his departure exacerbated preexisting factional disputes in the cabinet and disagreements among the coalition. Worse still, following the October 2001 elections, de la Rúa was forced to form a minority government that relied on the support of the Peronist opposition to pass laws. With a weak and divided elite that was struggling to maintain consent to rule amid a paralysis in the legislature, as well a series of high-profile corruption cases among the political elite, the struggling middle class sensed "political opportunities" (Oberschall, 1973:128) to take advantage of these elite divisions and make their voices heard about their own plight. The Radical President cut an isolated figure who had lost credibility even with many of his own allies. Together with increased networking possibilities for opposition activists (which had not existed to the same extent in the 1990s when the macroeconomic situation was relatively stable and Carlos Menem presided over a relatively strong and united government), these elite divisions gave confidence to oppositional movements and activists to upscale their activities and to "ordinary citizens" to join them (Onuch, 2014).

Effectively, this paralysis ended in May 2003, when the *Frente para la Victoria* gained control of both the Houses in parliament. Newly appointed

President Néstor Kirchner gave the Executive additional powers. He was soon to gain high approval ratings (Singer and Fara, 2008:756–760) and henceforth the opportunity for these internal divisions to be exploited was closed to oppositional groups. There was a notable decline in street mobilizations and collective resistance, both among the middle class and broader society after 2003, which some attribute to the fact that after Kirchner's election, people came to believe the crisis of legitimacy had ended (Mazzoni, 2008:222) and the middle class were persuaded that their "political rights" had been restored. Interestingly, Mazzoni also points out that their ongoing impoverishment was not accompanied by their prolonged political radicalization because these citizens had not developed a sophisticated enough understanding of their *social* (as opposed to *political*) citizenship. Instead, she argues, their radicalization resulted from what was deemed to be a violation of their *political* rights, rather than an encroachment on their right to live free from financial hardship (which was not necessarily understood as a "right" in itself). Further, once impoverished, their lack of comprehension of their social citizenship meant that the middle class expected little from the state in terms of welfare support and were driven by the value of financial self-sufficiency – a core component of their middle-class *habitus.*

In short, while declining material conditions provided the oxygen for the fire of collective actions that the impoverished middle class participated in during the 2001–02 crisis, the spark was ignited by contingent political events which helped them to see their impoverishment in political terms. This made them increasingly likely to transfer blame for their problems away from themselves and onto the agents of neoliberal capitalism such as politicians, government and international financial institutions like the IMF. For the pauperized middle class these contingent events included: first, the State of Siege declared by President de la Rúa on 19 December 2001, which outraged many and evoked memories of the civil-military dictatorship. Second, the confiscation of savings by the banks during the *Corralito* provided a very clear example of how financial institutions, backed by government policy, had been complicit in the gross injustice that had resulted in their financial hardship. Both brought into focus the exploited nature of their relationship with capital, as well as the gaping deficit of legitimacy among liberal democracy's "representative" institutions.

As described earlier, Davies (1971) and Gurr's (1970) "relative deprivation" theories regarding the sudden reversal of raised expectations creating rebellion seem to have some resonance here and help to explain the general differences between impoverished citizens' responses to their situations in Argentina in the 1990s and those in 2001–02. In the former period, while some middle-class sectors benefited hugely during the Menem presidency (such as those linked to the finance sectors and because under the Convertibility Plan foreign holidays and imported luxury goods became very cheap), those who suffered a decline in quality of life (often due to unemployment) tended to experience impoverishment gradually and incrementally, as savings ran down or the value of wages eroded (Svampa, 2005). Protests were also channeled through reformist organizations like trade unions, and impoverishment occurred amid *low* expectations as a result of the deep economic recession of the Lost Decade of the 1980s and the hyperinflation of 1989–91 (Adamovsky, 2009).

In 2001–02, by contrast, millions fell below the poverty line in a far more sudden and violent manner. It was also a personal descent that followed many years of *raised* expectations. As mentioned earlier, during the 1990s, it became easy to believe that Argentina was finally nearing the greatness for which in the national imaginary, it had always been destined. This was due to, among other factors, the rapid modernization of its infrastructure during this decade (shopping centers, airports and hotels), the expansion of services such as satellite TV and mobile phones, and its close relationship with the USA. Becoming accustomed to macroeconomic success for the first time in decades due to the country's strong annual growth of 4%–10% during the 1990s (except 1995) also relegitimized this feeling (Armony and Armony, 2005:42).

The policy of *convertibility* under President Menem's government also helped ensure that those sectors of the middle class enjoyed unprecedented purchasing power. Aside from being able to purchase cheap luxury imported goods, technology and consumer durables, low borrowing costs and sudden availability of credit in light of the artificially strong value of the peso added to their sense of material enrichment. It also helped convince many that the Menem government was correct when it repeatedly assured them that all this meant that the country had reached the "First World" at last. As Argentina became the IMF's new poster child for neoliberal reforms, Menem declared in 1992, "Our country is the leader of a new order. A new, home-grown Argentina will join the First World as a number-one country. The leader of new changes. The leader of a leap toward the future."

However, following the country's sovereign debt default in early 2002, the peg to the US dollar ended and the peso was subject to a 75% devaluation. The subsequent price hikes suddenly pushed imported consumer durables out of reach, and it quickly became clear that the hopes and aspirations for the better material future that many had harbored during the 1990s had been built on false promises and ill-considered economic policies (Vilas, 2005:252). This brought an abrupt end to citizens' perceived upward mobility and the high living standards that many in the middle class had become used to. It also exacerbated the perception and tangibility of social descent. This was not only difficult to cope with psychologically, but also provoked a ferocious response in the outburst of collective protests during 2001–02. Unlike the reformist demands of the unions and movements in the 1990s, those of 2001–02 were far more radical, articulating goals of direct democracy, neighborhood-level self-management and – as encompassed in the ¡*Qué se vayan todos!* slogan – questioning the whole system of representative democracy and neoliberal economics.

A further factor that helps to explain the difference in struggling middle class responses between 1995 and 2002 is that it takes "society" time to implement the social policy responses and aid programs necessary to help individuals cope with economic shocks (Powers, 1999:534). Citizens' responses are likely to be more radical when crises occur more abruptly, as was the case in late 2001 and 2002. During the 1990s, the ranks of the poor swelled gradually with each neoliberal policy reform that removed another welfare safety net, privatized another industry (shedding jobs) or placed further pressure on wages, charities, local authorities and other organizations. These intensified NGO and charitable organizations' interventions to ameliorate the problem accordingly and were relatively successful because they had time to plan a systematic response to the subsequent social problems that these policies spawned. The incremental nature of rising poverty meant that these organizations maintained the capacity to carry out their functions and plan for greater demand for their "service." This was aided by the fact that strong upward *structural* mobility among those in middle-income jobs also meant that thousands of middle-class citizens moved in the opposite direction and toward economic self-sufficiency once again.

However, the economic explosion that rocked the country between October 2000 and the end of 2002 was much more abrupt and violent in nature. Therefore, the agencies that were charged with the responsibility of looking after the millions of people who suddenly became poor found themselves unable to provide the degree of support needed. The welfare institutions that are necessary to offer aid to deprived citizens and essentially "buy-off" the risk of social revolt under liberal-democratic capitalist regimes was exposed (Gough, 1979) became impotent and financial misery deeper and more tangible, potentially generating greater anger and fueling the desire to join protest movements.

The Role of Middle-Class Identity Construction in Political Mobilization and Demobilization

Historically, Argentina enjoyed the largest, most politically influential middle class in Latin America. Following several waves of European immigration during the first half of the twentieth century, this embedded an aspirational mindset and successive generations of upward mobility. Social mobility was further encouraged through income redistribution and ISI policies as well as free university education which aided the growth of a domestic middle class under Peronism during the 1940s and 1950s.

Historian Ezequiel Adamovsky (2009) describes how the Argentinian middle class is not a social class but an identity. "Born out of politics" as a reaction to the rise of General Juan Perón and his *Justicialista* movement, when elements of the ruling elites took fright at the way that he first as Labor Minister (1943–45), then as President (1946–55) went further than expected when politicizing and mobilizing large swathes of the working class in the industrial urban centers, encouraging workers to strike against large employers, trebling social security coverage to five million people, expanding labor rights and leading to wage increases of 30% under his administration (McGuire, 1997). Together with his anti-clericalism and nationalization of large corporations, one of the ways that the ruling class responded was to attempt to imbue a middle-class identity in order to co-opt sectors of the aspirational working class and dilute the subaltern resistance, for instance, by advancing ideals of "progress," "whiteness" and "decency" and depicting Peronism as promoting the breakdown of social norms by creating indiscipline, immorality, laziness, violence and backwardness. The opposition to Perón also seized on underlying racial prejudices by associating it with the "threat" of the *Mestizo* shanty town-dwelling poor. Symbolic violence permeated everyday language and elite culture, with Peronist supporters derided as *cabecitas negras* (little blackheads). A simultaneous revival of the nineteenth-century "civilization vs barbarism" dichotomy of former Argentinian President Domingo Sarmiento under which two alternative projects for the country's future (one of "civilization"; a white, European-looking, "progressive," urban-centered middle-class culture) as opposed to "barbarism"; the rural, *Mestizo*, "backward" gaucho or blue-collar worker) were presented and the former advocated.

In radio, television and film, there was a concerted effort to promote middle-class values and lifestyles. In social science, Argentina's first-ever survey of social class by Gino Germani grossly exaggerated the size of the middle class, yet its flawed results were presented as "scientific" and promoted by the state following the *Revolucion Libertadora* civil-military uprising which eventually overthrew Perón in 1955. The UCR or "Radicals," alongside the Peronist/Justicialist Party, was the main political force to dominate Argentinian democratic politics in the latter twenty-first century and was traditionally understood to represent middle-class interests. Alongside the domestic bourgeoisie, they used modernization theory to win over the middle class during an intense period of "deperonization" (Adamovsky, 2009). It proved to be a rather effective strategy that resonated with a significant part of the aspirational population. Curiously, this fervent opposition to Perón also emerged even among many who gained economically from Peronism. Here lay the origins of a deep social fissure representing two distinct visions for national projects that opened up that continues to prevail today. This "rift," known as *la grieta,* pitted Peronism vs Radicalism, Sarmientan "Barbarism vs Civilization," "Europeanism vs Latin Americanism" and the "Mestizo vs White." It was at this stage that many in the aspiring urban working-class immigrant communities latched on to this middle-class identity, which as part of a national project can be understood to be the origin for why so many Argentinians of all socioeconomic backgrounds describe themselves as such.

The question of whether as a framing mechanism, the notion of being middle class has been more of an obstacle or enabler of collective demand-making in Argentina is a complex one. Certainly, it was largely avoided in communiqués and discourse among the assemblies and protest movements during 2002, for instance, with appeals instead more often being made to "the people" or those participants self-identifying as "neighbors." This was even true of the "savers" movement, which tended to limit its demands via *escraches* (public shaming protests) purely to the return of confiscated deposits by the banks, rarely extending solidarity to the broader uprisings (Svampa and Corral, 2006). There were pragmatic reasons for the avoidance of narrow class-based demand making, namely, to elicit sympathy from non-savers. The air of rebellion of those days meant that being seen to solely defend the interests of one class was deemed intolerable (Schilman and Icart, 2005).

Curiously, middle-class collective identity has rarely been used to mobilize politically and has usually been expressed covertly in the public protest arena. Attempts to do so explicitly have been disastrous, for instance, the brief existence of the Middle Class Movement in 1956 (Adamovsky, 2009) which failed spectacularly and which was unable to muster more than a few hundred members (many of whom were actually from the upper class).

The absence of class-based demand-making during the 2001 uprisings occurred in spite of the fact that such individual identities persevered with two-thirds maintaining self-identification (CCR Survey – see Grimson and Kessler, 2005). To understand the idiosyncratic distinction between the public performance of class which was expressed through identity with "the people" in 2001 and strong private "middle-class" identities, we must return to the intersectionality between nation and class in Argentina. Dating back to the time of General Juan Perón and how "the worker" was eulogized and the mythical idea of *el pueblo argentino*, political parties of all descriptions have tended to avoid directing their campaigns at any one specific social group or class, especially since Peronism, because the idea of the "middle class" began to adopt anti-popular connotations. Second, there has been little need to make such appeals directly to the middle class. Argentina's national identity was and remains closely associated with the middle class due to the majority of the country's white European origins. Therefore when politicians address "the people," the middle class recognize that they are a part of it and implicitly being addressed. Third, post-Perón politicians have developed subtle linguistic or aesthetic mechanisms to indicate that they are targeting the middle class when they do so.

This distinction has weakened over time and in the run up to the 2001 crisis for the first time since the 1950s, there were explicit attempts to both mobilize and placate the middle class as a collective entity. At the level of elite politics, Eduardo Duhalde (Peronist leader) began defending the middle class in his speeches during 2001 and in Mendoza, the Middle Class Housing Plan was enacted. A national TV campaign was launched to "defend the middle class" by a small political party and even the *Partido Obrero* (Workers Party) tried to win them over later that year. The Argentinian Confederation of Medium-Sized Companies (CAME) began to openly call for a rebellion "in defense of the impoverished middle class" in December 2001. The Middle Class Defense Front was formed in Rosario but didn't last long or gather support from beyond a few neighbors and in leading daily, *Página 12* the cartoon strip, "Rep" openly called upon readers to join a revolt of the middle class in a series of cartoons (Adamovsky, 2009).

However, in reality, middle-class mobilization didn't have to be forced during the 2001 uprisings. It was an organic response to their proletarianization. Pereyra (2003) asserts that it was the night of 19 December during the *cacerolazos* protests "that the middle class found each other on the streets and realized that there was no longer a middle class." It was this Lacanian sense of "presence through absence" that helped signify a collective middle-class identity and for such citizens to develop a consciousness of what had happened to them. This acted as a kind of social awakening in that their unemployment and impoverishment was no longer understood as a private problem but one that was being experienced collectively and thus could be attributed to a systemic failure.

The Role of National Identity Construction

At this point and to make further sense of the collective protest responses that newly poor citizens adopted during the crisis of 2001–02, it is important to mention the relevance of "national identity" construction and, in particular, the myths associated with "national greatness" in the Argentinian imaginary (Armony and Armony, 2005). Most accounts of the political mobilization of the middle class at this time can be categorized as either (i) "emotional/defensive" – as an outpouring of collective anger at having incurred personal financial or material loss during the crisis; (ii) "misguided/blame" – as collective frustration with politicians for having made bad economic decisions and for failing to represent them effectively; or (iii) "institutional" – due to public demands for accountability which were met with elected authorities' unresponsiveness due to the weakness of Argentina's institutions under *Menemismo*. However, each of these explanations fails to recognize the cultural frames and cognitive patterns that underlay the connection between civil and political society which influenced the way that citizens behaved in the context of economic and political crisis.

National identity construction in Argentina traces its origins to the influx of millions of European immigrants who settled in what they optimistically believed to be a rich, young, "progressive" American country during the early to mid-1900s. Initially joining the ranks of the country's industrial working class, they were soon aided by Peronist redistribution policies and acquired middle-class lifestyles, values and aspirations. At the same time, the country's political leaders from President Alvear in the 1920s through Perón in the 1940s and 1950s alongside the popular press proclaimed that Argentina was to become "a leading nation in the world." A myth of past and future national grandeur definitively shaped public discourse. However, when the decadence of the second half of the twentieth century set in (due to the saturation of the ISI economic model and many argue its looting by the neoliberal-extractivist one), the notion of the "Argentinian Dream'" faded and was replaced by a narrative of victimization in the minds of its people.

The belief that "there is always some kind of 'other' which is liable for robbing its citizens of their glorious destiny" began to take root (ibid. 2005:44). Presented as an "enemy within" or as a "foreign influence," this "other" has adopted various and sometimes overlapping forms throughout modern Argentinian history. Targeted by ruling elites and subsequently followed by sectors of the middle and lower classes, scapegoats have included foreign imperialism, the political class, the shanty town-dwelling poor and the *Mestizo* or Mapuche indigenous people. The latter has been singled out for particular attention by President Macri's government. *Cambiemos* Security Minister Patricia Bullrich labeled them as "extremely violent" (TeleSur, 2018) and linked them to terrorist groups (with little foundation) since 2015 as foreign multinationals such as Benetton have sought to expand their territorial control over what the Mapuche People claim are their "ancestral lands." State forces have repeatedly repressed their communities to support foreign capital in what Harvey describes as "accumulation by dispossession" (2003). Raids by state forces led to the killing of a young member of the community, Rafael Nahuel and the alleged forced disappearance of Santiago Maldonado, which saw protests erupt not just in Argentina but around the world (*Página 12*, 2017).

During the 2001–02 crisis, this neurosis played itself out with dramatic effect, especially among the pauperized middle class. They tended to direct blame for their personal pauperization at the "political class" that had, for them, long been responsible for the country's unfulfilled potential (Armony and Armony, 2015). However, the culprits were perhaps "too obvious," in the sense that it was much easier to personify them in "politicians" and "institutions" such as the IMF, rather than in the unobservable processes and workings of capitalism. It is true that political corruption, poor policy decisions and the unrelenting pressure of international financial institutions all played a part in the proletarian-ization of millions of Argentinians, but these merely obscured the true, underlying systemic cause of their impoverishment.

Another facet of Argentinian national identity – partly forged by the widely accessible education system that Peronism encouraged – was its association with the perception of upward social mobility. This had been enjoyed by three generations of the middle class by the time Menem ar-rived in power in 1989. To be Argentinian, its people believed, was to be able to socially aspire. However, the 2001–02 crisis was so profound that it marked a watershed for the application of these national imaginaries to the reality of everyday life. During this period, the ideological glue that maintained society's social fabric fell apart (Grimson and Kessler, 2005:88) as the impoverished middle class were forced to come to terms not just with their personal dislocation from society but also with three other painful realizations.

First, they saw that President Menem's so frequently repeated asser-tions in the 1990s that "Argentina belongs to the First World" and that he had managed to bring stability to the country were nothing but myths that they had been tricked into believing. Second, they realized that this crisis was so acute that neither they nor their children would probably be able to become upwardly mobile again. Third, they understood that the conviction that they belonged to the middle class had existed only in their minds. The collective sense of anger at this new social reality, the identification of a common (although misconstrued) enemy in the "polit-ical class" and the realization that they could no longer trust their lead-ers who had falsely claimed to act in their economic interests, therefore, became generative causes of the collective responses that many adopted.

Many impoverished middle-class citizens were moved from passivity into action and tried to participate in and rebuild society's economic and political structures through the establishment of self-organized neigh-borhood assemblies, factory cooperatives, the barter system as a means of alternative currency exchange and so on.

2001 as a Crisis of Neoliberal or Capitalist Hegemony?

It was this inherent weakness in the institutions of the Argentinian state that helped cultivate the crisis of political legitimacy that became explicit during the crisis of 2001–02. This created a crisis of neoliberal hegemony, which still has not been fully resolved (Levitsky and Murillo, 2005; Mazzoni, 2009). It is important at this juncture to be precise about some semantic intricacies. First, 2001–02 did not represent a full-blown "crisis of hegemony of capitalism" in its cultural and political forms. Despite sincere and widely supported attempts to create new political and eco-nomic models based upon participatory democracy through the popular assemblies and forms of economic production (workers' self-managed companies) and means of exchange to replace the money form (barter clubs), the survival of capitalism itself was never actually challenged in practice, not even in public discourse (outside far-Left circles).

Indeed, in terms of the ownership of production and social relations, a situation of "dual power" – which is necessary for a hegemonic crisis to exist – was absent in Argentina (Astarita, 2008). Only a fraction of workers (10,000 out of a working population of approximately 11 million) participated in the worker occupations and the highly politicized "recovered companies' movement," despite becoming a *cause celebre* of resistance among organized labor. This movement was also influential in that it prompted the Kirchner governments to establish thousands of depoliticized state-subsidized cooperatives that incorporated 300,000 workers (Ozarow and Croucher, 2014), partly in an attempt to co-opt the notion of *autogestion* and deradicalize what was becoming a "dangerous" grassroots autonomous movement. Yet, not even this movement represented an attack on the foundations of capitalist production (private property), as it only sought workers' control once the bosses *had already abandoned* their factories and workplaces. Not a single instance of workers seizing control of their factory and overthrowing their managers while the firm was operating under normal, profit-making conditions occurred. Capitalist ideas still dominated in Argentina in 2001–02, and ultimately, no alternative hegemony was able to replace it.

What *was* under threat at that time instead, was a specific set of *neoliberal* policies. It was these policies (privatization, concentration of industry, eroding of labor rights and social security, structural adjustment etc.), together with the abandonment of the state for those who needed its protection, which could be most easily identified as having caused suffering in citizens' daily lives. It is in this sense – with both this policy recipe and the representative model of democracy being the focus of attack – that the crisis of legitimacy represented a crisis of *neoliberal* hegemony, rather than a hegemonic crisis *per se* (Mazzoni, 2009).

Further, in terms of the postcrisis economic model to emerge under the Kirchner governments which followed (2003–15), these governments exhibited a range of continuities (and wholly neoliberal characteristics) which embedded Argentina even more deeply in the international capitalist economy. For instance, trade and investment deals were conducted with China and other powers. The Kirchners entered into alliances with both domestic and foreign manufacturing and agro-mineral elites such as Monsanto and Chevron, which often brought them into conflict with indigenous communities as these multinationals attacked their land and dispossessed them of it on occasion, sanctioned by the state. Their administrations also reproduced an unequal class structure through the promotion of commodity exports, transference of the national debt burden onto the pensions system and maintaining a low proportion of workers within the collective bargaining system. Nor did they nationalize industry (outside key sectors such as aviation with *Aerolineas Argentinas* or oil with Repsol/*YPF*). Indeed, the nation was returned to its traditional position as an agro-exporter in the global supply chain (Wylde, 2011). In general, they did deliver material improvements for the middle and popular sectors, reducing inequality (in terms of Gini Coefficient) and reversing the tendency of the 1990s (Kessler, 2016). However, acutely underreported evidence suggests that in Argentina and across Latin America during the Pink Tide governments, actually the wealthiest in society actually became even richer once undeclared income and tax avoidance schemes are accounted for (Salama, 2015).

Yet on the other hand, Argentina started to break from neoliberalism by integrating some of the demands of the ¡*Qué se vayan todos!* movement at the time (Schaumberg, 2014). These included the expansion of local participatory budgeting; the state's promotion of thousands of cooperative businesses, which came to account for 10% of the country's GDP (Silveira, 2011); the part-nationalization of key industries such as the Spanish-owned oil company, Repsol, in 2012; and the then government's insistence on distributing aid programs to millions of the poorest rather than paying off certain international creditors like the North American "vulture funds" that had held the country to ransom by suing the government for debt payments they claimed they were owed plus interest and penalty fees in US federal courts. The baton of hegemonic control passed from one faction of the ruling class (the international bourgeoisie) to another (the domestic bourgeoisie).

While social movements were unable to fill the political vacuum left by the 2001–02 uprisings with a new social and political order, they *did* successfully manage to condition the rehabilitation of the capitalist state and the incoming reformist Kirchner government away from neoliberalism as many of the demands asserted by mobilized citizens and social and labor movements were incorporated into the state agenda. Yet as Dinerstein explains (2014), the emancipatory nature of the ¡*Qué se vayan todos!* uprisings produced an *excess* that had no grammar in the logic of state power and policy. Thus, it could not be fully "translated" into law, with many of the demands being appropriated or even repressed. Many of the social and industrial policies that were implemented later constituted the foundations for creating a new *stability* that deradicalized the spirit of the iconic slogan and remain what she describes as the "hidden transcripts" of Argentina's political recovery in the postcrisis period.

During 2001–02, the mediating role that would normally have been fulfilled by state and civil society institutions like the Church, reformist political parties and trade unions in order to secure consent from the population to be governed by the ruling class was conspicuous in their absence. This led vast swathes of the struggling middle class to circumvent these institutions (which they had completely lost faith in) and to identifying the other side of the political superstructure (the state), as the source of their national problems. This tendency had already been identified by Menem in the 1990s as he too tried to distance himself from "the political class" during his election. Indeed, the practical experience of many grass-roots social movements like the popular assemblies that emerged during 2001–02 and participants in them was to reject any kind of alliance with the state or to collaborate with what its participants viewed as "agents of the political system." Instead, they purposively tended to organize outside the established structures (Svampa and Corral, 2006:146).[9]

Gramsci's theory is thus pivotal to understanding how and why newly poor citizens decided to either politically resist or passively accept their declining social conditions. When the dominant class successfully ensured that individuals perceived their pauperization as either a natural consequence of "how things are," a result of their own deficiencies as human beings, or even as a "temporary state" which will soon be overcome (as the struggling middle class were more inclined to believe in the 1990s), then they were far more likely to internalize their problems and adopt remedial self-improvement measures from among the economic opportunities available to them. However, where these dominant elites are unable to gain consent to implement their own preferred ideology, citizens began to question their allegiances and become conscious (albeit only for a few months at most during the revolt of 2001–02) that they had been supporting the dominant class' interests rather than their own.

Postcrisis Demobilization (2002) and the Kirchners in Power (2003–15)

The 2001–02 crisis mobilized millions of impoverished middle-class citizens alongside multiple sectors of society into seeking collective economic solutions to the problems generated by neoliberal capitalism and representative democracy. There was an insurrectionary mood in the air in Argentina's urban centers and for a period of several months in 2002, it was far from certain that the old order would remain in place. A radical transformation in society looked far more likely. However, the initial failure of the ruling class to maintain its consent to rule was soon overcome through a combination of accommodative and repressive strategies. Most importantly, despite the profound level of political crisis, although significant and widely supported counterhegemonic experiments in popular democracy (the neighborhood assemblies and even the efforts to create an inter-neighborhood coordinating assembly) and noncapitalist forms of production (factory cooperatives, the barter system etc.) started to emerge and enjoyed mass participation in 2002, as mentioned earlier, ultimately no alternative hegemony (socialist or otherwise) was able to replace the existing one. This was as much due to the rejection of the idea that "the state" could any longer act as a potential vehicle for change as it was the lack of desire to overthrow it. Arguably, middle-class citizens were also naturalized into taking orders from their employers or owners of capital, so lacked the capacity to seize power and rule themselves too.

Nevertheless, widespread alienation and exasperation that things could not change among Argentinian society at the time, as well as the lack of ideological coherence that was articulated from the grassroots resistance, fueled the failure to replace the existing order. As Schaumberg contends (2008:383), the state's reconstruction of clientelist networks and political co-optation was what shifted popular consensus from the widely used slogan of ¡*Qué se vayan todos!* during the uprisings of 2001–02 to resignation by 2003 and "all that can be done now is electing the *mal menor* [the lesser evil]."

The most important policies of appeasement and social control that were enacted to restore the dominant class' ideological hegemony after 2002 were implemented by the state itself. In its role as the guarantor of private property rights, the enforcer of contracts that exploit labor (albeit legally), the institution that eliminates barriers to the mobility of capital and labor, as well as in supporting the stabilization of the money system, state power is essentially capitalist because it maintains the conditions necessary for capital accumulation (Harvey, 2001:274). Indeed, not only in Argentina but in all the other countries mentioned earlier where mass pauperization has arisen following economic crises, the state has played a vital role in ensuring that hegemonic order was preserved.

In Argentina, strategies of appeasement that affected the middle-class and broader sectors were pursued first by President Eduardo Duhalde (2002–03) and then by President Néstor Kirchner (2003–07). The desire of both these men to prevent Argentina's bourgeoning social revolution from below from developing into a serious challenge to the existing order were expressed in their respective presidential inauguration speeches. Duhalde announced that his new government would pursue three priorities: "Rebuild political and institutional authority, guarantee social order and lay the foundations for the change of the economic and social model" (Ares, 2002). Meanwhile, Kirchner (2003 in *La Nación*) proposed "in our project we place central importance to the idea of rebuilding a national capitalism... I want a normal Argentina. I want us to be a serious country".

These strategies varied in terms of their success. For example, the expansion of welfare benefits was generally not taken up by the struggling middle class (who either didn't qualify for them or refused to be stigmatized by accepting such handouts), nor was the Programme for Unemployed Heads of Households (*Plan Jefes*), which was targeted at pacifying the indigent poor (Roca, 2003). However, these policies delivered by the interim government of Eduardo Duhalde (2002–03) did serve to break down the solidarity between classes that was so crucial to the success of the uprisings. By playing off one social sector against another, the state divided the various social struggles that existed while also opening up tensions between the impoverished middle class and the structural poor. Many in the former came to see the social programs as a reward for the idleness for the latter (Adamovsky, 2009). However, other strategies were highly successful in terms of appeasing the impoverished middle class, including those savers who had lost deposits in the *Corralito* by encouraging them to desist from further collective action.

These included, first, from mid-2002 the government announced that those who had personal debts to the banks in dollars (in the form of mortgages or loans) could repay them in devalued peso currency at a rate of one US dollar to one peso. This benefited many individuals, especially those who had accumulated debt during the 1990s when credit was so easy to obtain. With the official exchange rate now at almost four pesos to the dollar (as opposed to the pre-2002 parity), the value of their personal debts disintegrated. Meanwhile, the international banks with branches in Argentina bore the brunt of the losses (Blustein, 2005:192). This was apparently a pragmatic decision by the Duhalde government which, like that of his successor Néstor Kirchner, seemed less interested in supporting international financial capital and instead created an alliance with the domestic bourgeoisie.

Second, in March 2003, the Supreme Court issued a landmark ruling that overturned a government decree that had forced US dollar denominated bank accounts to be converted to pesos. This paved the way for hundreds of thousands of savers to legally reclaim the deposits that had been taken from them after the *Corralito*. This removed the *raison d'être* of the *escrache* protests that had been organized by several middle-class savers' groups, including the ABAE (Argentinian Association of Defrauded Bank Depositors), which many of the struggling middle class participated in until that point.

Third, although export driven in the early months immediately after currency devaluation, an impressive investment and private consumption-led macroeconomic recovery from late 2002 onward (Weisbrot and Sandoval, 2007) meant that from early 2003 more jobs were created and the disastrous anticipated consequences of the crisis were largely avoided. This removed the sense of chaos and Armageddon that had fueled the protests of earlier days (Vilas, 2005:258). Unemployment fell from its peak of 22% in 2003 to just 13% in 2005 (INDEC, 2018), but although two million mainly formal, salaried posts were created in the recovery period (Benza, 2016), the number of "superior middle-class" jobs ("autonomous professions," small business owners, middle managers and salaried professionals) available actually reduced during the 2003–11 recovery (INDEC, 2018). Thus, the struggling sectors of the middle class suffered ongoing downward or stagnant occupational mobility, yet with their possession of higher human and cultural capital they usually stood at the front of the queue to secure the low-paying, low-skilled jobs that were available at the time, while displacing the structural poor in the process (Porcú, 2003). The unemployed among the middle class were thus provided with work and, as the months went by, the daily grind to make ends meet became the principal preoccupation as many started to re-build their livelihoods.

As the middle class returned to the labor market after 2003, it fur-ther diluted the prospects of their participation in collective action in opposition to either the government or their bosses. The fact that the low-skilled jobs that they tended to acquire at the time were almost exclusively nonunionized, service sector roles mean that relatively lit-tle damage could be exerted by voluntarily withdrawing their labor as part of any industrial action. The threat of their militancy was fur-ther reduced at the time because a large reserve army of unskilled labor (mainly the unemployed structural poor) remained, waiting in the wings to replace them and thus instilled discipline among newly poor (and other) workers at that time. Furthermore, by being offered work it meant that those in the newly pauperized stratum not only had less spare time to engage in political activities but also ensured the end of any potential involvement in *piquetero* groups of unemployed and structurally poor workers. At that time, the *piqueteros*, via their road-blocking protest tactics in urban centers, posed the greater threat to the production process which they were regularly able to paralyze by impeding the circulation of transport. This prevented workers from arriving at work or the necessary supply of goods to be delivered to fac-tories, shops and businesses for production. It was they, rather than tra-ditional trade unions, who were causing more political and economic disruption during this period.

Aside from tactics of appeasement, the state also responded with re-pressive tactics against those involved in collective action, especially un-der the Duhalde Presidency during 2002 and early 2003. The main targets were the more radical or autonomous actions, such as those *piquetero* groups that refused to be co-opted by the government, which contributed to the overall demobilization of the social movements under the early years of Kirchnerismo. One example of this was the Unemployed Work-ers' Collective (CTD) Anibal Verón, which organized a roadblock at the Pueyrredón Bridge, Avellaneda, on 26 June 2002. During this protest, two young unemployed activists, Maximiliano Kosteki and Darío Santil-lán, were assassinated by the Greater Buenos Aires police, while another 90 were injured and many more imprisoned. The massacre on the bridge that day acted as a watershed moment. Not only did it spark indignation among broad sectors of society, but many of the social movements never fully recovered, often splintering over questions of how to deal with the aftermath. Several of the most emblematic worker-recovered companies were also symbolically targeted for attempted violent police eviction – like the Zanon Factory in Neuquén, Patagonia and the Bauen Hotel in

Buenos Aires – perhaps because they acted as a "threat of a good example" and demonstrated that alternative ways of democratically producing without bosses were possible. Meanwhile, while under the Kirchner governments the use of state repression against such movements was curtailed (both Néstor Kirchner and Cristina Kirchner claimed to be on the side of the movements), the two presidents often shifted the blame onto provincial governments when sporadic acts of state violence occurred to crush certain protests.

Fourth and perhaps most crucially, it was the election of reformist, center-left Néstor Kirchner as president in May 2003 that resecured hegemonic control for the bourgeoisie (albeit its domestic rather than international financial wing). He was also able to gain the support of many of the new urban poor (Mazzoni, 2007:188), despite the ongoing general disdain for politicians who had been indicted by the middle class. While only 22% of the electorate voted for Kirchner in the first round of the presidential race (the leading candidate Carlos Menem pulled out in order to avoid certain defeat in the runoff against him), the newly elected president successfully managed to pose as an "anti-establishment candidate," even though the reality was that as a Peronist he represented the hegemonic and most institutionalized political force in Argentina.

His personal popularity was attributed only in small part to the rapid macroeconomic recovery (pulling millions out of poverty, creating jobs and the fastest economic growth in the western hemisphere, averaging 10% between 2003 and 2007). He also found favor because he managed to present himself as the antithesis of everything that had preceded him and all the characteristics of dishonesty, pretension, excess and frivolity that *Menemismo* stood for in the 1990s and that de la Rúa had also unsuccessfully sought to repudiate between 1999 and 2001. Kirchner created a new electoral center-left Peronist ticket – *Frente para la Victoria* – to distinguish his brand of *Justicialismo* (Peronism) from that of Menem. He also toned down references to the legacy of Perón (so as to capture support from non-Peronist middle sectors) and alluded to a new generation of leaders, so as to convey sufficient distance between himself and the old political establishment. Finally, in responding to the civic mobilization of 2001–02, he successfully convinced the people that he was prepared to listen to their concerns. Initial measures that he took in office proved popular with large sectors of the middle class and beyond. These included reopening the trials of the ex-military leaders for the Disappearances of 30,000 people during the 1976–83 dictatorship (but who had previously been pardoned by President Menem) and removing many of the corrupt Supreme Court judges.

Many of the counterhegemonic structures that struggling middle-class citizens helped to create were soon co-opted by the state, deradicalizing their goals and demobilizing their protests as they became institutionalized. For example, the City of Buenos Aires government and municipal governments across the country introduced and sponsored participatory budgeting as a gesture to show that it wanted to incorporate the will of its residents into local decision-making. In practice, the extent to which citizens' decisions made during participatory budgeting reflected the "popular will" was more questionable (Centier, 2012). Furthermore, some of the *piquetero* groups with whom the impoverished middle class had stood during the 2001–02 protests were partially demobilized as its leaders such as Luis D'Elia (of *Federación de Tierra y Vivienda*) accepted invitations to join the new Kirchner government's cabinet in 2003. By granting major concessions to the less autonomous and anti-capitalist elements of the social movements while ignoring or repressing its more radical elements, the state apparatus delivered a textbook example of how to successfully split the challenging movement from below. The attempted containment or repression of autonomous, self-organized movements confirms the Kirchners' famously stated desire for the restoration of "normal capitalism" after the crisis. It also exemplified a reconstituted form of social control that Peronist governments have historically implemented, this time in its segmented neo-corporatist incarnation and which have been described here.

However, it is worth noting that in recent years, in the context of neo-liberalism and a tightening labor market, fragmentation of the working class, informalization and unemployment since the 1990s and the pro-union Kirchner governments (2008–15) with the credibility to institute tripartite negotiation with the unions, the nature of this relationship has changed. On the one hand, the distinction between the reduced number of insiders (beneficiaries of the corporatist agreement) and the swelled ranks of outsiders has continued and even been reinforced. It has been most formal-sector workers who are covered by union-negotiated collective contracts who have gained in exchange for accepted (rather than negotiated) macroeconomic policy and inflation targets. However, on the other hand, as Etchemendy and Collier (2007) explain, these gains have been limited to a smaller percentage of the overall labor force and have involved union organizational inducements and formal-sector workers' wage benefits rather than more general social welfare programs that cover the employed workforce. The corporatist model has thus become more "segmented."

So what else happened following Néstor Kirchner's election to explain the demobilization of the insurgency? Despite nearly 2,000 *cacerolazos* being recorded in the weeks following the *Corralito*, the level of social conflict dwindled so sharply during early 2003 that by the time of Kirchner's election in May that year, political resistance had largely shifted from the streets to the ballot box. The insurrection was over, not least in terms of involvement from the pauperized middle class, and capitalism had survived intact. As Argentinian historian de Lucía (2002:102) described, "this is a country where the mechanisms of social integration that enable a return to the hegemonic consensus have proved themselves to be highly efficient."

Before looking at the different specific factors that help account for the middle class' political demobilization, it is worth asking what underlying reasons might explain it. In other words, were the middle class fundamentally capable of achieving transformative change in the long term through their demand-making? A "community psychology" approach questions this by pointing to differences in how struggling middle class and structurally impoverished communities confronted their situations (Saforcada *et al.*, 2007). Among shanty town residents, internal solidarity and mutual aid are embedded in their ways of life as a survival strategy, given the conditions of indigence under which they exist. Their associated movements such as the piqueteros did not merely organize protest actions like road-blocking, but operated numerous community activities such as worker cooperatives and social centers as meeting places. Unlike the movements of the middle class, the piqueteros outlasted the crisis, partly because these activities provided more sustainable collective vehicles for organizing and survival. Yet for those in the middle class who suffered rather sudden pauperization after the initial few months of political revolt, they slid back toward private coping strategies. Some claim this was due to a deep-rooted individualism and belief in self-sufficiency. This prevented those outside the progressive middle class from continuing to participate in sustained political alternatives to the traditional political parties, which in 2001–02, they had repudiated as intensely as anyone else but which they reverted to supporting years later.

Developing this idea further, Mazzoni (2008) points to how it was a series of conservative and individualist values that post-2001 impoverished middle-class interviewees possessed but also saw as integral to their class identity (private property, individual freedom, respect for law and order) which contributed to them receding from the 2001–02 collective mobilizations and to eventually capitulate away from their anti-systemic ideals, to supporting the reformist Kirchner government in many cases. Over time, this led to a breakdown in social solidarity and helped to prevent a more revolutionary challenge from being posed. This author further describes them as "low-impact citizens" (2008: 219) due to their advanced political critique and intensity of their verbal demands, yet limited expectations of their social and economic citizenship (what the state should provide for them) or desire to actually take the necessary political action to change things. Further, their minimalist understanding of citizenship as "political" (principally centered around the act of voting in their representatives with whom, despite the crisis of representation they continued to demonstrate paternalistic sentiments toward), acts as a further limitation to the radicalization of their collective demand-making.

Precrisis collective middle-class action reflected these conservative attitudes. The neighborhood associations in Buenos Aires maintained preserving their property prices and security as core objectives, for example, collaborating with the police to prevent prostitution or the "occupation" of properties by marginalized groups. Shortly after the crisis, Almeyda (2004) posed two possible scenarios for the conservative middle class who became radicalized during the 2001 uprisings. Either their profound disenchantment with neoliberal capitalism and experiences of solidarity will remain in their collective memory and set the scene for their political trajectories in the decade that followed it, or their radicalization will reverse after the euphoria of the protests die away and they will be influenced by embedded, reactionary and including racist characteristics once again. Which path they pursued will become clearer later.

First Néstor Kirchner and then, following his untimely death, his wife Cristina Fernández de Kirchner's two administrations (2007–15), managed to overcome their ideological ambiguity by presenting themselves as "on the side of the movements." For example, both governments attacked the international financial elites and speculative capital, which they blamed for causing the 2001 economic crisis. They also took several measures to regulate the economy and protect domestic industry, such as providing generous subsidies to domestic industry (Rivera-Quiñones, 2014), part-nationalizing the Spanish-owned oil company YPF/Repsol and taking the pensions system back into state hands.

It is also worth exploring how the three Kirchner governments were able to capture either tacit or active support from the middle class. This was largely secured between 2003 and at least 2011 through a "consumption pact" in which the government expanded their consumption capacity in what Boos (2017) describes as "a reciprocal process of hegemonic integration rather than a unidirectional strategy from above." This was achieved, on the one hand, through the restoration of high economic growth which brought with it the creation of two million jobs and a 58% increase in average real-terms private-sector wages since 2003 (greater still in the public sector), and also thanks to national wage agreements with the CGT union confederation.

Interestingly, sales figures in both Argentina's supermarkets and shopping malls grew strongly throughout the Kirchnerist decade until they started tailing off after 2012 (along with aggregate private demand), opening up fissures in middle-class support as the consumption pact became exhausted. If one takes supermarket sales as representative of the general population, and shopping mall sales to be an indicator of middle- and upper-class demand, the latter grew especially strongly during 2010 and 2011, consolidating these groups' co-optation into Cristina Kirchner's 2011 election victory (Boos, 2017).

However, Kirchnerist public policy interventions were also crucial to achieving this. If one considers the Argentinian middle class to be a political identity (Adamovsky, 2009) and also the legacy of the 1990s Convertibility model to have positioned consumption capacity or the notion of the "consumer-citizen" at the heart of the reconstruction of this identity, then the increased ability to consume is, from a Gramscian perspective, a form of material integration of the dominated classes into consenting to the hegemony of the day. Thus, there was continuity between Menemismo in the 1990s and the Kirchner governments in terms of how the concept of citizenship was acted out and reproduced, the difference being that the latter also sought to endow previously disenfranchised sectors of the population with new social and economic rights as part of its social integration model. Consumption stimulation policies included the *Ahora 12* (Now 12) credit program that started in 2014 and facilitates payment in 12 interest-free quotas and which proved highly successful, leading to 200,000 shops participating, with US$3 billion spent up until 2015 alone. The program was limited only to those with credit cards (the middle and upper class) and was subsequently continued and even expanded by the Macri government after 2016.

A second policy, *Renovar* (Renovate), involved the government encouraging the purchase of new white goods by paying for consumers' old but still functioning fridges, washing machines and so on; and a third policy, "SUBEneficio," allowed consumers who owned public transport payment cards to enjoy discounts in shops. Other programs that ran concurrently to encourage a social integration model via consumption (and also sought to constrain inflation) and which benefited broader sectors included the price-capping schemes that involved agreements between the government and national supermarket chains. *Precios Cuidados* (Caring for Prices) and *Mirar para Cuidar* (Looking out to Care for you) were two examples. Other moves included strengthening the powers of consumer rights organizations and most importantly (slightly predating Néstor Kirchner's election but then being rolled out exponentially) were energy bill subsidies which increased as a proportion of government spending from 0.8% to 18.8% between 2003 and 2014, leading to a 50% increase in electricity consumption, for instance (Boos, 2017).

Middle-Class–led Political Mobilizations under the Kirchners

The emancipatory and radical goals of the protests of 2001–02 and the solidarity that was constructed between the structural poor and the struggling middle class which was such a prominent feature of it, seem to have been quickly forgotten by many in the latter stratum. But is this really the case? How is the period and the hopes and dreams of its protagonists remembered? These will be explored further later on. When preoccupations about crime and the sanctity of private property were fueled by a wave of high-profile kidnappings, including the murder of student Axel Blumberg, this saw concerns transformed into a sizable protest movement during the Blumberg demonstrations of 2004 and 2006. These attracted a strong middle class presence around the authoritarian demands for harsher penal laws, a transfer of power to the police and security forces and a repressive clampdown on crime. The shanty town poor were scapegoated, and symbolic violence and fearmongering against them became a regular feature of media hysteria (Guano, 2004). Perpetuated by sectors of the struggling middle class, anti-poor discourse also served as an attempt to negate the rapidly disappearing social boundaries that had left them facing the reality of their downward social mobility. This discourse created, constructed or emphasized points of distinction with the poor, so as to reinforce their justification for their membership of the middle class.

Then, in 2008, Cristina Kirchner's government attempted to raise export taxes (*retenciones*) on agricultural producers from 35% to 44%. The middle class, including many who had been on the streets in 2001, poured out onto the streets in opposition against what was framed as undue government interference in the free market (Adamovsky, 2009). The aim of this move was to raise revenues for social investment by increasing the government's share of returns from rising world grain prices, while reducing domestic food prices to lower the cost of living for the poorest and make staple foods affordable to domestic consumers.

A further wave of anti-government protests that featured a strong middle class presence occurred in September and November 2012, then again in April 2013 when hundreds of thousands of people joined *cacerolazos*. These were largely promoted by social networking sites (without the intervention of political parties or elite mobilizing vehicles) and took place in all major cities around the country. Sparked by increased dollar currency controls and the *Once* train crash in which 51 people died (which revealed the extent of alleged government corruption), they marked the most sizable street mobilizations since December 2001 but promoted very different objectives. Rather than solidarity and the transformation of society's neoliberal structures, these protests focused around inward-looking calls for the removal of President Cristina Kirchner who they accused of corruption and authoritarianism, and more self-interested concerns such as the reduction of crime and inflation alongside the ending of currency controls. The protests themselves remained nonparty political but occurred during a period of comparative economic stability but acute political polarization. They also marked a restoration of participants' confidence in opposition politicians that advocated conservative agendas. Svampa (2012) notes that while the demands were very different, the protests symbolized the fact that many of the preoccupations of 2001 such as lack of democratic accountability had remained unresolved. While middle class participation in each of these three protests was significant, there was a higher presence of upper middle-class citizens in 2012, for instance, compared to 2001 when they were more multisectoral.

It was also during these protests that the social and political polarization (known as *la grieta* in Argentina) that had been intensifying for several years, spilled out onto the streets. The dividing lines, themes of contention and social composition of the "pro-" and "anti-government" camps evoked the reemergence of historical racialized and ideological tensions dating back to the 1930s, which pitted those in the subaltern classes against each other to the benefit of the economic elites.

Many participants interviewed on television accused the shanty town poor for rising insecurity, opposed the government's proposals to limit the Clarín Group's monopoly in the media via the AudioVisual Media Law (which was designed to bestow independent media a greater voice), and demonstrated their disapproval at the government's restrictions on dollar transactions which aimed at protecting the value of the national currency (Goni and Watts, 2012).

Yet, each of the three cases of struggling or recuperated middle class mobilization since 2001 has in its majority adopted strongly conservative positions. These have either scapegoated the structural poor or opposed government proposals to increase public spending on social programs and wealth redistribution. One of the themes that will be addressed later is what the lessons are for progressive social movements internationally, in terms of mobilizing middle-class citizens. Which sustainable vehicles can be adopted to support their continuity so as to prevent it from disappearing or its objectives from becoming more conservative in the postcrisis years, despite originally being born of proposals to radically change society?

Cristina Fernández de Kirchner's second government (2011–15) quickly lost popularity as underlying economic problems begin to surface, inflation spiraled and growth began to stall after 2011. Further, the trade union confederations, including both the former Kirchner ally – the General Confederation of Labor (CGT) and the Argentinian Workers' Central (CTA) *Autónoma* – responded to the rising cost of living with general strikes in pursuit of wage rises. Meanwhile, the political parties that opposed the government remained highly divided, as demonstrated by the 2011 Presidential election result, during which Fernández de Kirchner gained 54.1% of the vote, far ahead of her next nearest rival, Hermes Binner of the Socialist Party on 16.8%. Opposition and collective grievance-forming was also cultivated via opposition media outlets, with journalists such as Jorge Lanata and his investigative television program *Periodismo para Todos* (first aired in 2012) gaining millions of viewers.

It wasn't until the creation of the *Cambiemos* coalition in 2015, led by the then Governor of the City of Buenos Aires Mauricio Macri and his Republican Proposal (PRO) Party, the UCR and Civic Coalition (CC), that serious attempts were made to challenge *Kirchnerismo* electorally. An earlier effort had been made to build an anti-Kirchner alliance of center-left and broadly social democratic parties in 2013 called UNEN, but it failed to draw sufficient support.

What seems clear is that it was the Kirchners' post-neoliberal neo-developmentalist project that managed to salvage the capitalist hegemony. However, as some authors report, it has still only been weakly consented to since 2001–02 given the persistently low confidence in its governing institutions, according to *Latinobarómetro* (2013) polling data. Furthermore, the capitalist accumulation model that underpins the Kirchners' economic model is heavily dependent on high global market prices and demand for agro-exports as well as continued growth in China. For example, 10% of the country's GDP currently emanated from the soya industry, most of the demand for which comes from the Chinese (Rivera-Quiñones, 2014). As the *Cambiemos* government (2015–) has discovered subsequently, these favorable conditions reversed, so the cracks in the hegemony have started to open up again as the economy is exposed to new challenges and sometimes the return of old challenges.

Macri's Election Victory and Administration (2015–)

The ascendency of the pro-business conservative Mauricio Macri to Argentina's presidency on 10 December 2015 spelled the end of 12 years of center-left Peronist governments. His narrow defeat of Cristina Kirchner's preferred candidate, Daniel Scioli by just 51%–49%, was made possible through the carefully constructed coalition of opposition parties as described above. In particular, the inclusion of the near-defunct UCR as a junior partner was crucial. Incorporating this ailing but historically second major force in Argentine politics allowed him to access the Party's national, provincial and neighborhood mobilizing infrastructure and activists. It also meant that the upper class could gain control of an electoral coalition that was capable of winning elections without the need for alliances with popular sectors for the first time since 1916.

Together with a supportive *Clarin* media group that was fiercely critical of the Kirchner government, Mr. Macri was also able to exploit genuine concerns about growing inflation, crime and government corruption (despite facing 214 separate charges upon election himself, ranging from "fraud and illicit association" to "abuse of public office," as well as being implicated in the Panama Papers scandal), in order to gain support from many in the middle class during the election campaign. These demands, key to the middle class' anti-government protests of 2012–13 were then adopted as flagship policies by *Cambiemos* which promised "change" but remained deliberately vague in terms of the policy detail of its so-called "happiness revolution." However, pledges included a liberalization of the economy, to stimulate growth, control high inflation, ending poverty and attract foreign investment.

Yet, the result was also indicative of a deeply polarized society in which historic social fault lines were revived and two very distinct visions for the national project divided the country. Many in the middle class voted for *Cambiemos*, not necessarily because they were enthusiastic about what it offered, but rather because they couldn't stand Cristina Kirchner or her supporters in power any longer because they were seen to represent the antithesis of the white, European, outward-looking, embodiment of "civilization" envisioned by Sarmiento.

Once in office, President Macri immediately appointed a host of CEOs and business leaders from multinationals such as Shell, HSBC, JP Morgan and Coca Cola to his cabinet. Taking advantage of the postelection honeymoon period as well as the impotence of the opposition, the new government delivered a series of structural adjustment reforms; first, currency controls were removed, provoking a sharp devaluation of the Argentine peso and provoking a 54% increase in the cost of living. Second, export taxes (*retenciones*) on grain, beef, soya, mining and fish, which had been used to fund both the Kirchners' public spending and debt repayments while also ensuring food sovereignty for the population, were significantly reduced or ended. Third, mass public-sector redundancies commenced, numbering tens of thousands. Fourth, the US vulture funds which had been holding Argentina's economy to ransom – after successfully suing in US courts for extortionate profits on bond holdings – were paid back in order to bring the country's "technical debt default" to an end and attract foreign investors. Fifth and perhaps most controversially of all, the Energy Minister Juan José Aranguren announced that he would halve the US$16 billion subsidy bill. Gas tariffs quadrupled for most consumers and more still for small businesses, while those for electricity increased six-fold in what soon became known as the *Tarifazo*.

Meanwhile, one enduring legacy of *Kirchnerismo* was the institutionalization of noncontributory social programs for the unemployed and the most vulnerable households. The new government had to preserve these, even expanding Universal Child Benefit (AUH) to act as a buffer against the severe impact of many of these adjustment policies for the poorest families with children.

In terms of its macroeconomic performance, Macri's administration has not achieved what it had hoped. Inflation is higher in 2018– standing at 31% (CEPALStat, 2018) – than when the government took over, poverty has increased by 1.4 million to one-third of the population (*El País*, 2017), thousands of small businesses have closed, the anticipated foreign investment didn't materialize and unemployment has increased to 9.1% in 2018 (INDEC, 2018). Growth did increase slightly in 2016, but the country was in danger of falling back into recession again a couple of years later. According to INDEC (2018), Argentina's trade balance presented a US$3.4 billion deficit during the first four months of 2018 alone, having experienced 16 successive months of deficit and the highest levels for 40 years.

Perhaps most concerning has been Argentina's currency crisis, with the peso losing 53% of its value in 2018 and its external debt having soared by one-third since 2016 to US$220 billion (INDEC, 2018). This prompted the government to sign a US$50 billion "standby" agreement with the IMF in July 2018 in return for a similar conditionality to that which its predecessors agreed in the 1990s (a shrinking of the state, austerity, return to fiscal balance etc.). Severely damaging his credibility, President Macri saw his approval ratings shrink to 62.3% negative in July 2018 (Ámbito, 2018). However, in spite of significant declines in standards of living for most sectors of the population and a general strike in mid-2018, *Cambiemos* has managed to maintain support for its project from significant parts of the middle class (and even a minority of the "working class"). This has been largely due to an intelligently delivered communications strategy which has included the annulment of the AudioVisual Media Law so as to restrict the diffusion of critical media outlets, generally maintaining support from key newspapers such as *Clarín* and *La Nación*, allegedly employing an army of employees to monitor and intervene in social media exchanges in favor of the government (Reyes, 2018) while discrediting the opposition, combined with the selected use of physical repression against anti-government mobilizations such as the deployment of the military police to crush the December 2017 anti-pension reform protests.

As the middle class continues to be squeezed, dissent is growing. Aside from the 2017 and 2018 general strikes, numerous strikes in the professions have taken place since 2016, including a dozen public-sector strikes led by the ATE union, and several national teachers' strikes. Further, of all the protest movements to emerge, perhaps the most politically damaging for the government has been the establishment of scores of *multisectoriales* (multisector assemblies) locally across the country. In attempting to reignite the politically pluralist, horizontalist and cross-class spirit of self-organization that was present in the 2001–02 neighborhood assembly movement, the *multisectoriales* have been key to organizing neighborhood-level opposition to the government's neoliberal project since the July 2016 *Ruidazo* (noise-maker) pot-banging protests. Taking the utility bill increases as a symbolic target to coalesce around, sizable crowds gather in public squares and intersections in both working-class and middle-class neighborhoods and urban centers nationally. These assemblies include pensioners, consumer protection groups, small- and medium-sized enterprises, students, trade unionists and professional associations. They could provide the embryonic territorially based mobilizing vehicles if and when Argentina experiences a sudden debt crisis again, following the intervention of the IMF in the economy once again, following its record indebtedness and currency crisis in 2018.

In later chapters, important questions will be answered about how the social attitudes, political stances and protest actions of the proletarianized middle class transformed from their progressive, class solidarity-inspired and autonomist nature in 2001–02, to the more conservative, insular and reactionary politics by 2012. Further, still through support for the election of President Macri in 2015.

Gramsci and Argentina's Middle-Class Resistance

The approach taken in this book is a heuristic one, through which the forming of middle-class citizens' grievances, targeting of their anger, measuring of their demands and, ultimately, the shape of their resistance to economic crisis and personal hardship or downward mobility are all based upon their daily experiences, perceptions and interactions, something that Gramsci terms their "experiential rationality" (Nilsen, 2009). He explains that this consists of two contradictory states of mind. First, they are guided by their "good sense," that's to say their consciousness about the reality of their position within the social world and the submerged aspects of their consciousness as a subjugated class, which serves as a basis for resistance that guides their instinctive behavior. However, as discussed, hegemonic projects that seek to be implemented by dominant social groups (but which are either accepted, reshaped or resisted from subaltern classes) mystify one's social position and manufacture the consent of exploited sectors. When the struggling middle class become subject to this and accept their own subjugation as "the natural way of things," their behavior is guided instead by a second but predominant state of mind which Gramsci labels "common sense" (1998:327).

A pivotal issue which must be answered in order to explain middle-class citizens' political participation in radical movements lies in first understanding their false consciousness (and why they may falsely self-identify as "middle class" and believe their interests to be shared with the dominant class rather than the working class). What Cox describes as "the local rationality" (1999) – through which actions that promote ways of doing, thinking and being that citizens develop to oppose the conventional wisdoms that constitute the hegemonic elements of "common sense" – will be explored in doing so. In Gramscian terms, one of the questions asked is, How do the behavioral patterns that stem from citizens' "good sense" come to override those inherent in their "common sense" and how did these account for their fluctuating political participation and views over the period in question?

Certainly, individual class identity was an important factor in the performance of contentious politics and the form of collective action that citizens took part in during 2001–02. Among the range of movements, the *piquetero* protests were universally understood to be a movement of the unemployed, demanding food, work, housing and social welfare plans. The worker-recovered companies' movement was largely blue-collar based. However, the neighborhood assemblies were a more attractive proposition for many of the middle class. These were seen as a more acceptable and sophisticated form of subversion through direct democracy, in which the nation's political, economic and social problems were discussed in mass gatherings of citizens on street corners or open public spaces, and decisions were made about both how to reallocate local resources and which political actions to pursue as part of the contemporary struggle against a delegitimized national ruling class. *Cacerolazo* protests also came to symbolize middle-class discontent both in 2001–02 and during subsequent protests in Argentina like the 2008 "Countryside Conflict" and again in the 2012–13 anti-government protests. The symbolic banging of a saucepan allowed citizens to express their anger with the government, while saving face regarding any personal financial difficulties they were experiencing. Through the *cacerolazos,* they could enunciate their individual middle-class identity through a distinct protest repertoire which distinguished them from trade union, blue-collar or unemployed citizens' groups while simultaneously "announcing" their individual class identity. To that end, the use of the saucepan has become a psychologically comforting form of protest in the repertoire of collective action for those who believe themselves to be middle class (Ozarow, 2019).

However, this distinction ultimately served to weaken, not strengthen, the overall outcome of the uprisings, because the movement was internally divided, not in terms of who it saw as its enemy, but its internal coherence and subjectivity at the time. Proletarianized middle-class citizens were potentially unable to connect with their "good sense" (which, as Gramsci posits, uniquely resides in the "working class," as the only true revolutionary agent).

One caveat should be added here. It must be recognized that in reality, one's subjective class consciousness is likely to be partial, possibly even "confused" or "multiple" and contradictory. Among struggling middle-class citizens, who – it is claimed here – have sunk into the ranks of the working class, its members will certainly maintain their attachments to middle-class culture, their home ownership and distinct understanding of political citizenship, all of which differ enormously from the *piquetero* shanty town dweller, who is barely able to cover his or her basic needs. Historically, cases of full class consciousness are extremely rare, so neither the proletarianized middle class (nor the remainder of the existing Argentinian working class) would ever fully achieve a nondifferentiated working-class consciousness. Instead, what is sought here is to understand how their subjective economic and political consciousness converged or diverged at different moments in time, even if they may retain a distinct middle-class identity at the cultural and social levels.

Argentina's New Rural Poor under Neoliberalism

While the focus of this book is Argentina's new *urban* poor's political responses to neoliberalism, research on the politicization of the new *rural* poor or its struggling middle class remains acutely neglected and merits some analysis here. Indeed, movements from both sectors cannot be divorced from the other and coalesced at two key points: the 2008 agrarian protests (*Crisis del Campo*) and the Agricultural Women's Movement (*Mujeres Agropecurias en Lucha*), active since the mid-1990s.

The 2008 protests, which lasted from March until July, were triggered by the reforms made to the export tax by Cristina Fernández de Kircher's government, with an increase from 35% to 44% on soya and other primary agricultural goods (Rzezak, 2008; Hora, 2010). This was objected to by rural communities especially in La Pampa, the key soya-producing region and an indefinite strike with accompanying protest actions was announced by the four key agrarian unions: FAA (Agrarian Federation of Argentina), SRA (Rural society of Argentina), CRA (Rural Confederation of Argentina) and COINAGRO (Inter-Cooperative Agricultural Federation of Argentina). This extended schedule of protests was characterized by roadblocks (*tractorazos*), lockouts of goods flowing out of La Pampa into urban areas, piquetero forms of protest and later marches and protests in key cities, including Buenos Aires, with the solidarity of urban communities, among them many in the impoverished *urban* middle class.

There is debate over further underlying causes of this protest movement. Some authors (Giarracca, Teubal and Palmisano, 2008; Rzezak, 2008) argue that it was an act of loss aversion, which was felt more profoundly by this traditionally wealthy sector of Argentinian society, who had experience a long period of prosperity with the high international soya prices between the mid-1990s and throughout the 2000s, but who were largely untouched by the 2001 crisis. Others (Giarracca, Teubal and Palmisano, 2008; Hora, 2008; Cerbino, 2018) place more importance on the political alienation of the rural sector and see the protest as the height of their discontent with their lack of political representation. Cerbino (2018) views this as a historical phenomenon, having developed since the mid-twentieth century, while Hora (2010) and Giarracca, Teubal and Palmisano (2008) understand the contentious actions to be more concretely oppositional to the Kirchner governments, who they claim were dismissive and especially harsh in their framing of the rural sector (Katz, 2008; Hora, 2010). It is widely seen as unusual that the middle and upper classes involved adapted working-class protest techniques such as the roadblock. More specifically, Cerbino (2018) explores how the legacy of the 2001 protests may have emboldened their decision to deploy these methods.

It is essential to point out the heterogeneous nature of the protestors (Hora, 2008; Giarracca, Teubal and Palmasino, 2008; Olivera, 2017). This was true both among the unions themselves which were ideologically very different and consisted of different social classes from small- and medium-sized producers whom one could describe as including the "new rural poor," (FAA) to large rentist land owners (SRA). The later involvement of the urban middle classes who took to the streets in *cacerolazos* in support of the rural sector is seen in different lights by the different authors. For instance, Hora (2008) stresses the opportunism of the anti-Peronist right, which saw a chance to weaken the Kirchner government and object what they saw to be overly interventionist economic policies (Giarracca, Teubal and Palmisano, 2008; Rzekak, 2008).

The Agrarian Women's Protest (*Mujeres Agropecuarias en Lucha*) represented a different section of Argentina's struggling middle-class society; the women of small- and medium-sized households, who were producing both soya and other agricultural goods. The protest movement was characterized by the strong leadership of Lucy de Cornelis and consisted of marches and occupations of public spaces, such as the main plazas, in Santa Fe (particularly between 1995 and 2000), *tractorazos*, their intelligent use of the media and other political associations, including the FAA and Chaceros Federados, to further their cause (Telechea and Muñoz, 2011).

They took to protest in the face of an increasingly precarious economic situation, during the expansion of large agro-business which was crowding out small and medium producers. This contrasted with their previous stability and the historical importance of their families and this downward social mobility being perceived strongly given that their parents had often helped to found Argentina's agricultural sector (Giarracca and Teubal, 2001; Lattuada, 2001; Lapegna, 2015; Olivera, 2017). The decrease in state support (Lattuada, 2001; Olivera, 2017), particularly via subsidies and the Menem government's reliance on borrowing high-interest loans, provoked a debt crisis among the agricultural sector in the 1990s. Often, this led to the expropriation and auction of their land, encouraged by high demand in the agro-business sector (Giarracca and Teubal, 2001; Lapegna, 2015). Some authors lean toward more structuralist interpretations, placing the Agrarian Women's Protest in the field of regional research that explores the effects of increasingly neoliberal policies and extractivism within Latin America (Svampa, 2008; Lapegna, 2015; Olivera, 2017). Giarracca and Teubal (2001) explain that the strength of the movement resided in the resilience of the women themselves, in that their strong identity and their families' historical presence in the rural sector played important roles. Critical views derive from feminist and postcolonial scholars, given the increasing involvement of these movements with those of indigenous rights (Giarracca, 2002), aligning with the wider trend in Latin America.

Summary

In this chapter, the international origins of new poverty have been traced to the neoliberal processes that were practiced in the global north since the late 1970s. Four waves of the phenomenon in Argentina have been identified, the most severe of which was that which followed the economic crisis in 2001–02. The need to reconceptualize poverty in light of structural adjustment in the 1980s and 1990s and its consequent impoverishment of millions of nonpoor citizens was highlighted. The importance of distinguishing the "new" from "structural" poor in order to enact suitable policy responses in each case was discussed, because their differentiated characteristics mean that the coping strategies enacted when pauperized are profoundly different. Various theoretical approaches to how and why citizens who are confronted with impoverishment may be moved to enact either self-improvement or protest responses and engage in these actions (either privately or collectively) have been analyzed. The sociopolitical nature of particular regimes and how they can influence whether protest movements emerge in response to economic shocks in a variety of societies in recent times has been discussed, and numerous social movement theories have been critically reviewed. The Gramscian theoretical framework has also been outlined, and the objective of understanding how proletarianized middle-class false consciousness develops so as to prevent uniting their seemingly disparate struggles from unifying with those of working-class and structurally poor movements has been highlighted.

Notes

1 A protectionist economic policy under which high tariffs were placed on imported goods so as to encourage economic autarky and domestic production. It was most famously (although not initially) pursued by General Juan Perón during his two initial presidential terms (1946–55).
2 Withdrawals were restricted to US$250 per week for a period of 90 days in order to prevent a run on the banks when Argentina defaulted on repaying its sovereign debt. Later on, savers' dollar deposits were forcefully converted into Argentinian pesos after the currency devaluation but consequently lost up to three times their original value (Blustein, 2005). As a result, many Argentinians forfeited thousands of dollars in life savings.
3 In this book, the term "working class" refer to those who have to sell their labor power for a wage that makes profit for someone else, and neither exert control over the means of production or their own working practices.
4 The Unsatisfied Basic Needs figures are taken from INDEC's periodic survey data to assess housing conditions, education levels and employment dependency ratios within households as an indicator of "structural poverty." See the Encuesta Permanente de Hogares (EPH) at www.indec.gov.ar.
5 Based upon INDEC data: www.iprofesional.com/notas/128955-Pirmide-social-revelan-qu-es-ser-hoy-un-clase-media-y-cunto-se-debe-ganar-para-formar-parte.
6 The Labor Party was established by trade union leaders just days after the protests, and together with two other political parties that supported Perón's return. They subsequently co-formed the Peronist Party a few months later.
7 Whom they pejoratively labeled the *cabecitas negras* (the little black heads).
8 Nevertheless, unlike most Latin American countries, the landowning class (*terratenientes*) has remained unthreatened ever since Argentina's independence in 1810, and their land was never expropriated under Perón's governments.
9 Although some neighbourhood assemblies adopted less radical social commentaries and *did* take pragmatic decisions about whether to engage with groups such as NGOs or municipal governments.

References

Adamovsky, Ezequiel (2009) *Historia de la Clase Media Argentina*. Buenos Aires, Planeta.

Aguirre, Patricia (2008) 'Social Assistance as Seen by the Buenos Aires Poor and New Urban Poor during Convertibility' *Anthropology of Food S4* [Online], 4 May 2008.

Almeyda, Guillermo (2004) *La Protesta Social En La Argentina* (1990–2004), Buenos Aires, Continente-Pax Ediciones.

Ámbito (2018) 'Por la situación económica se acentúa la caída de imagen de Macri y su gestión.' 2nd July 2018.

Anderson, Perry (1976) 'The Antinomies of Antonio Gramsci' *New Left Review*, Vol. 100, pp. 5–78.

Arakaki, Agustín (2016) 'Cuatro décadas de Necesidades Básicas Insatisfechas en Argentina' *Trabajo y Sociedad* 27. Santiago de Estero, UNSE.

Ares, Carlos (2002) 'Duhalde: 'Argentina está quebrada'' *El País*, 3rd January 2002.

Argentinean Ministry of the Economy (2002) 'Índice de salaries y coeficiente de variación salarial' *Información de Prensa, INDEC*, 29th November 2002.

Armony, Ariel and Armony, Victor (2005) 'Indictments, Myths, and Citizen Mobilization in Argentina: A Discourse Analysis' *Latin American Politics and Society*, Vol. 47 (4), pp. 27–54.

Astarita, Ronaldo (2008) 'La peligrosa ilusión del poder dual en la actual situación política' http://rolandoastarita.com. Last accessed 13th October 2018.

Auyero, Javier (2001) *Poor People's Politics: Peronist Survival Networks and the Legacy of Evita*. Durham, NC, Duke University Press.

Balsa, Javier (2006) 'Las tres lógicas de la construcción de la hegemonía' *Revista Theomai*, Vol. 14, pp. 16–36.

Barbetta, Pablo and Bidaseca, Karina (2004) 'Reflexiones sobre el 19 y el 20 de Diciembre de 2001 '¿Piquete y cacerola, la lucha es una sola': Emergencia discursiva o nueva subjetividad?' *Revista Argentina de Sociología*, Vol. 2, pp. 67–88.

Benza, Gabriela (2016) 'La estructura de clases argentina durante la década 2003–2013' in G. Kessler (ed.), *La Sociedad Argentina Hoy*. Buenos Aires: Siglo XXI. p. 111–139

Blustein, Paul (2005) *And the Money Kept Rolling In (and Out): Wall Street, the IMF, and the Bankrupting of Argentina*. New York, Public Affairs.

Boos, Tobias (2017) 'Pact of Consumption: Kirchnerism and the Argentinian Middle Class' *Journal fur Entwicklungspolitik*, Vol. 33 (4), pp. 37–62.

Bourdieu, Pierre (1977) *Outline of a Theory of Practice*. Cambridge, Cambridge University Press.

———— (1998) *On Television and Journalism*. London, Pluto Press.

Bourdieu, Pierre, Darbel, Alain, Rivet, Jean-Paul and Seibel, Claude (1963) *Travails et travailleurs en Algerie*. The Hague, Mouton.Bulmer-Thomas, Victor (1996) *The New Economic Model in Latin America and Its Impact on Income Distribution and Poverty*. London, Macmillan Press.

Burawoy, Michael (2008) 'Durable Domination: Gramsci Meets Bourdieu' http://burawoy.berkeley.edu/Bourdieu/Lecture%202.pdf. Last accessed 13th October 2018.

Centier, Ryan (2012) 'Techniques of Absence in Participatory Budgeting: Space, Difference and Governmentality across Buenos Aires' *Bulletin of Latin American Research*, Vol. 21 (2), pp. 142–159.

CEPALStat (2018) http://estadisticas.cepal.org/cepalstat.

Cerbino, Gonzalo S. (2018) 'Burguesía Agraria: Conflictividad Política y Quiebres Institucionales. Argentina, 1975–2008' *Polis Revista Latinoamericana*, Vol. 31 pp. 257–278.

Cox, Laurence (1999) *Building Counter Culture: The Radical Praxis of Social Movement Milieu*. Helsinki, IntoEbooks.

Davies, James C. (1971) *When Men Revolt and Why*. New York, Free Press.

Dinerstein, Ana (2014) 'Disagreement and Hope: The Hidden Transcripts in the Grammar of Political Recovery in Post-crisis Argentina' in C. Levey, D. Ozarow and C. Wylde (eds.), *Argentina Since the 2001 Crisis: Recovering the Past, Reclaiming the Future*. New York, Palgrave Macmillan. pp. 115–133.

Dorling, Danny (2010) *Injustice: Why Social Inequality Persists*. Bristol, The Policy Press.

Eder, Klaus (1993) *The New Politics of Class*. London, Sage Publications.

El País (2017) 'La pobreza creció en 1,5 millones de personas desde que llegó Mauricio Macri' 9th March 2017.

Etchemendy, Sebastian and Collier, Ruth (2007) 'Down But Not Out: Union Resurgence and Segmented Neocorporatism in Argentina (2003–2007)' *Politics and Society*, Vol. 35 (3), pp. 363–401.

Eurostat Database (2018) Luxembourg, European Union. https://ec.europa.eu/eurostat.

Eyerman, Ron (1981) 'False Consciousness and Ideology in Marxist Theory' *Acta Sociólogica*, Vol. 24 (1–2), pp. 43–56.

Filgueira, Carlos (1999) 'Bienestar y ciudadanía: viejas y nuevas vulnerabilidades' in V. Tokman and G. O'Donnell (eds.), *Pobreza y desigualdad en América Latina: temas y nuevos desafíos*. Buenos Aires, Paidós, pp. 147–169.

Fiszbein, Ariel, Giovagnoli, Paula and Aduriz, Isidro (2003) 'The Argentinean Crisis and Its Impact on Welfare' *CEPAL Review*, Vol. 79, pp. 143–158.

Freire, Pablo (1970) *Pedagogy of the Oppressed*. London, Continuum Publishing Company.

Giarracca, Norma (2002) 'Movimientos Sociales y Protestas en Los Mundos Rurales Latinoamericanos: Nuevo escenarios y nuevos enfoques' *Sociologías*, Vol. 4 (8), pp. 246–274.

Giarracca, Norma and Miguel Teubal (2001) 'Crisis and Agrarian Protest in Argentina: The Movimiento Mujeres Agropecuarias en Lucha.' *Latin American Perspectives* Vol 28 (6) pp. 38–53

Giarracca, Norma, Teubal, Miguel and Palmasino, Tomas (2008) 'Paro Agrario: Crónica de un Conflicto Alargado' *Realidad Económica*, Vol. 237, pp. 33–54.

Goldstone, Jack, Gurr, Ted and Moshiri, Farrokh (1991) *Revolutions of the Late Twentieth Century*. Boulder, CO, Westview Press.

Goni, Uki and Watts, Jonathan (2012) 'Argentina Protests: Up to Half a Million Rally against Fernández de Kirchner' *The Guardian*, 9th November 2012.

Gough, Ian (1979) 'Introduction – What is Political Economy? What is the Welfare State?' in I. Gough. *The Political Economy of the Welfare State*. London, Palgrave Macmillan, pp. 1–15.

Gramsci, Antonio (1998 [1929–1935]) *Selections from the Prison Notebooks*. London, Lawrence and Wishart.

Green, Duncan (2003) *The Silent Revolution: The Rise and Crisis of Market Economics in Latin America*. New York, Latin American Bureau.

Grimson, Alejandro and Kessler, Gabriel (2005) *On Argentina and the Southern Cone: Neoliberalism and National Imaginations*. Abingdon, Routledge.

Guano, Emanuela (2004) 'The Denial of Citizenship: Barbaric Buenos Aires and the Middle-Class Imaginary' *City & Society*, Vol. 16 (1), pp. 69–97.

Guess, Raymond (1981) *The Idea of a Critical Theory: Habermas and the Frankfurt School*. Cambridge, Cambridge University Press.

Gurr, Ted (1970) *Why Men Rebel*. Princeton NJ, Princeton University Press

Hardt, Michael and Negri, Antonio (2004) *Multitude: War and Democracy in the Age of Empire*. New York, Penguin Press.

Harvey, David (2001) *Spaces of Capital: Towards a Critical Geography*. New York, Routledge.

——— (2003). *The New Imperialism*. Oxford, Oxford University Press.

Herman, Edward and Chomsky, Noam (1988) *Manufacturing Consent: The Political Economy of the Mass Media*. New York, Pantheon Books.

Hora, Roy (2010) 'La Crisis del Campo del Otoño de 2008' *Desarrollo Económico*, Vol. 50 (197), pp. 81–111.

INDEC, (2018) Instituto Nacional de Estadística y Censos Database www.indec. gov.ar.

Justo, Marcelo (2017) 'Una Pregunta Que Recorrió El Mundo' *Página 12*, 2nd October 2017.

Katz, Claudio (2008) 'Argentina: The Clash Over Rent' *International Journal of Socialist Renewal*. 19th May 2008

Katzman, Ruben (1989) 'La heterogeneidad de la pobreza. El caso de Montevideo' *Revista de la CEPAL*, Vol. 37, pp. 141–152, Santiago de Chile.

Kelly, Caroline and Breinlinger, Sara (1996) *The Social Psychology of Collective Action: Identity, Injustice and Gender*. London, Taylor & Francis.

Kessler, Gabriel (2016) *La sociedad argentina hoy. Radiografía de una nueva estructura*. Buenos Aires, Siglo XXI-Osde.

Kessler, Gabriel and Di Virgilio, Maria (2008) 'La nueva pobreza urbana: dinámica global, regional y argentina en las últimas dos décadas' *Revista de la CEPAL*, Vol. 95, pp. 31–50.

Kirchner, Nestor (2003) 'Presidential Address' www.lanacion.com.ar/498849-el-texto-completo-del-discurso-presidencial. Last accessed 13th October 2018.

Kliksberg, Bernardo (2000) *La lucha contra la pobreza en América Latina: Deterioro social de las clases medias y experiencias de las comunidades judías*, (ed.), Buenos Aires, Inter-American Development Bank.

La Nación (2003) 'El texto completo del discurso presidencial' 25th May 2003.

Laclau, Ernesto and Mouffe, Chantal (1985) *Hegemony and Socialist Strategy*. Verso, London.

Lapegna, Pablo (2015) 'Popular Demobilization, Agribusiness Mobilization, and the Agrarian Boom in Post-Neoliberal Argentina' *Journal of World-Systems Research*, Vol. 21 (1), pp. 69–87.

LatinoBarómetro (2013) *Databank and Annual Reports*. www.LatinoBarómetro.org.

Lattuada, Mario (2001) 'Articulación de Intereses y Movimientos Sociales en Argentina: El Caso Del Movimiento de Mujeres Agropecuarias en Lucha (MMAL)' *Revista Internacional de Sociología*, Vol. 30, pp. 107–137.

Lenin, Vladimir (1902) *What is to be Done? Burning Questions of Our Movement.* Stuttgart, Dietz.

Levitsky, Steven and Murillo, Maria (2005) 'Building Castles in the Sand?' in S. Levitsky and M. Muriilo (eds.), *Argentine Democracy: The Politics of Institutional Weakness* Pennsylvania State University Press, pp. 21–44.

Lokshin, Michael and Yemtsov, Ruslan (2004) 'Household Strategies of Coping with Shocks in Post-crisis Russia' *Review of Development Economics*, Vol. 8 (1), pp. 15–32.

de Lucía, Daniel (2002) 'La revuelta de diciembre: hipótesis y perspectivas' *Herramienta*, n.19.

Lukács, George (1920) *History and Class Consciousness*, [1971]. Cambridge, MIT Press.

Luxemburg, Rosa (1906) *The Mass Strike, The Political Party and the Trade Union.* New York, Harper & Row.

Mansbridge, Jane (2001) 'The Making of Oppositional Consciousness' in J.J. Mansbridge and A. Morris (eds.), *Oppositional Consciousness: The Subjective Roots of Social Protest.* Chicago, University of Chicago Press, pp. 1–19.

Marx, Karl and Engels, Freidrich (1844) *The Holy Family.* Frankfurt am Main, Literarische Anstalt.

———— (1845) *The German Ideology* [1968]. Moscow, Progress Publishers.

Mazzoni, Maria (2007) 'Política y Empobrecimiento' *Revista de la Facultad*, Vol. 13, pp. 185–211, Argentina, Universidad Nacional de Comahue.

———— (2008) 'Ciudadanos de bajo impacto' *Revista de la Facultad*, Vol. 14, pp. 211–225, Argentina, Universidad Nacional, Comahue.

———— (2009) 'La relación justa entre lo orgánico y lo ocasional en la configuración de poder vigente' *Revista de la Facultad*, Vol. 15, pp. 141–163, Argentina, Universidad Nacional, Comahue.

McAdam, Doug (1982) *Political Process and the Development of Black Insurgency 1930–1970.* Chicago, IL, University of Chicago Press.

McAdam, Doug, McCarthy, John and Zald, Mayer (1996) *Comparative Perspectives on Social Movements: Political Opportunities, Mobilizing Structures and Cultural Framings.* Cambridge, Cambridge University Press.

McCarthy, Doug and Zald, Meyer (1977) 'Resource Mobilization and Social Movements: A Partial Theory' *American Journal of Sociology*, Vol. 82 (6), pp. 1212–1241.

McCoy, Drew (1980) *The Elusive Republic: Political Economy in Jeffersonian America.* Chapel Hill, University of North Carolina.

McGuire, James (1997) *Peronism Without Peron: Unions, Parties and Democracy in Argentina.* Stanford, CA, Stanford University Press.

Melucci, Alberto (1989) *Nomads of the Present: Social Movements and Individual Needs in Contemporary Society.* London, Hutchinson Radius.

Miliband, Ralph (1969) *The State in Capitalist Society.* New York, Basic Books.

Minujín, Alberto (1993) *Cuesta Abajo. Los Nuevos Pobres.* Buenos Aires, Editorial Losada.

———— (1995) 'Squeezed: The Middle Class in Latin America' *Environment and Urbanization*, Vol. 7 (2), pp. 153–166.

Munck, Ronaldo (1987) *Argentina from Anarchism to Peronism*. London, Zed Books.

Nilsen, A. Gunvald (2009) 'The Authors and the Actors of their Own Drama: Towards a Marxist Theory of Social Movements' *Capital and Class*, Vol. 33, pp. 109–139.

Nye, Ivan (1958). *Family Relationships and Delinquent Behavior*. New York, Wiley.

Oberschall, Anthony (1973) *Social Conflict and Social Movements*. Englewood Cliffs, NJ, Prentice Hall.

O'Donnell, Guillermo (1994) 'Delegative Democracy' *Journal of Democracy*, Vol. 5 (1), pp. 55–69.

Olivera, Gabriela (2017) 'Políticas Neoliberales y Agronegocio en Argentina (1991–2001)'. *Trabajos y Comunicaciones*, Vol. 45, p. e033.

Onuch, Olga (2014) "'It's the Economy, Stupid,' or Is It? The Role of Political Crisis in Mass Mobilization: The Case of Argentina in 2001' in D. Ozarow, C. Levey, and C. Wylde (eds.), *Argentina Since the 2001 Crisis: Recovering the Past, Reclaiming the Future*. London, Palgrave Macmillan. pp. 89–113.

Orwell, George (1937) *The Road to Wigan Pier*. London, Victor Gollancz.

Ozarow, Daniel (2019) 'Banging the Other Side of the Saucepan: Changing Political Activism among Argentina's Middle Class 2001–13' in F. Montero-Diaz and F. Winter (eds.), *Citizenship in the Latin American Upper and Middle Classes: Ethnographic Perspectives on Culture, Politics, and Consumption*. Routledge, Oxon.

Ozarow, Daniel and Croucher, Richard (2014) 'Workers' Self-Management, Recovered Companies and the Sociology of Work' *Sociology*, Vol. 48 (5), pp. 989–1006.

Palomino, Hector (2005) 'Los sindicatos y los movimientos sociales emergentes del colapso neoliberal en Argentina' in E. Toledo (ed.), *Sindicatos y Nuevos Movimientos Sociales en América Latina*, Buenos Aires, CLACSO, pp. 19–52.

Parkin, Frank (1968) *Middle-Class Radicalism*. Manchester, Manchester University Press.

Pereyra, Daniel (2003) *Argentina Rebelde: Crónicas y Enseñanzas de la Revuelta Social*, Buenos Aires, El Viejo Topo.

Porcú, Patricia (2003) 'Proceso de movilidad descendente de los noventa. El impacto de la pérdida del trabajo en los hogares pobres' Masters Thesis, Buenos Aires, FLACSO.

Powers, Nancy (1999), 'Coping with Economic Hardship in Argentina: How Material Interests Affect Individuals' Political interests' *Canadian Journal of Political Science*, Vol. 32, pp. 521–549.

Pressman, Steven (2007) 'The Decline of the Middle Class: An International Perspective' *The Journal of Economic Issues*, Vol. 41 (1), pp. 181–200.

Reyes, Rodrigo (2018) 'Investigación exclusiva: el call center de Marcos Peña por dentro' *InfoBae*, 11th February 2018.

Richards, David and Gelleny, Ronald (2006) 'Banking Crises, Collective Protest and Rebellion' *Canadian Journal of Political Science*, Vol. 39 (4), pp. 777–801.

Rivera-Quiñones, Miguel (2014) 'The Political Economy of Kirchnerist Post-Neoliberalism and the Relentless Power of Transnational Corporations: The Case of the Soy Complex' in D. Ozarow, C. Levey, and C. Wylde (eds.), *Argentina Since the 2001 Crisis: Recovering the Past, Reclaiming the Future.* London, Palgrave Macmillan. pp. 67–86.

Roca, Emilia (2003) 'Plan Jefas y Jefes de Hogar Desocupados: ¿política de empleo o política social?' Paper presented to the Asociación Argentina de Especialistas en Estudios del Trabajo, Buenos Aires.

Ryan, Charlotte (2005) 'Building Theorist-Activist Collaboration in the Media Arena: A Success Story' in D. Croteau, W. Hoynes, and C. Ryan (eds.), *Rhyming Hope and History: Academics, Activists and Social Movement Scholarship.* Minnesota, University of Minnesota Press.

Rzezak, Hernan (2008) 'El Conflicto entre el Gobierno y el camp en Argentina' *Iberóforum. Revista de Ciencias Sociales de la Universidad Iberoamericana,* Vol. 3 (6) pp. 81–106.

Saforcada, Enrique et al. (2007) 'Community Psychology in the River Plate Region (Argentina-Uruguay)', *International Community Psychology* pp. 99–116.

Salama, Pierre (2015) 'Se redujo la desigualdad en América Latina? Notas Sobre una Ilusión' *Nueva Sociedad,* Vol. 257, pp. 85–95.

Schaumberg, Heike (2008) 'The Making of Grassroots Politics and Power in Argentina' *Bulletin of Latin American Research,* Vol. 27 (3), pp. 368–387.

——— (2014) 'Since the 'Argentinazo': From Spontaneous Uprising to Transition, or a Crisis Intermezzo?' in D. Ozarow, C. Levey, and C. Wylde (eds.), *Argentina Since the 2001 Crisis: Recovering the Past, Reclaiming the Future.* London, Palgrave Macmillan. pp. 135–154

Schilman, Fernanda and Icart, Ignasi (2005) *Convivir con el capital financiero: corralito y movimientos ahorristas.* Madrid, Editorial Fundamentos.

Schutz, Alfred (1987) *Le chercheur et le quotidien*, Paris, Meridiens Klincksieck.

Silveira, Fabian (2011) *Argentina: Worker Cooperatives Rehabilitate Both Employment and Dignity.* Geneva, CICOPA.

Silverman, Bretam and Yanowitch, Murray (2000) *New Rich, New urban poor, New Russia: Winners and Losers on the Russian Road to Capitalism.* New York, M.E. Sharpe.

Singer, Matthew and Fara, Carlos (2008) 'The Presidential and Legislative Elections in Argentina' *Electoral Studies,* Vol. 27 (4), pp. 756–760.

Snow, David, and Benford, Robert (1988) 'Ideology, Frame Resonance, and Participant Mobilization' *International Social Movement Research,* Vol. 1, pp. 197–217.

Snow, David, Rochford, Burke, Worden, Steven, and Benford, Robert (1986) 'Frame Alignment Processes, Micro-Mobilization and Movement Participation' *American Sociological Review,* Vol. 51, pp. 464–481.

Svampa, Maristella (2005) *La sociedad excluyente. La Argentina bajo el signo del neoliberalismo.* Buenos Aires, Taurus.

——— (2008) 'Argentina: Una Cartografía de las Resistencias' (2003–2008). *Revista Osal,* Vol. 24 pp. 17–49.

——— (2012) 'Negro sobre blanco' *Perfil,* 16th September 2012.

Svampa, Maristella and Corral, Damian (2006) 'Political Mobilization in Neighborhood Assemblies' in E. Epstein and D. Pion-Berlin (eds.), *Broken Promises? The Argentinean Crisis and Argentinean Democracy.* New York, Lexington Books, pp. 117–141.

Tajfel, Henri and Turner, John (1986) 'The Social Identity Theory of Intergroup Behavior' in S. Worchel and W. Austin (eds.), *The Social Psychology of Intergroup Relations*. Canada, Brooks/Cole, pp. 7–24.

Telechea, Roxana and Muñoz, Roberto (2011) 'Protesta Agraria: Los Casos del Movimiento de Mujeres Agropecuarias en Lucha y Chaceros Federados. Argentina, 1995–2008' *Revista Izquierdas*, Vol. 10. pp. 1–29.

TeleSur (2018). 'Mapuches argentinos rechazan ser criminalizados por el gobierno' 13th January 2018.

Tikhonova, Natalie (2004) 'Social Exclusion in Russia' in N. Manning and N. Tikhonova (eds.), *Poverty and Social Exclusion in the New Russia*. Aldershot, Ashgate, Routledge.

Tilly, Charles (1978) *From Mobilization to Revolution*. Reading, MN, Addison-Wesley Publishing.

Torrado, Susana (2005) *Historia de la Familia en la Argentina*. Buenos Aires, Ediciones de la Flor.

Touraine, Alain (1981). *The Voice and the Eye: An Analysis of Social Movements*. Cambridge: Cambridge University Press.

United Nations Development Programme (2004) 'Slipping into Poverty: A Neglected Issue in Anti-Poverty Strategies' *One Pager*, Brasilia, International Poverty Center.

Vilas, Carlos (2005) 'Pobreza, desigualdad y sustentabilidad democrática' *Revista Mexicana de Sociología*, Vol. 67 (2), pp. 229–269, Universidad Nacional Autónoma de México-Instituto de Investigaciones Sociales.

Weisbrot, Mark and Sandoval, Luis (2007) *Argentina's Economic Recovery: Policy Choices and Implications*. Washington, DC, CEPR.

Wright, Erik (1978) *Crisis, Class and the State*. London, Verso.

Wylde, Christopher (2011) 'State, Society, and Markets in Argentina: The Political Economy of Neodesarrollismo under Néstor Kirchner, 2003–2007' *Bulletin of Latin American Research*, Vol. 30 (4), pp. 436–452.

3 "Crying for Argentina" (or for Themselves?) Mobilization and the 2001–02 Saucepan Revolt

> Then came the music. Little by little, at first emanating only from the kitchens of a few houses, the sounds of ladles banging pans rang out from windows and balconies. Then, multiplying from house to house, the clamour took over the streets of Buenos Aires... With only the sound of kitchen metalware and with no weapons apart from themselves, they launched this chorus of indignation. Incited by no one in particular, this crowd spilled out into the neighborhoods, the city, the whole country itself. The police responded with bullets. Yet the people, who they never expected to become so powerful, brought down the government. These invisible people, as unlikely as it seemed, had taken over the stage.
>
> Eduardo Galeano, "Los Invisibles" *El Mundo* 30/12/2001

This is how Eduardo Galeano, author of *Open Veins of Latin America* (1971) and one of the region's most famous writers, beautifully captured the historic *que se vayan todos* uprising that began on 19 December 2001. The people are described as "invisible" because they had been ignored for nearly three decades, while, other than what I describe as the "segmented mobilizations" had remained relatively docile, as neoliberalism reaped misery in Argentina and much of the region. However, the people, including the middle class suddenly became protagonists in the revolt of those days – a rebellion that became one of the most significant moments of mass mobilization in Argentina's history.

This chapter explores the diachronic shifts in patterns of mobilization and demobilization under neoliberalism in Argentina. The analysis is divided in the following ways. First, we analyze the in-group behavior of impoverished middle-class citizens from the start of the presidency of Carlos Menem and deepening of neoliberal reforms from 1989 up until the eve of the 2001 crisis. Particular emphasis is placed on the 1990s period with a range of generative social, economic and political factors interrogated which account for the shift in expressions of private and collective actions of 2001.

Second, the results of the analysis of the World Bank survey data and the *Latinobarómetro* surveys are scrutinized to understand specifically why decisions were taken to engage in collective actions during the 2001–02 uprisings. Among the explanations explored are the changes in the experience of impoverishment, severity of economic need, the emergence of a "impoverished middle class" collective identity as well as shared grievances, the impact of the accompanying crisis of representation and transformed political and economic climate, reduced tolerance of hardship, growing opportunities for participation in collective actions, and how underlying social attitudes and opinions militated toward politicized and collective responses rather than private and individual ones. However, the private considerations of those within this sector are also examined. Some citizens confined their strategies to individual coping, while others developed more radical or politicized critiques of their own downward mobility and the problems faced by the nation. The differences, therefore, become the focus, and variations in individual biographies, financial situations, labor market and social influences on their households and localized opportunities to participate in different actions are analyzed to help comprehend these differentiated responses. Differences are also highlighted between how the impoverished middle class mobilized to resist their situations compared to the structural urban poor, both in terms of their involvement in collective protest and also by way of how they activated their social, human and financial capital to enact economic coping strategies.

From Behind Closed Doors and "Segmented Mobilization" to Blowing the Doors Off (1989–2002)

The Menemist decade was met with fierce and sustained resistance from below, especially from 1993 onward. In fact, a study of 5,268 collective protests in Argentina between 1989 and 2003 indicates that the average annual number of protest actions was actually higher *among the general population* during the 1990s than during the economic and political crisis years of 2000–03 (GEPSAC, 2006). The principal movements involved were the trade unions (especially blue-collar labor in declining national industries, public-sector unions and white-collar workers like teachers, civil servants, and those aligned with the CTA) and unemployed workers' organizations. However, protests tended to be confined to these sectors without becoming generalized. The period marked, what we shall call, "segmented mobilization." Yet, during the latter period, levels of protest and collective self-help snowballed among the middle sectors, including the new poor, amid what were to become distinctly multisectoral protests (Svampa and Corral, 2006; Adamovsky, 2009).

Although longitudinal quantitative data that breaks down involvement in collective actions by class or social strata do not exist, a general intensification of impoverished middle class collective and protest activity during the crisis can be inferred from the proliferation of specific actions that contained a disproportionately high level of involvement from those in this stratum. For example, the number of barter clubs soared (largely due to contingent factors like the shortage of liquidity after the *Corralito* and sovereign debt default) from half a dozen in 1995 (totaling several hundred participants) to 500 clubs (400,000 participants) in 2000, to 4,500 clubs (2.6 million participants) in 2002 (Hintze, 2003). Similarly, the number of *cacerolazo* protests (the method favored by the middle class) exploded from a nominal pre-December 2001 figure to 2,014 in the first three months of 2002 alone. Further, although barely any permanent popular or neighborhood assemblies existed before 2001, 272 were established in 2002 (Nueva Mayoría, 2006). Middle-class savers' protests also became widespread that year (Svampa and Corral, 2006). These figures suggest that "opportunities for participation in" (or the "supply of") collective actions available during 2002 were vastly greater than that in the 1990s.

Svampa (2005) observes that responses to pauperization among the middle class tended to involve a retreat into private spaces in the 1990s, but then adopted more collectivist forms of action after 2001. The earlier decade is described as a period during which Argentinian citizens were greatly exposed to and influenced by the Zeitgeist of neoliberal values of individualism and personal responsibility for one's successes and failures. Therefore, citizens suffering unemployment and impoverishment tended to internalize culpability for their problems and feel enormous shame in admitting social descent (Minujín and Anguita, 2004; Grimson and Kessler, 2005). Amid the culture of risk and opportunity, those from within the middle class who faced material adversity tended to respond privately in the 1990s rather than to publicly expose their failings through a collective presence on the streets. If they did join protest movements, these tended to be as part of the labor movement resistance or small business associations' protests against structural adjustment, for example, the teachers' hunger strike and *carpa blanca* protest installation outside the National Congress building in 1997 which made up part of the "segmented mobilizations" against structural adjustment and austerity.

Indeed, one of the mantras of President Menem's administration was "save yourself" rather than relying on what he framed as a corrupt political class and the use of the "wasteful state" to support citizen needs (Armony and Armony, 2005). The middle class was also encouraged to accrue a sufficient level of savings to act as an "insurance policy" to cushion any potential fall or sudden impoverishment, should their "risks" (setting up businesses, speculating on the stock exchange or purchasing property) not pay off. As an added incentive to take risks, these savings were backed up against the US dollar under the government's Convertibility 1991–2001 policy.

This sense of embarrassment about their social fall meant that new poverty tended to only manifest itself physically "behind closed doors" in the 1990s (Minujín, 1995). Pauperization was more of an atomized experience, as nationally, poverty levels initially fell sharply when Menem came to power but then rose slowly during the decade. The perception among many, therefore, was that hardship was only happening "to them." However, by the start of the new millennium, the political and macroeconomic climate had been transformed beyond recognition. After two years of deep recession, with unemployment reaching almost one in four by 2002 (INDEC), a systematic critique of neoliberalism's flaws had emerged. The idea that the structural adjustment of the 1990s had both damaged society and created poverty began to be countenanced by many intellectuals. Popular culture (Adamovsky, 2009), such as the popular TV series *Los Simuladores* and hit songs by artists such as La Renga and León Gieco, also abounded in critical social commentaries. A wave of civil society organizations also sprang up in opposition to Argentina's economic trajectory, and their discourse was sprinkled with such rhetoric. Therefore, unlike the new poor of the 1990s who blamed themselves for making "bad choices," those of the post-2001/02 era, influenced by sympathetic social and cultural narratives and influential political currents at the time, tended to shed this guilt and place their personal descent within a broader historical and economic context, emphasizing the structural explanations for their "fall" (Svampa, 2005:143). The result was a radical shift in the positioning of their subjectivity, away from one of autonomous rationality and toward one of having become the innocent victims of their country's economic woes, for which the corrupt political establishment was deemed responsible.

Another notable difference was that during the 1990s, those citizens who became newly impoverished were more inclined to participate in collective forms of resistance following encouragement "from above" by organizations such as small business associations and trade unions. In contrast, during the early 2000s, such resistance was more autonomous and self-organized (Adamovsky, 2009). Interviews with newly impoverished people in the 1990s reveal that these organizations articulated their collective demands to the government. By contrast, the newly poor citizens who remained outside of their membership structures felt especially powerless and detached from these mobilizations; they tended to, instead, resist their pauperization through private means, almost exclusively relying on individual self-improvement strategies to do so (Svampa, 2005:143).

By late 2001 symbolic acts of collective resistance to the neoliberal program that were carried out in *private* spaces soon began to emerge and were followed by millions. These included the *apagones* (the voluntary, mass switching off of lights at home) after appeals from the National Coalition Against Poverty (FRENAPO) to protest at soaring utility bills and personal impoverishment. They were so widely followed that they even managed to halve electricity use during one such protest in December 2001 (Almeyra, 2004:165). Further, after the *voto bronco* (the angry vote) in October 2001 – when half of voters either spoiled their ballot papers or abstained completely (despite the legal obligation to vote) or voted for far-left parties during the legislative elections to vent their widespread anger and dissatisfaction with the political establishment – the new poor began to realize the impact of the collective strength of these acts of "private protest." These were made from the comfort of their own homes or in the voting booth. Unlike the new poor of a decade earlier, through participation in these actions, it became clear that they were not suffering alone and that millions of others shared their anger. New layers of the struggling middle class who had not been previously involved in strikes or trade union protests now began to feel part of the movement. This imbued many with the confidence to join more direct actions and street protests that followed the 19 and 20 December uprisings.

These citizens also came to realize that to participate in self-improvement actions alongside others no longer carried the stigma that it did a decade earlier. Individually, many reached the conclusion that only through collective action could they regain control of their fate and confront the structures in society that had caused their individual financial problems. The closed doors of new poverty had been "flung open" (Grimson and Kessler, 2005:99). Given the severity of the political and economic crisis, the stigma attached to openly admitting one's social descent melted away, as did this barrier to participation in collective self-help or protest actions. Shared grievances and a collective identity started to form, with a corresponding shift in blame attribution for their plight away from themselves to the government, IMF, banks and other external agents, which also cultivated a greater tendency to join protests in 2001 onward compared to the 1990s.

Further, collective protests such as the *cacerolazos* and neighborhood assemblies were construed as "new" methods of manifesting dissent,[1] which were sufficiently distinct from the traditional forms used by the working class and structurally poor. This allowed them to be involved while still reasserting their middle-class identity and restoring the important role of the middle class on the national political scene. It, therefore, became much more acceptable to attend these forms of collective action, which had not existed in the 1990s.

However, the radicalism of the impoverished middle class and their participation in protest actions during the 2002 crisis must also be placed into historical context. Many authors characterize the uprisings of 19 and 20 December 2001 as "spontaneous" (Dinerstein, 2003). However, while they were certainly initially an impromptu response to President de la Rúa's imposition of Martial Law following nationwide lootings (in the sense that they were self-organized without any group, party or union having called them), the strategies and tactics used in these protests did not emerge in a historical vacuum. As Tilly (2006) describes, protests are both shaped by the nature of political regimes and also agents' (either conscious or subconscious) recourse to a collective memory of social movements' experiences and repertoires of protest which have been acquired through previous struggles. From the "repertoires of territorialized protests" that developed as a response to hyperinflation during the 1980s through to the *vecinazo* protests in Greater Buenos Aires and then the *puebladas* (popular uprisings) following mass unemployment in the 1990s all involved neighborhood-based organizational methods such as public assemblies and mass street protests, which were relatively new in twentieth-century Argentina.

Yet, by 2001, they had been incorporated into the collective action repertoires of broad sectors of the population, and this included the middle class, when they too faced adverse economic conditions (Adamovsky, 2009). In any case, far from completely acquiescing to their descent in the 1990s, diverse elements of the struggling middle sectors had stood at the forefront of resistance to structural adjustment. Examples include small- and medium-sized agro-industry rural producers that joined the *Tractorazo* protest[2] in 1993, teachers and civil servants who were active in the CTA union confederation, and various business associations, which participated in the 1995 general strike. To some extent, therefore, by the time of the economic crisis in 2001–02, engagement in protest had become a more naturalized response to economic crises by newly poor Argentinians than during earlier decades. The scale of participation also transformed, with many of those who had until that point confined their responses to the private realm having begun to experiment in collective protests. In this sense, the 2001–02 scenario should not be considered a historically distinct period of struggling middle class collective resistance but rather as an upsurge of the existing one.

In summary, to understand the struggling middle-class responses to their impoverishment in the 1990s compared to the 2001–02 crisis, it must be stressed that they were informed not simply by their material hardship, nor the extent of their material need, but also by a range of contextual generative factors. The increased tendency to engage in collective actions and join protest movements during 2001–02 was influenced by the fact that impoverishment was experienced more tangibly and so their anger at their material loss was more potent (itself partly due to the hollowness of powerful national identity myths being exposed).

There was also a transformation in how one's pauperization was subjectively perceived, as it occurred at the same time as a crisis of political legitimacy; thus, the attribution for material losses was more likely to shift away from themselves and instead moved toward politicians and systemic causation. This shift in subjectivities bestowed the impoverished middle class with a target for their anger, to whom they could remonstrate through street mobilizations. Further, due to the scale of the economic crisis, and the sheer number of people who were suffering profound social descent leading up to 2001–02, it became easier for a collective identity to emerge, and the self-belief that demanding and achieving change to grow was possible when acting alongside others grew. This was especially true in light of the weak and fractured position of the ruling elites, which provided additional confidence that their actions would have an impact. As economic self-improvement channels such as employment were undermined during the 2001–02 crisis, political tolerance of their hardship declined at the same time, as opportunities to become involved in collective self-help and protest actions mushroomed. These factors all combined and cultivated a diachronic shift which transformed patterns of in-group new poor behavior.

The *Argentinazo* of 2001 and the "extraordinary year" of 2002

> Know that it's possible, will it to happen,
> Get rid of your fears, cast them away;
> Paint your face with the color of hope,
> Tempt your future with your heart
>   Diego Torres, 2002

In the midst of the depths of the 2002 crisis, the words of the smash hit *Color Esperanza* (Color Hope) struck a chord with every Argentinian who had been affected by it. The lyrics imparted an upbeat message of hope to those who had lost everything and who were struggling to resurrect their lives. Needless to say, following its release, the song quickly rose to number one in the charts. And it stayed there. Amid the desperation and terror felt by the middle class at the time, the success of Diego Torres' song represented the sparks of optimism that were yearned for.

For some, this hope of a brighter future was reflected through participation in the plethora of collective protests and self-organized solidarity economy actions that sprang up around local neighborhoods at the time. Through these, many didn't simply imagine but actually lived out the kind of transformations they wanted to see in society. The collective actions discussed earlier involved the removal of hierarchies, the advent of direct democracy and greater equality. For others, this "hope" found its home in a newfound religion. Many impoverished middle-class people were seduced by evangelical, religious sects who claim to have quick-fix solutions to their problems (Elustono, 2006). For others still, it concerned pastimes, simply spending more time with family or other private ways of coping. Drawing upon World Bank and *Latinobarómetro* survey data, here, the in-group responses of impoverished middle class citizens to the 2001–02 crisis are examined, in addition to the biographical factors that help explain differences in individual behavior among this stratum at the time.

Evidence from the period suggests that for the middle class, their hardship only became a generative factor in their decision to join the protests when other contextual events were also accounted for. Drawing upon Argentina's national annual household survey data (EPH), together with data from the *Grupo de Estudios sobre Protesta Social y Acción Colectiva* (GEPSAC) at the Gino Germani Research Institute of the University of Buenos Aires, Figure 3.1 illustrates that there seems to be no association

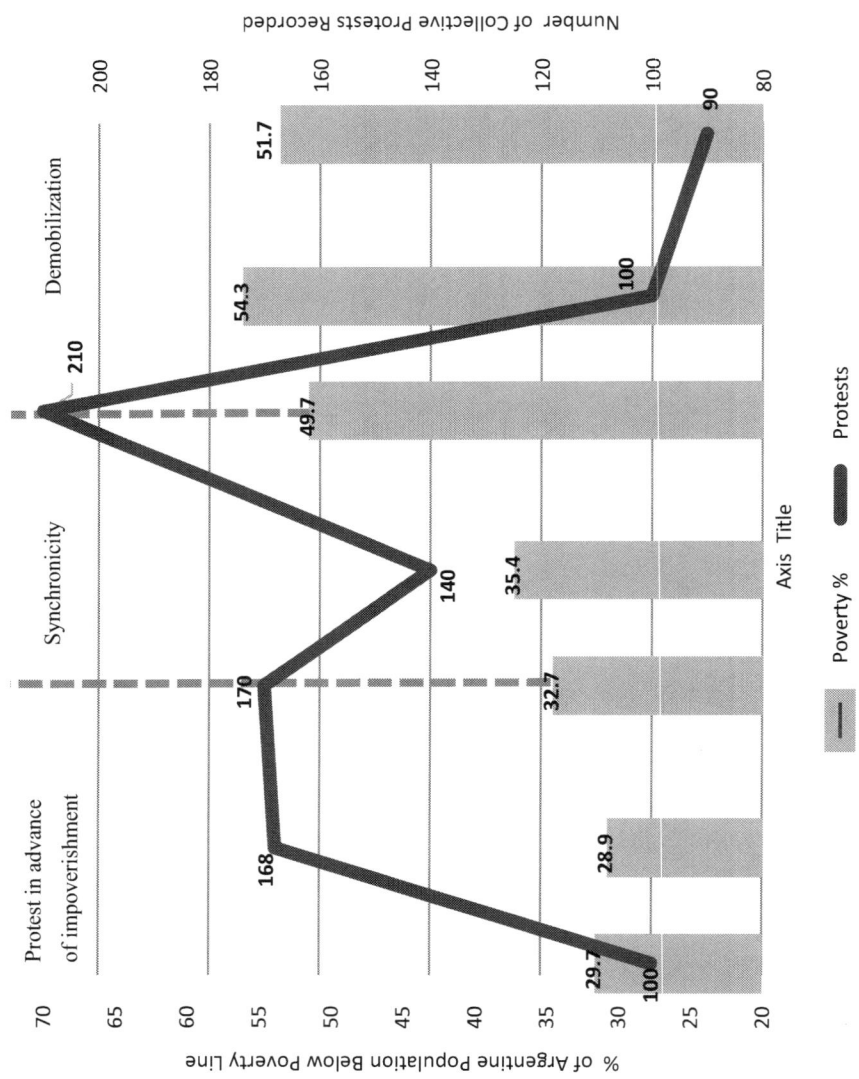

Figure 3.1 Impoverishment and the Number of Collective Protest Actions in Argentina during the Economic Crisis in 2000–03.

Source: Author, based on annual poverty figures from INDEC's *Encuesta Permanente de Hogares* and protest figures from GEPSAC (2006).

between the change in the proportion of the population that fell below the poverty line and the number of recorded collective protest actions that took place around the country during between 2000 and 2003.

This is best illustrated by observing a breakdown of the period in question into three different years. The first (May 2000 to May 2001) could be classified as a period of "protest in advance of impoverishment." Rapidly increasing levels of protest occurred (from 100 to 170 protests per quarter), yet during a time of stable poverty levels (increasing only slightly from 29.7% to 32.7%). In contrast, the second period during the following 12 months (May 2001 to May 2002) witnessed "synchronicity" between sharply rising poverty levels (from 32.7% to 49.7%) and increasing protest (170–210 such actions per quarter). Finally, the third year under observation, May 2002 to May 2003, can be interpreted as a period of "demobilization." It saw the number of organized protest actions slump back to below the levels that were prevalent at the start of the crisis (90 protests per quarter), even though the rate of poverty barely changed, and over half the population remained below the poverty line. Analysis of these three contrasting periods and the absence of a clear-cut relationship between poverty levels and protest indicate that pauperization alone is unlikely to actively generate politicization in terms of how citizens view or respond to their declining economic circumstances.

Further evidence against purely material motivations for protest is provided in numerous other sources. Collective protest had almost completely died away by 2004 (Grimson and Kessler, 2005; Vilas, 2005:254), even though real wage levels in that year were below half of what they had been in 2001 (OJF, 2010). Further, the number of protests grew strongly during 2000 and 2001, despite the fact that salaries were far higher in real terms than at any point subsequently until they recovered their pre-crisis levels in 2009. The fact that material living conditions were lower between 2002 and 2009 than they were in 2001, yet the protest movement became demobilized during that time, reinforces the argument that economic grievances were not, on their own, a generative factor in the decisions made about what actions to take in response to pauperization.

Form of Resistance

Argentina's impoverished middle class responded to their economic hardship by engaging in collective actions in huge numbers. In the six-month survey period between May and November 2002 alone (after the uprisings peaked at the start of the year), some 28.3% did so. Citizens appeared to contest their political grievances by implicitly applying the organizing principle of subsidiarity, that is to say by responding personally and locally most commonly, before demanding solutions from their political leaders nationally. Perhaps, unsurprisingly, *individual* strategies were most freely used, employed by *all* those in the sample. Of the collective

Table 3.1 Action Category Pursued by Impoverished
         Middle-Class Households, Argentina (June to
         November 2002) as Percent of Households

Type of Action	Individual	Collective	All Actions
Self-improvement	100	12.4	100
Protest	N/A	20.1	20.1
All Actions	100	28.3	100

Source: Author, based upon World Bank ISCA survey data.
*Columns and rows do not "add up" because some households
    took part in multiple actions.

responses, 12.4% joined self-improvement activities, while 20.1% joined protests (see Table 3.1).

Another way that this "subsidiarity principle" applied is in terms of where these activities were physically conducted. While citizens applied solutions most frequently at the *household* level, the next most common form of collective participation was at a second level of engagement – the *locality*, through involvement in community job centers, barter clubs or neighborhood assemblies. However, actions that adopted a more national focus (demonstrations against the central government, commercial banks' national headquarters etc.) were least commonly used and fell into this third tier of action. As the action became more "politicized," its unit of spatial organization grew evermore distant from the household and was undertaken by a diminishing number of participants. Based on the results, Figure 3.2 illustrates how the pauperized middle class organized their resistance.

One of the most intriguing findings, given the focus on seeking to understand impoverished middle-class mobilization, were the observations about their modes of organization in Argentina compared to those of their structurally poor counterparts. While no significant difference was detected in terms of their propensity to protest, they were almost twice as likely to take part in collective actions (either self-improvement or protest), with 28.3% doing so compared to 15.1% of the structural poor. This indicates first that the middle class who encountered hardship possessed a more deeply held conviction that their problems could be resolved by working alongside others during the 2002 crisis to improve their circumstances. Second, it seems to prove the suggestion made earlier that it was no longer as relevant to speak of the "hidden" nature of new poverty as it was in the 1990s, when it was seen as shameful, and citizens were more likely to resign themselves to confronting their situations privately (Svampa, 2006). Nevertheless, the fact that over two-thirds refrained from any collective action at all implies that many still felt too embarrassed to put themselves on a pedestal by publicly conceding their descent during the crisis.

FREQUENCY ORGANIZATIONAL UNIT ORIENTATION ACTION

HOUSEHOLD

LOCAL

NATIONAL

Individual ⟷ Collective

Self-help ⟷ Protest

Most Common ⟷ Least Common

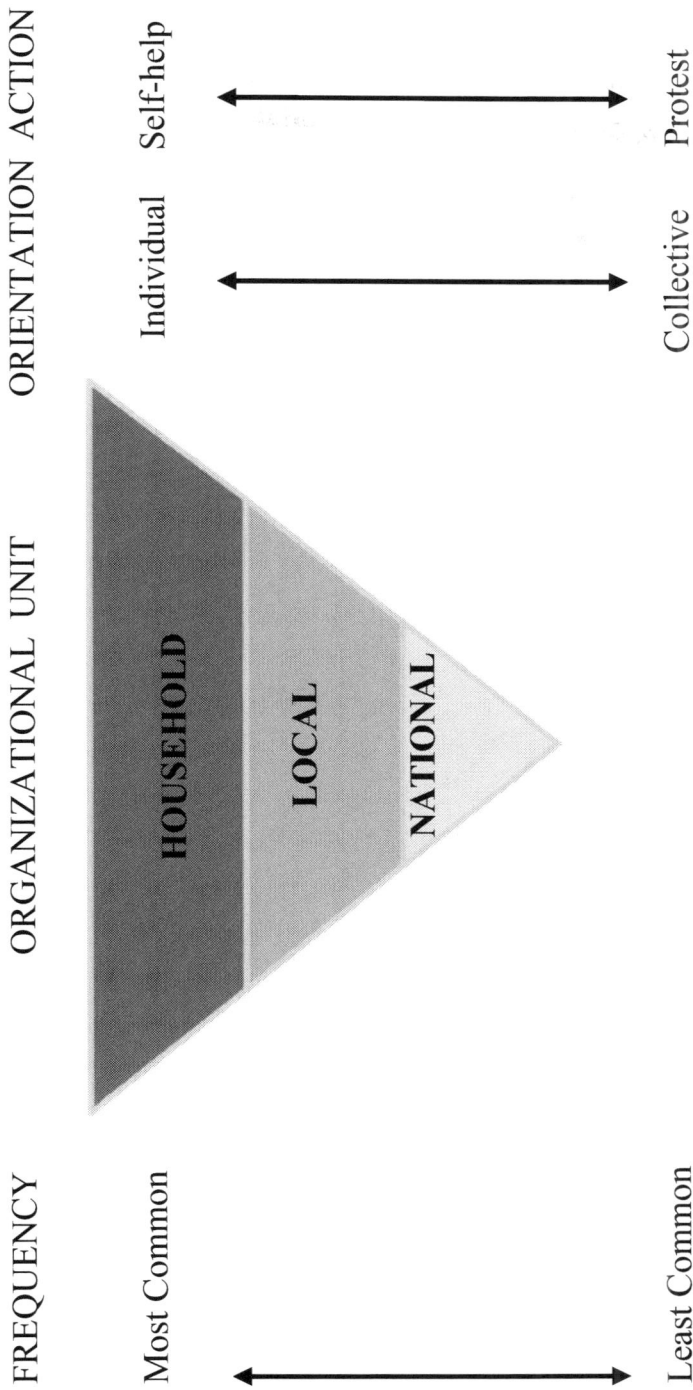

Figure 3.2 Modes of Resistance among the Impoverished Middle Class in 2002.
Source: Ozarow (2014:191), based upon World Bank ISCA Survey data.

Factors Affecting Pauperized Middle Class In-Group Decision-Making in 2001–02

Here, the collective behaviors of the Pauperized middle class are analyzed (their response tendencies as a social stratum in 2002), with their underlying attitudes, compared to those held by those citizens in the same personal situation in 1995 and 2005. The results analyze five different diachronic and situational factors that influenced decisions about whether to join protest movements and their increased propensity to do so in 2001–02: (1) their experience of impoverishment, (2) changing subjectivities and blame attribution, (3) impact of the political crisis of legitimacy on tolerance of hardship, (4) the fluctuation in opportunities to join collective and private actions and, finally, (5) the changes in their social attitudes and political stances.

The Experience of Impoverishment Did Not Generate a Protest Response on its Own

Becoming poor (in income terms) was not a sufficient stimulus in isolation to induce participation in collective action. Comparing household responses between the period immediately *before* their impoverishment (October 2001 to May 2002) and the period immediately *following* it (June 2002 to November 2002) revealed no significant change in either the level of participation in collective protest actions ($p = 0.98$), which remained at 20% or collective self-improvement responses ($p = 0.37$), or collective actions per se ($p = 0.17$). So, given that economic grievances alone were not sufficient to politicize action among Argentina's pauperized middle class, what does the data suggest *were* the alternative explanations for the political protests during the 2001–02 crisis?

Transformed Subjectivities: From Self-Blame to External Attribution

As described earlier, during the 1990s, many newly poor Argentinians tended to accept that their hardship was due to their own personal deficiencies. This provoked a retreat into private self-help responses (entrepreneurial, psychological, consumer-based etc.) as a way of coping. However, Table 3.2 suggests that by 2002 they had systematically reassessed their situations and instead attributed their descent to third-party authorities or to structural causes for which they bore no responsibility. In other words, they underwent a process of identifying how their pauperization related to the general economic and political climate and attributed blame accordingly in different moments. In 2002, 70% arrived at the conclusion that it was their government that was culpable for having caused the crisis that led to their impoverishment, while others came to

Table 3.2 Who the Impoverished Middle Class Blamed
for the Economic Crisis in 2002

Government's economic policy	70%
IMF	38%
Globalization	26%
The banks	21%
Lack of domestic production	20%
Lack of individual enterprise	18%
Lack of investment	15%
WTO	7%

Source: Ozarow (2014: 192), based on data from *Latinobarómetro*.

understand it as grounded in the actions of the international financial institutions, banks and processes of globalization that sustain global capitalism. Less than one-fifth saw themselves individually at fault (through a lack of enterprise) in any way see "Lack of individual enterprise" above.

The proportion that held "no confidence" in the government to run their affairs climbed sharply from 49% to 82% (p = <0.01), a dramatic loss of faith in their elected leaders between 1995 and 2002. Certainly, such distrust was already high in the former year, but the statistics illustrate that following events such as the national debt default, state repression during the December 2001 uprisings and the *Corralito*; the government had almost completely lost its authority to rule among those who had become poor. This helped to politicize the way in which the impoverished middle class perceived their hardship and transformed action from the private realm of individual coping strategies in the 1990s toward a preference for public, collective and protest actions by 2002. It should be noted, however, that confidence in government remained incredibly low throughout the ten-year period under study (1995–2005), despite a slight improvement during the macroeconomic boom in 2005 (see later section).

Crisis of Political Legitimacy Reduced Tolerance of Hardship

Figure 3.3 depicts how between 1995 and 2002 disillusionment with the establishment extended far beyond a mere loss of faith in the government and substantiates claims that the political situation amounted to a crisis of legitimacy. It shows how trust in each of Argentina's key institutions dramatically collapsed among newly poor citizens as measured by the proportion who had "a lot" or "some" confidence in them.[3] This also reinforces one of the protestors' main slogans during the crisis *¡qué se vayan todos!* and that at least among this sector, the notion was strongly supported in broad terms (although how it was actually understood by many will be discussed later in greater depth). This loss of faith was especially acute among those authorities with explicitly "political" objectives (government, parliament, political parties and trade unions).

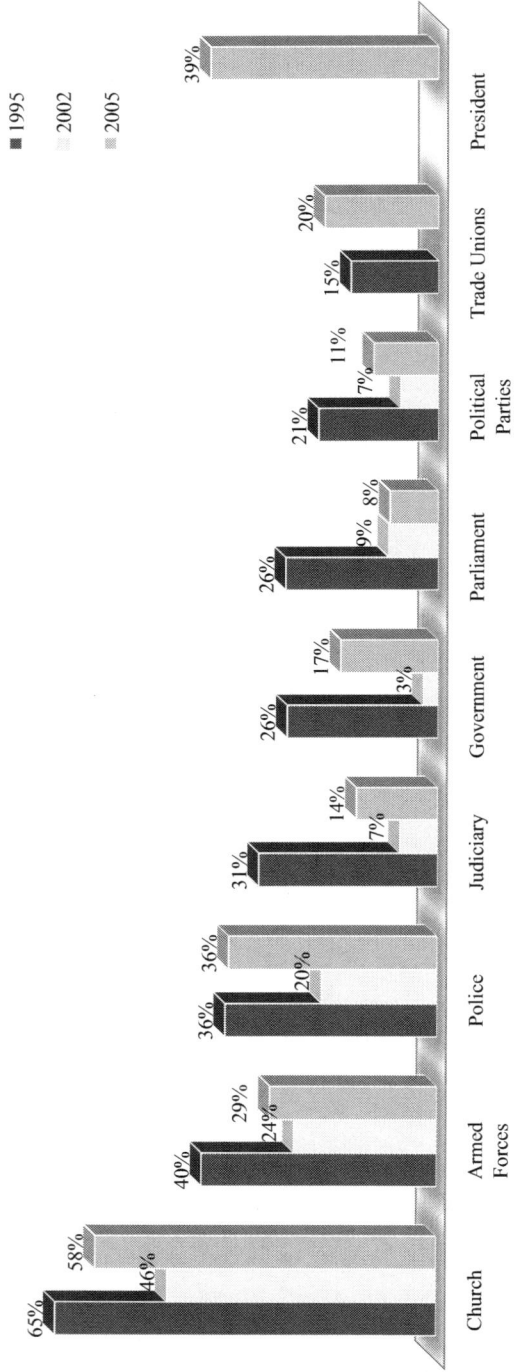

Figure 3.3 Confidence in Argentina's Institutions among the Impoverished Middle Class, 1995–2005.
Source: Ozarow (2014:193), based on *Latinobarómetro* data.

This loss of legitimacy in Argentina's institutions in 2002 must be understood in the context of the radical demand of the protest movement to dismiss the entire political and legislative class, as well as through the movements' efforts to begin to construct and participate in counterhegemonic economic, social and political movements to replace them. How this occurred in each institution between 1995 and the crisis in 2002 is discussed in turn; the collapse in confidence in the explicitly "politically representative" institutions is particularly evident.

PARLIAMENT

The functioning of parliament (especially Congress) was virtually paralyzed at the time due to the minority government that resulted from the October 2001 legislative elections and the fragmented distribution of seats as well as President de la Rúa's failure to oversee a workable governing alliance. Coupled with the general disdain with which most politicians were viewed among the pauperized middle class (and society at large) for being self-serving and incompetent, it is unsurprising that the proportion of those who had "a lot" or "some" confidence in parliament fell statistically significantly from 26% to 9% ($p = $ <0.01).

POLITICAL PARTIES

The struggling middle class had also lost faith in the old political parties to represent them by 2002 (although confidence was already low in 1995), as their support dropped from 21% to 7% ($p = $ <0.01) over the period. The implosion of the Radical Party, which lost all credibility following the crisis and was then wiped out in the 2003 legislative election, in 2002 was far from the only political party to be affected. The Peronist Party was seen as having been complicit in the march of neoliberalism and the country's self-destruction under President Menem, and the failure of the traditional Left to present a united slate as an electoral alternative and the fact that several Trotskyite groups were blamed for having infiltrated and sought to manipulate the popular assemblies contributed further to the demise of political parties. They were understood as vehicles for building up personal power bases rather than for listening to and representing citizens' voices in the minds of many. Citizens were also angry that many politicians seemed to lack convictions, transferring between parties regularly.

TRADE UNIONS

Figures are not available for confidence in the trade unions in 2002, but, perhaps surprisingly, of all the institutions, the unions were held in the lowest regard by the impoverished middle class in 1995 (with just 15% having confidence in them). Instead, they were seen as fundamental to the defense of state apparatus, which was so categorically rejected in 2002. This negative reputation also originates from the corporatist structures of Argentinian capitalism and the association of the main union confederation (CGT) with one political party – *Justicialismo* (Peronism), as discussed earlier. In addition, the CGT was widely criticized for having capitulated to neoliberalism during the 1990s due to its pact-making with President Menem (Duhalde, 2009). Furthermore, the unions were always more heavily associated with supporting industrial workers rather than being seen as genuine defenders of the struggling middle class who tended to be "professional" and services-sector based. Unionization rates and support in the latter lagged behind. The *Argentinazo*, therefore, marked the end of what Touraine would call the "grand politics" (1992:55) and opened up a new era of political self-organization, that filled the hole that was left when the reformist organs of representative democracy – including the political parties and trade unions – were no longer seen to be acting on the people's behalf.

"Non-representative" and "Non-political" Institutions

Then, there were the state's institutions that had less explicitly "political" aims.

THE CHURCH

Among these, the Catholic Church enjoyed the highest approval rating, although this fell significantly from 65% to 46% ($p = 0.01$). The Church's main function when the government lost legitimacy to rule during the crisis was to help maintain social order by supporting the functioning of failing state institutions; for example, they provided welfare aid to those in most desperate need and acted as a mediator during stand-offs between protesters and the police (Benclowicz, 2006). However, the fact that support for the Church declined so sharply demonstrates, on the one hand, just how profound the crisis of legitimacy was (stretching beyond the overtly "political" state structures), and on the other, arguably, how many of the impoverished middle class and others involved in the protest movement also criticized the social conservatism that lay at its heart, which was contradictory to the progressive ideals shared by many (although certainly not all) participants. This was a decade before Pope Francis, an Argentinian, became pontiff, who is seen as representing the more "progressive" side of the institution and who is held in high esteem by many Argentinians today.

ARMED FORCES AND POLICE

Support for the armed forces also collapsed. Views were divided among the population between those who praised the army for having pledged to "defend democracy" after beating back the *Carapintada* mutinies[4] in the late 1980s and early 1990s, and those who could never forgive them for having slaughtered 30,000 citizens during the military dictatorship. Having earned the confidence of 40% of the impoverished middle class in 1995, faith in the military slipped to just 25% in 2002 (p = < 0.01). While the armed forces may have returned to the barracks after the dictatorship fell in 1983, it was no secret that there were some 10,000 soldiers on standby to crush the revolt of 20 December 2001 (Katz, 2001). Ultimately, they were not needed, as it was the riot police that finally suppressed the uprisings after they alongside some vigilante shop-owners were responsible for murdering 39 citizens during those days. Confidence in the police subsequently fell from 36% to 19% (p = 0.01). Awareness that the armed forces were, in reality, a wholly undemocratic and repressive power was reignited during 2002 in light of these events.

JUDICIARY

However, aside from the government, the most acute disintegration of confidence was reserved for the judiciary, whose support rating was obliterated, falling from 31% to 6% between 1995 and 2002 (p = < 0.01). Not a single survey participant mentioned that they had "a lot" of faith in the judicial system in 2002. A series of high-profile corruption cases in which many wealthy businessmen and politicians were seemingly granted impunity during that period created the perception that the legal system was protecting the ruling class to the detriment of normal Argentinians. A few examples of such cases were (1) the 1994 terrorist attack on the AMIA Jewish community center in Buenos Aires, which left 85 people dead but for which no one has ever been found guilty, and for which the investigation has been plagued with both proven and alleged corruption by the police and politicians and (2) the ongoing bitter taste left by the *Ley del Punto Final* (1986), in which prosecutions against many of the generals responsible for the 30,000 disappearances under the dictatorship were lifted during the late 1990s. Their underlying exasperation with the justice system exploded when thousands of the new poor had their savings confiscated by the banks during the *Corralito* (which was, after all, "legal"). The judicial process that they pursued to claim their deposits back (which was just beginning in 2002 at the time of the surveys) seemed to be wrought with complexities which made claimants doubt the fairness of the judicial system even further.

In summary, the political crisis of legitimacy that has been identified helps to explain why the new poor were more likely to take a collective protest action in 2002 than in the 1990s which reduced the political tolerance with which they were prepared to endure their hardship.

Scale of the Crisis and Reduced Tolerance of Hardship

The completely different macroeconomic landscape in 2001–02 also played a role in reducing the tolerance that such citizens were prepared to demonstrate before seeking recourse to collective protest. Powers

(1999:533) argued that many in the 1990s put up with high personal economic costs due to having credited President Menem's government with having stabilized the economy, controlled the hyperinflation and turbulence of the 1980s and achieved a restoration of growth. Many were reluctant to criticize their own government for their impoverishment or would have felt moved to protest against it accordingly.

Support for their government's economic management at this time is attested to in the fact that in 1995, 77% of the new poor believed that the country's economic problems were either being solved or would be resolved given more time. Yet, as Table 3.2 indicates, by 2002 virtually the same proportion held their government's economic policies responsible for having caused the crisis. Economic, social and political volatility coupled with the specter of hyperinflation returning after the devaluation, made it appear that the government had completely lost control of the economy by the time of the *Argentinazo*.

In his statistical analysis of Latin American elections, Fabian Echegaray (2005) found that rather than one's own household economic circumstances, the most significant economic issue to influence individuals' voting choices and political opinions was actually inflation. Unlike 1995, in 2002, the specter of hyperinflation returned as prices for imported goods soared after currency devaluation and food costs rocketed by 34.6% (CEPAL, 2003). This may help to explain citizens' relative political radicalism in 2002 compared to 1995, despite their personal impoverishment in both cases.

Therefore, this economic context was an important consideration for Argentina's struggling middle class when deciding how to resist their plight. During the 1990s, they tended to blame themselves for their own misfortunes because of their belief that their government was managing the economy well, so they responded privately to their hardship. Yet, in contrast, in the case of 2001–02, the perceived economic incompetence of their government meant that they relinquished personal responsibility for their hardship and took collective action to protest their condition.

As described earlier, in the mid-1990s, many impoverished middle-class citizens' mindset was that they were experiencing their pauperization in isolation and not to *others*. During a decade when Convertibility generated the sense of societal prosperity and the economy was growing, the focus became enacting *individual* strategies to overcome their circumstances (Svampa, 2005). By 2002, however, it had become clear that impoverishment was a much more obviously "shared" experience in the midst of a social and economic crisis. This is reflected in the data, with the proportion of respondents who stated that poverty was the main "problem for society," more than doubling from 4% to 8.9% at this time; reducing the stigma with which to find oneself in poverty was regarded, and raising the possibility that taking action alongside others rather than alone was considered an option.

Figure 3.4 shows which issues were deemed to be "the main problem facing the country" among our stratum of interest and how this changed

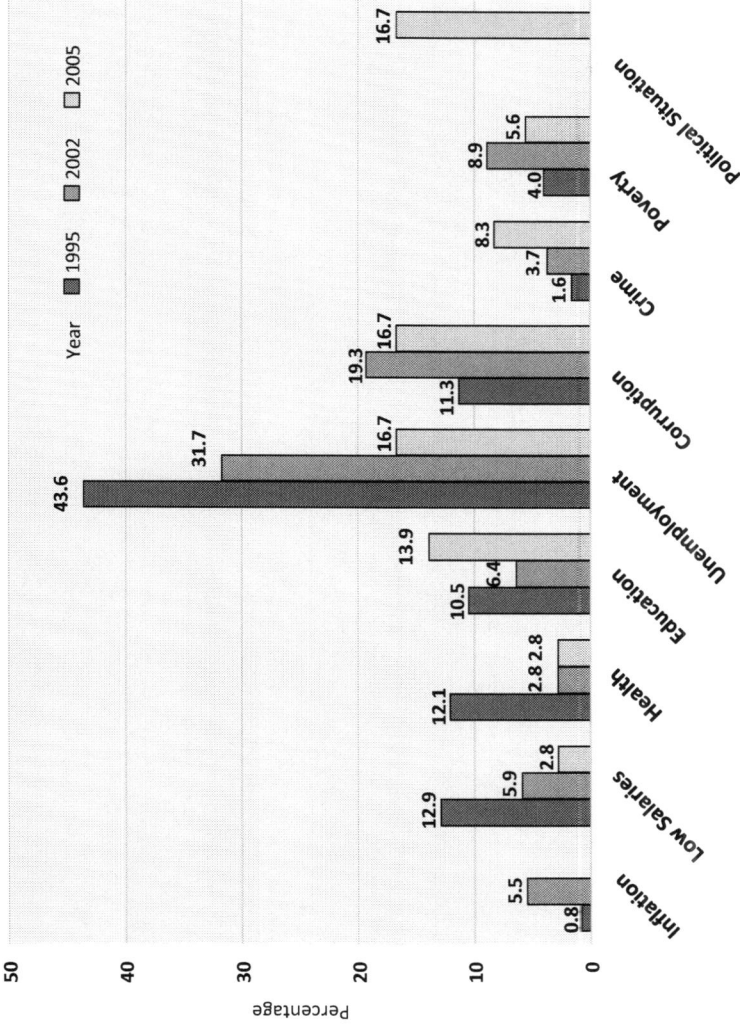

Figure 3.4 What was "the Main Problem Facing the Country" among the Impoverished Middle Class (1995–2005).

Source: Author, based on *Latinobarómetro* data.

between 1995, 2002 and 2005. It is interesting to note that in 2002 there was a strong, relative reduction in the naming of issues that the pauperized middle class could have imagined were attributable to their *own* inadequacies or those which could have been perceived as the "individual's responsibility" (certainly by neoliberal advocates such as Murray, 1984, who support the latter view), as opposed to being attributed to the government or other external processes and institutions. For instance, unemployment was cited by 43.6% in 1995, but this fell to 31.7% in 2002; yet there was an accompanying sharp rise in the citing of issues that could only objectively be seen as the responsibility of government policy and ineptitude, such as corruption (including government corruption), which almost doubled as the headline issue of concern from 11.3% to 19.3% between those years. The politically sensitive issue of inflation, seen by citizens as an indicator of government competence over the economy, was cited six times by as many new poor in 2002 as was the case in 1995. This change in perception added further impetus to the "transfer of attribution thesis," with a greater propensity to judge their economic woes to be a "political" problem that demanded a protest response in 2002.

An "Opportunities Approach": Undermining of Self-Help and Proliferation of Collective Protest

So far, we have seen how the experience of becoming poor did not itself generate a protest response from Argentina's pauperized middle class. Alternative explanations for which evidence has been found include their transformed subjectivity and attribution shift in which they relinquished self-responsibility for their circumstances and instead blamed the government and other external agents, how the crisis of representation and economic collapse reduced tolerance of their hardship and how the scale of the crisis aided the cultivation of a shared grievances and collective identity formation. However, the fourth alternative aligns more closely with the "political opportunities" school of social movement thought.

It was found that the decision about whether to engage in forms of protest action or not was also influenced by the extent to which opportunities for individual economic coping strategies were undermined and those for collective action engagement (whether protest or self-help) increased, thus confirming such propositions by Powers (1999) and others in the literature. Notably, the proportion of new poor who agreed with the statement "success in life depends on hard work" dwindled from 60% in 1995 to 45% in 2002 ($p = 0.01$). Official INDEC figures help to explain this sentiment. Whereas GDP had fallen by one-fifth in two years and 40% of Argentinians found themselves underemployed or unemployed during 2002, during the 1990s, the macroeconomy generally grew strongly and unemployment was at just 29%, even at the worst point of that decade. By 2002, skilled jobs (the kind that the new poor had undertaken before the crisis) were particularly scarce, meaning that elements of their human capital like their superior qualifications and skills counted for little when so few such jobs were available. Belief in individual hard work, self-sufficiency and education in order to achieve upward mobility are common to the middle class across cultures, but these values have been especially inculcated in the Argentinian middle class because of its predominantly immigrant ancestry and unusually open access to the education system (Mafud, 1985:24–26). A discourse analysis of national identity perceptions by predominantly middle-class citizens on Internet forums reveals that they overwhelmingly attach "hard work, honesty and generosity" to notions of what it means to be an ordinary citizen (Armony and Armony, 2005:38).

Aside from belief in hard work, the second resource upon which the Argentinian middle class had traditionally relied in order to achieve upward mobility and withstand economic strife was its accumulated social and cultural capital. The importance of mobilizing social networks as a means of gaining employment and upward occupational mobility in Argentina originated in the nineteenth century when the creole elites legally monopolized the most prestigious occupations in society (Toledo and Bastourre, 2006). Among the newly created, closely knit immigrant communities from Spain, Italy, Russia and elsewhere in Europe (who eventually comprised much of the middle class), such strategies eventually became culturally embedded in the collective *habitus* of the country's middle class. Unlike the traditional poor, who obtain the informal provision of goods and services through political clientelist networks (Auyero, 2001), neither are the new poor concentrated geographically (something that clientelism requires to function effectively), nor has it traditionally been possible to direct social policy at them specifically, because income targeting cannot distinguish the new poor from the structural poor (as they are likely to share similar income levels). Furthermore, the impoverished middle class are far less inclined to accept such clientelist or assistentialist forms of self-improvement than the structural poor (Aguirre, 2008). It is for these reasons that in the absence of these alternatives, stocks of social capital and, in particular, social and professional networks are exploited by the new poor during such times.

However, the value of their social capital also depreciated at this time as the networks of well-connected professional acquaintances who the new poor had previously benefited from to leverage employment, promotions and business recommendations dried up as very few businesses were able to recruit new staff. Accordingly, those who believed that "success in life depends on who you know" fell from 75% in 1995 to 60% in 2002 ($p = 0.01$). Further, the kinds of rudimentary favors that they required during the crisis (like food and money) were not those that their professional contacts could provide, and, in any case, they may have often been too embarrassed to ask these well-off peers for assistance with such necessities. Moreover, many could no longer afford to socialize in these professional networks as a means of maintaining this reciprocal and traditional means of middle-class favor-giving. Thus, despite their value during times of macroeconomic stability, in the context of crisis, their social capital became a superfluous resource (Kessler and Di Virgilio, 2008). Ever fewer believed that it was possible to recoup their lost socioeconomic status through their own efforts or connections, as the options of gaining skilled employment or support from personal acquaintances to do so were seriously undermined in 2002. Thus tolerance of hardship weakened, and protest was increasingly favored as a form of collective demand-making to improve their situation. This was also the case because they were forced to adopt "unacceptable" choices such as consuming less, working (if at all) in unskilled jobs and sacrificing leisure time.

A further incentive to join the protest movement arose following the curtailment of private protest channels. The option to vote for an opposition party as an expression of discontent was commonly taken up among the new poor during the 1990s. For instance, in 1995, 73% believed that "voting can change the way things will be in the future." Further, this belief in the vote as a viable protest option is supported by the fact that 80.5% of the new poor intended to vote for an opposition party that year, compared to just 19.5% who were going to vote for the governing Peronists. The UCR (Radical Civic Union or "Radicals") was the main opposition party in Congress, and, between them, the Peronists and Radicals shared 199 out of the 257 seats available in the Chamber of Deputies. Given that the UCR was viewed as the historic party of the urban middle class[5] (Powers, 1999:538; Lupu and Stokes, 2009) and that it already had strong support in parliament, it is no wonder that four-fifths of the pauperized middle class viewed them or FREPASO (Front for a Country in Solidarity; the other main electoral front which formed in 1994 and which enjoyed growing support throughout the late 1990s, becoming part of the *Alianza* government in 1999), as viable electoral options in 1995.

Although *Latinobarómetro* data about new poor voting patterns are unavailable for 2002, what is certain is that after the events of December 2001, the Radical Party became completely discredited, having been blamed (along with its leader, then President de la Rúa) for implementing the reforms that sparked the debt default and social crisis at the end of 2001. For example, in late 2000, a political scandal broke in which Argentina's secret service (SIDE) was found to have paid huge bribes to a number of senators so as to pass the controversial Labor Reform Act. SIDE's director, Fernando de Santibañes, was a personal friend of de la Rúa (Bazza, 2000), and so the mud stuck to both him and the UCR. With the Radicals entering a period of profound internal crisis and fragmentation between its left and right-leaning factions, the party hemorrhaged members, and two of its former protagonists left to form their own parties:

Elisa Carrió (ARI in 2001), followed by Ricardo López Murphy (who helped establish *Recrear* in 2002).

At the ballot box, the Radicals' percentage of the vote virtually halved between 2001 and 2003, and its 2003 Presidential Candidate Leopoldo Moreau received just 2.3% of the votes (Argentinian Interior Ministry figures). Once FREPASO disbanded in 2001, the pauperized middle class was left without a political party that they could trust to represent them (or to vote for) by 2002. Being able to vent their grievances and have their political energies channeled through the ballot box was no longer an option, nor was the reassurance that at least elected politicians were representing their feelings. Furthermore, the *voto bronca* in October 2001 demonstrates the complete disintegration of trust in the political establishment and in its parties, which contributed toward the crisis of legitimacy. This also made manifesting discontent through protest more likely at that point.

Although political scientists understand the mass abstention during the *voto bronca* to have been an act of protest in itself (in a country where voting is a legal obligation), it spoke more about what Argentinians were *against* than what they were *for*. Many of the struggling middle class participated in the direct democracy experiments that were embodied in the popular assemblies, worker-recovered companies, participatory budgeting and other acts of collective protest, precisely *because of* a collapse of faith in the political organs of representation. These *did* offer a positive alternative reconceptualization of political decision-making; only this time, it involved the principles of horizontalism and local grassroots participation in deciding how resources should be allocated. In 2001 and 2002, the vote (as an individual protest form) was therefore not a mechanism that was perceived to be able to actually bring about desired change on its own. Hence, alternative ways of "doing politics" (rather than being the passive recipients of it) were conceived.

Thus, we see how as both the opportunities available to pursue and the belief *in* private self-improvement or protest routes declined in 2001–02, simultaneously, spaces emerged to engage in collective solutions to overcome their pauperization and also protest their condition alongside others, shaping citizen behavior in new ways.

Factors Affecting Individual Pauperized Middle Class Decision-Making in 2001–02

Now that the tendencies toward social movement involvement among Argentina's pauperized middle class in 2001–02 have been outlined, our attention turns to an analysis of *who* did so within this socially and demographically diverse strata and *what* factors helped to generate protest participation for some, while others desisted.

"Relative" Poverty Stimulates Protest But "Absolute" Poverty Generates Self-Improvement Action

The process of becoming poor (economic grievances) did not itself spark the decision to engage in collective protest actions ($p = 0.98$), nor did the extent of material deprivation experienced. Those in the middle class who became poor but who survived just below the poverty line were just as likely to join protests as those Argentinians who ended up living in more profound income poverty ($p = 0.7$). Interestingly, those with lower incomes *did* pursue a wider range of economic coping strategies ($p = 0.01$), probably because many of the taboos that prevent self-help action among the middle class (like hostility to the idea of accepting charity or the embarrassment of borrowing money from acquaintances) are overcome as the sheer need to subsist takes precedence. As Brecht (1928) put it, "food comes first, then morality."

However, evidence was found to support relative deprivation theory and Davies' J-curve theory discussed earlier. The d*egree of income fall* experienced (how suddenly impoverishment arose) was (as opposed to *degree of material deprivation they fell into*) found to be a generative factor in the politicization of responses. In those households with no real-terms income loss (which slipped below the poverty line solely due to rising prices), 16% subsequently joined a protest; however, among those who lost between half and all of their income, this rose significantly to 28% ($p = 0.05$).

This result has two further theoretical implications. First, it supports the proposition that there is an intrinsic link between the *success of* economic self-help actions (in terms of generating household income) and the likelihood of joining protest movements. When self-help strategies fail to recoup sufficient household income or recover quality of life after a shock (either because they are unsuccessful or unavailable, or because their income fall occurs so quickly that affected households don't have time to enact adequate coping strategies), then protest emerges as a desirable and viable action.

Second, it suggests that responses become politicized when poverty becomes more "real" in terms of how tangibly it affects daily life. More abrupt income falls mean greater privations in daily life, so the sacrifices made by those affected become increasingly unacceptable. The undertaking of economic coping strategies to cushion their fall may have been undermined, or the disorientation caused by such a sudden fall could have prevented them from doing so. They then became less politically tolerant of their hardship. Under such circumstances, such citizens may be more likely to become conscious of the injustice which they are subject to, experience anger more intensely and understand collective demand-making to be an important alternative to confront and seek improvements to their situations. For instance, those living with children were more driven to join protests (28%) than those without under-18s in the household (16%) ($p = 0.01$). Those who found themselves unable to provide sufficiently for their children may have been moved to protest by feelings of responsibility and indignation about the impact of the crisis on them. Isolated prior practical experiences of struggle corroborate this association between the suddenness of impoverishment and the radicalism of response action. For example, the oil workers of the state-owned YPF Company in the Patagonian town of Cutral Có had traditionally represented the country's labor aristocracy and received high salaries, but in response to mass redundancy in the mid-1990s they took drastic measures by blocking the public highroads in protests that soon turned violent, an event that marked the formation of the *piqueteros* movement (Almeyra, 2004:62).

Finally, the results showed that those in greater depths of poverty also tended to pursue more *collective* self-improvement actions. In the context of a macroeconomic crisis where few skilled jobs were available, for those on the lowest incomes (usually the unemployed or underemployed), joining collective actions like barter clubs – especially when understood as a substitute form of "work" (Bombal and Luzzi, 2006), or recovered companies and workers' cooperatives – was an attractive option, because these provided a means of subsistence, a sense of self-worth and permitted a recovery of professional identities. The exception was those households that lost almost all (90%–100%) of their income who had quite low collective protest participation rates. They were also the households that conducted a wider range of individual economic self-improvement actions, including, in very rare cases, becoming a *cartonero* (cardboard and waste picker). Therefore, at this level of impoverishment, survival strategies become more pressing, and possibly choices are made in terms of a more "efficient" use of their time in order to generate income directly rather than joining collective protests.

Biographical Histories: The "Activist" and "Non-activist" Dichotomy

Pauperization invoked two polarized sets of responses between those who are termed here as "non-activists"[6] (for whom becoming poor appears to have induced a demoralizing and alienating impact, which sapped their desire to take action to resist their circumstances) and a second group of "activists"[7] (for whom hardship actually energized into taking action, whether by joining protests or pursuing self-help routes). This typology was expressed in numerous ways.

Citizens who pursued a low range (0–2) of self-help activities also tended to avoid participating in collective protests entirely, with only 13% doing so. Yet among those who pursued a wider range (3–11) of self-help strategies, the proportion who also engaged in collective protests more than doubled to 31% ($p = <0.01$). Moreover, despite the extra energies they exerted to both sets of activities, this activist group also dedicated longer hours to paid employment. The psychological explanations for the differences between the ways that these "activists" or non-activists reacted to their deteriorating financial circumstances must be explored further. Some social psychologists suggest that certain individuals were more prone to suffering mental paralysis or a denial of their reality during periods of national and personal crises like that which occurred in Argentina (Plotkin, 2003). Others assert that a denial of their new-found impoverishment makes impoverished middle class citizens remain intransigent in the face of their pauperization and so failed to change their behavior (immediately at least). This "cultural lag" (Bourdieu *et al.*, 1963:307–308; Kessler and Di Virgilio, 2008:41) may explain why many in the non-activist group were less responsive to what was happening to them that might have been expected.

Meanwhile, those who had experience of involvement in communal organizations (in its broadest sense and encompassing political, social and religious organizations) pre-*Argentinazo* were more likely to have engaged in protest action during 2002. Fifty-four percent of the impoverished middle class with such backgrounds did so, compared to just 19% of those without ($p = <0.01$). This builds on a previous empirical work that demonstrates the link between civic and political engagement in Latin America (Klesner, 2007) which showed how the social capital acquired and reciprocated through involvement in non-political organizations encourages participation in explicitly *political* activities.

These findings also build on a work that has been produced on the importance of previous political activism (Di Marco 2003:123), in particular that of those who participated in the neighborhood assemblies (as a form of collective protest); 60% had prior experience of political involvement. Interestingly, those with parents who were tortured or "disappeared" during the military dictatorship of 1976–83 were also more likely to participate. The reasons for this are not explored but are most likely accounted for by the heightened exposure to political ideas and networking (referring back to the idea that sites of collective action acted as locations of information exchange). Children of the last dictatorship's victims may well have belonged to HIJOS[8] or a related human rights campaign *before* the crisis and thus have been more likely to become involved in the assemblies (or other collective actions), having become politicized during the search for "justice" for their biological parents. Mazzoni (2007:291) found that citizens with a history of involvement in collective organizations tended to also be more predisposed to taking collective action in response to impoverishment because they possessed "collectivist outlooks" and recognized, from past experience, that the only way to improve their prospects was by acting together.

However, it was not possible to determine exactly which kinds of organizations participants belonged to (trade unions, political parties etc.) using the data. An association was also found between those who engaged in collective self-help activities and those who took part in collective protest (suggesting that participation in one led to involvement in the other). Of those who participated in collective protests, 21% had also participated in a collective self-improvement action, whereas among those who did not engage in collective protest only 10% had taken part in collective self-improvement of some kind ($p = 0.05$). One possible explanation for this is that collective self-improvement activities acted as "sites for the exchange of information, ideas and social networking opportunities," or about protest actions that were taking place. Therefore, aside from helping to alleviate their hardship, collective activities like barter clubs, soup kitchens and cooperative businesses may have played a secondary function by acting as recruitment grounds for protest actions through the cross-fertilization of resistance, with the same networking pattern repeated in the opposite direction among those who initially participated in a protest, then leading them to take part in a collective self-improvement activity.

These barter clubs, recovered factories, cooperative businesses and other collective coping strategies also played a third role, aiding participants to rediscover their sense of belonging and self-worth, especially for those new poor who were made unemployed. Through their involvement, they were able to both develop their abilities and have them appreciated by others as outlined above. For example, Parysow and Bogani (2002) researched a barter club in Bernal (a large town in Greater Buenos Aires) and found that having faced traumatic self-identity crises as a result of their loss of employment, belonging to the clubs had helped the middle class participants to establish a new, replacement identity, based on solidarity and trust. In this way, the workplace relationships that they had been deprived of were also replaced. The authors concluded that barter was a way of avoiding isolation and of achieving recognition of their profession, which they were able to practice at the clubs, and sometimes even impart knowledge of their own skills or in exchange for others' goods or services. Thus, aside from being an economic survival strategy, the barter clubs became a "transitory refuge" that such citizens could escape to so as to avoid being perceived – and perceiving themselves – as "unemployed."

Further, these were loci at which the interaction with others who had also experienced pauperization would have promoted a heightened sensitivity to the fact that social descent had burdened many of their peers, and so would have prompted a realization that they were not alone. By coming into contact with others who had been through a similar experience as theirs, it helped the new poor to foster a collective identity, and they became more confident about attending protests, either against their hardship or the general political situation. They also met people whom they could identify with – in their same situation – and whom they could attend these protests with. Thus, the new poor often became more conscious of the general injustices in society and the injustice of their own experience too, prompting them to join movements and collective protests at the time. As suggested earlier, as "sites of social integration" (Almeyra, 2004:167), they mixed with the long-term poor for the first time, while engaging in collective actions like barter clubs, community kitchens (*ollas populares*) and assemblies.

The practical experience of doing so heightened their discovery of a shared consciousness and in terms of their increasingly common experiences and ever more comparable social and economic conditions that they were exposed to. Through interactions at these sites during 2002, many started to feel a strong sense of solidarity with working-class and unemployed workers' movements, whom they recognized were also the exploited "victims" of capitalism (Palomino, 2005:19). Thus, proletarianized middle class citizens often began to develop a shared class consciousness with other subaltern sectors, even if they continued to openly deny their proletarianization at the ontological level of observable "reality."

Yet some of those non-activists among the seven million new poor Argentinians from 2001 to 2002 who quickly disengaged from all collective or community involvement as they hit rock bottom may also have experienced anomie (Durkheim, 1897) – a fragmentation of their social identity, and a temporary or possibly permanent withdrawal from aspects of society, as they perceived its norms (especially their middle-class values) being violated. Dichotomous psychological and behavioral traits tend to self-perpetuate. On the one hand, engagement in collective self-improvement activities breeds involvement in protest; on the other, those who fail to accept their new reality and retreat into individual coping strategies tend to fall into a spiral of withdrawal and self-imposed exclusion. This has worrying consequences for social inclusion if they did not quickly escape from this frame of mind. This will be reflected upon further later on. For some, it was better to resign themselves to defeat than to join the social revolt or seek more self-improvement strategies and face potential disappointment if they were not able to achieve upward social mobility again. It must be remembered that in 2002, just 18% of the new poor thought that their prospects would improve in the following 12 months, whereas 47% were convinced things would get worse.

Furthermore, as we have seen earlier, over half (55%) no longer believed that "success in life depends on hard work" in 2002. In an atmosphere of such pessimism and a breakdown in society's meritocratic functioning, these "non-activists" may well have become more risk-averse and lowered their expectations of a brighter future. This risk aversion would have reduced their participation in all types of action and was an especially potent demobilizing force, given the psychological damage that had been caused by having had their expectations raised so extensively during the 1990s but left unfulfilled and crushed during the 2001–02 crisis. Understandably, then, having their hopes lifted and then denied wasn't something that any of the middle class would have wanted to go through again after 2002. The answer for many was disillusionment and passivity rather than investing their energies in protesting for social change. How the pauperized middle class were affected by this anomie will be explored further later on.

Collective Self-Improvement Activities as Protest-Mobilizing Vehicles?

The finding that there is an association between participation in collective economic self-improvement strategies and collective protest actions is potentially an important one for movements wishing to mobilize and maintain the involvement of the middle class. It suggests that they should dedicate resources to establishing collective self-help projects as mobilizing vehicles for protest. Promoting involvement in such initiatives can form a "base" for practical, relevant and continuous activity from which people can make forays into political protest, even though encouraging such forms of action has often been neglected in the past by labor and other movements due to the fact that the public face of such mobilizations has focused so strongly on protests and "campaigning" (Croucher, 1987). For example, the "indoor relief" and "poor houses" which were used to punish sections of the unemployed and destitute by the British authorities became sites of widespread resistance and protest in the early twentieth century. Ultimately, protests are by their nature "sporadic" and not permanent, yet collective self-help activities can be more continuous and transcend the fluctuating levels of class struggle which result in peaks and troughs of political dissent (and which partly themselves depend on the extent to which the dominant class is able to maintain hegemonic control at different moments).

In relation to Argentina in 2002, the popular assemblies often acted as organizational nerve centers through which protests were either agreed upon or publicized. However, while scores of such assemblies operated throughout the country during 2002 (although largely concentrated in the City of Buenos Aires – see Table 3.5), as the latter part of that year came around and 2003 began, many of them disbanded,[9] with other collective actions soon dying away too as a consequence. They had lost one of their main coordinating and awareness-raising platforms. There was also a positive correlation observable between the numbers of barter clubs (and participants in them) and the number of collective protests that took place, as illustrated by the figures on barter club participation mentioned earlier. While it would be spurious to conclude that the rise and fall in protest levels was *because of* the changing level of participation in barter clubs, the idea that these acted as a base from which protest actions grew needs to be explored further.

Among the most concrete examples of how collective self-help activities can provide a springboard for involvement in protest actions are those means established by the *piqueteros*. One *piquetero* group – MTD de la Matanza – made the transition from a purely political movement to a self-managed cooperative in the longer term while still maintaining its clearly emancipatory aims. This subsequently crystallized their organization so that its participants remained "politicized" while also overcoming labor market precariousness by providing jobs to those involved. Further, the project has reinforced the social bonds and solidarity needed to reactivate its members into taking protest action at appropriate moments. In addition, it has successfully contributed toward building a counterhegemonic economic model while minimizing their level of compromise with the capitalist state or risk of being co-opted by it, a common preoccupation of Argentina's social movements, especially those movements with high levels of middle-class participation, as well as those, more recently, in Spain and Greece, for instance. By pooling social welfare that the state provides to individual cooperative members (the *Planes*) and reallocating it for use in self-contained community projects, state assistance does not threaten their independence and self-management. On the contrary, it has actually given the group an initial income source from which to launch its own collective social enterprise (Forto and Cáceres, 2006).

Gender – No Generative Impact on Response

Gender was not found to have influenced the kind of household response pursued. Just over one-fifth of men and women belonged to households that participated in collective protest actions ($p = 0.4$). There was also no gendered difference in terms of whether they took part in collective self-improvement activities ($p = 0.6$). However, some words of caution are due here. The result pertains not to the actions that newly poor men and women in postcrisis Argentina took as individuals but rather to the actions of the *households* to which they belonged (which was the closest dependent variable that could actually be tested with the available data). Therefore, due to data limitations, conclusions cannot be drawn about gender differences upon individual responses per se.

Previous work has been conducted from a gender perspective on participation in specific movements during 2002. For instance, Gómez and Helmsing (2008:2496) found that up to 85% of barter club participants were women. Their higher propensity to engage in such actions was due to the fact that women's assigned gender roles in Argentinian society were such that they tended to be seen as guardians of household welfare (Ford and Picasso, 2002). Therefore, during periods of pauperization, such as that which occurred during the crisis, it was they who were more likely to be made responsible for generating additional household income so that the well-being of its members could be restored. Bartering was also an action that many women felt particularly comfortable with, because it allowed those who *did* undertake traditional gendered household activities to combine them with hobbies like cooking foods or knitting garments for exchange as well as with wider opportunities for socializing (Parysow and Bogani, 2002).

Among the households that suffered economically, although stable employment was particularly difficult to secure during the depths of the economic crisis in 2002, Argentina's deeply ingrained *machista* culture meant that the male was expected to focus his attention on securing a return to formal, full-time employment as the main breadwinner – which often took much longer time (Stobbe, 2005) – while women were given the duty of ensuring that the household's short-term economic well-being was preserved by seeking temporary self-improvement openings (whether individual or collective), such as informal or part-time work and self-employment.

Some authors claim that women demonstrated "greater passion" during these events because they felt more responsibility than their husbands for the impact that the crisis was having on their children (Briones and Mendoza, 2003:17). While men remained disorientated by the crisis, women often both became the household's wage earners and also sought longer term and larger scale changes that could only be brought about through collective protest.

Age – Propensity among the Elderly to Avail Private Self-Help Activities, while the Young Take Flight

Table 3.3 illustrates how age impacted upon response. The elderly (65 years and over) tended to belong to households that took part in a significantly wider range of individual self-improvement strategies, with 66% doing so compared to 33% or less among other age groups ($p = 0.00$). This result can probably be explained firstly by the fact that, as an age group,

Table 3.3 Proportion of Impoverished Middle-Class Argentinians Belonging to Households that Participated in Different Actions in May–November 2002 (by age)

Age Category	Individual Self-Improvement (Wide Range/Strategies) (%)	Collective Self-Improvement (%)	Collective Protest (%)
18–34	33	16	18
35–49	27	9	21
50–64	33	10	25
65 and over	66	0	11

Source: Author, based upon World Bank ISCA Survey data.

they were much less likely to be "working" or "studying" because most were retired. In practice, this meant that they had more time available to dedicate to the pursuit of different economic coping strategies. Second, a breakdown of their coping strategies indicates that they were more likely to rent out their homes and "cash in" dividends or other kinds of investments than any other age group. Third, the results indicate that they were more likely to draw upon favors from acquaintances so as to buy goods and services on trust than other age groups.

Critically, they were far more likely to obtain help from friends and acquaintances (pursued by 33% of those 65 and over, but just 15% of young adults, 8% of those aged 35–49 and only 4% of those aged 50–64 ($p = 0.04$)). This suggests that their networks of social capital did not diminish in the same way that it did for members of other age groups, which meant they could still exploit it to pursue individual coping strategies to a greater extent than other groups. Furthermore, the results showed that of all age groups, the elderly were also most likely to withdraw savings, sell or pawn their possessions and access government aid. Consequently, they were also much less likely to belong to households that engaged in collective self-improvement activities because they were not in as much financial need, given their ability to obtain alternative income sources for the household through exploiting their own personal networks and individual solutions.

The particular susceptibility to impoverishment among the elderly in the 1990s (due to the reductions in state pensions) was contrasted with the fact that during the 2001–02 crisis, they were generally shielded from its most severe impacts (in terms of the extent of income loss). While the elderly suffered an especially low standard of living both before and during 2002, they did not encounter a particularly harsh *deterioration* in their circumstances compared to other age groups.

The lower level of household participation in collective protest among older people might also be explained by cross-referencing the earlier result, which indicated that more sudden losses of income are more likely to generate a protest response. However, the relative income stability that households with older people benefited from – due to pension income still being available on the one hand, and the multiple use of social capital to pursue a wider range of individual coping strategies, on the other – meant that such external shocks to the household were cushioned and impoverishment was *relatively* easier to adapt to compared to other age categories. Second, generally speaking, the elderly were usually physically less able to take to the streets in revolt, which surely also explains their preference for self-improvement actions ahead of protest. Separate studies (Jennings and Markus, 1988) indicate that political activity in the life cycle tends to peak during the mid-fifties, then declines into the sixties and seventies, when protest activity takes more individual forms such as letter writing.

In terms of attitudes and outlooks, unsurprisingly, there was generally a great deal of gloom among the struggling middle class with respect to their future in 2002 (see Table 3.4). Young adults were more optimistic about their future compared to those in the middle-aged category, who were more pessimistic than anyone else ($p = 0.09$). The reasons for this are numerous, but principally due to concern among the middle aged for their future employment prospects, given age discrimination in the labor market (Gómez, 2003), the erosion of their human capital and an "it's too late for me" mentality. On the other hand, emigration was seen as an exit strategy that gave particular cause for hope to younger age groups, partly explaining their (relative) optimism overall. 52% of 18–34-year-olds and their families "seriously considered" emigrating in 2002, while this fell to 44% among those aged 35–49, 39% of 50–64-year-olds and just 17% of those aged 65 and over ($p = 0.1$). This option was also considered more by the young adult age group (those who were the children or grandchildren of immigrants), both because of the more fluid concept of "nationality" that they had been brought up with (Feijóo, 2003:46), and in practical terms because such ancestry made it easier to obtain European Union (EU) citizenship (and the right to legally work and reside in any EU member-state) for second- or third-generation immigrants (Melamed, 2002:25).

The reasons why emigration was a particularly attractive option for young adults are due to a combination of "push" and "pull" factors. For example, on the "push side" (those which encouraged them to leave the country), the survey data illustrate that the unemployment rate among young adult new poor was an astonishing 42%, far higher than any other age group, meaning that they had more reason to seek job opportunities overseas. The rate was just 15% among 35–49-year-olds and 27% among 50–64-year-olds ($p =$ <0.01), so this was possibly a key factor. Further, not only did young people (18–34) have fewer job opportunities, but the data suggest that they had fewer family commitments (dependents) to keep them from leaving Argentina. Novick and Murias (2005:46) corroborate this and found that it was this age group who were more frustrated by the barriers to their professional or academic progress that an economic collapse entailed.

Table 3.4 Impact of Age upon Optimism for Future Prospects among the Impoverished Middle Class in 2002

Age Category	Better (%)	Same (%)	Worse (%)
18–34	20	39	41
35–49	19	33	48
50–64	13	27	60

Source: Author, based upon *Latinobarómetro* data.

They would also generally have been in better health to start a new life overseas than their older cohorts. Whether younger people were particularly attracted to emigrate by "pull factors" such as supportive family networks abroad could not be determined from the survey data alone, although it has been demonstrated that many Western countries which operated Highly Skilled Migrant Programmes at the time facilitated immigration prospects particularly for young professionals. Younger Argentinians also tended to be more likely to apply for EU passports (Melamed, 2002) which granted them the right to live and work in European countries.

Territoriality and Collective Action – City of Buenos Aires as the Hub but not for the New Poor

The choices that impoverished middle-class citizens took with regard to joining social movements as part of how they resisted their situations were not influenced by whether such opportunities physically existed within their province or the proximity to them from their residence. Nueva Mayoría data (2006) convey a marked geographical variation in the number of permanent neighborhood assemblies, *cacerolazo* protests and barter clubs in Argentina's provinces in 2002 (Table 3.5). Notwithstanding reliability problems concerning the accurate recording of all possible actions and not accounting for regional differentials in transport, infrastructure, terrain or distance to population hubs, the figures provide a tentative indication of the ease with which it was possible to locate and thus join these different actions within one's local proximity.

The data unequivocally posit the City of Buenos Aires as the district with the greatest concentration of actions, boasting 41% of neighborhood assemblies and 26% of *cacerolazo* protests, despite only containing 7% of the national population. Its residents also had the shortest average distance to travel (calculated by dividing each region's land mass by the number of collective actions that took place there at the time), in order to take part in collective actions (just 200 square meters). Greater Buenos Aires comprised a vastly disproportionate presence of barter clubs (60% of the total national figure) and offered relatively close physical proximity to collective actions, as did Santa Fe Province.

Among the *general survey universe*, in accordance with the above, citizens were significantly more likely to take part in collective protests if they lived in the Autonomous City of Buenos Aires (CABA) (31%) compared to Greater Buenos Aires (21%) or Argentina's remaining provinces (21%) (p = <0.01). However, among the impoverished middle class, no such variation was identified, and they were no more likely to join the protest movement in the CABA than anywhere else. Given that many of the major institutions that became targets of their anger (such as commercial banks' headquarters, the Supreme Court, Congress and the Presidential Palace) were situated in city centers, especially in the CABA, the fact that territorial opportunities made

Table 3.5 Geographical Distribution of Collective Actions in 2002

District	Popular Assemblies	Percent Total	Cacerolazo Protests	Percent Total	Barter Clubs	Percent Total	Population as Percent National	km² per Collective Action
City of Buenos Aires	112	41	529	26	208	4	7	0.2
Buenos Aires Province	105	39	329	16	3,000	60	38	90
Santa Fe	37	14	261	13	900	18	8	111
Cordoba	11	4	187	9	95	2	8	564
Rio Negro	2	1	38	2	180	4	2	923
Mendoza	0	0	129	6	65	1	4	767
Other	5	1	541	28	559	10	4	
Total	**277**	**100**	**2,094**	**100**	**5,356**	**100**	**33** **100**	

Source: Centro de Estudios Nueva Mayoria (2006).

no difference to their propensity to protest was surprising. In attempting to explain this, first, it must be acknowledged that the period of data collection (June 2002 to November 2002) was one of *demobilization* and, also, there was a relative shift in the "sites" of new poor-led protest, away from the major urban centers such as CABA toward the provinces.

So, why did struggling middle class-led protests in the provinces (that is to say, outside of CABA and Conurbano) increase through the course of 2002 yet remain unchanged in Argentina's capital city? Notably, the number of *cacerolazo, escrache* or other protest marches that were most likely to target strategic urban locations such as the courts, banks or parliament had fallen sharply by the time of the second survey, at the end of 2002. This can be ascribed firstly to the fact that at the tail end of that year, savings had been partially returned to many victims of the *Corralito,* second because the banks which had been the target for many of the new poor-led protests had become subject to a government-instigated judicial process (Vilas, 2005:258) and third because many of the individual politicians who were seen as being responsible for the crisis, such as President de la Rúa and Economy Minister Domingo Cavallo, had either resigned or been removed from office and were no longer targets in the same way.

For these reasons, many citizens were appeased during 2002 to some degree, and this reduced the magnetism that the national governing institutions based in the City of Buenos Aires held as protest loci. The fourth reason that may explain the provincialization of new poor citizens' protest is that many of the *escraches* that occurred later in 2002 targeted the private country estates of politicians, bankers or judges who were identified as being corrupt and who, it was felt, had to be removed from office due to their perceived role in the crisis.

Position within the Labor Market: Politicization through Work

Labor market difficulties have been a key trigger of new impoverishment ever since it was first theorized (Minujín, 1995:164). One of its most striking features internationally is that it leaves millions of well-educated, often highly experienced individuals either unemployed or working in a job for which they are tremendously overqualified. In referring to the contemporary situation in the USA, where underemployment, unemployment and new poverty are also a prominent part of the social landscape, Nobel Prize-winner Paul Krugman (2006) summarized the climate perfectly when he declared that we had entered the "marvellous world of the graduate waiter, taxi driver and flight attendant."

The study uncovered that spending time in the workplace had a politicizing impact on responses to pauperization. As Figure 3.5 illustrates, pauperized middle class Argentinians who dedicated longer hours to paid work demonstrated a greater propensity to join the protest movement, whereas those households which spent less time doing so were more likely to confine

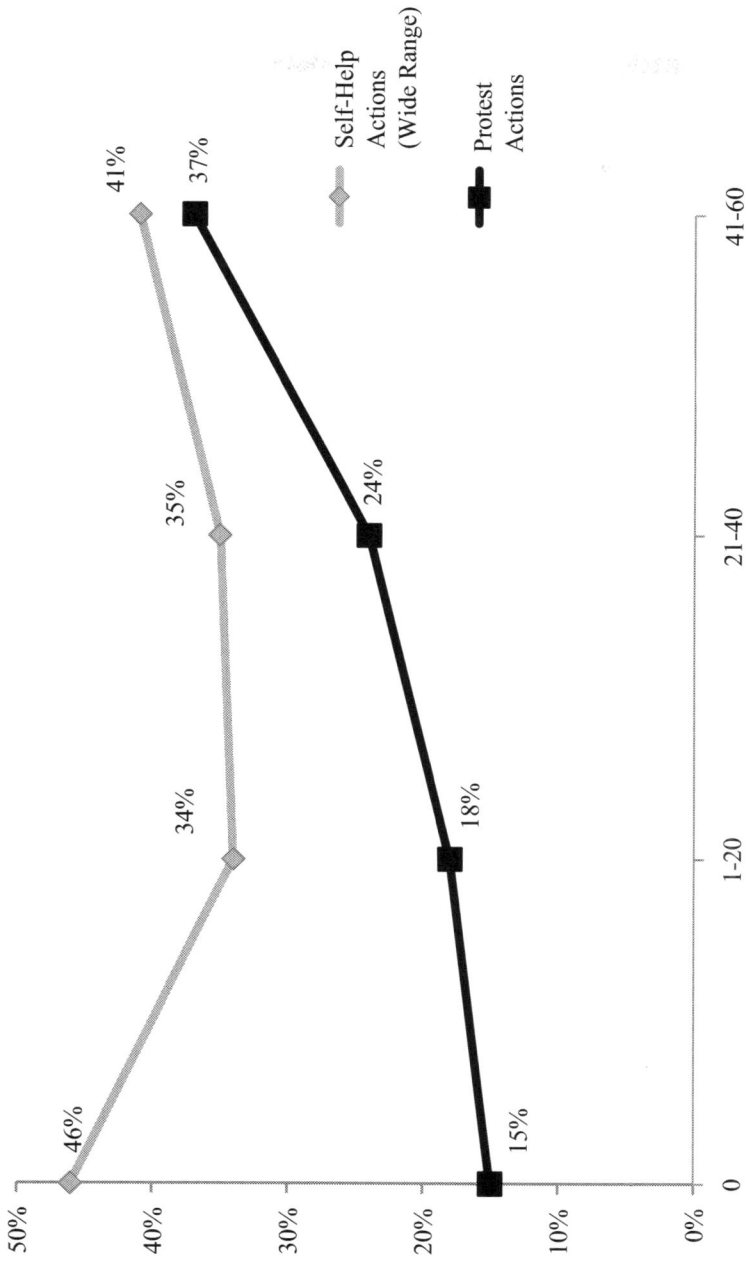

Figure 3.5 Working Hours and Responses to Impoverishment in Argentina, 2002.
Source: Ozarow (2014: 197), based on World Bank ISCA Survey, 2002.

their responses to self-help measures alone. Where no one was employed (the household's average working hours was zero), 46% of the new poor engaged in a wide range (3–11) of self-help actions, yet just 15% took part in protests. Whereas, under these circumstances, the impoverished middle class were three times more likely to enact higher ranges of economic coping strategies than political protest responses, this ratio decreased to 2:1 when households were working 1–20 hours per week, 1.5:1 at 21–40 hours, and then among those who worked the longest hours (41–60 hours), a protest response became equally as likely, with 37% joining protests compared to 41% engaging in wider ranges of self-help actions. At first sight, this seems surprising because it contradicts the rational assumption that working more means less "spare time" available to engage in political activities.

Initially, this result looks puzzling and somewhat "irrational." Why were those who were working longer hours more likely to engage in protest actions if they had less time available? Four alternative propositions that may explain this relationship between work and politicization are proposed for further inquiry. First of all, in trying to understand which sectors within the pauperized middle class population were more likely to be mobilized by the call to protest, it is crucial to analyze the success of the "frame-alignment processes" that were used by social movement leaders. These helped such citizens to understand the causes of their impoverishment as being attributable to systemic factors rather than to their own responsibility as individuals. This process of attributing blame establishes the link between individual grievances and action, by framing the injustice in a way that resonates with the personal concerns of a disadvantaged group (in this case, the new poor) in a congruent and complementary manner. In examining who was moved to join the protest movement at this time, what is important is that the "frame" had to seem relevant to the participants' experience and fit within their cultural narrations (Snow and Benford, 1988).

One should remember that – as mentioned on numerous occasions – the ethos of hard work and self-reliance has always been fundamental to the Argentinian middle-class habitus, particularly given their predominantly immigrant ancestry (Mafud, 1985:24–26). It is therefore possible that when referring to the personal injustices afflicting the hard-working, impoverished members of the middle class who had been the victims of the crisis, these mobilizing messages from the assemblies, *cacerolazos* and *escraches* resonated most strongly with those who worked the longest hours. When they apportioned blame to the politicians, bankers, IMF and virtually *all* of neoliberalism's institutions in an attempt at "motivational framing," that would convey the message that they "deserved better" leaders and representative institutions. Therefore, these would also be the most salient mobilizing frames to those who had suffered impoverishment and dramatic declines in living standards *in spite of* their hard work, which contravened the meritocratic values they held. Indeed, those who worked more hours yet remained impoverished may have been more likely to have become conscious of the nature of their exploitation at the hands of their bosses and in relation to capital than those who were also newly pauperized but worked fewer (or zero) hours. Therefore, this raised level of class consciousness may have radicalized the solutions that they sought to improve their own circumstances. How "economic" issues, such as falling incomes and increased working hours, can become the catalyst for "political" demands, like democratic rights, was analyzed over a century ago, when Rosa Luxemburg (1906) discussed the idea with reference to the 1905 Revolution in Russia. This is entirely relevant to Argentina, where the new poor (who had to work longer hours yet remained in poverty), initially took a lead role in demanding a replacement of the country's existing representative political structures with the notion of direct democracy.

The second possibility is that spending more time in the presence of work colleagues increased their exposure to others with similar grievances to them. Evidence suggests that the workplace thus acted as an important social interaction site, which cultivated collective grievance and identity-forming, as well as helped to raise awareness of the existence of protest actions either through word of mouth or possibly a trade union source and increased the confidence to join them. The third hypothesis is that those dedicating more time to their job will have sacrificed more of their social lives. This reduced their tolerance of hardship, provoked greater anger and ignited political action. Fourth, in terms of overcoming free rider barriers to collective action, those working longer hours may have been more motivated to protest to defend their interests by the fear of losing their job during the crisis because they were the ones at risk of forfeiting higher levels of income than those working (and earning) less through doing nothing about the state of the country.

No association was found between the head of household's employment status and the decision to participate in collective protest ($p = 0.96$); however, those with an employed head were more likely to pursue collective self-help strategies ($p = 0.03$). Those with unemployed or inactive heads were more likely to pursue a wider range of individual coping strategies (40%) compared to those with a working head of household (29%) ($p = 0.06$). One way of understanding this result is with reference to the *a priori* proposition that the workplace acted as a site through which information about the occurrence of collective self-improvement activities was disseminated. Although the data itself do not provide such explanations, one can insinuate that, through interaction with work colleagues during their employment, the head of the household may not only have been more likely to join protests due to the discovery of shared grievances with fellow workers, but they may also have persuaded other household members to join them. Such behavioral patterns were *less* likely among those who did not go to work. Unemployed heads of households would have been less exposed to such environments where they could discover the possibility of engaging in collective action; hence, they and their families resorted more to *individualist* solutions. Further, unemployed or inactive newly poor citizens also tended to resort to establishing a microenterprise or going self-employed as a private way of dealing with their hardship.

Increased Propensity of Public-Sector Employment Histories for Collective Action

Whether impoverished middle-class citizens worked in the public or private sector in 2002 had no impact on the question of whether they participated in the rebellion at the time ($p = 0.4$). Although trade union density and militancy were greater in the public sector, the incidence of trade union protest (strikes, demonstrations etc.) as a proportion of all societal protests actually fell sharply from almost 40% to 25% between 2001 and 2002, while the level of mobilization among civil society and *piquetero* organizations intensified in relative terms, increasing from 170 to 210 protests between May 2001 and May 2002 (GEPSAC, 2006). This, therefore, reduced the relevance that the strength of the unions in the public sector had in terms of whether those working for the state were more likely to join protests in general.

However, two intriguing results lie behind this finding. First, the results point to the fact that there was not necessarily a "collectivist" ethos among those with public-sector backgrounds – at least not to the extent that it influenced action. Working in the public sector had no bearing on whether *all* types of collective actions (protests and self-improvement combined) were pursued.

Second, what *did* make some difference to the propensity toward protest choices was the background sector of their employment history *before* the economic crisis deepened in October 2001 (as opposed to the sector they were actually working in *at the time* of the ISCA Survey). Taking this variable into account, among those with public-sector backgrounds from before the crisis, 30% engaged in a protest of some kind *after* their impoverishment, but this figure was considerably (and statistically significantly) lower, at 18%, among those who had a previous employment history in the private sector ($p = 0.07$). Among those working for state or local government enterprises, there may have been a more "collectivist" spirit derived from the public-sector ethos or simply because there was more of a culture of joining collective protest actions given that the trade unions in the public sector had headed national strike statistics since the 1980s (Atzeni and Ghigliani, 2008). However, whether or not the collective repertoires of protest (Tilly, 1986:390) that were learned through the public-sector industrial struggles against the cuts of the 1990s actually empowered the struggling middle class with such labor histories to take collective protest action compared to their colleagues with private sector backgrounds needs to be explored in greater depth.

Type of Household Income Source: The Waged Participate in Fewer Self-Help Activities

Impoverished middle class households *without* a waged income source tended to take part in a wider range of economic coping strategies than those that *did* possess such an income source. Fifty-seven percent of the unemployed or inactive in this category belonged to households that resorted to wider ranges of coping strategies, but this figure fell to just 35% among those *with* a waged income source (p = <0.01). Waged work is the self-improvement strategy from which the vast majority of household income is derived; those in households that did not benefit from such an income source were generally forced to be more creative when exploring alternative income sources. Those households with someone working had an average monthly household income of $164 pesos (US$47), a significantly higher salary than those without waged work ($140 or US$40) (p = 0.01). In any case, those without paid work often had more time available to undertake alternative strategies, which also explains why their households undertook wider ranges of self-improvement activities.

Mapping the Impoverished Middle Class and Contextualizing Their Responses

At this juncture, it is important to construct an overall picture of Argentina's "new poverty map." This map is elaborated in terms of which sectors of society were most affected by the crisis. Then, three further areas are explored in order to contextualize the findings about how citizens responded to pauperization during the crisis in 2002. It also aids research on the new poor, which has largely been qualitative in nature until now. First, comparisons are drawn between the actions of the new poor and those of their long-term poor counterparts. Then, the question of how the impoverished middle class leveraged their superior capital assets as a survival strategy in ways that were not possible for those who lived in conditions of abstract poverty in the shanty towns is discussed. Finally, the data concerning impoverished middle class uptake of state benefits at the time are analyzed, and insights are offered into their underlying values, attitudes and opinions about welfare aid, with a view to contributing toward "new poor" social policy debates.

During the period of data collection, the official per capita monthly income poverty line was $232 pesos, which at the exchange rate of 1 dollar to $3.5 pesos (at the time) equates to approximately US$2 per day (US$66 per month). The income distribution among the impoverished middle class reveals a negatively skewed distribution with an average monthly per capita income of $158 pesos (US$45), a median of $176 pesos (US$50) and a mode of $205 pesos (US$60). These figures suggest a mixed picture in terms of the severity of deprivation that was experienced. Generally, this stratum avoided extreme income poverty (less than US$1 per day[10]). One-quarter of them fell only fractionally below the poverty line (with a per capita household income of $208 pesos/US$60 or above), and half had a monthly income of $176 pesos (US$50) or more. Nevertheless, absolute income poverty *did* afflict 28% of the new poor, a worrying proportion in any case.

The Face of New Poverty in 2002: Young, Female and Public Sector

Women, young adults and public-sector workers faced a disproportionate risk of being affected by new poverty during the crisis. This confirms qualitative studies which argue that external shocks generate such tendencies (Minujín, 2007; Koldorf, 2008).

Women accounted for 60% of those in this stratum, compared to just 40% of men ($p = 0.01$). The feminization of new poverty seems to have primarily been due to Argentinian women earning lower incomes than men at the time, just $109 pesos (US$31) per month compared to men's $198 pesos (US$57). However, this disparity was not because they were less skilled but that they were being actively discriminated against in the labor market. For example, while no significant gender difference was observed in terms of their qualifications, men earned $4.71 pesos (US$1.35) *per hour*, but for women the rate was 32% lower at just $3.20 pesos (92 cents). This disparity is almost identical to the gendered salary difference (33%) that was calculated by SIEMPRO (Bermúdez, 2003) at the time. Little research has been carried out that particularly addresses the question of gender differentials within the impoverished middle class social stratum, either in Argentina or elsewhere. The rare exception is Koldorf's (2008) study in the city of Rosario, which found that women had suffered especially harshly as a result of the neoliberal policies that generated new poverty since *Menemismo* in the 1990s. Despite the evidence that women were disproportionately affected in terms of new poverty *incidence* (that is to say, statistically "in income terms") during this period, detrimental qualitative effects of the crisis on their living standards remained "hidden" from the survey results. These include the fact that they experienced increased levels of domestic violence (Kliksberg, 2006) and that they encountered significant "double burden" effects. This was because they were expected to both generate additional sources of household income *and* intensify their regular domestic duties, for example, due to having an additional household member to look after at home due to husbands or dependents losing their jobs, or their children's additional emotional needs in a time of widespread anxiety and national turmoil (Bonder and Rosenfeld, 2003:35).

Historically, such wage inequalities are often increased during crises, when employers show discretion and give favorable treatment to male "breadwinners" in terms of jobs and wages (Grytten and Brautaset, 2000). Indeed, the gender pay gap in the immediate precrisis years between 1998 and 2001 was never higher than 29% (Weisburd *et al.*, 2011), which clearly became more acute as the crisis took hold. Women may also have struggled to access financial credit in order to start their own microenterprises to a greater degree than their male counterparts (Jelin, 1998:99–100).

Young adults (aged 18–34) were also significantly overrepresented, making up 55% of the stratum (p = <0.01). Among 15–29-year-olds, unemployment doubled between 1999 and 2002, reaching 27.3% during the crisis, the highest proportion of all age groups (CEPAL in Minujín, 2007). This helps explain why this age group was particularly exposed to pauperization. During periods of high unemployment like this, young adults are particularly prone to joblessness because of their relative lack of labor market experience (Weller, 2003). Employment opportunities that do open up during such periods tend to be low skilled and low paid, so these provide the only sources of work available to new entrants to the labor market, especially young adults (CEPAL, 2004). In addition, crisis periods like Argentina's are often associated with inflation, so the fact that young people tend to have lower incomes means that as consumers they also tend to experience more severe deprivation than other groups whose members are cushioned by higher incomes, assets or savings.

Meanwhile, the elderly made up just 3% of the sample and were disproportionately unaffected. This result is explained by the fact that their pensions and/or savings acted as a cushion to pauperization.[11] Unlike pensions, alternative sources of income such as employment had to be *negotiated* rather than being *guaranteed,* so the elderly were less likely to have fallen into poverty than other age groups whose income sources were more vulnerable to the effects of the crisis.[12] During the 2002 crisis, the elderly were generally shielded from its most severe impacts (in terms of the extent of income loss) compared to other age groups, because they were relatively unaffected by its main economic consequences, such as sharply reduced salaries, redundancy and loss of businesses. For example, the 2000 Argentinian Census records show that the rate of economic activity for the over-65 age group was just 22%, whereas it was between 72% and 79% for all other age groups. Exceptions existed, of course, for example, in cases where children or even grandchildren with whom they lived had lost their jobs, in which case many elderly citizens become the main income-provider, relying on their often-meager pensions to support their families.

Middle-aged citizens (50–64 years) were not overrepresented in this stratum; however, there are two points to make about this which may help to explain the result or, rather, some of the real-life experiences that it obscures. First, the survey data largely only reveal information about *economic* well-being and does not examine other variables, such as the particularly acute emotional anguish that those in this age group experienced due to the psychological burdens of poverty, seeing their children's hopes for a bright future extinguished (Briones and Mendoza, 2003:17) or being unable to sufficiently care for their children and parents.

Second, as mentioned earlier, survey data only refer to the impact of new poverty "within the first few months" of pauperization in 2002 as a snapshot of this moment in time. Interviews with middle-aged Argentinians conveyed how, as an age group, they tended not to suffer particularly badly during the early stages of the crisis; however, when job opportunities were created, and the economy grew again, they found it relatively harder to escape impoverishment in the longer term compared to their younger cohorts, because of age discrimination in the labor market and an erosion of the value of their human capital. In addition, the practical impossibility of other exit routes such as emigration prevented upward mobility from being redeemed to the same degree as it did for their younger cohorts who were able to leave.

Those working in the public sector were disproportionately vulnerable to becoming poor (they made up 39% of the impoverished middle class but just 28% of the general survey population, $p = 0.01$.). State workers were found to be more greatly exposed to pauperization because while both public and private sectors suffered severe recession during 2001 and 2002 after the country's debt default, under pressure from the IMF, public spending was slashed from 35.7% to 29.3% of GDP or from an average of 2,582 pesos (US$738) to 1,613 pesos (US$461) per capita in 2002, according to the ministry of the economy. This helps to explain why public-sector salaries fell 15% faster than they did in the (formal) private sector between May and October 2002 and why state workers were more vulnerable to impoverishment.

However, while the survey revealed that 14% of the new poor worked in the agricultural, mining, construction or manufacturing industries and 86% in the services sector, this was not significantly different from the general population. Argentinians were thus equally likely to become poor regardless of the economic sector in which they worked ($p = 0.11$).

Superior Capital Assets as a Mode of Struggling Middle Class Survival

Here, the coping strategies undertaken by pauperized middle class citizens are compared to those of the structural poor in 2002. Only 28% of the former actually saw their incomes diminish below the then "dollar-a-day" marker of absolute poverty. However, among Argentinians who did not possess the resources that they enjoyed (superior education and adequate housing), the absolute poverty rate was twice as high (55%). This indicates that the impoverished middle class enjoyed a greater capacity to gain alternative income sources by accessing possibilities which simply did not exist to the same extent for the structural poor. Furthermore, the latter were often unable to take advantage of their social, human and physical capital as effectively and sought recourse to different "resources of poverty" (de la Rocha, 1994). For instance, the conditions for exchanging favors and seeking recourse to social networks are rather more favorable in areas where extreme poverty is concentrated, such as the shanty towns, where many of the structural poor reside.

The results also point toward the fact that the reason why extreme income poverty was generally avoided by the pauperized middle class was because they tended to gain some kind of work source during late 2002 (albeit precarious, part-time or underemployment). As Table 3.6 indicates, 83% of poor middle class households possessed an employment or informal work source within the first six months of impoverishment. Despite this, clearly the wages received (or hours worked) were not enough to keep them from falling into poverty, which confirms the suggestion made earlier that the impoverished middle class was able to replace the structural poor in the low-skilled and low-paid services jobs that remained available, due to their superior levels of human capital.

Table 3.6 compares new and structurally poor levels of engagement in active self-help strategies. The new poor middle class largely managed to escape extreme poverty because their waged income was 17% higher, in itself, perhaps due to their possession of superior human capital.[13] The statistics also illustrate that they were significantly more likely to access credit, bank loans, rental earnings and savings or sell/pawn assets as part of their coping strategies. It was probably their higher rates of home ownership, salaries, formal employment and professional networks that leveraged them such access. Drawing upon such economic capital was simply a less realistic option for the structural poor, because they were not socially connected to those with businesses and jobs and sometimes did not own the deeds to their (precarious) homes. Nor would their homes have had much monetary value to provide collateral to gain credit or investment income to the same extent. The pauperized middle class also benefited from more pensionable income than their structurally poor counterparts.

Interestingly, the results show that social networking strategies were undertaken by twice as many structurally poor than new poor – 32%

Table 3.6 Self-Improvement Strategies among the New Poor/Impoverished Middle Class and Structural Poor (June to November 2002)

Strategy	New Poor (%)	Structural Poor (%)
Work or employment	83	77
Social networks (gifts/loans from those outside household)	17	32*
Financial capital (credit card/bank loan/ savings/sale of assets)	16***	8
Advance payment (on trust)	10	6
State aid (non-pension benefits)	5	22*
Barter	3	4
Cartonero	0	4

Source: Ozarow (2014:98), based on World Bank's ISCA Survey, 2002.

Chi-square statistic identifies a significant difference between new and structural poor at *0.01 **0.05 and ***0.1 levels.

compared to 17% ($p = 0.01$). Although this seems surprising because the impoverished middle class were much more well connected to professional networks and those with status or financial resources, it seems to support the notion from earlier that many were simply too ashamed to approach such acquaintances for help following impoverishment.

The survey also indicated that the new poor (29%) were significantly more likely to become self-employed than the structural poor (13%), substantiating several qualitative sources which point to the symbolic importance that they gave to (often informal) *cuentapropismo or* self-employment as a response to unemployment in light of the scarce opportunities for labor market reintegration during 2002 (Bayon, 2003).

In the Argentinian middle-class psyche of the early 2000s, to be unemployed was synonymous with being "outside the system," which evoked feelings of horror, even in the aftermath of the crisis and especially among the new poor, who had never experienced unemployment (Whitson, 2007:129). Because it was extremely difficult to gain quality employment during 2002–03 rather than return to the formal labor market, many newly unemployed professionals opted for *cuentapropismo*, such as starting small businesses, as an alternative way to recover the social mobility that allowed them to recover dignity and avoid such exclusion. It was also comparatively easier for them to do so because, unlike many of the structurally poor, they often possessed the necessary physical capital such as telephones, PCs and homes, as well as the relevant employment experience and social networks for them to flourish.

Rejection of State Benefits and Charity

The impoverished middle class were also highly ambivalent about accepting state aid to ameliorate their hardship. Only 5% of their strata were enrolled in state welfare programs in 2002 compared to 22% of the structural poor ($p = 0.01$). *Plan Jefes y Jefas de Hogar Desocupados* (Programme for Unemployed Heads of Households)[14] was launched in mid-2002 and became the flagship state aid program of the President Duhalde's interim government. However, just 1.3% of the middle class poor were enrolled specifically in this program. An analysis of its beneficiaries reveals that those in this stratum expressed great reluctance to apply for such assistance. Of those who were eligible, according to the survey, one-quarter refused to register and many more experienced difficulties when doing so. An additional 9% of households applied for the benefit (of whom 81% were actually eligible) but were not actually able to receive it. There were clear teething problems identified with how the plan was implemented.

The data reveal two interesting trends about the extent to which the *Plan Jefes* failed the middle class as a social policy. First, in practical terms, they found it extremely difficult to obtain. Of those who were eligible but not receiving it, 32% were told that they must wait longer to qualify. Another 27% were told by local offices that as there were limited places available, and their office had "exceeded their local quota" so could not provide the benefit to them. A further 41% had been told that they *would* receive the benefits but had not done so yet due to "delays." This suggests that the problems of delivering aid to the struggling middle class are more complicated than assisting the structural poor and represent both a lack of cultural sensitivity toward such applicants, on the one hand, as well as eligibility difficulties, on the other. Aguirre (2008) describes how the impoverished middle class tend to find it hard to access "focalized" government assistance programs in the first place, because in recent years Argentinian welfare aid has generally been aimed at those with "basic needs requirements" rather than being means tested by income. These stipulations act as a particular deterrent to the new poor (who by definition are "income deprived" but "basic needs satisfied"), so they tend not to be eligible.

Second, the data confirm the idea that – despite being seen as their "right as taxpayers" – the middle class largely tend to avoid aid programs because they do not want to be seen as "good-for-nothings." The structural poor, on the other hand, see such aid as coming from "some distant place as a gift" that is to be accepted (Aguirre, 2008). This rejection of state aid programs by the new poor is also represented by figures showing that of those in the sample who did not register for *Plan Jefes*, intriguingly, 23% simply "did not want the Plan" despite being entitled to it. A further 6.4% were either unaware of the program or unsure how to apply for it, and 71% had work or did not qualify for some other reason.

The general rejection of such charity support was often a result of a desire to maintain their middle-class identity, which entailed them giving preference to strategies that were believed to symbolize the "middle-class values" of self-sufficiency and individual enterprise (Svampa, 2005). Therefore, options such as self-employment and *negotiating access* to public goods or benefits (excluding the taboos of financial or food aid) through their own efforts and utilizing their sophisticated accumulated social and cultural capitals were strongly favored over "assistentialist" means (those that resorted to welfare aid). Assistentialism or becoming an *ambulante* (street vendor) were understood to incur an unacceptable loss of dignity and were therefore only reserved for "the real poor."

As Kessler and Di Virgilio emphasize (2008:41), drawing upon Bourdieu's notion of "the embodied state" (1986), the new poor thus enjoyed advantages of access that were closed to the structural poor, because (for example) they possess greater knowledge about how to "play the system" or are skilled at framing their demands for public goods in ways that are more likely to obtain results. When trying to access state or municipal institutions for resolution of disputes regarding (non-aid) entitlements, attempting to gain access to hospital treatments or seeking a place for their child at the best school, they enjoyed considerable success by utilizing their more sophisticated cultural capital, littering their claims with references to "rights," or emphasizing their social position or qualifications to resource gatekeepers. Such coping mechanisms were further aided by them often having friends "in the right places" within organizations and therefore greater social capital available to exploit.

Notes

1 The *cacerolazos* were commonly used in Argentina in 2001–02 but originated in anti-government protests by women opposing Salvador Allende's government in Chile in 1971. However, I traced a much earlier reference to banging saucepans as a form of protest in an 1977 interview with a woman about a local suicide in a small English fishing village in East Anglia in 1901 whereby she mentioned how local villagers gathered outside the home of a man who had stood accused of wife beating and infidelity and during which they 'banged tins' outside his home as a form of public shaming (Lummins, 1977).

2 Thousands of protestors drove their tractors to the Plaza de Mayo square in Buenos Aires.

3 "Confidence" in the eyes of survey participants according to *Latinobarómetro* refers to the degree of trust held in an institution to fulfil its function under the liberal democratic system. For example, "confidence in Congress" is understood as faith in the lower house of parliament to reflect the interests of the country's citizens through the approval and delivery of legislation.

4 The *Carapintadas* was a faction of the military that staged a series of attempted mutinies between 1987 and 1990 after democracy had been restored. The reasons ranged from pay grievances to demanding impunity against prosecution for human rights violations during the Dirty War under the 1976–83 military dictatorship. Some even called for the full-scale restoration of military rule.

5 While the Peronist *Partido Justicialista* (Justicialist Party) officially embraces all classes, it has always reserved its strongest supportive rhetoric for the working class, channelled through its historic alignment with the country's main union confederation – the CGT.

6 To suggest a sense of a continuum in terms of the level of civic engagement that citizens possess, I use the term "non-activist" because many still took part in *some* collective actions.

7 "Activists" is used not in the sense that they belonged to a political party or interest group but to describe someone who took part in a lot of actions at this particular time, even if they were an "ordinary" citizen.

8 The organization run by children of the "Disappeared" that campaigns for the perpetrators of the murders committed by Argentina's government during the 1976–83 military dictatorship to be brought to justice.

9 The reasons ranged from participants' becoming alienated from the assemblies by the growing influence and dogmatism of sectarian left-wing parties (Almeyra, 2004:175) to the creeping devolution of decision-making power away from the local assemblies toward first the "Citywide Assemblies" and then the *Colombres* (the supreme decision-making body of all Citywide

Assemblies) which put others off (Svampa and Corral, 2006:131). Pereyra (2003:169) suggests that by June 2002, the cold Argentinian winter and the relocation of the assemblies away from streets, parks and public spaces to abandoned buildings or community centers created a loss of visibility and public display of solidarity.

10 The internationally recognized income representing "absolute poverty" was US$1 per day at the time of the crisis, but the Wold Bank has since revised it to US$1.25.

11 Indeed, while approximately 77.5% of Argentinians over the age of 65 were drawing a pension in 2001 (Rofman, 2002:3), this was almost certainly higher among the impoverished middle class, who would have fitted the middle-class profile of having worked in formal employment and contributed to private as well as state pensions.

12 Although I found that older people were less likely to have become pauperized in 2002, the statistic does not signify that their *material conditions* were necessarily superior to those of other age groups, but rather they suffered a less harsh deterioration of their preexisting living standards *compared to* other age groups.

13 Those included in the "new poor" sample had either finished secondary school or a university education, whereas the structural poor had either incomplete secondary or primary or no education at all.

14 In response to soaring unemployment and in order to try to placate the protests, in May 2002, the Argentinian government launched *Plan Jefes y Jefas de Hogar Desocupados* (Programme for Unemployed Heads of Households). This state benefit granted a monthly monetary cash transfer of $150 pesos to unemployed heads of households, conditional upon the recipient carrying out up to 20 hours a week of communitarian activities, such as public works or childcare (Roca *et al.*, 2003).

References

Adamovsky, Ezequiel (2009) *Historia de la Clase Media Argentina*. Buenos Aires, Planeta.

Aguirre, Pierre (2008) 'Social Assistance as Seen by the Buenos Aires Poor and New Urban complete Poor during Convertibility' in *Anthropology of Food* S4 [Online], 4th May 2008.

Almeyra, Guillermo (2004) *La Protesta Social En La Argentina (1990–2004)*. Buenos Aires, Continente-Pax Ediciones.

Armony, Ariel and Armony, Victor (2005) 'Indictments, Myths, and Citizen Mobilization in Argentina: A Discourse Analysis,' *Latin American Politics and Society*, Vol. 47 (4), pp. 27–54.

Atzeni, Maurizio and Ghigliani, Pablo (2008) *Nature and Limits of Trade Unions' Mobilizations in Contemporary Argentina*. Netherlands. LaborAgain Publications, International Institute of Social History.

Auyero, Javier (2001) *Poor People's Politics: Peronist Survival Networks and the Legacy of Evita*. Durham, NC, Duke University Press.

Bayón, Cristina (2003) 'La erosión de las certezas previas: significados, percepciones e impactos del desempleo en la experiencia Argentina' *Perfiles Latinoamericanos*, 22nd June 2003.

Bazza, G. (2000) 'Bajaron los mercados pero no por la renuncia de Santibañes' *Clarín*, 20th October 2000.

Benclowicz, Jose (2006) 'Destellos de contra-hegemonía antes del Argentinazo' *Rebelión*, 30th January 2006.

Bermúdez, I. (2003) SIEMPRO Report, 'Las mujeres ganan 33% menos, aunque están más capacitadas' *Clarín*, 13th March 2003.

Bombal, Inés and Luzzi, Mariana (2006) 'Middle-Class Use of Barter Clubs: A Real Alternative or Just Survival?' in E. Epstein and D. Pion-Berlin (eds.), *Broken Promises? The Argentine Crisis and Argentine Democracy*. New York, Lexington Books, pp. 141–163.

Bonder, Gloria and Rosenfeld, Monica (2003) *Equidad de Género en Argentina*. Buenos Aires, United Nations Development Programme.

Bourdieu, Pierre (1986) 'The Forms of Capital' in J. Richardson (ed.), *Handbook of Theory and Research for the Sociology of Education*. New York, Greenwood, pp. 241–258.

Bourdieu, Pierre, Darbel, Alain, Rivet, Jean-Paul and Seibel, Claude (1963) *Travails et travailleurs en Algerie*. Mouton, The Hague.

Brecht, Bertolt (1928) *The Three Penny Opera*. Bayonne, NJ: Troubleman Unlimited.

Briones, Claudia and Mendoza, Marcela (2003) *Urban Middle-Class Women's Responses to Political Crisis in Buenos Aires*. Memphis, TN, University of Memphis Center for Research on Women.

Centro de Estudios Nueva Mayoría (2006) 'La desaparición de los cacerolazos, las asambleas populares, y el fenómeno del trueque, tras la salida de la crisis 2001–2002' CENM, 21st December 2006.

CEPAL (2003) *Anuario Estadístico de América Latina y el Cáribe 2002*. Santiago, United Nations.

Croucher, Richard (1987) *We Refuse to Starve in Silence: A History of the National Unemployed Workers' Movement, 1920–46*. London, Lawrence & Wishart Ltd.

de la Rocha, Mercedes (1994) *The Resources of Poverty: Women and Survival in a Mexican City*. Oxford, Blackwell Publishing.

Di Marco, Graciela ed. (2003) *Movimientos Sociales en la Argentina: la Politización de la Sociedad Civil*. Buenos Aires, Jorge Baudino Ediciones.

Dinerstein, Ana (2003) '¡Qué se vayan todos! Popular Insurrection and the Asambleas Barriales in Argentina' *Bulletin of Latin American Research*, Vol. 22 (2), pp. 187–200.

Duhalde, Santiago (2009) 'La respuesta de los sindicatos estatales al neoliberalismo en Argentina (1989–1995)' *Trabajo y Sociedad*, Vol. 13 (XII), pp. 1–14.

Durkheim, Emile (1897) *Le Suicide*. Paris, Ancienne Librairie Germer Bailliere

Echegaray, Fabian (2005) *Economic Crises and Electoral Responses in Latin America*. Lanham, MD, University Press of America.

Elustono, Georgina (2006) 'En los últimos 15 años se registraron 900 nuevos cultos' *Clarín*, 23rd April 2006.

Feijóo, Maria (2003) *Nuevo País, Nueva Pobreza*. Buenos Aires, Fondo de Cultura Económica.

Ford, Myriam and Picasso, Maria (2002) 'Representaciones sociales acerca de la pobreza, el trabajo y la identidad' in *Proceedings from the seminar Las Caras de la Pobreza* (pp. 233–253). Buenos Aires, Universidad Católica Argentina.

Forto, Mariela and Cáceres, Victoria. Dir (2006) *Sin Trabajo en el Barrio*. Matanza, Buenos Aires, Colectivo DocSur.

GEPSAC (2006) *Transformaciones de la protesta social en Argentina 1989–2003, Grupo de Estudios Sobre Protesta Social y Acción Colectiva, Instituto de Investigaciones Gino Germani*. University of Buenos Aires.

Gómez, Claudio (2003) 'Derecho a la igualdad y la discriminación en razón de la edad' *Suplemento de Derecho Constitucional*, Vol 115, pp. 21–26, Buenos Aires.

Gómez, Georgina and Helmsing, Bert. (2008) 'Selective spatial closure and Local Economic Development: What Do We Learn from the Argentinean Local Currency Systems?' *World Development*, Vol. 36, (11), pp. 2489–2511.

Grimson, Alejandro and Kessler, Gabriel (2005) *On Argentina and the Southern Cone: Neoliberalism and National Imaginations*. Abingdon, Routledge.

Grytten, Ola and Brautaset, Camilla (2000) 'Family Households and Unemployment in Norway during Years of Crisis: New Estimates 1926–1939' *The History of the Family*, Vol. 5 (1), pp. 23–53.

Hintze, Susana. ed. (2003) *Trueque y Economía Solidaria*. Buenos Aires, Prometeo, Universidad Nacional de General Sarmiento.

INDEC (Instituto Nacional de Estadística y Censos) www.indec.gov.ar

Jennings, Kent and Markus, Gregory (1988) 'Political Involvement in the Later Years: A Longitudinal Survey' *American Journal of Political Science*, Vol. 32 (2), pp. 302–316.

Katz, Claudio (2001) 'El significado del Argentinazo', *Lahaine.org*

Kessler, Gabriel and Di Virgilio, Maria (2008) 'La nueva pobreza urbana: dinámica global, regional y Argentina en las últimas dos décadas' *Revista de la CEPAL*, Vol. 95, pp. 31–50.

Klesner, Joseph (2007) 'Social Capital and Political Participation in Latin America: Evidence from Argentina, Mexico, Chile and Peru' *Latin American Research Review*, Vol. 42 (2), pp. 1–32.

Kliksberg, Bernardo (2006) 'La violencia doméstica en Latinoamérica: un escándalo ético' *Clarín*, 15th October 2006.

Koldorf, Ana. ed. (2008) *Familia y nueva pobreza desde una perspectiva de género*. Rosario, Prohistoria.

Krugman, Paul (2006) 'The Great Wealth Transfer' *Rolling Stone Magazine*, Vol. 1015, pp. 44–50.

Lummins, Trevor (1977) 'The Occupational Community of East Anglian Fishermen' *British Journal of Sociology*, Vol. 28 (1), pp. 51–74.

Lupu, Noam and Stokes, Susan (2009) 'The Social Bases of Political Parties in Argentina, 1912–2003' *Latin American Research Review*, Vol. 44 (1), pp. 58–87.

Luxemburg, Rosa (1906) *The Mass Strike, the Political Party and the Trade Union*. New York, Harper & Row.

Mafud, Julio (1985) *Sociología de la clase media Argentina*. Buenos Aires, Distal.

Mazzoni, Maria (2007) 'Política y Empobrecimiento' *Revista de la Facultad*, Vol. 13, pp. 185–211. Argentina, Universidad Nacional de Comahue.

Melamed, Diego (2002) *Irse: Cómo y por qué los argentinos se están yendo del país*, Buenos Aires, Editorial Sudamericana.

Minujín, Alberto (1995) 'Squeezed: the Middle Class in Latin America' *Environment and Urbanization*, Vol. 7 (2), pp. 153–166.

——— (2007) *Vulnerabilidad y resiliencia de la clase media en América Latina*. New York, The New School.

Minujín Alberto and Anguita, Eduardo (2004) *La Clase Media: Seducida y abandonada.* Buenos Aires, EDHASA.

Murray, Charles (1984) *Losing Ground.* New York, Basic Books.

Novick, Susana and Murias, Maria (2005) 'Dos estudios sobre la emigración reciente en la Argentina' IIGG, University of Buenos Aires.

OJF Asociados, www.ojf.com/

Ozarow, Daniel (2014) 'When All They Thought Was Solid Melted into Air: Resisting Pauperization in Argentina during the 2002 Crisis' *Latin American Research Review*, Vol. 49 (2), pp. 178–202.

Palomino, Héctor (2005) 'Los sindicatos y los movimientos sociales emergentes del colapso neoliberal en Argentina' in E. Toledo (ed.), *Sindicatos y Nuevos Movimientos Sociales en América Latina.* Buenos Aires, CLACSO, pp. 19–52.

Parysow, Javier and Bogani, Esteban (2002) 'Perspectivas de desarrollo económico y social para las mujeres pobres y empobrecidas en los clubes del Trueque' in *Conference Proceedings of the Seminar Las Caras de la Pobreza*, Buenos Aires, pp. 215–230.

Plotkin, Mariano. ed. (2003) *Argentina on the Couch: Psychiatry, State, and Society, 1880 to the Present.* Albuquerque, University of New Mexico Press.

Powers, Nancy (1999) 'Coping with Economic Hardship in Argentina: How Material Interests Affect Individuals' Political Interests' *Canadian Journal of Political Science*, Vol. 32, pp. 521–549.

Rofman, Rafael (2002) *The Pension System and the Crisis in Argentina: Learning the Lessons.* Washington DC, World Bank.

Snow, David and Benford, Robert (1988) 'Ideology, Frame Resonance, and Participant Mobilization' *International Social Movement Research*, Vol. 1, pp. 197–217.

Stobbe, Lineke (2005) 'Doing Machismo: Legitimating Speech Acts as a Selection Discourse' *Gender, Work and Organization*, Vol. 12 (2), pp. 105–123.

Svampa, Maristella (2005) *La sociedad excluyente. La Argentina bajo el signo del neoliberalismo.* Buenos Aires, Taurus.

——— (2006) 'La Argentina: Movimientios sociales e izquierdas' *Entre Voces* Vol. 5, Quito.

Svampa, Maristella and Corral, Damian (2006) 'Political Mobilization in Neighborhood Assemblies' in E. Epstein and D. Pion-Berlin (eds.), *Broken Promises? The Argentinean Crisis and Argentinean Democracy.* New York, Lexington Books, pp. 117–141.

Tilly, Charles (1986) *The Contentious French.* Cambridge, MA, Harvard University Press.

——— (2006) *Regimes and Repertoires.* London, University of Chicago Press.

Toledo, Fernando and Bastourre, Diego (2006) 'Capital Social y recomposición laboral en Argentina. Un análisis para el periodo 1995–2000' *Convergencia*, Vol. 13 (40), pp. 141–171.

Touraine, Alain (1992) 'Comunicación política y crisis de representatividad' in Ferry, Jean-Marc and Wolton, Dominique (eds). (eds.), *El Nuevo espacio público.* Barcelona, Gedisa.

Vilas, Carlos (2005) 'Pobreza, desigualdad y sustentabilidad democrática' *Revista Mexicana de Sociología*, Vol. 67 (2), pp. 229–269.

Weisburd, Leopoldo et al. (2011) *Problemas de género en la Argentina del siglo XXI: feminización de la pobreza e inequidad del mercado laboral.* Buenos Aires, University of Buenos Aires.

Weller, Jurgen (2003) *Inserción Laboral en Cinco Países Latinoamericanos.* Santiago, Chile, CEPAL.

Whitson, Rita (2007) 'Beyond the Crisis: Economic Globalization and Informal Work in Urban Argentina' *Journal of Latin American Geography*, Vol. 6 (2), pp. 121–136.

4 Banging on the Other Side of the Saucepan

The Struggling Middle Class under *Kirchnerismo* and *Macrismo* (2003–18)

Kristina = Chavez
Chau K thieves
Government, if you hear cacerolazos tonight you have nothing to fear.
It's just your imagination
Kristina you are a mare, a whore and a montonera!
No to the diKtatorship

Home-made placards on anti-government
cacerolazo protest, 8th November 2012

This chapter triangulates both *Latinobarómetro* Survey data (2005) and three sets of in-depth interviews (2007, 2011 and 2016) to explore the demobilization and remobilization of Argentina's struggling middle class between 2003 and 2018. It is broken down into four separate periods: first, the post-2001 crisis appeasement, normalization and withdrawal from the streets during the first two years of Néstor Kirchner's government (2003–05). Second, the generally low level of social conflict but periodic outbursts of rebellion that plagued the latter half of Néstor's government and the first term of Cristina' Kirchner's following the Blumberg protests and Countryside Conflict (2006–11). Third, the remobilization of the middle class in Cristina's second term during the sustained anti-government protests (2012–15). And finally, the opening years of Mauricio Macri's government (2016–18) which sparked the largest, most multisectoral protests since 2001. Within each period, a set of emerging themes are analyzed, which help to explain the varying degrees of political mobilization and demobilization. As far as possible, the same themes are returned to across the time frame.

Demobilization: Postcrisis Aftermath and President Néstor Kirchner's Honeymoon (2003–05)

Following the 2001–02 crisis of legitimacy, the categorical rejection of the entire political establishment and the attempts to reconstruct society's political and economic institutions by establishing potentially counterhegemonic, parallel organizing structures,[1] how was a new post-neoliberal capitalist hegemony reasserted and consent granted for it from the population (including the new poor) in the immediate aftermath?

Recovery of Confidence by 2005, but only in the Non-politically Representative Institutions

Interestingly, Argentina's less overtly "political" institutions mostly obtained a significant recovery in confidence between 2002 and 2005, although they remained low. For example, confidence in the police was restored to 1995 levels at 36% ($p = 0.02$), in public administration it grew strongly from 16% to 36% ($p = 0.03$), as did trust in private companies from 17% to 36% ($p = <0.01$). The Church also recovered most of the confidence lost since 2002. However, support for the armed forces ($p = 0.18$) and the judiciary ($p = 0.54$) did not improve between 2002 and 2005 and remained far lower than they were back in 1995.

Here lies the crucial point. Between 2002 and 2005, not one of the country's overtly *democratic* organs experienced a recovery of confidence among the new poor despite the strong macroeconomic recovery. As illustrated in Figure 3.3, faith in parliament remained abysmally low, at just 8%. There was no significant change in the support for political parties (just 11%), and while faith in the "government" increased from a pitifully low base of 3% to just 17% ($p = < 0.01$), 83% of the new poor remained disappointed with their government in 2005. Trade union support remained low (20%) and hadn't increased since 2002, suggesting that there was an long-standing pessimism felt by squeezed middle-class Argentinians about the ability of trade unions to defend their specific labor demands. At least among the new poor, an underlying "crisis of representation" endured long after the *Argentinazo*.

Néstor Kirchner as the "Cesarist" Savior for Some, but Crisis of Legitimacy Persists

Crucially, it was "confidence in the President" that surpassed every other political institution – parliament, parties, trade unions and the government. Thirty-nine percent of the new poor possessed "some" or "a lot" of confidence in him in 2005 according to the survey. Faith was relative, given that the majority still had "little" or "no" confidence though. Moreover, 49% of the new poor "approved" of President Kirchner in 2005 compared to just 9% who did so for President Duhalde in 2002 ($p = <0.01$). Further, Néstor Kirchner was broadly popular among society in general (in separate polls) with support ranging from 74% to 79% (*Clarín*, 30/12/2005). He was credited for Argentina's postcrisis macroeconomic "miracle" and positioning himself on the side of the people in his rhetoric and policies (Armony and Armony, 2005).

These results signal firstly that an underlying "crisis of representation" in the political structures persisted in 2005 (even though faith was restored in most of the non-political institutions). Second, as Gramsci (1998) wrote, in moments of organic crisis,[2] social classes separate themselves from the old political parties and the gap is filled by one of two possibilities: (1) either popular revolutionary fervor or (2) the rise of a "Cesarist" figure who represents "the collective will" in whom the masses instill their trust and who appeases the revolution. This strong leader should represent a powerful political party, but who is ultimately accountable to "the people." In Argentina, after a brief spell of the former during late 2001 and 2002, Gramsci's prediction materialized, and this "Cesarist" character soon appeared in the form of this charismatic and populist Presidential Candidate, Néstor Kirchner. Once elected, he pacified the challenge from below and largely due to his personal popularity, was able to restore "consent to govern" by the ruling class, albeit by the national, rather than international bourgeoisie. Resistance from the struggling middle class alongside most of society was thus demobilized and depoliticized.

An alternative understanding is offered by Leon Trotsky (1939). He described how when underdeveloped countries are exposed to an opening up of the economy to overseas competition for prolonged periods as it had been under neoliberalism since 1976, foreign capital becomes the predominant social force. The domestic bourgeoisie becomes very weak, but the working class, although weakened, remains relatively strong. In such situations, Trotsky explains that the political elites are faced with the option of either siding with foreign capital and suppressing the working class (which is what they did during the military dictatorship of 1976–83, so as to force through the neoliberal agenda) or instead they get the working class onside, in order to gain the political and social space within which to establish a project of "national capitalism." Trotsky described both these forms of rule as Bonapartism – the second of which is the national popular project that Kirchner moved toward (within the limitations of the globalized economy). His policies included expanding state intervention, improved wage pacts with the unions, redistributive income policies, social plans to protect and integrate the most vulnerable, support for the social economy, founding a new state-owned energy company, ENARSA, in 2004, and reducing trade with the USA and European Union and favoring closer ties with MERCOSUR – the regional trading block in Latin America.

Faltering Support for "Democracy"

Perhaps, the most concerning finding was that rather than citizens simply losing confidence in the government and entire political system in 2001–02, the scale of the *crisis of legitimacy* then became so acute that among the new poor it even led to a significant fall in support for democracy as a political system in subsequent years.

In Argentina's historical context, democracy had been the exception as opposed to the rule, having been littered with periods of military dictatorships during the twentieth century (Rock, 1991). Given that the country had only reestablished its democracy in 1983, this faltering support for Argentina's democracy is something which must surely confound leading theorists of political transition such as Linz and Stepan (1996). With reference to South America, these authors claimed that in the new democratic era, citizens no longer judge a particular political system by the policy successes or failures of its governments, because democracy has become "the only game in town." Yet between 1995 and 2002, the proportion of new poor who "wholeheartedly supported democracy at any cost" fell from 81% to 72%, with those who believed either that there "was a place for authoritarianism in certain circumstances" or "had no strong feelings in favor of democracy" increasing from 19% to 28% ($p = 0.1$).

Notably between 2002 and 2005, first, "confidence in the government" barely increased, rising from 3% to just 17% ($p = <0.01$). Second, despite President Néstor Kirchner's popularity and the thriving macroeconomic situation in 2005, the proportion of impoverished middle class citizens who "wholeheartedly supported democracy" did not recover in these three years from applying to just one in six ($p = 0.9$), remaining significantly lower than it was during the 1990s.

The "crisis of representation" continued to exist long after the 2001–02 uprisings. The use of abstention as a protest tool against the political establishment was widely used during the 2001 "angry vote" among them, but its legacy endured in 2005. Then, only 40% of the sample were willing to use a vote for an opposition party to protest at their declining personal circumstances, compared to 80% in 1995 ($p = 0.01$). This demonstrated that political parties were generally unable to capitalize on struggling middle class discontent, probably because the whole political class had been tarnished by corruption and economic implosion. Furthermore, just 28.6% of the sample voted for Néstor Kirchner's *Frente para la Victoria* (which had become the largest force in parliament by 2003), suggesting that they were far from enamored with the way he was managing the country. Indeed, despite its positioning as the natural party of the middle class, those from it who became poor tended to remain largely disillusioned with the Radicals. According to Eduardo Fidanza, director of Argentinian consultancy *Poliarquía*, a large part of this impoverished middle-class stratum (which he claims made up approximately 15% of the electorate) began voting for ex-Radical leaders such as Carrió and her *Acuerdo Cívico y Social* electoral front, or for López Murphy in the postcrisis decade (Fidanza, 2009).

Failure of the Left to Capitalize and Slide toward Conservative Values

How the underlying social and political attitudes of the new poor changed since the crisis must also be investigated in order to help to explain the period of demobilization.

First, in spite of the crisis of legitimacy, economic catastrophe, a personal financial abyss and near universal condemnation of the neoliberal model that brought Argentina to its knees, Argentina's impoverished middle class' political identities (in terms of their self-defined position on the political spectrum) remained constant and "centrist" between 2002 and 2005. Both the organized political Left and the country's traditionally weakly, "institutionalized" conservative Right failed (in the short term at least) to capitalize on the financial impoverishment of the middle sectors. About one-fifth found themselves "on the Left" and the same proportion "on the Right" with over half *generally* maintaining centrist positions. However, some evidence suggests that the crisis in 2002 did provoke some respondents to move further away from the center and toward the extremes of the political spectrum. In 1995, the data on the ranking of political position elicited an interquartile range (IQR) of 2 (as it did in 2005), but in 2002 the IQR had increased to 3.

The decline in postcrisis support for the electoral Left among the *general population* has been researched elsewhere. In the election years, the combined result of far-left parties such as *Izquierda Unida, Autodeterminación y Libertad, Partido Obrero* and others dropped from 3.5% (2003) to 1% (2005), having fallen from 7.5% in 2001. Due to the wide, but momentary diffusion of Autonomist or Open Marxist currents of thinking both within the movements and intellectual environment, during 2001–02, these countenanced against electoral politics; otherwise, the Left's performance may have been stronger in 2001 and 2003.

The decline of the non-Peronist Left was not due so much to a loss of faith in its principles, but rather its *political parties*, which were becoming ever more sectarian and disunited. Meanwhile, left-wing commentators like Petras (2004) have also criticized the "impoverished middle class" for abandoning their radical ideals and becoming submerged in "conservative," security-related preoccupations following macroeconomic recovery after 2003. When this happened, their concerns switched to those of (i) their private property, (ii) their own and their family's personal safety and (iii) the security of their (often recently acquired and often precarious) employment. Their perspectives became more individualistic and inward-looking, values upon which the political Right have traditionally thrived. Thus, the collectivist ideals that were so popular during 2001–02 were slowly abandoned, and a race to the bottom ensued as competition for jobs increased in the postcrisis labor market. Solidarity broke down and the popular slogan *¡piquetes y cacerolas, la lucha es una sola!* (unemployed picketeers and middle-class pot-bangers, we share one struggle), which once echoed around the streets of Buenos Aires and which as a principle was even enshrined in the Resolution of the First Inter-Neighborhood Assembly on 17 March 2002 (Pereyra, 2003:153), almost completely disappeared. Nevertheless, it must be noted that a sizable "progressive" middle class (which tended to support *Kirchnerismo* from 2003) persisted. For several years, solidarity with the poor persisted, not just rhetorically, but also within certain Kirchnerist movements like *Nuevo Encuentro* and autonomist sociopolitical organizations like the *Frente Popular Dario Santillan*. Young adults from middle-class backgrounds, volunteered in shanty towns or in multisectoral political projects, aimed at social change with interclass solidarity thriving among small-scale initiatives for several years.

Figure 3.1 illustrated how the collective mobilizations quickly faded away, especially between late 2002 and mid-2003. However, it was also the case that particular social and political attitudes of many of the new poor became increasingly reactionary during that period. The new poor, who had joined the popular resistance in 2001 and 2002, began to turn against the structural poor with whom they had once seen as allies from 2003 as they fought to compete for the same kinds of low-skilled jobs available at the time. This led to a rise in expressions of racism and anti-immigration feeling among them. By late 2002, 42% of those surveyed felt that "immigrants[3] were to blame for taking away their jobs."

By 2003, many of the new poor also came to believe that those inhabiting the shanty towns had become a threat to their personal safety, dividing them further. Fed by a media frenzy that depicted the shanty town poor as "dangerous and foreign," the middle class including those in our survey became defensive about law and order and increasingly concerned about the encroachment of these structural poor upon the "respectable" middle-class districts and the exaggerated threat that they could occupy their homes (Guano, 2004:69).

Meanwhile, conservative protest leaders such as millionaire Juan Carlos Blumberg were promoting the criminalization of the indigent poor (Lladós, 2006), a depiction that many of the new poor concurred with for the historical and cultural reasons explained in Chapter 2. By supporting this discourse themselves, they often symbolically differentiated themselves from the structural poor in terms of their race (their "whiteness" as opposed to the shanty town *negro*[4]), national origins (their Argentinian backgrounds and European ancestry as opposed to the recent immigrant background of many of the structural poor), and level of education. Highlighting these differences acted as a psychological coping strategy that many used in a scenario where – in terms of their income and job status – they were almost indistinguishable (Guano, 2004).

Many of these propositions concerning the growing racism and fear of the poor are reflected in the survey results. For example, during that time, the proportion who cited "crime" as their main concern doubled from 4% to 8%. Furthermore, the number who had either "been the victim of a crime, assault or attack or knew someone who had in the last twelve months" rose from 53% in 2002 to 64% in 2005 ($p = 0.01$). The statistic had stood at just 30% in 1995. Those citing that crime had "increased in the last twelve months" remained well into the 90% bracket in both 2002 and 2005. However, the moral panic about crime was not based on evidence of any actual increase. In fact, the statistics suggest that the homicide rate in Argentina and crime rates for other offenses, as well as the number of prisoners, actually fell from 2001 to 2005 (Presidencia de la Nación, 2009). So the fear and perception of insecurity, while understandable and real to some extent, was certainly exaggerated due to the proliferation of media coverage and sensationalism which served to increase division between them.

The data show that other issues which are traditional rallying points for the political right had also appeared by 2005, such as the concern that "immigrants are the main problem in our society," which was not judged to have been of importance by any of the impoverished middle class sample in either 1995 or 2002. Consequently, the middle class came to feel increasingly under attack, less trusting of others and more disposed to seek individualist self-improvement solutions rather than those which called upon cooperation with other members of the community. It is little wonder, then, that among those who continued to struggle to get by, social solidarity diminished, and the associated fear and instability were used as rallying cries for political gain by Blumberg and later by Mauricio Macri and other conservative politicians.

Demobilization with Sporadic Revolts: Néstor Kirchner and Cristina Kirchner Governments (2006–11)

In this section, I explore a number of themes based upon my first two extended fieldwork visits to Argentina in 2007 and 2011. Following embeddedness in struggling middle-class communities, in-depth interviews and observation, inductively emerging themes that relate to the demobilization of middle-class collective protest once political and economic "normality" had been restored during the Kirchner governments are discussed in turn. The latter half or President Néstor Kirchner's administration (2006–07) and President Cristina Fernández de Kirchner's first term (2007–11) are the focus. However, I recognize that there were several outbreaks of revolt in this period, during which time non-activists, principally from the middle class, also joined large-scale protests in significant numbers, namely during the Blumberg protests (2006) and the Countryside Conflict (2008). Given that the interviews also took place shortly before the anti-government protests of 2012 and 2013, what they revealed also helps to inform about motivations for those revolts and how the social and political attitudes shifted in the preceding years and months.

Ongoing but Diluted Crisis of Representation

First of all, the endurance of a low-intensity crisis of representation was palpable during both data collection periods, but more so in 2011. All but one-sixth of participants expressed complete disdain for politicians,

parties and politics in general. However, in the absence of an accompanying economic crisis, the anger and urgency "to get rid of them all" was
not present as it was in 2001. Further, as we shall see later, polling well
in surveys, and capturing the votes of over half the electorate, Presidents
Néstor Kirchner and Cristina Kirchner, respectively, were able to garner
support from significant parts of the population. Among the struggling
middle class, by 2011, opposition to them was stronger than in the general
population. Generally, their sense of political citizenship was understood
to have been violated due to a corrupt-ridden, self-serving political class
that had benefited from impunity.

> You know there is corruption elsewhere but here it's like they go on
> TV and actually tell you 'I am going to rob you, and I'll keep doing
> it again and again.'
>
> Ana, 50, Buenos Aires

> Politics is a money-making scheme for them. For example, there are
> politicians who get hold of cash and land in the south you see? Then
> they put on the pretence that they are just about getting by like we do,
> that they still earn the same as before. But they don't. They receive
> backhanders and all that. All the temptations that exist you see? It's
> what happens when you get to power here.
>
> Milagros, 30, Posadas

> An honest person won't make it as a politician in Argentina. There
> is corruption everywhere. Anyone who does make it, it's because
> they've been involved somehow. I'm sure of it.
>
> Vanesa, 26, La Plata

Some associated "politics" with words such as "corruption" and "dirt,"
just as they had in the immediate aftermath of the 2001 crisis when the
narrative of "the polluted nation" with endemic corruption had pene-
trated multiple layers of society (Visacovsky, 2019).

> One lot govern and then another, but the politicians are like a weed.
> They just keep coming back. But that's politics. Politics is garbage.
>
> Julieta, 86, La Plata

> Dirt. Quite simply, they are dirt.
>
> Graciela, 57, Buenos Aires

This underlying sense of repugnance toward the political class and its
representative institutions (which as we saw from the earlier survey result, didn't recover between 2002 and 2005) but intensified and became

progressively bitter in participants' discourse between 2007 and 2011. Among the over 40s, it tended to engender a sense of powerlessness, demobilizing citizens from taking action to address perceived injustices. Corruption and to have an ineffective political class seemed to be naturalized in their minds. They knew it was wrong, but most felt a profound sense of resignation.

> I'm not going to become the next Robin Hood. In the grand scheme of things I am nobody. I learned that through bitter experience. Politics here turns you apolitical... I don't believe you can change anything anyway.
>
> Santiago, 60, Buenos Aires

> You reach the point where you realize that it's all just a spider's web you can't escape from. So I'll just go and take my dog for a walk, enjoy my life, mess around and let them get on with it. So there you have it mate, I don't have enough money to get by, but I can't do a thing about it. And all this leads you to care less and less every day about anyone but yourself.
>
> Jorge, 36, La Plata

The exception to this apathy was participation in collective moments of mass "rage." Such protests galvanized opposition like the 2008 Countryside Conflict. Although when questioned about it in 2011, only three of the interviewees actually took part, with four involved in Blumberg's 2006 march on the Plaza de Mayo.

However, several nuances were observed. First, there was a generational affect. While older interviewees reminisced about a bygone age when politicians were more honest (a period generally associated with the pre-neoliberal era and elected presidents like Frondizi, 1958–62, and Illia 1963–66) and felt disempowered as we saw above, the anger at the political elites among younger interview participants actually *increased* their propensity to become involved in longer term activism for *some*. Three of six of the young adults under 26 (and who were children at the time of the 2001–02 crisis) were engaged in political parties or movements. One, Romina, age 21, who I interviewed in Rosario was scathing of endemic corruption by the political elites. She became politicized at university, joined a sociopolitical organization called the Santiago Pampillón Front and regularly took part in collective protests and solidarity actions, including roadblocks in support of the poor and unemployed.

However, for other young adults, especially those who felt disillusioned that the 2001 uprisings didn't lead to the desired profound social change, further corruption and failure to "represent them" led them to pursue "exit routes" as opposed to actively expressing opposition through "voice" (Hirschman, 1970). For instance, Federico dreamed of moving abroad as he had become completely despondent with his country:

> If the political situation were to deteriorate, I wouldn't participate in any protests. No, because I just want to get out of this country and the truth is that I don't want anything more to do with it. You could say I am completely disinterested... I'm completely resigned, they are all awful governments whoever comes along. My country is condemned and so am I.
>
> Federico, 26, Buenos Aires

Milagros (30, Posadas) told me that she was interested in politics but has never joined a political party because she would have to "provide favors for men that I wouldn't want to" in order to climb the ranks.

In terms of the general powerlessness many felt at the political scenario, political alienation made most of those interviewed (including those who had participated in the 2001–02 protests), either retreat into individual self-help strategies or if they did participate in solidarity actions with the structural poor, these tended to be "non-political." They were channeled into those activities which don't challenge the systemic causes of poverty, but which are encouraged by neoliberalism as mechanisms of dealing with social contention. Many mentioned that they regularly give to children begging on the street or donate to soup kitchens, charity or the Church or pro-bono support that related to their own profession. Laura (49, Buenos Aires) was an education consultant who described how she provided her such professional services voluntarily, to the poorest families, for instance.

Even among the minority who recognized that there were a few good politicians, the metaphor of "contamination" was present. They linked it to the notion that the "powers that be" would never permit real change to occur because they would find a way to discredit or even physically remove individuals who tried to do so.

In the following case, the risk of facing sanction put Graciela (57, Buenos Aires) off involvement in politics:

> No, I don't get involved at any level because they end up discrediting anyone who wants to do good, whether it be as a member of the residents' association, for the neighborhood or for the country. There were people who tried to do the right thing in the government. Then they sacked them and washed their hands of it. There is no way [to make a change]. It's like a cancer that takes over your body. The bad cells eat the good ones.

A handful praised Roberto Lavagna, Economy Minister (2002–05), for having masterminded Argentina's postcrisis recovery. However, they were also angry that he was removed by President Kirchner as he was "becoming too popular."

The notion of "stay out of politics for your own good" (*no te metas*), which was propagated by the military dictatorship (1976–83) in its attempts to depoliticize society, was implicit in the responses of many of the middle-aged or older interviews.

For example, Santiago (60, Buenos Aires) made reference to characters he admired who sought to make transformative social changes (John F. Kennedy and John Lennon) but whom were duly assassinated.

> Here you will be lynched to death if you get too involved. If you stay away and just think about things passively, you will survive.

Or in this older participant who was very critical of the Kirchner government,

> The insecurity today is that of Juan Manuel de Rosas. What do I mean? If you are influential and gaining support from the people as an anti-Kirchner activist, some relation of yours will suffer a misfortune. They won't kill you directly, that would be too obvious. You can be sure of that.
>
> Carlos, 78, Buenos Aires

I wondered what he would have made of the mysterious death of prosecutor Alberto Nisman four years later in 2015. He was found dead at his home the day before he was due to present evidence against President Cristina Kirchner and the Kirchner government in the AMIA-bombing case.

Another important continuity from the 2002 to 2005 survey results were the echoes of the crisis of representation. Interviewees struggled to mention a single current politician who they felt represented them. Only a handful did so, citing Cristina Kirchner or then opposition Deputy Elisa Carrió. Historical figures like Perón, Che Guevara or Radical presidents like Alfonsín (1983–89) or Frondizi (1958–62) were referenced. The most serious condemnation was deferred for other political institutions like trade unions which half the sample viewed negatively and were often described as "mafias" (see more later). A small minority expressed faith in charities, the Church, the media or their trade union, but most commonly they felt completely unrepresented by any institution.

Meanwhile, it is worth passing comment on the analysis of participants' sentiments toward Argentina's *non-representative* institutions such as the media, police, the Church, judiciary and army. Here, the findings corroborate the strong recovery of confidence identified in the 2002–05 survey data and that this extended into 2007 and 2011. Certainly, there was a tendency in the sample toward the view that corruption, and inefficiency was a structural problem that had continued to "infect" the whole of society. The justice system came in for especially harsh criticism (for instance, the failure to bring justice in the AMIA-bombing case from 1994 was cited by a handful to represent how slow and corrupt the judicial process was). Several claimed that the police worked hand in hand with thieves. For instance, Graciela (57, Buenos Aires) cited the ineffectiveness of the security forces and the example of how the national and local police forces were in dispute over which should handle the protests that were blocking the distribution of the *Clarín* newspaper that was taking place at the time (in April 2011).

Jorge (36, La Plata) used the example of the national statistics agency (INDEC) which at the time was being accused of having the statistics it published (poverty, inflation etc.) manipulated by government interference.

A third of the sample explicitly mentioned that the little they were able to save, they no longer deposited in the banks, as they feared that another *Corralito* could occur in the future. This comment was typical from a woman who lost her life savings in that event:

> To break your back working these days just isn't worth it any more. Even if you manage to save a bit, what's the point? Where do you put the money? If you are going to work hard in order to have a better quality of life ok, but you can't conceive of the future here.
>
> Daniela, 59, Buenos Aires

Many also lamented how Argentina was not a serious country, including those who compared it to my own (the UK) which they stated they wished Argentina could be more like in terms of the professionalism and efficacy of its justice system, security forces and politicians' behavior:

> The circus has always been here. It's never left us. Look what they did do those who kept their money in the banks. They don't respect pensioners' savings either. That's why I insist that you [the British] are a serious country. We aren't!
>
> Sofía, 31, Santa Fe City

A second distinction observed was an urban-rural divide in terms of how "politics" was viewed. In the rural village of Piedras Blancas in Entre Rios, politics and political institutions generally were judged much more positively by interviewees compared to those from the urban centers. In fact, only one of the 24 city residents spoke positively about the political process, and she was originally from a small, rural town in Cordoba. We saw above a whole range of manifestations of how urban dwellers had little or no faith in the process. In the village, politics was described more holistically:

> I believe that politics is everything. From getting changed, to painting your house, to participating in a decision-making commission. Politics is life.
>
> Diego, 42, Piedras Blancas

Several other villagers were keen to make the distinction between politics itself and those representatives who conduct it. Sometimes having confidence in them, and other times not. Discourse was more favorable to the system of representative democracy that was viewed as rotten in the cities. In Piedras Blancas, politics was judged more as one reserved more for key personalities. Systemic explanations for failings of representation were virtually ignored. This was apparently due to the more paternalistic relationship that the villagers had with their politicians and conformity with the idea of near total delegation of responsibility to them upon election.

> Politics is beautiful in theory but not always in practice as it is people who can mean it is conducted badly... In our case the village Intendant *will* listen to you if you have a problem for instance.
>
> Martin, 50, Piedras Blancas

> There is a side to politics that is good. Politics is good for the country. But the problem in Argentina are the 'politicians', as people. There is a lot of corruption. That was what was questioned [in 2001] when they wanted to clean them out.
>
> Pablo, 58, Piedras Blancas

> I am not going to say that politics is filth like many do. Politics isn't dirty, the ones who contaminate it are the people. No, politics is necessary. It is necessary as are leaders.
>
> Micaela, 50, Piedras Blancas

The "ongoing diluted crisis of legitimacy" seems to have geo-territorial borders and stopped at the village gate.

Let us return to the ingredients of social movement theory. The "belief that change is possible through collective action" is outlined as a prerequisite for political mobilization (McAdam, 1982). At the time of the second set of interviews in 2011, some citizens felt so exasperated due to the level of corruption they perceived (and also due to disillusionment with how the 2001 uprising didn't deliver on its promise of profound change), that when questioned about how change could come about in Argentina (if not by the ballot box), many like Jorge mentioned that it was pointless to join protests but "divine intervention" was their only hope.

> Now I believe that change can only come from... well, I suppose it would have to be divine intervention, I don't know really. A tsunami that envelopes half of Argentina so that people say "hey, for goodness sake what do we do now?" We have to start from scratch. If not, then everything is so corrupt that there is no place where they aren't trying to rob you.
>
> Jorge, 36, La Plata

In an episode of tragic irony, two years later in April 2013, Jorge's city of La Plata suffered a flood of near biblical proportions in which 89 people died. He was to join the *cacerolazo* protests against the President's visit at the time, even though he had made clear in his 2011 interview that he'd never protest again. Another participant adopted similar language:

> The Mayans predicted that the world was going to change, you know? In 2012 another dimension will arrive and change the situation. Let's hope so. It's not only the politicians but there are vested interests all over the place that need to be taken on.
>
> Lucía, 63, Posadas

The Politicized Reluctant Voter Paradox

An interesting paradox was observed. Despite the near universal sense of "anti-politics" among interviewees and disdain they held for the political class, the act of voting seemed almost sacred, as a sense of civic duty. It continued to be central to their understanding of citizenship, even among those who were most scathing of politicians or could be categorized as apolitical. Historical factors were commonly cited as motivating them to vote, and valuing elections. The fear that not voting would lead to anarchy (understood as a breakdown of order and threat to their property), or even the legacy of the dictatorship (when cited as "the alternative") meant that they valued voting, even if there was no candidate or party they liked. In several cases, they mentioned that they and most people they knew were voting "to stop another candidate from winning, not for someone I actually believe in." This was encapsulated in the widely repeated phrase "the lesser evil" (*el mal menor*). This was the case even though all of the sample mentioned that they always make sure that they vote, even though they were adamant that voting won't change anything.

> I am going to struggle to vote this year I'm telling you… But we have to go and vote. We have to vote for somebody… Spoiling my vote? That's not the solution either. In reality we shouldn't vote for anyone but we haven't done that *en masse* since 2001 so we aren't going to change things that way.
>
> Lucía, 63, Posadas

The option to vote (as an *individual* protest) was taken up by all interview participants in both 2007 and 2011 and therefore acted as a demobilizer in terms of expressing their disagreement through *collective* protest. On the one hand, it provided an outlet for opposition and anger and, on the other, it made them complicit in the system and sometimes with the government that ruled over them. Not one interviewee said that they would spoil their ballot paper or abstain. This stood in contrast to October 2001 when the high level of voter abstention or "blank votes" in the legislative elections actually acted as a signal to citizens in creating awareness about the shared grievances being held by others and thus empowered them to take mass collective action two months later during the December uprisings.

Six of them were even somewhat conspiratorial, explaining that the winners were predetermined.

> To be honest I don't have a bloody clue. But I don't really care who I vote for either. That's the most pathetic thing. I don't care... because it's all fixed anyway.
>
> Jorge, 36, La Plata

Voting preferences were predictably mixed. Both the 2007 and 2011 sets of interviews were conducted during or just before presidential election campaigns, which focused minds. The Socialist Party and its leader Hermes Binner elicited support from at least one-quarter of the sample in the latter. This reflected the national election results during which they did especially well, coming second overall in the presidential elections. Interviewees were also impressed with what they had achieved in Santa Fe and Rosario, where the governors had been socialist since 1989. Their "honesty" and also the fact that they stood for progressive ideals, without being deterred by "combative" language, nor being "wholly socialist," were widely praised. Their success with those in the struggling middle class appears to have been due to how they represented a project that transcended left-right political divisions and appealed to specific unifying values while projecting a clear (in European terms, "social-democratic") vision for the country.

A similar number were drawn toward the personalities of Elisa Carrió of the Civic Coalition and Pino Solanas/Graciela Ocampo of *Proyecto Sur* (Project South). Carrió proved divisive, being loved for her honesty, transparency and for holding the government to account, but also hated in equal measure by those who were tired of her constant public denouncements of others and "negative" politics. Solanas and Ocampo were admired for presenting an alternative project while not coming from political backgrounds (Solanas was a film director, for instance), so he was seen as untainted by the corrupt political class.

Another observation was that participants spoke about their voting choices with a sense of individual superiority. They both insinuated and sometimes explicitly stated that *they* were the ones who knew the truth about Argentina's corrupt political elite and how to change it. This change would come about either by voting for a particular candidate or by pursuing some other kind of strategy that they "felt special" about knowing and which they explained none of their other countrymen were agitating for, such as changing the tax system, redistributing wealth or limiting periods of political office to a certain amount of time. They would accuse others of "electing badly," which is why the country was condemned. Yet the curious thing was, almost all of those interviewed shared the same belief about their counterparts, despite claiming that their awareness of "the truth" was unique.

> The same old faces keep coming back because we are the ones who vote them back in! So you can't blame them for re-standing if we always go and vote for them.
>
> Sofía, 31, Santa Fe City

> I read the newspapers on Saturdays and Sundays only. But you read through them all and think 'how can so many people support this politician when they know how corrupt they are?'
>
> Daniela, 59, Buenos Aires

Others accused their fellow Argentinians of "not thinking critically," and being "ignorant" or "selfish" in their political choices and actions.

> Of the five interviews you have done so far, how many others have answered you while truly thinking rather than just repeating what they saw on the television yesterday or last week?
>
> Carlos, 78, Buenos Aires

> But it's what we deserve. What we deserve. A society that doesn't think is a society that doesn't make demands, that doesn't put any limits... We are the fools. But as long as we can eat and go on holiday once a year to Brazil then we are as happy as Larry.
>
> Jorge, 36, La Plata

In summary, participants struggled to imagine a way of removing their corrupt politicians that didn't involve the ballot box. None of them advocated a revolution, nor a desire for one. The devolution of power to localities and the return of "assemblies" (not for their own sake as was the case in 2001–02, but to help make politicians more accountable) were posed by a small number. Therefore, voting had become completely re-naturalized in interviewee's minds since 2001, and their political imaginaries did not permit them to believe or desire anything beyond delegating responsibility for decision-making to elected representatives, despite holding them in such low esteem. This is why the "crisis or representation" from 2001 to 2002 endured in 2007 and 2011, but in a diluted form. Unlike 2001–02, when Argentinians lived out their dreams and hopes through participation in innovative collective actions of their own, including direct democracy in the neighborhood and popular assemblies, ten years later the "limits of the possible" did not extend any further than what they already knew.

Memory of Que Se Vayan Todos *Participation and Legacy for Subsequent Mobilization*

The 2001–02 uprisings rocked Argentinian society to its foundations. It brought about a genuine crisis for the ruling class. Under the popular slogan *que se vayan todos* (QSVT) (get rid of them all), millions took to the streets nationwide during the rebellion of 19 and 20 December 2001. A broad range of collective protests and solidarity economy actions then blossomed over the next 12 months. Although the demands were numerous, the slogan itself was debated at the time. Did it mean that the protestors wanted to solely get rid of all politicians? Or was this an attempt to remove the entire ruling elites and their institutions, from the politicians to the bankers, businesspeople, trade unionists, judges, and the lot? If so, what did they seek to replace them with? Further, what would happen if these politicians were to return? Some point to the fact that Argentina was undergoing a prerevolutionary situation with new forms of grassroots political and economic structures being established from below, such as the neighborhood assemblies, worker-recovered companies and national barter system. Some referred to Engels (1878) and claimed that the state was virtually absent at this time and that the government had lost authority to rule. The existing structures were "withering away" as some parts of society, especially via the assembly movement and the inter-neighborhood assembly, were preparing for *autogestión* – to govern themselves.

As Dr. Ezequiel Adamovsky, a historian and specialist on Argentina's middle class who also participated in the Cid Campeador Popular Assembly in 2002, told me, "the capacity of the people to radically transform society seemed very real at the time, at least among those who participated in the revolt." However, with the passing of time and restoration of normality (as well as the consolidation of capitalist, "postneoliberal" hegemony), interviewees looked back on those days and reflected upon the phrase *que se vayan todos* with a strong dose of cynicism. Indeed, the state and civil society apparatus exerted considerable effort, not just to extinguish the flames of rebellion at the time through policies of appeasement (see earlier section on Postcrisis demobilization, 2002, in Chapter 2) but also to dampen the very memory of "hope" of change that the revolt evoked in society. For instance, the media and politicians subsequently depicted the period as one of "anarchy" and "violence." Warning against any repeat of such turmoil and in sullying the memory of those days further, on the 15th anniversary on 19 December 2001, in 2016 ex-President Duhalde described how Argentina was then on the brink of "civil war." Even the ten-year commemorative events in Argentina itself were subdued, with a sprinkling of talks and protests organized by trade unions and left-wing groups to demand an end to impunity for the murderers of the 39 victims who were killed in the uprising (Zibechi, 2011). Internationally, the events were commemo-rated, for example, at a London conference that I co-organized: "Crisis, Response and Recovery: A Decade on from the Argentinazo 2001–11" at the University of London, which invited a series of papers that were later converted into an edited book (Ozarow, Levey and Wylde, 2014).

Participants were asked about their reflections of their understanding of the term *que se vayan todos*, whether they subscribed to it, and were also asked about their own household's participation in the 2001–02 pro-tests. The latter, or rather their recollections of them, were compared to the answers that they supplied in the World Bank Survey at the time (in 2002) and any discrepancies were noted. Patterns in the data were also explored regarding memories of participation and the impact these had on their political involvement (or not) in subsequent years. What is of in-terest here is clearly not to take the content of their descriptions as accu-rate representations of what they felt or experienced at the time. Instead, their value is precisely as memories. How their experiences are recalled as memory is a reconstruction of the past (Schacter, 1996).

Indeed, the problems of "recall bias" during ex post facto interviewing are numerous. Further, recalling "mixed emotions" such as those many experienced at the time (fear, hope for change especially through partici-pation in action, uncertainty etc.) is especially problematic. For instance, *current* experiences can color the memory of *prior* experiences (Robinson and Clore, 2002), and when one's current belief system supports a nega-tive bias, it can also taint the experienced emotion (Wilson, Meyers and Gilbert, 2003). In this instance, even if at the time, interviewees experi-enced their participation in the protests as "positive," perhaps inspired by hope and feeling exhilarated by the unity they enjoyed with other par-ticipants, they may recall them as negative because years later society as a whole and they as individuals generally look back on the uprising as having failed to achieve what they aimed to at the time. Further, the "peak experience" or "final experience" was negative, so this may also taint the memory of overall participation (Fredrickson and Kahneman, 1993). Given that many participants in the 2001–02 insurrection left the movements due to disillusionment or frustration (e.g., when the assem-blies began to get infiltrated by left-wing parties or when the barter cred-its system imploded following the influx of forged barter notes), they may feel negative about their overall experience even though these don't re-flect the actual emotions they experienced during the weeks or months of participation prior to it.

Moreover, research on memory of emotions suggests that over time people tend toward giving more unipolar assessments as positive or nega-tive (Thomas and Diener, 1990). When trying to recall "mixed emotions," people have to deal with both positive and negative information at once which can subconsciously generate feelings of discomfort and conflict. They subsequently enact coping strategies to reduce the intensity of this discomfort at the moment of recall by reevaluating the elements that underlie their mixed emotions, to create a less nuanced and more absolute emotion. People may also come to believe that emotionally ambiguous experiences eventually have to be "decided". For instance, a cultural narrative dictates that a wedding day should be remembered as an overwhelmingly happy experience as the negative emotions of the day are "explained away," e.g., as wedding day jitters, or the photographers' camera being stolen (Aaker, Drolet and Griffin, 2008).

In the case of those remembering the 2001–02 uprising, a self-defense mechanism that may have been enacted by interview participants was thus to remember all crisis events as "negative," including their own support at the time for the rebellion, because they don't want to admit that they were naive enough to have believed it was possible for the crisis to have an idealistic ending in terms of a more participatory, democratic and just society as the QSVT revolt sought to create.

Finally, through the process of "assimilation," perceptions of past events are affected not just by the present state of affairs but also past experience, feelings and attitudes (Warr and Knapper, 1968). Expectations can also impact upon perceptions. If Argentines were cynical about whether it was possible to change their society collectively *before* 2001, their attitudes may have been "confirmed" or "reinforced" by the fact that QSVT never became a reality – thus making them even more cynical than they were to start with. For those who did have genuine hope/expectation that things would change, they may have felt subsequent disillusionment, so may also remember events more negatively than they did at the time.

So, with this caveat in mind, in terms of how the QSVT revolt was recalled, I divide interviewee responses into three categories. First, those whose overriding recollection of events and the slogan was overwhelmingly negative, either as "anti-democratic," "anarchy" or as one of "selfishness." They professed to disagree with QSVT. This first category applied to 16 of the 30 participants. Second, were those who agreed with QSVT but have minimalist perceptions of the term, as nothing more than "a change of faces." This includes those who had broadly negative recollections and claim "never to have believed" in the term (even if they agreed with it). This applied to 10 of the 30 interviewees. The third category was for those who recalled positive emotions, either that the QSVT had made an important, positive change in Argentinian society or had made society more united in the longer term. This applied to 4 of the 30 participants.

Denunciations of QSVT

In terms of negative portrayals, an overarching theme recalled almost universally was that the period marked one of chaos, disorientation and emotional trauma.

The sensation of vulnerability and paranoia was overwhelming. To feel that at any moment of the day or night, you could lose everything. It was a cumulative process but towards the end became much more chaotic. I mean anything could have happened. You didn't know what to do or what decision to make, not only in terms of financially but in terms of life-choices either.

Federico, 26, Buenos Aires

Such sentiments dominated, even among those who had positive experiences in the social movements at the time:

Going back to 2002, that was a year of great upheaval, so depressing for us. 2002 was the year of desperation, of 'what can we do?'

Ana, 50, Buenos Aires

Words such as "disaster," "terror," "powerlessness," "collapse," "chaos" and "fear" permeated the descriptions that interviewees attached to the period. With these being the strongest "unipolar" emotions recalled, it was unsurprising that few recited positive experiences.

Participants' interpretations tended to link to their political allegiances, notably those who were activists in political parties, or those who came from families that were part of the political "establishment" tended to depict the uprising as "non-democratic," perhaps because of the existential threat that the idea of "getting rid of the political class" posed to them.

A young self-employed English teacher, Carolina, was an activist in the UCR Party that was in power at the time of the December 2001 uprisings and whose leader was forced to resign as national president back then. While she recognized the desperation of the population, she didn't see the protests as "popular" but related them instead to Argentina's long history of coup d'états and military intervention – as an undemocratic ousting of their leader.

To understand the 2001 crisis, you have to also take into account everything that happened in the past. Many people see the crisis in that way, and if you know just a bit of history then you see that there have been many coup d'états that things like this gave rise to.

Carolina, 23, Piedras Blancas

Indeed, cynicism toward the QSVT was generally more prominent among anti-Peronists than among those with Peronist sympathies. The latter tended to possess more positive memories.

Then there was a curious case of Matias, a young man who was a child at the time of the crisis, but whose father happened was a local Socialist Party leader. During our discussion, he was genuinely very supportive of the idea of participatory democracy, neighbors organizing in assemblies to take decisions themselves and of the ideals of horizontal decision-making that (re)emerged from the social movements during the 2001 crisis. In fact, he referenced his own party leader, Hermes Binner who had visited his city that week and who also espoused the idea of "reversing the political pyramid" to devolve power to the people.

Yet, Matias' denouncements of the protests that overthrew the president at the time were based around the fact that they "offered no solutions." When pushed on this and how in fact the movement offered a whole range of alternative social, political and economic experiments such as those mentioned earlier, he sought to justify his statement by separating those protests (which he condemned), from the autonomist movements like the assemblies that were born out of them (which he favored but which sought create an alternative way of living and producing in society). For him, the protests of December 2001 were empty because they offered no alternatives. The vast majority of the literature written about the *Argentinazo* promotes the idea that the initial insurgency and the counterhegemonic movements that they spawned were inseparable in terms of how they projected into the future their vision for the transformation in society that they wanted to see.

> I don't believe in the slogan. If by saying 'que se vayan todos', they really meant [get rid of them] *all* then someone elected this *all* and one assumes this was the majority. In a democratic system when someone is elected it's for a reason. They didn't just fall from the sky because they are enlightened. It's because the majority of Argentinians elected them. So, I would have preferred that they'd have done things another way,
>
> Matias, 20, Posadas

Democracy and rights-based framing was used by both supporters and opponents of the uprising. Authors have claimed that many in the middle class were moved to join the "spontaneous" uprising because they were so indignant at President de la Rua's declaration of the state of siege on 19 December 2001, precisely because it evoked memories of the 1976–83 military dictatorship (Armony and Armony, 2005). However, it wasn't only those with some stake in the party political system who portrayed the protests of those days as anti-democratic.

> No, I didn't support it because I have always thought that democracy has to prevail and be resolved from within the democratic process itself. I've been heavily involved in defending human rights. During the military period I went out and protested in a rage, but I never took part in the 2001 cacerolazos. I don't know, there was something about them... The people gave me the impression that they weren't participating, just reacting.
>
> Laura, 49, Buenos Aires

Only 10% of the sample (three participants) believed the uprising to be about "self-interest." It was generally accepted that there was a great deal of social solidarity at the time and that the QSVT was a multisectoral movement demanding fundamental political and social change. However, this minority dismissed the protests as being purely about "upper-class" interests for having lost money in the *Corralito*. Santiago (60, Buenos Aires) dismissed the *cacerolazos* as a "murga" (a popular local musical performance), while others also remembered things negatively:

> No, it wasn't a revolution. No. People were there who had never lost out financially, but at the time related to the piqueteros and the hungry who long before this had been blocking the roads. But those you refer to like the lawyers who lost everything always ignored the poor until then. So for me structural poverty was the real crisis, but it was already there. The uprising of those days was that of the upper-middle class, for their own interests and nothing more.
>
> Brian, 37, Rosario

> The cacerolazos? I hate them, because when there is hunger they aren't protesting. Only when it has to do with their own money. And that upsets me. If they went out to demand money for the poor, waving their saucepan then I would be the first in line to join them. But if it's only about their savings then they can forget it.
>
> Julieta, La Plata, 86

Yet, Svampa (2006) makes clear through her study of the *escrache* protests outside the banks, that only the savers' protests had more insular, self-interested financial motives, but that these were quite distinct and isolated from the general social movements at the time. The assemblies, *piqueteros*, community soup kitchens, worker-recovered companies and so on offered more idealistic visions of transformative social change and of solidarity between different social strata and even refused to count the savers' protests as part of their movement. Nevertheless, either due to being misinformed or due to "recall bias" (the images of depositors queuing outside and sometimes physically damaging banks being one of the most iconic and enduring of the *uprisings*), this was not *their* interpretation of events.

In my time in Argentina, I had dozens of conversations where locals lamented the self-centered nature of their fellow countrymen/women. "We Argentinians only react when we lose out financially [*nos toca en el bolsillo*]," they would tell me. This would usually be accompanied by them retorting their fellow citizens for having no social conscience, while also admitting (without batting an eyelid) that they don't protest or confront the government about social injustices either. For them, it was sufficient to give to charity or to street children to satisfy their own consciences.

For others, the QSVT was remembered as part of the same anarchy and chaos that rattled their beliefs in social order. They recalled the images of the hungry and sick, or images of either police violence or protestors throwing stones or building barricades. While these certainly happened, the stories of hope and of creating a new solidaristic world that were experienced at the time through the various social movements were virtually forgotten, and certainly only rarely appeared in the media or public discourse. Other criticisms included those who were part of the movement "merely wanting to put the Kirchners in power," which was a clear example of distorted memory bias as Néstor Kirchner was a virtually unknown provincial governor at the time (2001–02), and neither the presidential election, nor his candidacy were announced for many months after the December 2001 revolt.

A final element of QSVT that evoked much cynicism among those in this category were the notions of "participatory democracy," "autonomism" and "horizontal decision-making" without leaders or bosses. Advocated in academic discourse by those such as Zibechi (2003), Holloway (2002) and Hardt and Negri (2000), those of the alter-globalization movement and also the founding declarations of the movements that were either born or became part of the cartography of 2001–02 in Argentina themselves,[5] these ideas were much derided among this group of interviewees. This was despite the fact that the practice was broadly accepted and performed among the movements at the time (and elements of which, such as the "assembly" as the key decision-making body, endure today in Argentina). Those in this group asserted that "leaders" or "representatives" were necessary. Given that those harboring such feelings tallied over half of the overall sample, it provides further evidence that the crisis of representative democracy was well and truly over by 2007 and 2011. Even if a return to the status quo wasn't popular, counterhegemonic ideas of participatory democracy were dismissed as either "crazy," a form of "anarchy" or, most commonly, "impractical." The new poor of 2001–02 had been resocialized into accepting representative democracy.

> What a load of nonsense! I think this way, the guy opposite thinks another, and he disagrees with his neighbor... no, no! It's impossible if everyone has their own idea. So when you go and vote, at least you know who you are voting for you know? But this notion of arguing for your opinion against what the others think, no. For me it's crazy!
>
> Julieta, 86, La Plata

A handful saw merit in the idea of greater participation, not as a new system of direct democracy but *within* the representative democratic framework, either at a localized level or for daily decision-making on a small scale.

I agree with the idea of more participation but not in every circumstance. The reality is that we are accustomed to a different way. I believe that steps can be taken towards a more participatory model... simple things. Day-to-day decisions and those that affect the neighborhood no? But to open a debate on the macroeconomy or those that affected large numbers of people, no. It's impractical. It won't work. Some will say yes, others no, but they can't know if the idea is coherent with other parts of the plan.

Franco, 35, Posadas

Meanwhile in the small village of Piedras Blancas, there was near consensus around the paternalistic idea that "the Intendent" was the only one who should govern and that faith should be vested in him.

I think that here in the village what's needed is one person in charge of the people. Maybe a system where the people have more say is used more in the cities, (not rule by one person), but not here. Here until now, thank God that the Intendent we have does all that he can for us.

Veronica, 20, Piedras Blancas

I wasn't in favor with the idea of 'que se vayan todos' because we the people should stay out of it. In a small village you always have to have a representative to dialogue with those outside. The idea of a popular assembly just doesn't wash here.

Martin, 50 Piedras Blancas

Even those in the village who didn't like the way that the current Intendent was governing believed that power should nevertheless be concentrated in the post, albeit with a different person in charge.

For me all groups need to have leaders. I mean if twenty of us got together it would be very difficult to reach an agreement. I think the representative system we have today is fine but what's bad are the politicians who receive the salaries as they become corrupt... For instance, our Intendent receives $15,000 pesos (US$ 3,000) per month which for Piedras Blancas is an absolute fortune.

Diego, 42, Piedras Blancas

Supportive of QSVT as "A Change of Faces"

This second group, consisting of one-third of all those interviewed, admitted having supported the idea of QSVT in 2001. Many described how they participated in the protests of 19 December and often in related collective mobilizations. However, as with the last group, while it is not possible to tell what their beliefs were at the time (or whether they supported a more systemic challenge to the neoliberal and representative democratic hegemony), by the time of their interviews in 2007 and 2011, they interpreted QSVT simply as the need to have removed all the old politicians and to have replaced them with others. At the same time, they denied that there was a structural problem that needed to be addressed (which may or may not have been their actual view at the time). Effectively, there was a fetishization of the QSVT concept within this group. If individual political representatives could have been removed and others have taken their place, everything would have ended up ok, and Argentina would have achieved a healthy, functioning democracy.

The problem with this interpretation is that many of the "old faces" did indeed "come back" when national parliamentary representatives who were present in 2001 were either subsequently reelected as provincial senators or sometimes as deputies. This generated profound disillusionment and resignation. Judging from subsequent political trajectories disclosed to me by participants, for many it led them to withdraw from political activity. They expressed that if a rebellion as violent and massive as 2001 didn't work, things will now never change. Several cited the fact that if former President Carlos Menem (who was almost universally blamed for having initiated the neoliberal policies and indebtedness that caused the 2001 default) could re-stand for president on 27 April 2003 and lead the polling after the first round of national voting, then it devalued the entire rebellion.

> Here we had the 'que se vayan todos'. But in the end 'they all stayed' and carried on stealing from us you see? It [the revolt] was no use in the end... We wanted an end to all the corruption, that all the same politicians that had always been around should go. We wanted a change. A change in the people, a change in the mentality.
>
> Cristina, 59, Buenos Aires

> I don't know if it was so much 'que se vayan todos' but more 'let new ones come along'. It was as if we were tired of the same old faces you see? Menem stood for president again, are you kidding me?! Duhalde as president again?? Really?! We needed new faces, with new ideas.
>
> Romina, 21, Rosario

Perhaps as some kind of emotional self-defense mechanism to save face, almost all in this group admitted that even though they supported the uprising, they never truly believed that it was possible to "get rid of them all."

> I supported the idea a bit. But it wasn't the answer... you know why? Because even though you demanded it, it was never going to happen.

Yes, it's what we said at the time, and it came from the heart. We all wanted 'que se vayan todos' but it wasn't going to happen that way.

Graciela, 57, Buenos Aires

While the protests were reconstructed in their memory as having "failed," participants felt a sense of deception. In their discourse at least, this de-motivated them from taking part in further protest in the future.

I remember the very day it happened, when it all kicked off that night [in 2001]. Then on the 20 December when he [President De La Rua] confirmed his resignation, I recall listening to it on the radio stretched out on the bed. At that moment I thought 'finally some-thing good is happening in this country.' But things just went back to how they were before you see, so what's the point?

Jorge, 36, La Plata

Supportive of QSVT as (Partially) Successful

A small minority of the sample held positive memories of the period. That's to say, the positive memories outweighed the bad when undergoing the recall process of their "mixed emotions." They highlighted how aims were achieved in the long term, and Argentina either became a fairer, more just society with greater levels of citizen participation, greater unity among the population at the time, or because it made politicians more accountable and cautious of ignoring "the people."

The protests provided a harsh lesson for those in power. A lesson because no politician wants to be subject to that. It was a horrible situation for them to face. For instance, the government had a huge external debt, but after with Cristina and Nestor Kirchner, they searched for solutions to pay it off.

Milagros, 30, Posadas

Yes, I believe they were a success because not many [politicians] came back here in La Plata. Not many stood for election again. The protests proposed a change in government and a change in policy direction. These things happened. They also helped to change the mentality that people had, including the banks and other entities. Yes, it marked a watershed moment. It gives me goose-pimples to think of how everyone came together to protest at the time. I loved it and remember how it gave me hope.

Vanesa, 26, La Plata

Notably, all those in this category were women below 40 years old. Women tended to analyze their past and present in a more nuanced way, engaging in cautious self-reflexivity. The males interviewed, on the other hand, tended to respond to questions more spontaneously. They swayed toward unipolar recollections that were inevitably more negative, and these were recounted with both physical and verbal aggression.

Further, between 2007 and 2011, recollections generally became increasingly unipolar, tending toward increased feelings of disillusionment with what QSVT aimed to achieve and what the results were in practice. Their memories of the uprising also became increasingly cynical and less nostalgic. As we saw earlier, *current* experiences can color the memory of *prior* experiences, and when one's *current* belief system supports a negative bias, it can also taint the experienced emotion. In Argentina at the time of the 2007 interviews, none withstanding growing concern about crime (see later), the economy was booming, inflation was under control, and employment, growth and standards of living were all rising. Néstor Kirchner was generally a popular president, and the government (including the opposition) was broadly free of major corruption scandals.

However by the 2011 interviews, although they took place on the eve of the election that Cristina Fernández de Kirchner won convincingly, the macroeconomic indicators had all dipped, the Countryside Conflict (2008) dented confidence in the government, many of the corporate media conglomerates, especially Clarín Group and Cablevision – which reached two-thirds of Argentinian households and almost all of those in the middle class (LAMAC, 2012) – had turned against the government after it had passed the Audio-visual and Media Law (2009), influencing public opinion negatively especially among the middle class and its impoverished wing. Furthermore, Cristina's government was beginning to be tainted by similar corruption scandals to those that helped spark the social explosion of 2001.[6]

The QSVT Uprising and Socio-Territorial Impact

The impact of urban-led revolts on life in rural or countryside areas is often forgotten in academic discussions. This is especially true if they don't have direct implications for land reform or tackle agrarian or peasant questions (unlike the Russian Revolution of 1917 or French Revolution of 1789 did, for instance). Certainly, there has been little, if any previous work conducted on how the QSVT revolt of December 2001 was experienced by those living in such areas in Argentina. From the interviewees' accounts, it was lived much less intensely in the provinces and compared to Buenos Aires, our isolated village Piedras Blancas was associated with something distant. The performance of contention was deemed to have happened "over there" and didn't relate closely to interview participants' own heuristic experience, even if they understood that the grievances felt (debt default, elite corruption etc.) were issues of nationwide importance. Even if they sympathized with these, rural or provincial citizens felt a certain alienation from the overall "movement" because physical opportunities to participate in it were either limited or nonexistent. This presents a challenge to social movements. How can these movements become more inclusive and mobilize sympathetic citizens across vast geographical space? How can they help them to connect with the movement?

> God only listens to you in Buenos Aires. Maybe I would have joined the protests if I'd lived there. But there is a huge difference between Buenos Aires and living here you see? We watched it on television so partly lived it in that sense, but the feeling and passion weren't the same, even if we were all affected by what was going on.
>
> Magalí, 36, Posadas

For example, Romina, age 21, was interviewed in Rosario but in December 2001 was back in her small rural town (Cañada de Gomez, 75 km from the nearest city). While she was a child at the time, her words still have resonance:

> I remember! I have the image of the cacerolazo and the moment that President De La Rua came out onto the balcony of the Casa Rosada... But it was an 'another worldly' sensation.... I saw Buenos Aires as if it were another country you see? For me Buenos Aires was... it was another world. It wasn't my world. It wasn't Cañada. It's the same when I see news from other countries you see? Nothing to do with me, it doesn't affect me. Back then it was a strange sensation.

Meanwhile in isolated areas, there was less motivation to participate in the protests because they felt that their voices wouldn't be heard to the same extent. The geographical distance from loci of legislative or symbolic power also discouraged them from mobilization:

> In the cities they agitate more so as to get television coverage when they do a protest. They say 'if the TV cameras are going, let's join!' But here no one listens to you. Not here.
>
> Victoria, 51, Piedras Blancas

Participation in 2001 Collective Action, Political Trajectories and Effects on Mobilization

The next theme to emerge was that which was based upon the participants' experiences of their own household's involvement in collective actions during and since the 2001 crisis (as opposed to their memories of the general uprising per se). Coding was based around whether their memories were positive, negative or neutral and what impact this had both for their political trajectories and subsequent participation in collective actions. Unsurprisingly, synergies were identified between how they interpreted QSVT and whether they were nostalgic or cynical about their own personal experience in it. Their answers were also cross-referenced with those they provided in the 2002 World Bank survey to add a further longitudinal element to the analysis. One-third of the sample described how they engaged in either collective protests or collective self-improvement actions in the solidarity economy in 2001–02. This broadly reflected the 28% of the impoverished middle class who did so according to the survey over a similar time period.

Positive Experiences

Some participants spoke about the exhilaration of joining enormous crowds of protestors in the December 2001 rebellion and of their hope for change. One middle-aged woman pointed out that until that point she believed that she was alone in her social decent and hardship, describing the protests as a "liberation." However, the greatest nostalgia was actually reserved for their engagement with solidarity economy activities which were initially joined out of "financial need" and "curiosity" in equal measure.

Participants described the warmness of the personal interactions that they had with other Argentinians in the middle class who were experiencing a fall and also of mixing with those from other social sectors (the long-term poor), often for the first time. This endowed them with a sense of "togetherness" and common purpose although the activity as a means in itself was sometimes judged unfavorably and associated with backwardness. As one woman described her barter club experience:

> What I loved most were the interactions I had with other people. The 'how did you make that?' or the 'how does that work?' Sharing experiences was, for me was better than the bartering itself. It seemed like a step back in time.
>
> Micaela, 50, Piedras Blancas

Some also explained how it left them with a desire to participate in other solidarity economy activities as a means of breaking down differences. This offered support for the "sites of social integration and awareness-raising" thesis from Chapter 3.

> Everything about them [barter and other collective actions] was positive. I'd have liked to take part in more actions with others back then because they helped break down the fear between those attending who always had their fridge full and never lacked bread, milk or clothes, and the needy, who had always been hungry. I saw this going on and lived it in the flesh. It was a beautiful thing.
>
> Diego, 42, Piedras Blancas

Negative Experiences and Deterrent to Future Participation

The overwhelming majority described their own experiences negatively. Feeling "deceived," "manipulated" and in a number of cases explaining how being burned had deterred them from subsequent involvement in protests and social movements. Men evoked especially toxic memories of involvement in post-2001 movements, both quantitatively and qualitatively. Their sense of disappointment or anger was expressed more resolutely than the women, whom, while often conveying similar feelings, did so in a more measured way, with a greater tendency to also emphasize the positive aspects of participation. For men, it seemed to have hurt their pride more that they had been "cheated" in some way and it was this emotion that dominated their discourse and guided future collective behavior. The sense of not wanting to be hurt again was a common theme.

> In 2002 I got involved in the Participatory Budget programme that was organized by the City government. I felt it provided a space where as neighbors, we could have more of a say. But I was mistaken, *badly* mistaken. In general, the neighbors took part in the assembly movement, which left the Participatory Budget totally at the whim of different political party representatives. I mean the local party *punteros*[7] held the majority. They made me Green Spaces Commission delegate, I was only 18 and younger than everyone else, so I was really happy. Later in the year I stood for re-election for this post but all party representatives; Peronist, Radical, Left and Centre-Left banded together and elected another candidate. It was then that I realized that that the whole thing had been totally co-opted. I left feeling completely deceived.
>
> Federico, 26, Buenos Aires

I became friends with Federico and took an interest in his political trajectory in subsequent years. He recounted how badly the experience burned him at such a young age. He remained heavily interested in politics, became a doctor of political science, but as far as I know, he never attended a single protest or collective action again, instead retreating into private strategies, becoming despondent with political corruption and longing to leave Argentina to establish a new life overseas.

Five of those who attended neighborhood assemblies explained that they either left them because they felt their views were not listened to or that the meetings were being manipulated by political parties.

Women tended to focus on "micro" experiences of feeling defrauded by collective action they were involved in (either during or since 2001). For instance, one complained how the coordinator of a local campaign to get traffic lights installed in their road suddenly disappeared. Another that the apartment block associations' delegate was accused of fraud.

This elderly man blamed the failure of his community purchasing scheme on his own friends and their middle-class mentality:

> I buy my things from the Central Market and I tried to establish a community purchasing scheme among friends. But being middle class, many of them had anxieties that exceeded their possibilities and they ended up wanting more for less. They were unable to adapt to a communitarian system of sharing out equally, so the project failed.
>
> Juan, 86, Buenos Aires

While the experiences from 2001 to 2002 were the most embedded in their discourse, occasionally they recounted the failure of more historic involvement which also made them more cynical. Past failed experiences can remain in the memory and serve to make one more cautious about social movement involvement in the longer term.

> Here back in 1994 we tried to establish one [a neighborhood assembly]. But no, it didn't work. Because we all spent too much time criticising each other! 'This so-and-so robbed me last time me saw each other...!' You see [laughs]? So, no it didn't work.
>
> Diego, 42, Piedras Blancas

Many were explicit that their sense of deception meant that they would not join protests again as they didn't believe they would change anything. This woman explains that old-fashioned "who you know" private strategies would be more fruitful next time. She describes her experience of joining a savers' *escrache* protest after she'd had her dollar deposits confiscated by the banks:

> I took part to add to the numbers... so that we were stronger. In part I went along because I was furious, in part because others were there protesting already and it gave you confidence. But I realized that getting your savings back depended a lot on who you knew in the bank. If you had a connection to the Manager they would find a way. In my case, nothing. If this were to happen again I would search for my own solution because these protests were pointless. I doubt I'd join them ever again. I don't believe in anything in Argentina anymore. I'm not going to [gestures as if she is hitting a saucepan] with the others like I'm a caged animal.
>
> Daniela, 59, Buenos Aires

The Manipulated Protestor

Another theme that emerged in over half of the interviews in 2007 and 2011 was the idea that there was no such thing as a genuine protest and that the experience of 2001 had taught them that even those protests or organizations that claimed to be "autonomous" were in fact having their strings pulled behind the scenes. This cynicism was striking because Argentina's 2001–02 movement was globally acclaimed for precisely its "spontaneity" and rejection of political party, trade union or other interference from those associated with the political superstructure. Indeed, such claims stand in contrast to most accounts of those who took part at the time and with most academic analyzes. The sociologist Maristella Svampa (2014:158) described how 2001–02 was the moment when metaphorically speaking, Antonio Negri and the "multitude" defeated Gramsci (and the need for organized parties and alignments to organize a counterhegemony) and enjoyed a decisive victory over Lenin (and the Marxist-Leninist Party as the vanguard for the masses).

For instance, Franco and several others claimed that it was the Peronist government of the 1990s that generated the economic and political crisis, then when the Radicals took power, they were the same political force that started to stage food riots and lootings around Argentina. There is some evidence for the latter (see Auyero and Moran, 2007), in order to provoke a hard response from the government. Ultimately, it was President de la Rua's declaration of the "state of siege" which provoked a popular backlash and the December uprising. He continues,

> After two years, the same Party in a new guise [he refers to the 'Frente para la Victoria' which is part of the Peronist Party], returns to power but is the same one from whose administration the crisis originated. I mean they are cut from the same cloth. I believe those marches were provoked and set up so that the same party would end up coming back to power. It was a kind of coup.
>
> Franco, 35, Posadas

Several also claimed that the popular assemblies were controlled by the political parties, a bit like Federico did earlier. Another dismissed them as "a mass psychologist's couch where people went to let off steam." In this sense, interview participants struggled to decide which protests were "genuine" and which were "staged," so the solution that many came to was just to stay out altogether.

For a substantial number, the 2001 uprisings was one last throw of the dice for them as already cynical citizens have their faith restored and end corruption and rule by the same old elites. When this was perceived to have failed and old corrupt or self-serving practices renewed under *Kirchnerismo*, it marked a point of no return where their skepticism became engrained and irreversible. The loss of trust also definitively ended their political mobilization:

> In the moment itself you think you can change the world. Later on you realize that the difference you made is exactly zero.
>
> Brian, 37, Rosario

Among the most cynical, even figures like the Mothers of the Plaza de Mayo (who, as elderly women, were highly revered in society for having protested against the military dictatorship in the 1970s and 1980s in search of their disappeared children) came in for the most obtuse criticism.[8] As if to echo the lyrics of John Lennon in "God," where the singer lists a whole range of people and things he had once sworn by but no longer believes in (including the Maharishi, Bob Dylan and even the Beatles), Jorge makes an assertion that was equally as depressing:

> I don't believe in any organization with miraculous ideas. I only believe in those who are no longer here. Mother Theresa, in her, in Ghandi, in those people whom their actions are more than proven. I don't believe in anyone. Not in God, not in my own father [laughs]! And I think that it's precisely thinking that way that will keep me going.
>
> Jorge, 36, La Plata

Jorge and Brian were the two whose discourse most fervently represented this "manipulated protestor" sentiment. Yet, they hid a dirty secret. In their reconstruction of the past events, both denied proactively taking part in the December 2001 protests. Both stated that they went along "as observers" to check that "the protests were genuine" as if they had some kind of memory of being there, yet simultaneously they denied purposeful participation in their ex post facto interviews. Intriguingly, in the 2002 World Bank Survey, it stated that they *had* participated in the protests. This was a clear indication of the shame they felt to have been associated with them in subsequent years and how their memories had been distorted by intermediate events, opinions and feelings. A psychological coping strategy for the pain they perhaps both felt in having their illusions shattered.

Struggling Middle Class as "Occasional Citizens" and "Passive Dissidence"

Among the two-thirds of the sample who opposed the Kirchner government that they were living under in 2011 (this increased from half in 2007), there was a distinct discontinuity observed between participants' radical analysis of how society functions (often critical, anti-systemic, even Marxist), perceptions of their own subjugation and their fiery rhetoric, on the one hand, yet their lack of desire to any action taken to change it on the other.

Despite their wholesale disdain for the political class including in 2007 and 2011, their sophisticated understanding of their own political citizenship and of what was and wasn't acceptable behavior from them and recognition that they were *still* corrupt, paradoxically for them the act of "doing politics" was seemingly limited to the confines of "giving opinions" and "being consulted" by politicians. Few acted on those convictions in terms of collective protest participation. This confirmed Mazzoni's (2008) "low-impact citizens" thesis (see p. 77 of this book).

During the period in question (2007–11), however, unlike 2001–02, several factors intertwined that resulted in the vast majority desisting from taking any collective action against the government's alleged corruption or in protest against their own hardship. The lack of political opportunities to join such actions, the resignation many felt, plus the fact that all but one of the participants was much better off financially than they were during the economic crisis, also contributed to this.

Collective identity theory states that the conditions required for a social movement to emerge are where grievances are understood to be shared by multiple individuals and organizations and that there is the belief that those grievances can be overcome (Tajfel and Turner, 1986). It was evident through daily interactions during fieldwork that there was a strong awareness of the intensity of widespread discontentment by middle-class citizens among those interviewed. Dissident conversations in shops, on public transport or… about the state of society would be sprinkled with phrases such as "well with the government we have…" as a demonstration of passive resistance. However, it was the belief that protests would bring change that was lacking at the time. The boundaries between movements and the society and culture from which they emerge are indefinite and "fuzzy" (Marwell and Oliver, 1984).

Participation in these movements can range from more tangible actions, like marching in demonstrations or signing petitions, to less concrete forms of protest such as these forms of passive dissidence. It is within this latter realm that resistance remained. Part of the reason is that during the research period, incumbent President Cristina Kirchner was leading by far in the polls, then actually won 48% of the vote in the August 2011 presidential primaries, some 35% ahead of her nearest rival (*Dirección Nacional Electoral*, 2011). Neither had there been any major anti-government protests for the preceding three years. At times among government opponents, in the interview sample it was as if a cauldron of grievances was heating up that would explode at some point. Tensions had spilled out into the open, but in a highly restrained way.

Collective or individual protest, as a form of expressing their discontent with their own socioeconomic situation or with the government in general, tended to be only sporadic, for instance, against the 2008 proposal to raise *retenciones* (export tariffs), or at election time (through voting for an opposition party).

It was also common to hear participants complain incessantly about the state of the country and that it continued to be plagued by endemic corruption or that they were deeply unhappy with the political situation. Yet, they admitted that they took no action in practice:

> There is no unity of action. No 'well, let's all get together to do something about it!' The other day I heard that there was a telephone

workers strike because they wanted more pay. But among us there is no unity of action to demand that the government stop stealing from us!

Sofía, 31, Santa Fe City

Or they criticized other Argentinians for being selfish and individualistic (as part of the problem), while acting as if they held the moral high ground themselves. The point was that to an observer, their actions couldn't be distinguished from the rest!

'While I'm alright, I won't worry about anyone else ok?' That's how things are and why things are going downhill all the time.

Magalí, 36, Posadas

What I believe is that here people don't protest out of solidarity you know? It's a reaction from their pockets.

Laura, 49, Buenos Aires

How can this disparity between their high-intensity discourse and low-intensity action be explained? The *liberal* model of political citizenship tends to be hegemonic in contemporary constitutional democracies. Under this model, citizens restrict themselves to entrusting the business of law-making to representatives rather than engaging actively in decision-making. This notion was found to be almost universally accepted among the sample. With the exception of three cases, collective protest engagement was also minimal, with the then widely advocated notion of participatory democracy of 2001 now deemed unworkable. For these reasons, I term how participants relate to their citizenship as an "occasional" identity, invoked once every two years in the act of voting or via the occasional protest participation.

To some extent, the Kirchner governments since 2003 had attempted to translate some of the demands of the 2001 uprisings, especially for more active citizen participation in political and economic decision-making in the nation's institutions. The application of more "republican" conceptualizations of citizenship through their National Popular project is exemplified by the creation of the 2004 National Institute for the Associative and Social Economy, support for worker-recovered enterprises and cooperatives (Ozarow and Croucher, 2014) and the government's 2014 National Programme for Participatory Budgeting.

However, these were found to have had little resonance during the fieldwork. Among those interviewed, the reasons identified for only passive resistance or non-involvement in collective protest at the time of the interviews in 2007 or 2011 fell equally into three categories: (1) alienation or resignation, (2) fear and (3) Lowering of expectations and increased tolerance of either their own ongoing hardship of the political elite's alleged misdeeds.

First, alienation and resignation:

> I don't believe that the people have any power.... They don't have it. We have to make do with a system that grants us elections to vote for people who don't represent us but in reality, you don't even choose them anyway.
>
> Franco, 35, Posadas

In the cities, sometimes participants confessed that they simply didn't have time to join protests, despite their strong views. Returning to our "political opportunities idea" from Chapter 3, others stated that the place that they worked or studied was non-political, so it bestowed them fewer possibilities to be involved in the place where they spent most of their waking hours (workplace, university etc.). Meanwhile in Piedras Blancas village, all but the one political party activist expressed how they stay out of politics as there was more "perfect knowledge" of each other's political, social and private lives. Thus, to actively engage in politics was seen as risky, in terms of the potential fallout in a political environment that was highly partisan and clientelist:

> I prefer friendship to politics. If you get involved in politics here, you end up losing friends.
>
> Martin, 50, Piedras Blancas

> For me politics causes problems... Maybe, erm if you need help from other neighbors or even the Intendent, they could say "no" because you are in the wrong party. No, my policy is just to stay out of it.
>
> Veronica, 20, Piedras Blancas

Returning to the general sample, some, especially middle-aged women or older also put off taking part in post-2001 mobilizations due to fear of them turning violent. This woman explained how since then she preferred to simply sign petitions as a channel for her political actions:

> The thing is that if you remember the 2001 crisis, errrm, people died. Here, generally the demonstrations always end up badly because there are infiltrators. They infiltrate the protests so that things don't end well. So I'm scared of all that.
>
> Graciela, 57, Buenos Aires

Among the younger generation, awareness of the 1976–83 military dictatorship tended to make them appreciate their democratic rights, as well as understand protest as a legitimate and widely used tool in their repertoire of responses. For middle-aged and older participants, especially women, it made some more cautious about political involvement.

The second reason to emerge was that of a general lowering of expectations and heightened tolerance of corruption. This applied not just to politicians' behavior (to the point where even a low to medium level of corruption was rhetorically condemned, but in practice accepted), but tolerance of their own hardship.

> The thing is that for those of us who lived through military governments like that last one that was terrible, so terrible and killed so many people, anything is better. But in truth honest politicians don't exist. They just don't.
>
> Laura, 49, Buenos Aires

It was clear that many had reduced their professional and life expectations and (among the middle-aged and older), long-abandoned hopes of upward mobility, so were less demanding of the government too.

> My goals nowadays are modest. The zenith (*cumbre*) of my life has past. Thinking realistically about what I want from my life now; I'd have to say just to maintain what I already have. What has happened to me has killed off any hopes (*mató la illusion*) of anything more.
>
> Agustina, 48 Buenos Aires

Somewhat poetically, Carlos described how he was happier now that he had reconciled himself with a humble lifestyle, even if at times in the past he had been driven to take collective action to demand the salary or politicians that he felt he deserved.

> If in order to be economically better off, you constantly think about how life *should* be, then you'll go nowhere. My father always used to say, "We are at our most content when listening to music and when we know exactly what note comes next. If the note falls out of tune, it goes against our spirit and makes us anxious." I feel that way, it's the same in life. I know what to expect and where I'm going. I am happy.
>
> Carlos, 78, Buenos Aires

With seemingly little to personally gain through engagement in collective demand-making to improve their own circumstances, it is no wonder that many desisted from doing so.

Aside from this, some of the governments' fiercest critics actually expressed anti-imperialist and even anti-capitalist views, some of which one can regularly find in Kirchnerist discourse and policy. However, it was precisely these participants like Luis who were among their most critical voices. Somehow the government was failing to win over its natural allies.

The main problem we have is one of dependence. All our riches are being stolen by the Americans... by the English.

Luis, 57, Santa Fe City

For instance, this interviewee lamented that the English and Americans only get away with this because there is an Argentinian somewhere who is selling out to them. Joking that I had "come to study Argentina under a microscope, like a science experiment," he proceeded to spend the next few minutes claiming he was a "nationalist" while simultaneously complaining how inefficient everything is in Argentina and how he could barely stand living there. He then quipped that Argentinians "made a mistake by throwing boiling oil over the English" in 1807[9] and that if the English had successfully taken over Argentina during the English Invasions, their country would be much better off than they are today. What is notable from his interview is not only the contradiction between his nationalist but also anti-nationalist discourse, but that this reflected a number of schizophrenic elements of national identity (the myth of national greatness and arriving at the "First World" yet the reality of disenchantment). This was common to the "talk" of a wide number of interviewees.

Another example was Carlos, who provided a Marxist analysis of hegemony of which Gramsci would have been proud.

The world's wealth is overwhelmingly owned by just 270 powerful men. Via their minions, who own 10% of what they do, the rest of us are exploited day after day. They will only stop us from rising up by giving us just about enough of the crumbs to survive. So what worries them is the mass media. That the people read newspapers, listen to the radio or [sic] television... So they use these to gently shape their minds in order that the governments and the powerful maintain control. Basically the world is controlled that way.

Carlos, 78, Buenos Aires

Others praised the communist system in Cuba:

The Cubans are very sociable and community-minded. The health system is excellent.

Martin, 50, Piedras Blancas

Here you have to change jobs because you can't afford the petrol. But not in Cuba. Cuba is fantastic. I'm a believer in the 'this is my country and I'm going to live how I want like that do, not how capitalism wants me to' idea.

Jorge, 36, La Plata

Meanwhile, others still were indignant that wealth wasn't fairly distributed in Argentina, arguing that the rich should pay more. Yet in each case, the interviewees admitted that they were staunchly against the Kirchner government, despite its own strongly nationalist, left-wing and anti-imperialist rhetoric (and actions) that formed its National Popular political and economic program.

Those with such views should have made natural bedfellows for the Kirchner government, were often the most vitriolic in their opposition. The Kirchner governments, especially that of Cristina, had alienated their support base. Attention now turns to why they gained support from some, yet faced strong opposition from others?

Appeasement by Kirchnerismo

On 23 October 2011, Argentinians went to the polls. Cristina Fernández de Kirchner obtained a landslide victory in this second round vote, receiving 54.1% of votes cast, with her nearest rival, the Socialist Hermes Binner lagging far behind on 16.8%. Similarly, Néstor Kirchner had support ratings of 74%–79% at the height of his government, and it remained high until the end of his administration (*Clarín*, 2005). We also saw earlier how Néstor Kirchner gained the support of 49% of the struggling middle class in 2005 and that confidence in him recovered much faster than it did than for any other institution after the 2001–02 crisis among those in this sector. However, among the interview participants, only one-third expressed support in 2007, falling to one-quarter for his wife by 2011. Here the analysis focuses on how the Kirchners were able to do appease some among the struggling middle class and therefore help demobilize their prior anti-government opposition.

Interviewees recalled the early years of Néstor Kirchner's government favorably, including some of those who grew to oppose him. He was credited with clearing out the courts of corrupt judges, putting the military leaders back on trial for the torture and disappearances of thousands of people between 1976 and 1983, and other human rights-based policies which seemed to appeal to their strong sense of *political* citizenship and liberal values. Cristina Kirchner was also credited with other human rights policies that aligned with such values, including the legalization of equal marriage. Speaking in her defense in 2011, others mentioned that the economy was functioning well and that schools and public services were better financed than before. The fact that Cristina was a "strong leader who brought order" was also a factor for a small number, perhaps reflecting the conservative value of social order they possessed, despite her being viewed as a "progressive" figure who Carlos (78, Buenos Aires) even lamented had "brought communism to Argentina."

In line with national voting patterns, the Kirchner governments were perceived more favorably among younger participants, in the provinces outside Buenos Aires City, and by women. Romina was one of only two interviewees to praise the Kirchners' social policies (which were generally understood to be heavily targeted at the long-term poor). Dismissing the accusation that the nature of the majority of government programs was "assistentialist," she saw her own university grant and pensions also as "subsidies" and highlighted that many middle-class beneficiaries of these don't recognize them as such. She also praised Universal Childhood Benefit (*Asignación Universal por Hijo*) (AUH)[10] which was heavily criticized by many in the sample for "incentivising the poor to have more children" because, as she explained, it made payments dependent on school attendance, so improved the future prospects for such children. She also described why she liked Cristina Kirchner, echoing some of the explanations for Jeremy Corbyn's popularity in the UK:

> She never responds negatively to the attacks against her. For example, thousands of politicians criticise, criticise, criticise, but she has never stooped to their level in any of her speeches. The important thing is to be grown up in such situations.
>
> Romina, 21, Rosario

The government's policy on the external debt also drew support from some, but in general this extract sums up participants' feelings about the economy. Almost all were worried about future instability, which may help explain why the anti-government protests didn't emerge until economic instability (high inflation and a dip in growth) returned in 2012–13.

> The external debt was always a huge weight on our shoulders. The fact that it's now largely been paid off to an extent has alleviated us of this burden. We also have just a little more faith in this government now too. In any case, we are always on tenterhooks that the economy will change, we are always fearful of that…we don't feel that the state protects us and we are scared that anything could happen, as in other moments of our history.
>
> Marcos, 51, Buenos Aires

> It's like here we have to enjoy the seven years of fat cows because they will soon be followed by seven years of thin cows. That comes from the Bible, you know? Well I think that… I agree completely [with that analysis] of Argentina's experience you know? There is never any stability.
>
> Agustina, 48, Buenos Aires

This respondent, a hostel manager, was the only one who had attended the Countryside Conflict protests on the side of the government. He understood the need for the increase in export taxes so as to fund the social programs and was generally supportive of the Kirchners' attempts to redistribute wealth.

> The cake has started to be shared out more. Although not all of it is shared, before there was the cake and we had a small piece between us. Now we all get to share a quarter of it. By 'we' I mean as society, not 'we' the middle class.
>
> Brian 37, Rosario

However, *Kirchnerismo* struggled to appease much of the struggling middle class, especially by the 2011 interviews, as discourse became increasingly critical. Here some of the principle themes of their estrangement from the National Popular project are discussed.

Estrangement from Kirchnerismo

It was evident that the 2001–02 "inter-class" solidarity had dried up among all but the most progressive interviewees. The fact that the long-term poor and *piqueteros* were seen to be advantaged at their expense was a recurring bone of contention that will be elaborated upon in the next section. The sense was that these sectors were being given handouts "not to work," including for several of those who otherwise supported the Kirchner governments. Similar themes are raised by those who object to elements of the welfare state in Western Europe. The depiction of the poor as "lazy" and work-shy will be familiar to readers from there. Sometimes, "culture of poverty" arguments (Lewis, 1969) were used by interviewees or those referring to these citizens as a kind of "underclass" (Wilson, 1987) as distinct from the rest of the working class, but all the while blaming the situation on the Kirchner government.

> For me Cristina [Kirchner] hasn't done things badly. She's actually done things well, but the thing I object to is that they take resources off the people who kill themselves working, to then give to those who are destitute. I mean it's good to give to destitute people. However, with *Asignación Universal por Hijo* you can have seven or eight children they pay you for, and you never have to work again. It's an easy life!
>
> Veronica, 20, Piedras Blancas

Others argued that the government was "sending a message" that work doesn't pay and several – especially in Buenos Aires City – explained that it was bussing in the poor from the shanty towns to attend protest marches in exchange for *un chori y una coca* (a popular national delicacy, like a hotdog and coke). This phrase was repeated by several respondents, and whether or not completely true, the image reflected their embedded understandings of traditional Peronist clientelist practices toward the poor. Several criticized other aspects of the Kirchners' social policy and how it was "creating" rather than "reducing" poverty. This stood in contrast to the reality which was that poverty had fallen under the Kirchner governments from 50% in 2003, to 28% in 2007, to 25% in 2011, according to figures from prestigious and independent Catholic University of Argentina (Clarín, 2016).[11] While expectations of social change had generally been drastically reduced since 2002, the one exception was in terms of the generally high poverty levels in society, which the government was lambasted for by two-thirds of the interviewees and whom they held up to very high standards.

President Cristina Kirchner sometimes came in for a lot of criticism by those in the sample for allegedly wearing fashionable shoes or handbags, despite claiming to be helping the poor. These were references that were generally not made about male politicians and indicate an element of sexism in their discourse.

Other issues raised for opposition to the Kirchner governments included allegations that they were "vote-buying" (via the gifting of Argentinian passports to immigrants from surrounding countries), their failure to "control the unions" (see later), seeking to perpetuate their hold on power (with the transition from Néstor Kirchner to his wife, Cristina) and general corruption. The latter was mentioned by half of the interviewees. However, in all but two cases it was introduced in passing as a marginal issue, whereas it became a dominant rather than "in-passing" theme in the 2016 fieldwork (see later).

The fact that Argentinians had become highly tolerant of corruption was illustrated by the fact that on half of the occasions that it was mentioned as a problem, it was qualified with the positive changes that the government had made in the economy, almost as if to say "we know you are corrupt but so long as the economy is running well, we won't openly object to it."

> Things are progressing. The government is different from the Radicals in that sense. But in spite of that they are still corrupt. They are still stealing but within the grand scheme of things improving.
>
> Milagros, 30, Posadas

> There is a saying here. 'They are stealing from us but at least they are doing something good'. The current government steals less than the previous ones, but still steals you see? They haven't stopped doing it, but they are doing good things. It's something innate.
>
> Magalí, 36, Posadas

The Kirchner governments were deeply polarizing in their discourse and action. One of the problems that many analysts have pointed to, including Kirchneristas' own self-criticisms, was that they didn't seek to reach out sufficiently to unaligned sectors and instead tried to please their loyal supporter base too much (Filmus, 2016). This was evident from those struggling middle-class interview participants who felt alienated by the aggressive language and rhetoric that the Kirchner governments used, especially Cristina. They may be characteristics of charismatic "populist" leaders, but they didn't sit well with interviewees, nor did their recourse to executive powers or rule by presidential decree, (a constitutional right under Argentinian law), but one that was deemed "authoritarian" by several. Indeed, even though Presidents Menem and Macri frequently used presidential decrees too, this was overlooked by the same Kirchner critics.

> When the President speaks, she shouts. She is authoritarian. I don't need someone to sound like they are in the middle of an election campaign every time they speak to me or try to explain something.
>
> Graciela, 57, Buenos Aires

Meanwhile among *Kirchnerismo*'s harshest critics were those who accused it of having brought "communism" to Argentina, and for aligning with Hugo Chavez in Venezuela and other left-wing regimes. They spoke vitriolically about both Presidents Néstor and Cristina. One young man, whose mother was an ardent *kirchnerista,* described the endless arguments that they would engage in, to the point where discussing politics was banned in the household.

> [Néstor] Kirchner is loathsome, even in death. The day he died I ran out onto the balcony to celebrate! [Laughs].
>
> Federico, 26, Buenos Aires

The Tragic Hero: Struggling Middle-Class Victimhood as Neglected Citizens

In seeking to answer the demands of the 2001–02 uprisings and of social movements such as the *piqueteros, Kirchnerismo* used state benefits and workfare programs to extend social and economic citizenship rights to previously excluded sectors, such as the unemployed, informal workers and the poorest sectors of society. This post-neoliberal ethos (Wylde, 2016) distinguished them from traditional Peronist governments that had focused social coverage on formally employed labor. However, an unintended consequence was that many of the middle-class interview participants (who fell outside the scope of these plans) felt abandoned or neglected and thought that some of the values they held dear such as meritocracy, the right to private property and self-sufficiency were under attack. They were at pains to highlight that they didn't want to live off the state like their nemesis "the poor," but simultaneously expressed their anger that the state was supporting those who often didn't deserve it, while they themselves were capable of self-improvement without it.

> If they insist on giving the poor social plans so they can live, I don't understand why they don't also look to support the middle class, or say 'we'll do all we can to find you work.' Because unlike them [the poor] we don't sit here with our arms crossed waiting for money from above.
>
> Sofía, 31, Santa Fe

Daniela and Vanesa compare their own "worthiness" to that of the unemployed *piqueteros* in terms of the right to purchase a property. Daniela had lost her home several years earlier:

> When the piqueteros do their road-blocks to demand everything, you see them on their mobile phones sending messages. Now on the other hand there are people breaking their backs working and can't afford to buy a property. Something is wrong with the state. Today it's impossible to buy a house. Listen, sometimes we say to each other [pointing to her partner], 'I have my studio, let's sell it, get a mortgage and buy an apartment.' But there is no credit available. No credit. It is impossible here.
>
> Daniela, 59, Buenos Aires

> State aid? I'm against it [laughs]! I am against the kind of programmes that make people more ignorant. Now, if... if that support for example enables someone to buy a house, to help them to progress, then yes. There are professionals who don't have their own property, you see? But there are poor people who don't study, who have beautiful houses... But what about us professionals?
>
> Vanesa, 26, La Plata

Complaints were framed in terms of "those of us who work hard maintain the work-shy" via the governments system of social plans. Over half of the sample alluded to this in some form.

> Years ago, the social programmes helped people to find work. Nowadays a kind of assistentialism predominates. Working people work, but the government doesn't support them precisely because they work. The worker shouldn't be punished in order to grant gifts to the lazy.
>
> Martin, 50, Piedras Blancas

The poor were depicted as lazy and work-shy, and the widely repeated charge was made that the Kirchner government was encouraging this by them breeding a generation of children who never saw their parents work. However, these accusations did not stand up to scrutiny. For instance, around the time of the 2011 interviews, the level of employment among those with "low levels of education" (the group most targeted to receive state benefits) had increased in successive years from 63.6% in 2009, to 64.1% in 2010, to 64.9% in 2011 (INDEC database). This was in spite of the fact that these figures correspond to the precise years when Cristina Kirchner's government launched the AUH, which grated cash payments to unemployed people and those working below the minimum wage who have children (and to all families with disabled children). Second, in terms of the various social plans themselves, "paying the poor not to work" was simply a fallacy. AUH was a conditional cash program in which the payment would only be made if the parent made sure that their child complied with their vaccinations, maintained certain health standards and school attendance. *Jefes y Jefas de Hogar* (Heads of Household Benefit) worked on a similar basis, and often these programs helped to reduce unemployment by giving recipients enough of an income to be able to spend their time looking for work while paying for the basics for their children. Other plans such as *Manos a la Obra* and *Plan* (Plan Get to Work) and *Trabaja* (Work!) were workfare programs, generating employment for the jobless and poor through public works programs or assisting them with the creation of new cooperatives. Nevertheless, the point is that the idea of the government supporting the lazy became embedded for many and caused much indignation.

For many, their white, European origins, "middle-class status" and privileged ethnic backgrounds were precisely why they felt they were being discriminated against. In 2011, two-thirds of the 30 research participants saw themselves as "victims" of the Kirchner government. In stressing that it was "Peronist," they explained that Peronism was historically supportive of the non-European, *Mestizo* and *descamisado*.[12] In their discourse, respondents evoked the deep historical social fissures in Argentinian society which just as 70 years ago, existed in the form of symbolic racialized violence against internal "enemies" – the poor and the *piqueteros*. These were the same groups with whom many had marched on the streets a decade earlier. Other values and "rights" they held dear such as the freedom to circulate and get to work were also highlighted. Their victimhood and alleged "protection of the poor" by the authorities thus also adopted these incarnations.

> And that's another contradiction. Human rights. Human rights are for blacks [*negros*], not for all of us. If one of them kills me on the street corner, I was the 'victim of a mugging' and that's the end of it. If you grab one of these bastards and smash his head in, suddenly it's

all 'ah but what about his human rights?' Here you have to conform. But if you are *negro* the law won't touch you. The government has your back.

Hugo, 36, La Plata

If you are going somewhere and find the road closed off by a load of people with sticks and their faces covered [the piqueteros] they tell you 'you aren't getting through here.' But they are impeding my right to circulate! Who is going to defend *me*? No one.

Graciela, 57, Buenos Aires

Among many of the middle-aged participants in particular, their perception that they had been abandoned by the state was sufficient to contribute toward the loss of aspiration to reintegrate into the labor market or to even aspire for upward mobility again. It was as if they were saying, "if society's rules are stacked against me, why should I bother?" Politically, this led more to resignation than to the kinds of "deviant" or potentially illegal behavior and social disorder described by Merton (1968). However, as illustrated above, sometimes open racism and other behaviors that violated the norms of middle-class society started to creep in to their discourse and actions.

In the rural village of Piedras Blancas, the situation differed, and these attitudes were not in evidence. Rather, respondents there chose to emphasize utilizing their personal connections to the local political elite in order to obtain material favors or employment opportunities. There, it was seen as completely acceptable (largely due to the villagers' more intimate relationships with their political representatives), to appeal directly to the town Intendent for assistance – providing they were affiliated or sympathetic to his political party. The people I interviewed would tell me, "The neighbors over there are Radicals" or "You could talk to family x down the road, they are Peronists." Clientelism was seen as repugnant by the city dwellers in the impoverished middle-class sample. They explained that such strategies should be reserved for the "real poor" from whom they sharply distinguished themselves. Pursuing them was dismissed as "lacking merit" or as "anti-democratic."

The more sophisticated understanding of political citizenship that middle-class or new urban poor Argentinians had acquired (Mazzoni, 2008) and their cultural value of self-sufficiency inhibited these respondents from seeking access to state support through potentially advantageous political connections. However, this contrasted with the new *rural* poor in the village. A particular variant of clientelism existed here and was widely practiced. Villagers knew precisely what their possibilities were of eliciting a financial favor from the Intendent because he would already be aware of their political affiliation. Therefore, neither anger toward the national government nor the structural poor was in evidence to anywhere near the same degree, nor was the "retreatism" or "ritualism" associated with the breakdown of society's meritocratic rules to which they were a victim.

Having said all this, in the 2011 interviews (much less those of 2007), how they framed themselves as the "squeezed middle-class victim" and "neglected citizen" in the sense of a shared identity with potentially millions of others had not yet been forged. This is one of the reasons why their mass involvement in a protest movement for change (as an expression of their disagreement with their own financial circumstances and with how the government was "ruining" the country) had not emerged. So what was the process by which underlying discontent, fear and anger transformed into the mass mobilizations of 2012–13? How did such an identity crystallize and how did these ordinary citizens gain the confidence to engage in the protest actions that followed?

Anomie, Retreatism and Ritualism

Many also expressed a yearning to recover the material prosperity that they had enjoyed under Convertibility in the 1990s. Almost half of all participants complained that it was impossible to use socially acceptable means to achieve their desired living standards, although this was less pronounced among the young adults (only two of the seven under 30 years old felt this way). Older participants especially felt futility and despair, as their values of honesty and hard work were deemed to hold little currency. This despair had politically demobilizing consequences.

However, those with children described how they couldn't see many prospects for their own situation to improve due to the violation of these principles. Instead, they harbored hopes that children would be able to use their university degrees to achieve stability. In a number of cases, their adult children had emigrated to obtain success in their profession.

> Thinking of something that realistically I hope for given the little that I have… it'd be that my daughters have more than what I have had. That they can achieve what they deserve and not just be successful but also enjoy more stability in their lives than me.
>
> Agustina, 48, Buenos Aires

Almost all (23) mentioned how they felt Argentina's meritocratic society (another strongly held middle-class conviction) had been replaced by one which rewarded laziness, violence or corruption:

> It is as if here there is a mentality whereby an honest person is seen as a fool, while the one who screws everyone else is admired.
>
> Nicolas, 49, Buenos Aires

There was some disagreement about whether education, and particularly higher education, still had value in terms of achieving upward mobility and qualified jobs. Interestingly, here generally it was the younger Argentinians who were more pessimistic than their parents. Argentina's Minister for Education (2007–13) Daniel Filmus (1996) once described how education had become a "parachute where it was once a trampoline" for social mobility. This view was shared by many.

> Here in Argentina professionals don't earn anything, but in Chile if you have a professional title or university degree they actually value it.
>
> Vanesa, 26, La Plata

Responding to this Durkheimian *anomie* and a perceived breakdown of social norms, several adopted what Merton (1968) described as "retreatism" (rejecting the cultural goal of success and socially legitimate means of achieving it) or "ritualism" (accepting a lifestyle of hard work but rejecting the goal of monetary rewards). "Retreatism" had a distinct political dimension among our respondents because the reaction linked respondents' fates to the perceived discrimination against them as members of their social class. This encouraged them to differentiate themselves from those they saw as their social inferiors as a result. About two-thirds of participants (higher still among males) insinuated that traditionally excluded sectors of society were favored by the (then current) government of President Cristina Fernández de Kirchner, as its traditional and natural electoral constituency. The "generous" welfare and unemployment benefits they received, and supposed government impunity (despite acts of alleged corruption and criminality) were asserted.

Carolina spoke angrily about the injustice of being squeezed, although as a self-employed private English teacher most of her work involved payment in cash and a heavy dose of tax avoidance. She ominously predicts a social revolt against the government (which eventually occurred in 2012 and 2013):

> Something is going to explode at any moment. This government is giving out money, left, right and centre, take, take, take from the hardworking people who pay taxes. They are the ones who will rebel sometime soon because they are fed up with paying so that others can live for free.
>
> Carolina, 23 Piedras Blancas

One way that this anomie manifests itself was in terms of rebelling against the accepted social norms. A handful of interviewees used overtly racist language about structurally poor shanty town dwellers (who often have non-European origins). They linked that directly to pessimism about white middle-class prospects:

> This country is made for either those who have a load of money or those blacks [*negros*] who have nothing. The guy who works hard and wants to progress in life has no chance.
>
> Jorge, 36, La Plata

Such discourses became quantitatively more pronounced and more symbolically violent among the struggling middle-class interviewees between 2007 and 2011, especially among those who were living in more precarious financial or occupational conditions. As the macroeconomic context slowly deteriorated between 2007 and 2011, they felt their social position increasingly threatened "from below," so responded with increasing discursive contempt toward the structural poor. As traditional markers of social distinction (income, value of educational qualifications, recent job status, savings) eroded, they also became ever more desperate to emphasize how they were distinct from the "working class" or "traditional poor." The blurring of interclass boundaries is not a new phenomenon, but intensified after the 2001 crisis and, as we saw above, did so further still under the Kirchner governments' mandates. For instance, during this period, income and average purchasing power differentials between certain manual and clerical occupations eroded (Benza, 2016). The real-terms salaries of those with university degrees (including many of the impoverished middle class) fell by 26% between 2001 and 2010, yet for those with only primary education increased by 5% (INDEC database).

Growing Fear and Rhetoric against "the Other" as a Mobilizing Factor

On his television show *Filosofía, aquí y ahora*, the Argentinian philosopher and playwright, José Pablo Feinmann (2018) recently analyzed why the country's middle class had moved from their position of unity with the structural poor and unemployed in December 2001 under the slogan "¡piqueteros and caceroleros (pot-bangers), our struggle is the same!," to having identified this sector as an enemy a few years later.

He described this as the "Theory of Being," thus:

> The middle class faces an extremely harsh existential reality because it doesn't want to be what it is. Middle class. It wants to be something that it will never be. Upper class. But it is very fearful of becoming something that it isn't currently but could become. Lower class. Under these circumstances, what does it do? When the right-wing throws the middle class into poverty, the middle class unites with the poor and adopts that slogan. '¡piqueteros and caceroleros (pot-bangers), our

struggle is the same!' Populist governments come to power and the middle class is content until it starts to recover its purchasing power. At this point it gets tired of the populist government and unites with the upper class, which it believes it can become part of. Then, the upper class once again throws the middle class back into poverty, and the latter once again joins the poor to call for a populist government. The get out of this vicious circle the middle class must ask itself "who does it want to be? On whose side does it want to be?" once and for all. I would say that its destiny lies much closer with the 'poor class' than it believes. Because the upper class only ever governs in its own interests and if it has to send the middle class into poverty, it always will.

These processes were clearly observable during the 2007 and 2011 interviews. Since their 2001 unemployment or impoverishment, participants had recovered their consumption patterns and livelihoods (to varying degrees), albeit many were still struggling. Cross-class solidarity with the structural poor had virtually disappeared and had been replaced by fear and suspicion. All the while, as Gramsci would explain, they returned to believing that their class interests lay alongside those of the ruling class. The enemies whom the middle class identified with having caused their "fall" from the 2002 World Bank Survey, like the IMF, "globalization" and the banks, were barely mentioned in the 2007 or 2011 interviews. Instead, they were replaced with internal "enemies" – the poor and *piqueteros*, the same groups with whom many had marched a decade earlier.

Crime committed by the poor was mentioned by 14 of the 31 interviewees as their main preoccupation in 2011. Many uncritically repeated unsubstantiated related claims that certain mass media were propagating. Fear of crime is something that studies prove is grossly exaggerated in Argentina (UCA, 2017), but which tapped into deep-seated fears of "the other" that many middle-class citizens possessed. Making sense of their own disenfranchisement by articulating a consensus on how Argentina's modernity was being threatened by the presence of a *Mestizo* lower class (often as immigrants from Paraguay, Bolivia or Peru) and how this representation sought to reinforce the fading social difference between them through denying the latter its citizenship, was a theme that other researchers explored several years earlier (Guano, 2004) but appeared to have become what Gramsci calls "common sense" by 2011.

Tensions were aggravated further due to the fact that the personal interactions that those in the sample tended to have with structurally impoverished citizens were negative. They would see them blocking their road on a *piquete* protest or occasionally stealing from them. While Argentinian society provides channels for social integration, even if they shared a bus or a shopping queue, little actual interaction would take place. In the literature from the early 2000s, many impoverished middle-class participants described how their involvement in barter clubs, communal soup kitchens and other collective self-improvement actions acted as a mechanism through which the new poor began to meet with the long-term poor and working class, often for the first time. It helped to improve the image they had of each other. Improving the prospects for longer term cross-class solidarity partly depends on creating spaces for positive interactions and for facilitating mutual understanding.

In the rural village of Piedras Blancas, all but one of the six residents explained that crime wasn't a problem at all there, although they recognized that it was at a national level from what they saw in the media. Back in the urban centers, for some, these fears appeared to be stem from their concern about incursions on private property, sanctity of which was another deeply held (middle) class conviction.

> In general these foreigners come here from neighboring countries to usurp public spaces or do things that they shouldn't. Set up businesses in places you aren't allowed, or other land-grabbing practices. Then they go and demand money for housing which the state just cedes to.
>
> Graciela, 57, Buenos Aires

Others, especially older participants, associated the current immigrants from the Andean countries with "laziness." In this sense, the "other" was the work-shy non-Argentinian *Mestizo*, who they compared unfavorably with their countrymen/women. Conscious of their own European immigrant origins, those who made such critiques were careful to differentiate between the "immigrant" of the past, who upheld "Argentinian" values of hard work and honesty, with more recent immigrants who they associated with criminality. This concerned them because of how it placed in danger the country being able to achieve its national destiny as a modern country of progress that was headed toward the First World.

> No, no, the majority of immigrants don't work, eh? So how will the country progress that way? You can't! I'm telling you. People used to w-o-r-k. With what you earned you ate and lived. Nowadays they kick their kids out and teach them to be thieves or pickpockets. That is what we have to put up with today and it pains me because it is ruining the country.
>
> Julieta, 86, La Plata

The younger interviewees held more liberal attitudes with respect to immigration and the poor. However, the majority were more preoccupied about their personal safety than property:

> Today it's a struggle between social classes. I see it everywhere. You can't take anything new with you without someone pulling a gun on

you and threatening to kill you for two pesos. Today that is how things are. You have to keep your wits about you, it's complete insecurity.

Vanesa, 26, La Plata

Such fears transcended political alignment and were expressed, albeit more cautiously both among more "progressive" and avowedly "Kirchnerist" or left-wing interview participants and by friends and acquaintances in everyday conversations. Such sensibilities were conveyed more strongly in 2011 than in 2007.

Wishes to conceal their own economic decline and loss of membership of the middle class since the late 1990s, alongside their political alienation by the government, meant that many projected these fears onto the structural poor. There was evidence to support this Freudian "projection" which tends to come to the fore during political crises (Erikson, 1973:241), such as that Argentina was starting to experience during 2011 at the time of the interviews and which exploded on to the streets in 2012. They were defending themselves against their own unconscious impulses or qualities by participating in the symbolic violence used against the most marginalized in order to help grant themselves reassurance about the preservation of their own class position. The social bonds between the middle and other popular classes that proved the bedrock of the 2001 protests had broken down by 2011 and became a key theme of the 2012 protests. Those who had more negative views about the poor, depicting them as violent or criminals, also tended to be more strongly opposed to the Kirchner government, and generally held more conservative attitudes. For instance, they associated the shanty towns with sites of violence, crime and drugs and the poor people inhabiting them with the related character traits:

The problem with the shanty towns is the *people* who have moved there. Years ago, those who lived there were not thieves, but many started moving in and now more often than not it's the case.

Laura, 49, Buenos Aires

You know what? Those people don't work. They don't work, they are thieves, or they live off the social plans... Jefes y Jefas. Don't tell me that they don't have enough money, they have mobile phones, television sets, MP3 players and everything.

Daniela, 59, Buenos Aires

Several explained that the poor were once noble, but more recently had become much more violent and engaged in criminal behavior.

The poor bloke of yesteryear worked, knew how to read and write and sent his kids to school... Today's doesn't know how to read or write. He drugs himself up, he's an alcoholic so reproduces the next generation who will be even poorer. Before they would rob you in your home and say 'sir, kindly sit there,' then leave. And you'd sit there swearing and thinking 'he's robbing me but it will be ok.' Today they will just kill you for any old reason.

Jorge, 36, La Plata

There was more sympathy offered to two kinds of "poor people." First, young children. They were painted as innocent, unlike their parents who were often accused of being responsible for their children's plight. Second, those "poor" in the rural areas of Argentina's northern provinces. They were understood to be "genuine" because they were apparently not involved in crime and survived in conditions of indigence that participants felt ashamed of. Very few interviewees practiced acts of solidarity with the structural poor that moved beyond donating to charity or giving money to beggars or *ambulantes* (street traders).

Tellingly, many participants seemed visibly uncomfortable when I asked them what they felt they had in common with the shanty town poor. For the reasons explained by Feinmann earlier, several shied away from the question. Others failed to provide a single characteristic. Those mentioned tended to be somewhat abstract like "we both hope for a brighter future," whereas only three mentioned shared financial difficulties such as not being able to afford to buy a house, or that they have to both work for a living.

This breakdown in social solidarity also extended to protest movements. While only four interviewees explained that they had never sympathized with the *piqueteros* in any form (neither their demands, nor methods), nine expressed how they had been sympathetic or supportive of the *piqueteros* during the 2001 crisis, and also in the 1990s with the initial roadblocks began. Framed in "citizenship" terms of "liberal democracy," there was general agreement that the unemployed had the right to have their basic needs covered and to be provided with work. However, their concern for the protection of such rights for the *piqueteros* had since been superseded by their own anger that their "right" to freely move around the city themselves in order to be able to arrive at their workplace and exercise their "right to work" was being infringed by their constant roadblocks. One participant described their protest methods as "a revolutionary car tax against the middle class" (Laura, 49, Buenos Aires). All but two participants held negative views about them overall, this one being typical:

The more road-blocks you participate in, the more you get paid. They'll take you by bus. It's bad, really bad that they allow these guys to cover their faces and carry sticks. What the piqueteros do -and I'm not saying that their demands aren't just rather the *way* that they make them- they annoy so many people who *are* working... What you are restricting is the right to freedom of transit.

Graciela, 57, Buenos Aires

Some fragments of the "spirit of 2001" remained among these nine. For them, this notion that the average unemployed person's protest was initially "virtuous" but had become discredited over the years (especially due to their "manipulation" by *piquetero* and party leaders) was present. Several were concerned that those whose motives were "genuine," could not get their voices heard, so the roadblock was a legitimate tool in the collective repertoire of action (Tilly, 1986). In this sense, beliefs in autonomism and principle of self-organization (free from political party control), to which many subscribed in 2001–02 endured.

> I agree with many of their [*piquetero*] positions. But the time has arrived to look for other forms [of protest]. The road block has served its purpose, nowadays people are fed up with them. I believe that as a society we are too used to the 'now' culture. 'If you don't give me it now, I will block the road, I will protest against you, I'll occupy your building.' But for me this method has gone out of fashion.
>
> Brian, 37, Rosario

In particular, the *piqueteros* elicited greater sympathy when their demands centered on "work" or to "improve a school" (which interviewees labeled as "genuine" demands) as opposed to assistentialist claims for food (in accordance with their cherished value of self-improvement). The harshest critiques against them concerned the fact that as a handful alleged, they were able to earn more for being a *piquetero* than they were for having a paid job, thus violating their meritocratic principles. There was a greater tendency among those who lived in Buenos Aires City and La Plata (in Greater Buenos Aires) to depict them as violent. Tolerance was generally greater in the Provinces, perhaps because roadblocks were less frequent or were less of an inconvenience.

Fears about insecurity, the poor, violence, crime and drugs among the struggling middle class and their growing anger at the *piqueteros'* conduct had paradoxical impacts on their political mobilization. Post-2003 they served to divide the subaltern classes and demobilize the resistance as the solidarity of 2001–02 eroded. Then, during the Blumberg protests of 2004 and 2006, they became central to the struggling middle class' defensive political demands and acted as a mobilizer. Later, during fieldwork between 2007 and 2011 they became pent up frustrations before providing the fuel that set the 2012 and 2013 anti-government protests alight. The reasons for this will be discussed later on.

Deteriorating Sense of Community

Another theme to emerge that played against prospects for collective action during the period was the declining levels of trust in fellow citizens, or sense of neighborhood or national community. Certainly, the growing fear of crime generally made participants more suspicious of others and less likely to unite to take action in their collective defense. About half of the sample also perceived that they were being tricked or cheated in some way by broad sectors of society (taxi drivers in terms of the fare they were charged, salespeople knocking on their door, which tradespeople to use in their homes etc.). The notion that tricksters were endemic in Argentina's society from the political elites to educated white-collar criminals was famously depicted in the multi-award winning film *Nueve Reinas* (Bielinsky, 2000).

The idea that there was "no sense of community" in their neighborhood or that it was in decline was especially potent in Buenos Aires City and La Plata (Buenos Aires province). Several cited disputes that they had had with neighbors, but others explained that the sense of community was stronger in their (more isolated and rural) towns of origin, or in the provinces where they lived. A handful reported being involved in defensive campaigns with other neighbors to remove street artists, to install traffic lights or to protect themselves against spates of robberies. Many described how during the 2001 crisis both at the neighborhood and national level, citizens came together to confront their poverty but that since then society had become more fractured and individualistic.

> In the fight for survival, solidarity doesn't exist. People have become more… closed to outsiders and more insular within their homes. Crises takes their toll on families. They close down too. When a country goes to hell the people within it are left fighting among themselves.
>
> Santiago, 60, Buenos Aires

While a minority in the cities spoke about how they still believed that there was a community spirit where they lived, they also confessed that this rarely extended to communal acts of solidarity. Instead, it was confined to exchanging pleasantries and the odd favor with neighbors. Once again, the experience in Piedras Blancas village was distinct. There, neighbors unanimously described how there was a close-knit community (albeit slightly weaker than in years past) and strong social bonds. Crime was also reported to be low. The villagers were conscious of how their own situation compared to that of city dwellers, where crime was believed to be endemic.

The one caveat to this was the fierce, almost tribal political rivalry between the Radicals and Peronists in the village. Although there are historical fissures between supporters of these political forces, its manifestation in the village seems to emanate from the "all or nothing" scenario relating to "linking social capital" (Aldrich, 2012) and the fact that the villagers understood that the all-powerful Intendent would only offer support to those aligned to *his* political party. This problem seemed to have become more acute in recent years.

> It's a town with a lot of solidarity. If there is a problem we will all be there to help. We all know each other you see? In that sense things are great. But politics has diluted Piedras Blancas' solidarity. Before we were more united. We would all go to the match together, there would be events laid on, we'd all help each other out. But today there are political arguments that we never used to have.
>
> Diego, 42, Piedras Blancas

Micaela (50, Piedras Blancas) who was sympathetic to the incumbent Kirchner (Peronist) government provided an insightful example of just how ingrained the problem was:

> The Intendent is my cousin but he would never help me as he's a Radical. So I don't even bother asking.

Although the dynamics of political mobilization didn't exist in the same sense as they did in the cities, collective self-help activities were plentiful. Both the income data from World Bank Survey from 2002 and the interviewees themselves suggested that inequality was significantly lower in rural than in the urban areas. Class antagonisms were virtually nonexistent. There was only one person in the village whose property size and occupational status exceeded everyone else – The Intendent. Meanwhile, there were few boundaries (real or imagined) between those in the "middle" and "lower classes." For example, the nearest city (Paraná) was 80 km away and the village's shops sold no ostentatious goods, fashionable clothes or electronics. Living standards and access to culture and services were thus almost the same for all the villagers.

> Here in Piedras Blancas there are not two social classes. Just one. Here it is a poor society, I mean we are all equal.
>
> Micaela, 50, Piedras Blancas

> For me, everyone is the same here. Piedras Blancas doesn't have shanty towns… our village is our village. Nothing more, nothing less.
>
> Veronica, 20, Piedras Blancas

This sense of togetherness meant that people came together more in tough times. Collective protests in the village were almost unheard of due to its lack of proximity to decision-making centers and also because people would be easily identifiable (so it would create confrontation). The paternalistic society also had other manifestations which seemed to reduce any possibilities of collective action. For example, one of the most upsetting interviews I did was with 42-year-old Diego, who described himself as "self-made." Just a few weeks before meeting him, he had lost his wife to illness and now had to raise three children alone. Things got worse for Diego. He'd also recently been laid off from his Head of Production job at the village factory, where he had worked for 15 years. When interviewed, I noticed that he was sporting a t-shirt emblazoned with the logo of the very company that had made him redundant and caused so much hardship and anxiety for his family in their lowest ebb. When questioned about this, he explained that he maintained a sense of loyalty to the factory that was the industrial backbone of his small community. The way he described his redundancy was somewhat self-deprecating and without a hint of ill-feeling:

> Although the factory sacked me, I gave my life for it. I put in many, many hours, working continually and I suppose at some point I was no use to them anymore and they had to get rid of me. Or maybe I couldn't adjust to their new practices. I still love the company and wish it all the best because it's our crown jewel. When things go well for the factory, it benefits all of us in the village.
>
> Diego, 42, Piedras Blancas

The "Hidden Grammar" of 2001 and Autonomism

Several years after the crisis, Ana Dinerstein (2014) described how many of the demands expressed in *¡que se vayan todos!* by new "non-conformist subjectivities" came to be echoed in the Kirchner governments' 2003–15 political agenda through the recomposition of power and the establishment of a neo-hegemonic project. However, she also added that, on the other hand, although many of the radical forms of political involvement and participation from the 2001 to 2002 movements were de-radicalized and integrated into the National Popular project via cooptation or policies of appeasement (and less so via repression), not all could not be fully integrated into the logic of the state. She explained that it left behind a "space with no grammar, as an excess, as dissensus, as an anticipation of the unnameable alternative. Thus, both disagreement and hope remain the "hidden transcripts" in the grammar of the political recovery following the crisis."

One of the features of the post-2001 social movements was the profound skepticism toward the state and all of its institutions, including those that were part of the superstructure such as political parties of the Left and the trade unions. Among interview participants, the state was generally still viewed negatively and tainted with corruption. Some described how it is never there to help them. Others were repulsed by its exclusionary corporatist structures. The attempts to avoid engagement with it (as championed by many of the key "autonomist" movements) because it was so enmeshed with corrupt practices at all levels persisted for some.

> Wherever the state is involved there are problems. They [the Kirchners] changed certain policies but politicians didn't stop stealing, they didn't stop lying.
>
> Daniela, 59, Buenos Aires

In terms of which mobilizing vehicles were preferred as a channel for either existing or possible future political involvement, just as in 2001–02, a preference was manifested for loosely based self-organized collectives, and for all but the two political party activists among the interviewees, the latter were generally frowned upon and described as "little businesses" or lacking values because ideals have to be compromised to belong to them. Far-left parties barely appeared on interviewees' radar. They were only mentioned by a handful at all, and even then they were associated with the same dogmatism and sectarianism that they were in 2001.

> And I am sick of the Argentinian Left. Because it has created seventy three Lefts. Because every idiot goes and sets up a 'new left' you see? The Partido Obrero, El Partido Trabajador, El Partido of I don't know what. The Party that works and does solicarity acts, the Party that will never get anywhere because of the 70,000 fragments of the same thing. So you end up saying "no, I'm fed up with it".
>
> Jorge, 36, La Plata

Kirchnerismo (mis)translated the ideals of the 2001–02 revolt into the preexisting political superstructure (anti-establishmentism, rejection of neoliberalism, support for cooperative working, greater distribution of wealth, more control to workers and national industry, opposition to international financial capitalism). However, it also co-opted these ideals into the traditional Peronist infrastructure that was at the heart of the very "establishment" that the rebellion diametrically opposed. Such translation was thus antagonistic. About one-sixth of those interviewed described how they believed that one day, through collective action from below, a more democratic society could be constructed that rejected all "representative" structures (including political party machines and the "hegemony" of Peronism).

> I think the political class is set for retirement. There has to be a political renewal. I am excited by the movements of young people too, who are saying 'we are from a different age, with a different vision,

and we live in a different world to yours.' I mean I really believe that it's different to in the past when people would say 'today's youth are distinct.' This time it's for real... Out with the old faces!

Romina, 21, Rosario

Another legacy of the 2001 revolt was the cynicism toward the idea that the trade unions could act as a potential mobilizing vehicle for their "class interests." QSVT also encapsulated a repudiation of the unions (in particular, the union bureaucracies) and according to the survey data in Chapter 3, they were the institution to *least* recover confidence among the struggling middle class in the years following the crisis. But how did they fare between 2007 and 2011?

Revulsion toward the Unions

While writing this book in 2018, I happened to have meetings with several of Argentina's trade union leaders for a project on "the International Network for Comparative Analysis of Social Inequalities" (INCASI) in Latin America and Europe, funded by the European Commission. After one particular interview with Roberto Baradel, leader of the teachers' trade union in Buenos Aires Province, SUTEBA I shared a photo of the two of us on social media. Despite being met with lots of "likes," I also received a handful of private messages from "concerned" middle-class friends and acquaintances in Argentina. In one instance, I was told "I only wish they would bomb all the Argentinian trade unionists." Where did this indignation come from? After all, the trade unions are, objectively speaking, the only organ which collectively represents and mobilizes to defend the interests of working people. Is it possible for the unions to become a mobilizing vehicle for struggling middle-class interests?

The unions, and in particular their leaders, were generally held in very low regard among the sample. This view appeared to be fueled by regular demonization in the corporate media, memories of how a large part of the union movement colluded with the Menem government to effect socially damaging neoliberal policies in the 1990s, Peronist hegemony within the union movement via the CGT's corporatist relationship with the government (that many frowned upon) and the generalization to all "trade unionists" of the excessive practices (alleged corruption, ostentatious forms of dress or travel etc.) of certain leaders, especially Hugo Moyano, the leader of the CGT at the time.

Two-thirds of those spoken to held a negative image of the unions with "lazy," "self-interested," "nepotistic," "mafias" or "thugs" being the most common ways that union leaderships were described. Such depictions filtered through to "trade unionists" in general, with few interviewees able to distinguish between the leaderships and rank and file union members in their discourse. Such opinions were expressed most vehemently in

Buenos Aires City and La Plata (Greater Buenos Aires) and interestingly among women too, perhaps because they were most repelled by their perceived "aggressive" rhetoric and actions. There was an overwhelming feeling that the unions did not "represent" them.

> No, no! None of them represent me nor other workers. They represent trade unionists, no one else. And they are, errr worse thieves than the government is... there are people there who don't work, or don't want to, yet they earn more than the President. Take a look at the kinds of car they drive.
>
> Franco, 35, Posadas

Interestingly, even among some of the Kirchner government sympathizers or Peronists, they didn't have a good standing.

> It annoys me that they don't consult their members. I joined the strikes when I was a member out of obligation. If you refuse they will give you a hiding... The only thing I don't agree with this government about is that they are very close to the trade unions. It seems to me that the current ones don't represent the worker, only themselves.
>
> Brian, 37, Rosario

> They are layabouts. I have seen it myself. Here in the neighborhood they use the union for their own enrichment. They are layabouts.
>
> Diego, 42, Piedras Blancas

Moyano was singled out for especially harsh treatment. However, as the main face of the union movement, it was unsurprising that their view of unions generally was tainted by what they thought of him. I must have heard him being called every name under the sun. This was perhaps the worst:

> Moyano is a criminal, a mafia baron and a murderer.
>
> Carlos, 78, Buenos Aires

On several occasions, hatred of him and other union leaders seemed to be because of their humble origins. Participants jealousy may have owed to a perceived violation of their meritocratic values and individualism. A working-class truck driver had achieved wealth and power, thanks to his position in the union and collective efforts.

> He is a cretin. Does it seem right to you that his entire family can become millionaires because he is leader of the transport workers union?
>
> Julieta, 86, La Plata

I can't believe that such a badly spoken and uneducated bully has so much power.

> Vanesa, 26, La Plata

Others felt that the unions were too influential and that the government had lost control of them. Some conjured up images of Frankenstein's monster:

If the state creates a monster, feeds it and then it grows stronger, of course it will end up being consumed by it. The government is also scared because the unions have brought down governments before. You can't give the unions the same power as the President, but this is what has happened here.

> Graciela, 57, Buenos Aires

Some interviewees (one-quarter) were more charitable or nuanced in their perspectives, distinguishing between the notion of unions as positive, yet how they conducted their affairs in practice as highly questionable.

In theory, the idea of a trade union of people who come together to defend their interests is excellent, but not how they work in Argentina. Here they are merely branches of Mafia Central, Moyano. In my day, sixty years ago the railway workers and other unions that originated in socialism were clean, not like today.

> Carlos, 78, Buenos Aires

Laziness is the first thought that comes to mind! Corrupt! Frauds! Look, a trade union that is well implemented is another thing altogether but the ones they made here in Argentina are thieves and layabouts.

> Vanesa, 26, La Plata

Opinions tended to improve when asked about their own experience of having benefited or not from unions in their own workplace.

They fight for themselves, not for the people... I don't feel that any trade union represents me... However, in my union there is this guy who has been leader for thirty years. We get on well. He's never got his family involved or anything, and yes it's true that he really has done some good things.

> Cristina, 59, Buenos Aires

There also seemed to be a lot of stereotyping and lack of awareness about the diversity of the union movement. For instance, only three were aware that the CTA confederation existed separately from the CGT and that it was non-politically aligned and non-Peronist in ideology. All unions were "tarnished" with the same brush.

Only two participants were highly supportive of the unions, going as far as to criticize the media's demonization of trade unionists. One was currently a trade unionist and had been a trucker in the past, another was the young woman who was an activist in the *Santiago Pampillón Front*. She didn't belong to a union but took a more objective view of what they could do for her and exploited workers.

> Yes, the unions represent me. I don't belong to one as I work informally but I think their role is very important. For instance, I had a friend who worked in an ice cream parlour nearby and they didn't have a trade union. They were working long hours and sometimes weren't paid. Yet when they tried to form one my friend was sacked for her involvement and she had to take her ex-employer to court to win the case.
>
> Romina, 21, Rosario

A further five were moderately supportive. This was based on the fact that their own union had previously won them improvements to their pay and conditions.

> Yes, at the moment they are fighting for us, the teachers. Sometimes less so if they are aligned with the government, but our one is doing a good job and is gaining things for us.
>
> Lucía, 63, Posadas

In summary, the reputation that the unions held, especially among middle-aged and older workers, was abysmal. This negative image and partly due to the kinds of jobs interviewees had (self-employment, working informally, being retired) meant that their own involvement in unions was limited, so few were mobilized by them to participate in collective actions. The exceptions were specific sections of workers, such as the teachers (there were four teachers in the group and they held the unions in highest esteem due to the salary gains they had made themselves). However, it is unlikely that they will become a key mobilizing vehicle for the struggling middle class in future. The general lack of faith in any kind of organization or institution that claimed to represent them persisted from the 2001 revolt. Individualist conceptualizations of self-improvement were favored, as opposed to that of collective self-organization, in defense of their interests that predominated a decade earlier.

What Kinds of Political Mobilization were Favored?

Interviewees were somewhat cynical about the potential for "self-organized" protest to both be free of external manipulation or control or for it to bring about real change. Thus, they expressed a preference for participating in protests where direct achievements could be seen. Those that could be conducted from the privacy of their homes or computer screens like petitions or protest blackouts were favored. Between 2007 and 2011 demobilization was not absolute, and not all collective solutions and social movements were scorned upon. For example, while it was perhaps unsurprising that only one interviewee actively participated in the 2008 Countryside Conflict protests (as they tended remain localized and take the form of roadblocks by countryside workers themselves other than the main protest in Buenos Aires), they did garner significant support among the sample, including from those who sympathized with the Kirchner government on most other issues. The scale of the proposed increase in export taxes was widely deemed to be unjust. But there were also other factors that generated political mobilization that social movements should consider when considering how to stimulate involvement from struggling middle-class citizens in future:

Belief in Moral Not Economic Causes

Violations of perceptions of *political* citizenship rather than its social or economic components were more likely to mobilize them into joining collective protests and other political actions, corroborating earlier work by Mazzoni (2007). Certainly, the middle-class value of "self-sufficiency" appeared embedded in their belief systems. For this reason, a large majority expressed how either their own economic grievances or those of others should be dealt with through "hard work" and "personal responsibility" rather than political demand-making (see more later). However, they highlighted how they were more likely to join collective protest actions if civil or political rights were attacked or if motivated by a deep sense of injustice or moral causes. Laura held negative views about those whom in her opinion protested for "financial self-interest," but then gave examples of under what circumstances she would take part herself:

> If it were a question of human rights, then yes. Anything to do with the AMIA or the Israeli Embassy bombings, and I'm not even Jewish. The right to life for me, and human rights. Those are what I believe in.
>
> Laura, 49, Buenos Aires

Santiago echoed her belief:

> Here you can only fight for yourself, or at best I'd take to the streets if there was some kind of massacre. Those are the only cases where I'd go out to demand justice. Because I'd be defending a matter of life or death.
>
> Santiago, 60, Buenos Aires

The exception to this, and where the violation of social rights *did* ignite particular anger, was perceived gender discrimination. This was mentioned by all of the middle-aged women. Intersectional discrimination against older and female workers was widely experienced, and by some of the young adults in relation to labor market opportunities especially. In a country where the gender pay gap was 30% in 2011 (INDEC), these grievances were justified.

Curiously, these wouldn't manifest themselves as political mobilization until the enormous *Ni Una Menos* (Not One Less) protests in 2015–16, following the gruesome femicides of teenagers Chiara Paez and Lucía Perez that shocked the nation. This galvanized activists and non-activists alike and raised awareness of the extent of domestic violence and other elements of gender inequality in society. It also helped raise awareness of more subtle discrimination that women face. Protests occurred again in June and August 2018 during the two million-strong protests to legalize abortion, as parliamentarians voted in the Chamber of Deputies (in favor) and Chamber of Senators (against), respectively. Having stayed in touch with some of the research participants on social media, several of the women attended these. The debate on both sides was framed in terms of "saving lives." The anti-abortion campaign's main slogan was "Save both lives!" (that is to say that of the fetus) and the pro-abortion campaign emphasized "legal abortion to not die!" (emphasizing the hundreds of deaths of pregnant women who seek clandestine abortions). The idea of "death" has been a mobilizing frame that has had huge resonance in Argentina, including in commemorations of the 30,000 disappeared from the military dictatorship (1976–83). It would certainly be a useful one for the future movements of the impoverished middle class to utilize, as it was in Greece following the suicide of a Greek chemist, a 77-year-old Dimitris Christoulas in 2012, an impoverished middle-class citizen[13] who had grown depressed at his condition and that of his family and the nation, sparking enormous anger and huge nationwide protests.

Support for Solidarity Economy Projects that Involve Work and Self-Sufficiency

While the perceived assistentialism of the state's social plans was heavily condemned, attempts by people to come together and either protest for "work" or to use their initiative in collective self-improvement projects were roundly supported. Respondents reacted positively to the idea of fired employees occupying and then taking over their bankrupt firms and factories to save their own jobs and the practice of worker-recovered companies.

> I saw how the workers recovered the Zanon plant in Neuquén where I am from. You'd see how the people who worked there

would sell the tiles and got the factory back on its feet without the old owner. But that's what I like. That they protested and said 'I want to work because I need to!' Not 'give me more money, I don't want to grow!'

Vanesa, 26, La Plata

While many no longer believed in collective "protest," they viewed collective self-help initiatives such as barter clubs as a means of survival in a positive light. Where people are willing to work themselves out of their difficulties either on their own or alongside others, there was commendation.

The need to help each other in order to recover from a crisis is crucial. Standing on the others' neck in order to get ahead does no one any favors. That's how we got into the mess we are today. In crisis I mean. No, no, [if there were another crisis tomorrow] I would take part in barter, community purchasing and all of that.

Romina, 21, La Plata

However, such was the level of distrust of "the other" that certain respondents, like Santiago and Laura, were adamant that they could only rely upon themselves, and upon private coping strategies in future.

Seeing is Believing: Social Movement Participation

Returning to social movement theory, citizens must believe that change can happen through collective action to prompt their participation (McAdam, 1982). Outside the minority who were Kirchner government supporters, the sense of deflation and disillusionment since 2001 left many deterred from involvement in further political mobilization. However, where participants had seen concrete, visible examples of how protests or solidarity economy activities had made tangible changes to their communities or to national policy, it restored faith and sometimes prompted a reconnection to protest movements that had been absent for the best part of a decade, even among the most cynical. This woman emphasized the organic nature of a protest that she witnessed, that couldn't be manipulated for partisan reasons by parties or *punteros* because it happened on the spot:

During the blackouts last summer we went out into the street and blocked the road. We blocked the road! Everyone applauded the *cacerolazo* we did from their balconies. But it was a spontaneous thing you see? A form of protesting 'right now' and at least last time we did it, they turned the lights back on.

Daniela, 59, Buenos Aires

Julieta (86, La Plata) also described how impressed she was at how the local neighborhood assembly had made real changes to the parks, squares and public areas. Generally, those living in cities like Rosario, where participatory budgeting had been operating for a number of years, were impressed with the changes they had made. While there was a broad consensus that the idea of greater citizen participation in society was needed and that popular or neighborhood assemblies could play a role, very few took the idea of direct democracy seriously in of itself. Unlike in 2001, there was also a consensus around the fact that this process could only feed in to helping strengthen the failing representative democracy as opposed to replacing it altogether.

> I have some experience. In Rosario where I'm from we had the Participatory Budget. My city was where the project was first applied... and it works well... We can devolve certain decisions to a participatory model, erm but others not. I mean you can't debate macroeconomic issues and gain the influence of many more people because it is impractical... But certain elements and features could be incorporated for sure.
>
> Franco, 35, Posadas

Connected to this idea of needing "confidence" in order to engage in protest movements was that of the critical mass. Conducting passive forms of protest from one's own home were preferred by most, but some only joined street protests if they were convinced that the desired change would happen once enough people were already involved in it.

> The kind of protests where you make noise, switch off your lights, put out a flag, yes I take part in those. But not in those where... you can't see the results, or which won't actually change anything.
>
> Carlos, 78, Buenos Aires

The idea of citizens needing to recover the confidence that they are capable of changing things through their own firsthand experience of being part of improvements to their local area or policymaking was perhaps best summed up by one of the youngest of all those interviewed when he proposed that

> When people start to participate, to search for alternatives, it is then that they realize there is another way of doing things. It doesn't mean having to protest or cause a riot to solve a problem. I believe that eventually the people will win out because they will realize that their involvement is true and can change things.
>
> Matias, 21, Posadas

From Passive Dissidence to Anti-Government Mobilization (2012–15)

The anti-government protests of 2012 and 2013 marked a turning point in the political mobilization of the struggling middle class. To reiterate, there were a range of opinions and attitudes held by those within this stratum, but during the third fieldwork period in 2016, interviewees feelings had become overwhelming cynical by this time. A considerable majority of interviewees (especially in Buenos Aires where several hundred thousand-strong marches occurred), either supported or actually participated in the anti-government *cacerolazos* of those two years. Why and how was their passive dissidence that we observed earlier transformed into active collective protest?

In earlier interviews, many referred precisely to the fact that they needed to feel more confidence to do so. To rebel without a critical mass would be pointless. For instance, the following analogy represented the feelings of many:

> My relations in the USA always ask me 'why I don't rebel?' Well one feels a certain degree of impotence. Imagine that you are shepherding cows, sheep or whatever. You bring them along with you and they all follow. None of the animals rebels because they know that the consequences of doing so would be immediate and dangerous.
>
> Carlos, 78, Buenos Aires

For this reason, in 2011 a second element of the theory (the belief that they could bring about change; McAdam, 1982) was virtually absent among those in the sample who were critical of the government. Thus, the 2011 fieldwork period seemed to mark a time of "testing the water" for many of those interviewed, as they experimented with how far their anti-government feelings were tolerated or shared by making subtle comments in public exchanges – until such time that the depth of feeling became well established on the streets the following year.

When initially social media, then the corporate media, started to publicize the 2012 and 2013 protests, commitment to participating in them quickly snowballed as it was evident that the necessary critical mass they had been waiting for had been reached. Another factor that transformed this passive dissidence into mobilization was that between the fieldwork period and the 2012 protests, oppositional actors established diagnostic framing processes to attribute and personalize blame toward President Cristina Kirchner for middle-class citizens' underlying sense of political neglect. For instance, Jorge Lanata's fiercely anti-government TV show, *Periodismo Para Todos* (Journalism for Everyone) principally watched by a middle-class audience, launched in 2012 and quickly gained millions of viewers just weeks before the first anti-government mobilizations. His show launched several investigations into alleged government corruption and mocked and demonized the president and her aides.

It thus served, on the one hand, as a rallying point to help such citizens to understand that their grievances were shared by millions of others, and on the other, it legitimized their discontent and gave them the confidence to join collective actions that were initially organized via social media in 2012. For instance, by this time, it was felt that government-linked corruption had permeated virtually every orifice of society. Federico (32), who by 2016 had gained a PhD yet was working in a series of precarious jobs and was only able to save because he continued to live with his mother, explained how he felt about working in an education project for a water company:

> The project was very erratic. It was obvious that they were stealing funds and using dirty money. The woman who coordinated the project was a friend of the Company President. So, everyone assumed (not just me) that it was Julio de Vido's laundered funds. That made me feel very uncomfortable all the time I worked there... I felt very stressed and guilty about it too.

De Vido was Public Planning Minister during the three Kirchner administrations and is currently imprisoned for corruption.

For others, their hatred of the Kirchners related to an existential fear that they would lose their homes or other aspects of their (middle) class status. From having been "neglected citizens" in 2007 and more so in 2011, between then and 2016, panic and rumors abounded that the Kirchners could become responsible for nothing less than their social fall. As fanciful as it sounded, everything seemed to link back to them. Agustina joined the *cacerolazo* protests in 2012 and 2013:

> The parents of an acquaintance of mine from secondary school died. She was a professional translator. She had no siblings or children and was single. Their house was sold in an auction as they owed money and she ended up on the streets. Then the translation company she worked for closed. A year later she ended up in a lunatic's asylum (sic) and then a hospital, but when she was discharged had nowhere to live. So, my question is 'where is all the money they stole that could have saved her?' I'm not saying everyone is to blame as we all have things to do, but this [Kirchner] government is terrible.
>
> Agustina, 53, Buenos Aires

The sensation of crime and insecurity identified earlier from 2007 and 2011 remained a central theme in their narratives. Only this time, once again interviewees were even more adamant that the Kirchner governments were at fault. Criminals were believed to have free reign to rule as they wished. Recounting a news story from that week, Carlos lamented,

Kirchnerism was the worst government that Argentina has ever had. It corrupted the people and turned them into degenerates. It is their fault that nowadays people defend criminals. 'How could they kill that petty thief?!' But it's the thief who kills loads of people every day, thousands dead due to them but if you kill a thief, like that doctor who was mugged did last week, just you see what happens. They made him buy a house for the kid's mother just to so he could avoid going to jail!

Carlos, 82, Buenos Aires

It was common for participants to continue to embellish the specter of the historic civilization vs barbarity social fissure and how the Kirchners' represented the latter to their detriment. As educated, white citizens of European origin, most of the interviewees viewed their administrations as having worked against their interests, for the benefit of the poor, backward *Mestizo*. Another participant who joined the 2012–13 anti-government protests stated,

Those who supported Cristina were not intellectuals or… professionals. Anyone would support her for a *choripán* [hot dog] and 200 pesos [15 dollars]. I mean if you take a look at who she is surrounded by, it's the poor. Whenever she spoke at the Pink House, guess who was there outside screaming her name with adulation?

Daniela, 63, Buenos Aires

Certainly, if the underlying grievances were present in government opponents' discourse in the 2011 interviews, it was not yet highly personalized against President Cristina Kirchner in the way that it would become by 2012. The interviews were conducted shortly before her re-election (when she gained 54% of the votes in the presidential runoff) and as a figurehead she remained popular among the general public. Yet in later (2016) interviews, she became the clear target, and the way that they described her became increasingly venomous between 2011 and 2016. As Daniela added, "that bitch did nothing right." Mass oppositional movements tend to be more successful when a defined "enemy" is identified as "responsible" for injustices. This is what Cristina de Kirchner became.

While these protests in 2012 and 2013 were not officially organized by any political party (something that appealed to interviewees), and did not effect immediate change as President Kirchner's government remained rather intransient. However, they did set in motion a series of events in the realm of high politics which culminated in an attempt to answer many of their demands.

Electoral opposition was completely divided in 2011, but the 2012–13 mobilizations prompted the realization that a grassroots movement, antagonistic to the government, existed and required a channel that would unite these forces at the ballot box. Initially, a Broad Front (UNEN) alliance formed, between the Civic Coalition (CC-ARI) headed by one of the protests movements' most outspoken advocates, Elisa Carrió, together with other parties that enjoyed significant support among middle-class voters (including its historic electoral outlet, the UCR and the Socialist Party). When UNEN was dissolved in mid-2015, enough headwind had been generated for CC-ARI and UCR to join Governor of Buenos Aires City Mauricio Macri's conservative *Republican Proposal* (PRO) Party to form *Cambiemos* (Let's Change), uniting the political center with the right. This alliance then came to power in December 2015 and presented the demands of the 2012–13 protests – ending corruption, inflation, crime and currency controls – as its flagship manifesto pledges. "The Happiness Revolution is underway!" boomed Mauricio Macri amid a sea of yellow election campaign balloons moments after being declared the new president.

To this extent, following the 2012–13 protests, Argentina's middle class renewed its position as an important actor in the process of social change, something it has repeatedly managed to do when their class-based demands resonate with broader sections of society. The multisectoral alliance between the lower-middle class, organized labor, the indigent poor and unemployed on the streets during 2001–02 eventually provided the electoral basis for *Kirchnerismo*. This began to disintegrate after 2011 and in a similar way the 2012–13 movement led by the upper-middle class and supported by much of the nonprogressive middle class and pockets of the poor morphed into what became *Macrismo*.

The perceived injustice of having been neglected and that of corruption that were noted in the interviews were understood well by Mauricio Macri, who was able to construct an alliance of political forces to form *Cambiemos* in 2015. The way they tapped into these sentiments and values with both subtle and covert imagery and messaging to seduce the middle class (including struggling sectors of it) without alienating the rest of society or adopting a discourse that was deemed to be "anti-*pueblo*" was, alongside a heavily supportive media, key to Macri's 2015 election success. Notions of *emprendedorismo* (entrepreneurism), thus chimed with their values of self-sufficiency, of "decency" (which evoked the "civilization" that Sarmiento aspired to for Argentina) that of "returning to the world" (meaning the "First World," from which their immigrant grandparents came by ending the Latin American regionalist policy and developing closer ties with white, European and North American businesses and governments), also enticed middle-class voters. Social movements and political parties on the political left meanwhile failed to capitalize on alternative framing. Opposition candidate from the Kirchners' *Frente para la Victoria,* Daniel Scioli, was only able to capture 48.7% of the votes in the presidential runoff election and hence began a new era in Argentinian history.

Remobilization: The Struggling Middle Class under the *Cambiemos* Government (2016–18)

As outlined in Chapter 2, Argentina's fourth wave of new poverty commenced soon after the election of President Macri and *Cambiemos* 1.4 million citizens became pauperized within the first year of their government in 2016 due to the policies outlined earlier (*El País*, 2017). This made a mockery of the new government's slogan "Zero Poverty" and while the numbers of impoverished citizens dipped back a little in 2017, by late -2018 it rose to one in three Argentinians. The middle class was affected by public-sector job losses, small companies going out of business (especially due to the increases in 600% in utility prices in that year alone) and salary freezes. They lost 6%–9% purchasing power (EcoLatina, 2016) in real terms due to inflation, which would reach 42% by late 2018 following the mega devaluation.

Yet despite facing indictment on 214 separate charges upon election, ranging from "fraud and illicit association" to "abuse of public office," as well as delivering a plethora of deeply unpopular neoliberal policies, being implicated in the Panama Papers and suffering a fall in approval ratings of 10% since March 2016 to 43%, organized opposition on the streets by those from the middle class was severely limited. In the wake of over a decade of *Kirchnerismo*, many of the labor and social movements had remained deeply divided into pro- and non-Kirchnerist camps. This weakened the possibilities to mobilize an effective and united opposition to structural adjustment in the opening months of *Macrismo*, as the labor and social movements struggled to reconfigure themselves to adapt to their new reality.

In the second half of 2016, social movements, civil society groups and labor unions finally started to seize the opportunity to ignite a broad-based opposition movement linking up seemingly disparate struggles. The three factions of the divided Peronist umbrella labor union, the General Confederation of Workers (CGT), which split under Cristina Kirchner's presidency, announced their reunification on 22 August 2016. Meanwhile, fragments of middle-class resistance could be found via the State Workers Union (ATE) which organized several national strikes. Meanwhile, the two divisions of the Argentinian Workers Central (CTA) (consisting of autonomists, socialists, communists and a Peronist minority) organized a coordinated national strike against the government in October 2016. However, the CGT failed to participate due to Macri's successful attempts to buy out its support through the reimbursement of 29 billion pesos ($US 2 billion) of health insurance funds which had previously been retained by the state for such purposes.

On 2 September 2016, protestors repeated the heroic "Federal March" of 1994, in which they marched for three days from all four corners of the country and included cavalcades of workers, unemployed people's federations, indigenous movements, civil society groups, human rights organizations and those with sectoral interests from Argentina's provinces and which descended on the Plaza de Mayo in Buenos Aires to oppose adjustment, tariff hikes and unemployment.

Middle-class involvement also emanated from the establishment of scores of *multisectoriales* (multisector assemblies) across the country. In attempting to reignite the politically pluralist, horizontalist and cross-class spirit of self-organization that was present in the 2001–02 neighborhood assembly movement, the *multisectoriales* organized the July and August 2016 *Ruidazo* (Noise-maker) pot-banging protests against the utility bill hikes (the "Tarifazo"), in which sizable crowds gathered in public squares and intersections in both working-class and middle-class neighborhoods and urban centers across the country.

The final round of interviews took place toward the end of 2016, as the street mobilization against Cambiemos started to build. In general, there was tacit support for the new administration, certainly little outright opposition. For the time being, the new government appeared to have appeased them. The sample was split primarily into three camps. First, those who were supportive of *Cambiemos'* intentions and policy program. Second, those who were not happy with the way they were governing but were tolerant of it as they insisted on comparing it to how terrible they felt the previous government was. We will call them the *relativists*. Their political stance was, therefore, constructed in *relative* terms. In line with the strong support base that Macri enjoyed in Argentina's capital city, all the interview participants from Buenos Aires were located in these two groups. In both cases, it was clear that they feared a return of the Kirchners and wanted to avoid it at all costs. The third group of "government opponents" was much smaller and more heavily populated in the Provinces (again this corresponds to the national vote breakdown). They despised the Macri government and either maintained *some* sympathy for the previous government (in terms of its social and economic policies) or were outright supporters of it. None of the sample had felt moved to join any collective actions or movements at this point.

Cambiemos *Supporters*

Supporters of the government who had bought into their narrative, liked the fact that in contrast to the previous government, they were less polarizing and saw them as guardians of middle-class interests. Transparency and credentials were reoccurring themes, as were the comparisons:

> I really like the new Government, much more than the previous one. I think it's less corrupt. I think it's much more efficient, much more transparent. I think the officials have either knowledge or credentials to do their jobs. I think there is less… not none but *less* nepotism…

> I think they are trying to put the country into a sustainable develop-
> ment path, which is incredibly difficult. They [Macri government]
> are achieving consensus with the other political parties, mainly with
> mainstream Peronism, and dissident Peronism... Of course, in spite
> of the conflict over the utility price rises, it is still a kind of honey-
> moon for the middle and upper classes with this Government. They
> really suffered, or I think they did, with Kirchnerism.
>
> Federico, 32, Buenos Aires

Others liked the fact that the government included educated and apparently less corrupt officials, all the while comparing them to the past. They
also seem to possess low expectations of what to expect from their government and tended to be cautious rather than enthusiastic in endorsing
Cambiemos. Corruption was expected, what mattered was that they were
less corrupt than before.

> With Macri we don't know what he's going to do properly yet as he
> hasn't got into the swing, but I see he is surrounding himself with
> people who think. Maybe they will be more transparent, *less* corrupt,
> with *less* involvement in dirty business, hiding *less* from us.
>
> Daniela, 63, Buenos Aires

Almost all were prepared to accept the narrative that they would need to
make short-term sacrifices to their living standards, while austerity was
the order of the day, in order to create a more stable, prosperous country
in the future. Several cited the *pesada herencia* – the idea expounded by
Macri and *Cambiemos* that the previous government had run the country into the ground and that they would be its saviors (without raising
expectations too far). This was a discourse that was also promulgated
in Europe and North America during austerity and, like Argentina, was
largely accepted in the short term:

> 'If Macri wins' they used to say... 'There will be terrible austerity!' I
> knew that there would be austerity. It wasn't logical that I'd receive
> an electricity or gas bill for 50 pesos (four dollars) when in Cordoba,
> Entre Rios and Santa Fe they'd be paying so much more. They got
> rid of the subsidy but my question is, who were we subsidising? The
> Kirchners? Baez[14]?
>
> Agustina, 53, Buenos Aires

The Relativists

Among this second category, there was complete distrust of President
Macri. Awareness of his personal corruption and that of his administration was high and they were cynical about its election pledges. The

"lesser evil" notion was also evident. The legitimacy crisis described earlier seemed to never have ended for them as it seemed a case of "a plague on all your houses." However, despite their disdain for the current *Cambiemos* government, they hated the Kirchners even more and held the view that anything would be better than them.

> I knew that Macri was going to be President the minute he became President of Boca Juniors.[15] It was all in his plan to make himself popular and well-known, dating back 10, 15 or 20 years. It was an investment and helped benefit his family. However, he was the only hope that *Kirchnerismo* would go, even though he's dishonest. I repeat, this is better than *Kirchnerismo* but for Macri and those like the mining industry who have paid him to have influence, being President is all about doing business, about improving their situation and not that of the working man. The way he's dished out public works contracts to his friends is an example of that.
>
> Carlos, 82, Buenos Aires

The "politicized reluctant voter paradox" theme was also evident among many respondents, especially in this group. Argentina's presidential run-off system inflated this. Most voters had to hold their nose while voting for Macri, but strongly rejected the Kirchnerist candidate, Daniel Scioli, so felt they had no choice.

Government Opponents

In all three groups, their prior political stances in 2011 became entrenched by 2016. Government supporters focused on what they thought were the positive aspects of the opening year of the Macri government (liberalization of the markets, removal of currency controls, "professionalization" of government etc.), while opponents felt vindicated that their worst fears were coming true (unemployment, salary freezes, higher inflation, rolling back of human rights). Government opponents pointed out contradictions in the *Cambiemos* discourse and election pledges. Micaela quipped sarcastically,

> I'm half way through the month and don't have a peso left. I guess trickle-down theory moves slowly! The thing that gets me is that it's the way they [the government] have covered up so much that got them into power. 'You have to be patient' they tell us. But why should I be patient with them, that kind of thing is reserved for friends, not politicians.
>
> Micaela, 55, Piedras Blancas

While government supporters made clear that they were prepared to make personal sacrifices for the country's economic well-being and stressed that they knew what was coming when they voted, its opponents were angry that their personal financial situation was deteriorating and accused the government of lying. Romina, who had lived in Rosario but by 2016 had moved to Cordoba, angrily explained:

> The government nailed us. We ceded to a 20% salary increase [a loss in real terms] at the beginning of the year because they lied to us during the negotiations in order to sweeten us. Their lies do not surprise me, but it scares me to think that I have to continue to survive on my "salary."
>
> Romina, 26, Cordoba

Indeed, among this latter group there was disbelief that their fellow citizens had voted for a neoliberal government that they compared to that of Carlos Menem's in the 1990s. The lack of confidence they had in their country folk to "choose well" was a theme raised by many participants on all sides of the political divide in 2007 and 2011 and was reaffirmed in 2016.

Neither of the two latter groups were yet ready to convert their opposition to Macri's government into joining protest movements. For the relativists, this tended to be due to the concern that it would aid the return of Cristina Kirchner one day. For the government opponents, it was more about not having the confidence or a critical mass of opposition to the government, given it was in its early months and that the majority of the population were prepared to give them more time to improve the economic situation.

Continuities and changes were identified in other themes from the earlier 2007–11 interviews. Painting themselves as "professionals" or middle-class "victims" continued into 2016. This time, among the three-quarters of participants who were either government supporters or "relativists," the government was seen as their defender and they as citizens, were victims of circumstance, global factors or sometimes the *pesada herencia*. Whereas in years gone by, they saw themselves as "political victims" of the former government, this victim mentality had broadened to now cover their life opportunities, professional conditions or access to the state.

> A middle-class person from a non-developed country like mine, has to sell their soul or throw away all of their savings in order to do an overseas internship with an NGO, which is what I want to do.
>
> Federico, 32, Buenos Aires

> There is not a single professional who is treated well these days, who can charge a decent fee. Just look at the teachers, always on strike because they aren't remunerated well.
>
> Santiago, 65, Buenos Aires

Here it's full of people who receive a pension without ever having worked. Without completing the necessary years, maybe they have just worked for two or five or ten. Yet they receive the same as me, who worked for thirty eight! Prisoners and criminals receive more than me.

Carlos, 82, Buenos Aires

Elements of the "hidden grammar" of 2001 and the crisis of political legitimacy also persisted. For instance, politicians were generally still held in very low esteem. Among the government supporters, several mentioned that they only voted for Macri and were more tolerant of him because he wasn't a career politician but had a business background (ironically even though he and his family were about as close to the "establishment" as one could get, dating back to the 1976–83 dictatorship which it supported).

We thought well, Macri will come in, he's loaded and is a businessman. He won't have to rob anyone as he's already got money. That's what a lot of us thought, even though they had no plan for government.

Daniela, 63, Buenos Aires

For all those in the "relativist" camp (and for many in the pro- and anti-government camps to a lesser degree), it was as if nothing had changed since the days of QSVT, except that they were now demobilized politically. Vanesa (31) had emigrated to New Zealand in 2016 partly due to the lack of career opportunities in her field. However, a few weeks before she did so, she angrily explained:

The fact is that all Argentina's politicians smell of shit. It's simple. They make people ignorant, brainwash, and constantly make false promises to fill their own pockets while people are hungry. I don't give a crap what party they are from, they are all corrupt and if they weren't they wouldn't get to where they were.

Vanesa, 31, La Plata

However, she was one of the few who recognized that as struggling middle class, it was important to forge alliances with other sectors against a common class enemy.

I also couldn't give a toss about Lanata [the anti-Kirchner journalist]. The truth is that we are how we are today because our government is a reflection of the people. We fight among ourselves and everyone loses out in the meantime. Every 15 years we suffer a crisis... We argue over who has more or who has less between us and the foreign multinationals take advantage. We have scoundrels leading us and thanks to them we are easy prey.

The "other" and "anti-poor" discourse was still present, but certainly toned down from 2011. Ironically, the fact that the *Cambiemos* government had replaced *Kirchnerismo* helped to reduce tensions toward these sectors from the struggling middle class in two senses. First, with the Kirchners in power, especially Cristina, anger was targeted toward "the poor" due to the belief that they were favored over them as middle-class citizens. Most were also angered that the rules of society (meritocracy, fair justice system etc.) were still being violated. With Macri as president, barely any participants mentioned this. The other contradictory effect this "return to the rules of the game" had was that for some in the sample, the "retreatism" they experienced under *Kirchnerismo* was reversed. No longer feeling that they were second-class citizens reactivated their interest in active participation in political life and to involvement in other aspects of citizenship. In other words, in re-engaging them, it acted as a kind of precursor to them becoming involved in collective protests.

Second, Macri's neoliberal project was clearly hurting both the lower-middle class, the blue-collar working class and the structural poor. Thus, the green shoots of collective grievances and political alliances were starting to appear. This was evident in the formation of the neighborhood-based *multisectoriales* against the *Tarifazo* at the time in late 2016, for instance.

2018: A Return to the que se vayan todos?

According to a recent survey by Taquion Consultants in April 2018, there are strong signs of a return to a crisis of legitimacy in Argentina. Seventy-six percent of the overall population are not happy with how the country's democracy is functioning. When questioned about which institution or sector they most believed in, 54% stated "no one," followed by 12% who cited "journalists" and just 8.5% "politicians." Indeed, among those with university education, perhaps closest to our "middle-class subject group," the proportion who believe in "no one" reached 72%.

As the economy has deteriorated, inflation increased and the government's structural adjustment policies deepened, the squeezing of the population has sparked a new cycle of resistance from below on a scale not seen since 2013 and unprecedented since 2002. Three general strikes in April 2017, June 2018 and September 2018 were followed by millions of workers, including white-collar, professionals and highly skilled workers. Several *cacerolazos* or *ruidazo* protests against successive 1,500% utility price rises and ongoing austerity have drawn support from small business owners alongside consumers, pensioners, students and others in the struggling middle class alongside the structural poor and on several occasions, the *piqueteros*.

In December 2017, hundreds of thousands protested the Pension Reforms. These were met with brutal repression by the security forces, which made headlines around the world. They fired water canisters and rubber bullets arbitrarily into the crowds. Several protestors lost their eyes and pensioners and MPs were physically assaulted by the gendarmerie or police. The progressive sectors of the middle class have returned to the streets in enormous numbers in protests relating to human rights violations and alleged state complicity in the murders of activists or other citizens, especially that of the Disappearance of Santiago Maldonado and repression of the Mapuche communities. A new "green wave" of women-led protest against domestic violence, inequality and femicide culminated in up to two million protesting for the right to legal abortion in August 2018. Meanwhile, numerous strikes by state-sector workers, then teachers and university lecturers in August and September 2018 incorporated significant layers of the newly squeezed middle class.

When the Macri government called upon to IMF to bail out the economy with a US$57 billion standby agreement, tied to a series of conditions that included deeper public spending cuts, it set in motion a series of catastrophic financial events, including the peso crisis in mid-2018 which saw the national currency lose 52% of its value against the dollar since the start of that year alone, untold misery and the return of shop lootings as the poorest struggle to eat. This has sparked significant capital flight and to investors abandoning the country, with public debt as a proportion of GDP having soared from 35% in 2015, to nearly 100% (allowing for the currency devaluation) by late 2018. This has led many economists, analysts and politicians to question whether we are on the verge of witnessing another debt default and social crisis. Meanwhile, the parliamentary opposition, while growing in support, has failed to capitalize. Peronism remains deeply divided into at least three camps – the *Frente Renovador*, Federal Peronism and *Kirchnerismo*. Cristina Kirchner, while the most popular opposition leader nationally, remains a polarizing character. She and the *Frente para la Victoria/Unidad Ciudadana* have failed to make inroads into gaining middle-class support, in spite of the favorable economic and political conditions to do so. *Cambiemos* is riddled with corruption scandals, including over "fake voter registrations" allegations, while 17 current or former cabinet ministers are facing charges or accusations of corruption, including President Macri himself (Heguier, 2017).

Given how mobilized civil society has become, and how quickly Argentina is slipping toward the abyss, it may not be long before another QSVT uprising. The squeezed middle class will surely play an important role again.

Notes

1 While these were not organs of dual-power (thus, there was no counter-hegemonic challenge to capitalism per se), the Assembly movement (via the inter-neighborhood assembly) in particular had the potential to become an alternative mechanism for governance, but it died away before its potential

could be fulfilled. Hence, for a few months at least, the hegemonic order came to be profoundly questioned by a significant part of the Argentinian population, even though no alternative project was able to replace it.

2 An organic crisis of capitalism describes a deep and irreversible crisis that reflects an unraveling of the inherent contradictions within the system.

3 White, urban middle-class Argentinians often confuse their fellow Argentinians who migrate to the urban centers from the north of the country (and who tend to be racially *Mestizo*) with being "immigrants." Nevertheless, figures show that there *was* an influx of immigration, especially from neighboring Andean countries from 2003 as the economy started to grow strongly and the weak value of the peso meant that it was relatively easy to settle.

4 Translates into English as "of Black racial origin" in but is used by Argentinians to refer to those of Andean or indigenous descent.

5 See those of the Inter-neighbourhood Assembly, the National Movement of Recovered Companies (MNER) and those of various *piquetero* groups.

6 For instance, the 2008 conviction of Venezuelan-American businessman Antonini Wilson after his suitcases were inspected at an airport and contained almost US$1 million. This money was illegally provided by state oil company Petróleos de Venezuela, to be used for Kirchner's 2007 general election campaign. For details, visit https://archive.nytimes.com/query.nytimes.com/gst/fullpage-9803E3D6163DF937A35752C1A96E9C8B63.html.

7 *Puntero* means "political broker" – Argentinian slang for someone who acts as an intermediary between poor people and political parties in a clientelist relation.

8 At the time of the 2011 interviews, one of the two Mothers' groups, the *Asociación de las Madres de la Plaza de Mayo* was embroiled in the Schoklender Scandal regarding the alleged embezzlement of state funds.

9 The mythological story of how when the English Army sought to invade the River Plate region in 1806 and 1807, the locals poured cooking pots full of boiling water and oil over the invaders' heads from their houses to prevent their advance.

10 Universal Childhood Benefit (AUH) is a conditional cash transfer program for unemployed people and those working below the minimum wage who have children, or all families with disabled children.

11 The accuracy of economic figures provided by Argentinian government's statistics agency, INDEC, was called into question from the late 2000s due to discrepancies in their data collection methods. However, independent agencies like the UCA confirm that poverty did indeed fall strongly during this period.

12 "Shirtless" refers to the traditional poor from whom Peronist governments built their supporter base.

13 www.theguardian.com/world/2012/apr/05/greece-suicide-tributes-retired-pharmacist.

14 An Argentinian businessman and central figure in several corruption scandals liked to the Kirchner governments.

15 One of Argentina's most successful football clubs.

References

Aaker, Jennifer, Drolet, Amiee and Griffin, Dale (2008) 'Recalling Mixed Emotions' *Journal of Consumer Research*, Vol. 35 (2), pp. 268–278.

Aldrich, Daniel (2012) *Building Resilience: Social Capital in Post-Disaster Recovery*. Chicago, IL, University of Chicago.

Armony, Ariel and Armony, Victor (2005) 'Indictments, Myths, and Citizen Mobilization in Argentina: A Discourse Analysis' *Latin American Politics and Society*, Vol. 47 (4 Winter, 2005, pp. 27–54.

Auyero, Javier and Moran, Patrick (2007) 'The Dynamics of Collective Violence: Dissecting Food Riots in Contemporary Argentina' *Social Forces*, Vol. 85 (3), pp. 1341–1367.

Bielinsky, Fabian Dir. (2000) *Nueve Reinas*. California. Buena Vista International.

Clarín (2005) 'Una encuesta asegura que Kirchner es el Presidente con mayor popularidad en América' 21st September 2005.

Clarin (2016) 'Menem y Kirchner, mejor que De la Rúa y Cristina en el ranking de la pobreza' 9th October 2016.

Dinerstein, Ana (2014) 'Disagreement and Hope: The Hidden Transcripts in the Grammar of Political Recovery in Post-crisis Argentina' in D. Ozarow, C. Levey and C. Wylde (eds.), *Argentina since the 2001 Crisis*. New York, Palgrave Macmillan.

Ecolatina (2016) *Paritarias 2017: todo lo que sabemos hasta el momento*. Buenos Aires, InversorGlobal.

El País (2017) 'La pobreza creció en 1,5 millones de personas desde que llegó Mauricio Macri' 9th March 2017.

Engels, Friedrich. (1878) *Anti-Dühring*. Berlin. *Vorwärts*

Erikson, Erik (1973) *Childhood and Society*. New York, W. W. Norton & Co.

Filmus, Daniel (1996) *Estado, sociedad y educación en la Argentina de fin de siglo: procesos y desafíos*. Buenos Aires, Troquel.

———. ed. (2016) *Pensar el Kirchnerismo: Lo que hizo, lo que falta, lo que viene*. Buenos Aires, Siglo Veintiuno.

Feinmann, Jose (2018) *Filosofía, aquí y ahora*. Buenos Aires, Encuentro TV. 22nd April 2018.

Fidanza, Eduardo (2009) 'El ajedrez electoral argentino', *La Nación*, 9th June 2009.

Fredrickson, Barbara and Kahneman, Daniel (1993) 'Duration Neglect in Retrospective Evaluations of Affective Episodes' *Journal of Personality and Social Psychology*, Vol. 65 (1), pp. 45–55.

Gramsci, Antonio (1998 [1929–1935]) *Selections from the Prison Notebooks*. London, Lawrence and Wishart.

Guano, Emanuela (2004) 'The Denial of Citizenship: Barbaric Buenos Aires and the Middle-Class Imaginary' *City & Society*, Vol. 16 (1), pp. 69–97.

Hardt, Michael and Negri, Antonio (2000) *Empire*. Cambridge, MA, Harvard University Press.

Heguier, Jonathan (2017) 'Qué funcionarios del Gobierno de Macri deberían estar presos con la 'doctrina De Vido-Boudou'? *El Destape*. Buenos Aires. Talar Producciones. 3rd November 2017.

Holloway, John (2002) *Change the World without Taking Power*. London. Pluto Press.

INDEC (*Instituto Nacional de Estadística y Censos*) www.indec.gov.ar

LAMAC (2012) *Informe de TV Paga Nacional*. Florida. Latin American Multichannel Advertising Council. March 2012

Lewis, Oscar (1969) "The Culture of Poverty" in D. Mcynihn (ed.), *On Understanding Poverty: Perspectives from the Social Sciences*. New York: Basic Books.

Linz, Juan and Stepan, Alfred (1996) *Problems of Democratic Transition and Consolidation: Southern Europe, South America, and Post-Communist Europe.* Baltimore, MD, John Hopkins University Press.

Lladós, Jose Ignacio (2006) 'Blumberg reclamó seguridad a Kirchner' *La Nación*, 1st September 2006.

Marwell, Gerald and Oliver, Pamela (1984) 'Collective Action Theory and Social Movements Research' in L. G. Kriesberg (ed.), *Social Movements, Conflict and Change*, Greenwich, CT. Jai Press, pp. 1–27.

Mazzoni, Maria (2007) 'Política y Empobrecimiento' *Revista de la Facultad*, Vol. 13, pp. 185–211. Argentina, Universidad Nacional de Comahue.

——— (2008) 'Ciudadanos de bajo impacto' *Revista de la Facultad*, Vol. 14, pp. 211–225. Argentina, Universidad Nacional, Comahue.

McAdam, Doug (1982) *Political Process and the Development of Black Insurgency 1930–1970.* Chicago, IL, University of Chicago Press.

Merton, Robert (1968) *Social Theory and Social Structure.* New York, The Free Press.

Ozarow, Daniel and Croucher, Richard (2014) 'Workers' Self-management, Recovered Companies and the Sociology of Work' *Sociology*, Vol. 48 (5), pp. 989–1006.

Pereyra, Daniel (2003) *Argentina Rebelde: crónicas y enseñanzas de la revuelta social*, Buenos Aires, El Viejo Topo.

Presidencia de la Nación Argentina (2009) *Tasa de Delitos.* Buenos Aires. Ministry of Justice and Human Rights.

Rock, D. (1991) 'Argentina 1930–46' in L. Bethell (ed.), *The Cambridge History of Latin America, Vol. 8.* Cambridge, Cambridge University Press, p. 69.

Robinson, Michael and Clore, Gerald (2000) 'Episodic and Semantic Knowledge in Emotional Self-Report' *Journal of Personality and Social Psychology*, Vol. 83 (1), pp. 198–215.

Schacter, Daniel (1996) *Searching for Memory: The Brain, the Mind, and the Past.* New York: Basic Books.

Svampa, Maristella (2006) 'Réquiem para el ahorrista argentino?' in G. Massuh and S. Arrese (ed.), *La Normalidad.* Buenos Aires, Interzona Editora.

——— (2014) 'Revisiting Argentina 2001–13: From "¡Que se vayan todos!" to the Peronist Decade' in D. Ozarow, C. Levey, C. Wylde (eds.), *Argentina Since the 2001 Crisis*:Recovering the Past, Reclaiming the Future. New York, Palgrave Macmillan.pp. 155–173

Tajfel, Henri and Turner, John C. (1986) 'The Social Identity Theory of Intergroup Behaviour' in S. Worchel and W. Austin (eds.), *The Social Psychology of Intergroup Relations.* Monterey, CA, Brooks/Cole, pp. 7–24.

Taquion Consultants (2018) '¿La vuelta del que se vayan todos?' *PrimeroPlano*, 16th April 2018.

Thomas, David and Diener, Ed (1990) 'Memory Accuracy in the Recall of Emotions' *Journal of Personality and Social Psychology*, Vol. 59 (2), pp. 291–297.

Tilly, Charles (1986) *The Contentious French.* Cambridge, MA, Harvard University Press.

Trotsky, Leon (1939) 'The Bonapartist Philosophy of the State' *The New International*, Vol. 5 (6), pp. 166–169. New York.

UCA (2017) *Seguridad Ciudadana en la Argentina Urbana (2010–2016).* Buenos Aires, Catholic University of Argentina.

Visacovsky, Sergio (2019) 'The Days Argentina Stood Still' *Horizontes Antropológicos*, Vol. 24 (52) pp. 311–341

Warr, Peter and Knapper, Christopher (1968) *The Perception of People and Events*. London: Wiley.

Wilson, Timothy, Meyers, Jan and Gilbert, Daniel (2003) 'How Happy Was I, Anyway?? A Retrospective Impact Bias' *Social Cognition*, Vol. 21 (6), pp. 421–446.

Wilson, William (1987) *The Truly Disadvantaged: The Inner City, the Underclass and Public Policy*. Chicago, IL, University of Chicago Press.

Wylde, Christopher (2016) 'Post-Neoliberal Developmental Regimes in Latin America: Argentina under Cristina Fernandez de Kirchner' *New Political Economy*, Vol. 21 (3), 322–341.

Zibechi, Raul (2003) *Genealogía de la revuelta. Argentina, una sociedad en movimiento*. La Plata, Letra Libre.

——— (2011) 'Una década del argentinazo: impunidad en democracia' 16th December 2011.

Conclusions
Struggling Middle-Class Radicalism. Past, Present and Future

> We are supporting the *cacerolazos*, which were started by the middle class... It's not political, we don't do politics. It is just a social movement. We want equality for all...political, economic and social equality and decent health services.
>
> Male protestor, *Argentina in Revolt*, 2002

> Just as politics cannot be separated from life, life cannot be separated from politics. People who consider themselves to be non-political are no different; they've already been assimilated by the dominant political culture. They just don't feel it any more.
>
> Pramoedya Ananta Toer, 1978

It is a crisp, sunny winter's afternoon on 8 August 2014. I'm sitting in the café of the *Metro* TV studio in the Constitución district of Buenos Aires, waiting to be interviewed for the political talk show *Asuntos Públicos*. In the latest episode of Argentina's seemingly perpetual external debt odyssey, US Judge Thomas Griesa has just declared Argentina to be in "technical" default on its external debt by following the court case brought against them by North American hedge funds Aurelius Capital and NML Capital. In walks *Podemos* Founder, Juan Carlos Monedero who is to be interviewed on the same show. We get talking. Noticing that I am clutching a copy of my coedited book, *Argentina Since the 2001 Crisis*, he asks me if he can take a look. I of course oblige. Through his round spectacles that add to his intellectual aura, Monedero browses the back cover, then the first couple of pages of the introduction before he pauses pensively. Then in his Madrileño accent, he looks at me and says,

> You know Daniel, when we first founded *Podemos*; we studied the Argentina post-2001 case very carefully. We learned a great deal from their successes and mistakes, and about how to convert our *Indignado* uprisings into a movement that could affect profound social change through the electoral system.

The formation of *Podemos*, what has become one of Europe's leading progressive parties, and one that is strongly supported by the fallen middle class, and the young, is but one of countless international legacies left by Argentina's 2001 uprising and subsequent political developments. One of the lessons learned was how to tap in to the *anti-politics* sentiment that had fermented among many in the struggling middle class, such that as the two quotes at the start of this chapter portray, even "political acts" were justified by the actors themselves as being "non-political" and which held almost as much resonance in Spain post-2008 *Indignados* uprisings, as it did in Argentina during 2001.

In this current book, I have sought to ascertain what processes and conditions affect how professionals and other middle-class citizens have taken decisions about how to resist severe financial hardship or downward social mobility. Using the case of Argentina, we have asked why some choose to limit their responses to private and collective self-improvement strategies while others engage in individual protest actions or take to the streets to collectively defend their interests? Specific national contexts in which protest movements emerge were also compared and the conditions under which these movements are able to attract and mobilize recently pauperized citizens were explored.

So what were the motivating factors that mobilize middle-class participation in protests? In Argentina's case, economic grievances did not have a significant effect on their own. Neither the descent into poverty itself, nor the level of income deprivation experienced influenced this choice of action. Those who became poor, but survived just below the poverty line, were just as likely to join protests as those who had the lowest household incomes to start with. Indeed until the latest wave of middle-class protests in 2017–18, post-2001–02 mass mobilizations all occurred during moments of national affluence, including the 2006 the Blumberg demonstrations, the 2008 Countryside Conflict and even the 2012–13, anti-government protests that arose two years into a recovery following a brief dip. Few if any of the demands on each occasion were based upon material concerns, and anger about personal economic grievances was rarely expressed as a reason why interviewees would participate in protest movements.

Instead, post-material concerns such as corruption, crime, perceived government authoritarianism and then under the Macri government, for abortion rights for women alongside attacks on pensions and salaries were the key issues that motivated the middle-class to collective action. Perceived violations of their civil or political rights were mobilizing factors, whereas social and economic rights tended not to be. This was due to the Argentina's middle class' understanding of citizenship to be limited to its political and civil components. Their inherent beliefs in self-sufficiency minimized their expectations by way of what social and economic rights should be endowed to them or others and their liberal rather than republican understanding of citizenship made them much more sensitive to questions of alleged corruption, authoritarianism, human rights abuses and anti-liberalism compared to poverty, unemployment or, even to some extent, macroeconomic performance. However, the interaction of several other generative processes and features *did* mold the form of the response taken.

Fluctuating Consent to be Ruled by the Dominant Class

In explaining the collective group behavior of Argentina's struggling middle class, a notable distinction was made between various phases during the past 30 years. During the 1990s, those experiencing social descent either dealt with their situation behind closed doors or engaged in "segmented mobilization." From December 2001 to 2002, this "extraordinary year" marked a period of generalized and radicalized mobilization. The "post-crisis demobilization" phase followed in the opening years of *Kirchnerismo* (2003–05). Periods of "demobilization with sporadic revolts" (2006–11) and then "passive dissidence" turned into "anti-government mobilizations" (2012–15) before the latest period of "remobilization" (2016–18) under *Macrismo* took place. The oscillating sense of collective identity and transfer between progressive and reactionary attitudes has informed these fluctuating patterns of action. A principal factor that transformed economic grievances into political ones was the loss of the consent to rule by both elected officials and the institutions of power during the crisis of legitimacy in 2001–02. However, this broad-based consent was held intact during the two periods either side of it in the 1990s and mid-2000s and prevented resistance from becoming generalized on the same scale. The actions of the struggling middle class under neoliberalism or post-neoliberalism can, therefore, be described as constituting "cycles of protest and collective behavior" (Tarrow, 1998), which fluctuate depending on the spaces available for these actions.

Citizens perpetually reassessed who was to blame for their personal descent, attributing culpability either toward themselves or casting it toward their government, the banks, globalization and international financial institutions at different moments depending on the dominant hegemonic narrative and the spaces to act in alternative ways.

A key finding was that rather than automatically wishing to contest their economic circumstances through political action, the struggling middle class first underwent a cognitive process of assessing the broader macropolitical and macroeconomic conditions in which their impoverishment had occurred. Then, they responded either through collective protest, participation in the solidarity economy or through private responses at different moments.

Both qualitative and quantitative results showed that the struggling middle class who were involved in collective *self-improvement* activities or spent more time in the workplace were also more likely to join collective *protests*. Marx emphasizes the proximity of members of the working class to one another in their daily social environment as being important in terms of the development of a class consciousness and thus as an antecedent to collective action of all kinds (Elster, 1986:132). These collective activities and workplace "mobilizing sites" became incubators for the development of a shared class consciousness with the long-term poor. Recognition of an injustice is a vital precondition to participation in protest action (Mansbridge, 2001). Thus, those who had engaged in communal self-improvement actions were more likely to identify their declining circumstances as such as they could see that such a large number of other both structurally and recently impoverished citizens had also been affected as well as themselves, politicizing their responses.

Yet, in 2002, neither awareness about such injustices, nor the drive to pour onto the streets in protest were stimulated from above, or "formally" by official, resource-rich organizations like the trade unions or political parties (López-Levy, 2004), as resource mobilization theory advocates would assume. Instead, both then and since, these ways of thinking were developed through the informal conversations and "learned experiences" that were derived through their engagement in these "awareness-raising sites." That is to say, their collective self-help activities and the workplace became alternative "mobilizing vehicles" to reformist organizations like left-wing political parties or trade unions in terms of the protest movements they joined (popular assemblies, *escraches, cacerolazos* etc.). The notion of protests being called and organized by political parties or trade unions also remains held in suspicion by non-activist sectors of Argentina's middle class. In fact, the regard in which the struggling middle class held both these types of organization was extremely low and remains so today for the reasons elaborated upon in Chapter 4.

Those protests that *have* elicited extensive participation from Argentina's middle class in recent years have been "self-organized" or have purposely avoided direct party-political influence (the pro-abortion march in August 2018, protests against the pension reforms in December 2017 and the anti-government protests of 2012–13, for instance). They have tended to be organized through informal channels via social media, word of mouth or sometimes independent civil society organizations such as the *multisectoriales*. Similar mobilizing vehicles have also provided key information and dissemination channels for other national mass protest movements recently that were led by elements of the struggling middle class, such as the Arab Spring, Iceland's Kitchenware Revolution, Occupy Wall Street, Spain's *Indignados* uprising and occupation of the squares or Greece's *Amesi Dimokratia Tora!* movement (Mason, 2012).

However, none of these movements were entirely "spontaneous" as is often asserted. Instead, citizens can be better understood as having joined the protests while either consciously or unconsciously pursuing learned collective repertoires of action (Tilly, 1986), especially those that had been practiced in struggles against neoliberalism in previous decades. This was the case in Argentina in 2001–02, for instance, with participants conveying personal or collective memories of such prior involvement. Further, extemporaneous collective actions like those of 19 and 20 December require at least minimum levels of organization if they are to be maintained in the longer term (Atzeni, 2010:6). Some kind of leadership soon becomes necessary (Hyman, 1989). Yet while the reduced role of formal modes of organization did limit Argentina's 2001–02 movement in some ways, it proved to be a considerable strength too. This challenges some of the suppositions of resource mobilization theory, by seemingly refuting the links between organizational infrastructure, its political institutionalization and the propensity for protest that it creates.

In "Mobilization and Meaning" (1985), Ferree and Miller argue that people are more likely to correctly attribute their circumstances to "systems" rather than internalize their situation if they enjoy intense, regular contact with other similar people. In other words, evidence points to the fact that grassroots settings like the workplace and neighborhood (Tilly, 1978) and informal social networks can facilitate and structure collective action. They may also hold the potential for the "destruction of top-down sovereignty in favor of popular democracy" (Hardt and Negri, 2004:353). We asked how informal social interactions such as friendships and peer networks – upon which the results suggested much of the participation in collective protest by struggling middle class citizens was built, can help foster the development of collective identities, including that of being part of a downwardly mobile middle class. We explored how political radicalization can be fostered through such interactions and how can recently pauperized citizens from the middle class be brought together with other exploited groups, so that the process of social atomization which initially militated *against* collective protest action being taken in the 1990s, be reversed and solidarity reignited.

Findings also support J-curve theory, because those middle-class citizens who became poor during the 2001–02 economic crisis tended to experience more sudden descent, on the back of growing expectations and perceived prosperity throughout the 1990s, which was quickly brought to an end as the economy collapsed in December 2001. Because poverty was experienced more abruptly and intensely and was more tangible compared to that experienced in the 1990s or the mid-2010s, it prompted more intense outrage than the gradual social descent and incremental pauperization of a decade earlier. The same factor helps to explain why middle-class responses to hardship were so radical in Iceland following its 2008 banking collapse, for instance. The population enjoyed among the highest living standards in the world but suddenly lost jobs, businesses and life savings, as well as experiencing a political crisis in a similar way to Argentina in 2001.

The election of President Néstor Kirchner in May 2003 also played an important role in the reconstitution of citizens' subjective positioning of their own place in society, as well as of Argentina's role in the world. He broke with the long-standing tradition of promulgating the country's mythical "greatness" and of predicting a prosperous future for the individual (Armony and Armony, 2005:48). Instead, President Kirchner talked about a "dream" of an "ordinary" country: "I want a normal Argentina. I want a serious country" (Kirchner, 2003). By managing expectations and initiating economic stability, he was able to construct a more realistic vision for society. In turn, for this reason and following the defeat of the uprisings, citizens adopted more conciliatory outlooks: The radical demands of 2001–02 were placed into perspective and the ambition to achieve them dissipated. President Mauricio Macri went one step further during his 2015 election campaign, lowering expectations to the point where he stopped just short of stating that short-term hardship should be anticipated in exchange for "stabilising the macro-economy" through a kind of developmentalist approach that was similar to that of President Arturo Frondizi (1958–62), encouraging foreign investment and support for business. Many in the middle class put their faith in Macri and *Cambiemos*, but it is the violation of Macri's side of this new social contract (as the economy appears to be collapsing while standards of living also plummet) that helps to explain why increasing numbers are returning to the streets to protest against him as patience runs dry.

Macroeconomic and Political Context and Spaces for Action

The changing macropolitical and macroeconomic contexts in Argentina over time also created or restricted opportunities to engage in collective action, as the dominant class' ability to enforce its consent to rule expanded and contracted since the restoration of democracy in 1983.

These diachronic "spaces" are construed in four ways. First, fluctuating opportunities linked to different *ideological* economic models. In the early 1990s before the exhaustion of the neoliberal model and collapse of the economy, growth and "stability" created ample spaces for "individual self-improvement action" for the middle class, including those who were struggling. Employment was relatively high, credit easy to obtain and entrepreneurial opportunities existed due to strong domestic demand. However, when the economy went into free fall during the crisis in 2001–02, jobs (especially skilled ones) became scarce and official unemployment officially hit 21.5% (INDEC), it reduced individual self-help possibilities. These recovered between 2003 and 2012 with a consumer boom, employment growth and high growth under *Kirchnerismo* and post-neoliberalism, even if the economy didn't generate sufficient *skilled* opportunities. Thus, it engendered a recovery of occupational mobility for some, with downward trajectories for others. Meanwhile under *Macrismo* and the return of the neoliberal model, such possibilities have generally fallen again as the economy has stagnated, credit has dried up and internal demand has weakened due to the favoring of foreign capital. While self-employment opportunities have grown at the expense of salaried posts, these are generally precarious and low-paid.

Similarly, while individual protest options existed for the middle class in the 1990s, via a credible and apparently sympathetic main opposition Radical Party (UCR) to channel anger against downward mobility or impoverishment through the ballot box, by late 2001 the mainstream opposition had become discredited. The Peronists were tarnished by *Menemismo*, and the governing Radicals – and FREPASO as part of the ruling *Alianza* – were blamed for the crisis. So such spaces closed as reflected in the *voto bronca* in October 2001. The limitations placed on individual protest routes increased the likelihood of engagement in *collective* protests to voice their dissent at the time.

The 1990s macropolitical context generated a thriving individualist spirit and way of thinking at the time. This reduced social interaction, hindered the development of a consciousness of individual exploitation, limited confidence to protest and heightened the stigma of impoverishment, thus closing spaces for collective forms of action. However, such spaces soon opened up in 2001–02 due to short-term contingent factors, such as the *Corralito*, and especially the Declaration of the "state of siege" in late December 2001, which caused hundreds of thousands of middle-class citizens to take to the streets and made them question the legitimacy of the governing regime as well as the structural reasons for their descent. The election of Néstor Kirchner in May 2003, by contrast, closed many of these spaces once again, as he was largely able to recover citizens' consent to be governed by the dominant class, albeit by the *domestic* rather than *international* bourgeoisie. Since 2015, President Macri's attempts to reinvigorate this individualist spirit under the guise of *emprenderismo* have been less successful, and attempts to consolidate this as a hegemonic idea have been stunted by the slide into debt crisis and economic recession.

A second kind of space that can be understood here is the "physical" space, or "opportunities" available for certain actions within one's geographical proximity. While during 2001 and 2002 the sheer number of barter clubs, neighborhood assemblies, protests, worker-recovered companies, roadblocks and other collective actions soared, this should have facilitated participation because they were within closer proximity to where citizens lived and worked. However, this kind of space was found *not* to be a generative factor in terms of explanations for impoverished middle-class citizens' participation in social movements.

Third, those interdependent spaces that opened and closed to individual citizens to engage in political and economic actions. These continually shaped and reshaped spaces to participate in alternative ways. The desire to reverse declining material conditions was more likely to become "political" among impoverished middle-class citizens when they were unable to find sufficient economic mechanisms to be able to cope, or such opportunities were undermined, thus reducing tolerance of their hardship (Powers, 1999). When individual coping strategies that were used in the 1990s such as savings, finding work or utilizing social capital became restricted during 2001–02, spaces for collective protest action opened up as an alternative.

Fourth and finally, these "spaces" refer to how the struggling middle class (as individuals) were able to utilize their different biographical characteristics to access a particular type of action or, conversely, how these constrained spaces for involvement in alternative categories of action at different points in time. For example, emigrating and "exit" routes post-2001 were established by securing European Union (EU) citizenship rights. This, in turn, affected whether such citizens pursued alternative response actions.

Violation of Rights and Anomie

We saw how struggling middle-class Argentinians who participated in collective self-improvement actions simultaneously gained opportunities to also engage in collective protest actions in 2001–02. Welfare programs like *Plan Jefes y Jefas de Hogar Desocupados* were ineffective in terms of alleviating the financial needs of the poor middle class, yet served to break down the social solidarity in the initial postcrisis period. The expansion of such social plans eventually generated resentment toward the long-term poor and unemployed from the struggling middle class who could neither qualify for them nor registered for them in any case. Thus, they increasingly came to understand their own situation to be that of the "neglected citizen." Underlying this framing was the evoking of historical fissures as they saw themselves as victims of the Kirchner government that favored the shanty town poor and organized working class as the Peronists had done in the 1940s–70s. Together with the perception of rising crime and alleged government corruption, the Kirchner governments were perceived to be encouraging the violation of several cherished middle-class values or political and civil rights.

First, through its policy of what they believed were "limitations" on the free media (via the Media and Audiovisual Law that regulated corporate ownership of the media). Second, via "attacks" on the freedom of capital (due to the restrictions it placed on US dollar holdings to protect the national currency). Third, the perceived encouragement of the *piqueteros* (and its support for restricting "freedom of circulation and transit") and even the "right to arrive at work." These provided a toxic mix that Cristina Kirchner's government was indicted for, combined with supposed attacks on cherished values of meritocracy and equality before the law that fueled the anti-government protests of 2012–13. These preoccupations were successfully exploited by *Macrismo* in the 2015 election campaign as Mauricio Macri and *Cambiemos* pledged to overturn many of these Kirchnerist ills.

Similarly, the value of possessing strong social networks or working hard fell between 1995 and 2002. So as the value of possessing such capital or belief in such values declined, society's rules were perceived by some to be breaking down. Initially, this fostered participation in protest action but over the medium term, the vast majority withdrew into private and individualistic self-improvement spaces again, especially as the impact of "retreatism" and anomie deepened under Cristina Kirchner's government. While occasionally sporadic outbursts of dissent occurred under her presidency, only a minority continued to engage in collective self-help initiatives. However, more recently there are signs that as two million citizens have once again become impoverished since Mauricio Macri became President in December 2015, those whose living standards have deteriorated are politically mobilizing via the demonstrations against the *Tarifazo* (removal of subsidies on electricity, gas and water bills) in July 2016, protests against the Pension Reform (December 2017), general strikes (2017 and 2018) or actions against cuts to the university and education in general (2018), for instance.

Who Was Mobilized and Who Wasn't?

Within Argentina's struggling middle class, some citizens displayed a range of participation in protest movements, while others desisted from almost any involvement. Biographical characteristics do not *determine* behavior because these do not possess intrinsic properties which induce action in themselves in the absence of context. However, under certain generative conditions such as macroeconomic or political changes, these characteristics gained behavioral value in order to *become* either stimulants or barriers to collective actions as a response.

Relative Deprivation

Findings confirmed Davies' "relative deprivation" theory because they indicated that individuals in households who suffered a more sudden material descent tended to adopt collective protest actions compared to those who slipped into poverty. Those in this latter group were more likely to restrict their responses to economic self-improvement activities and desisted from joining social movements. Neither the event of becoming "income poor" nor the general level of material conditions in which they lived affected the propensity to protest. However, the "degree of their fall" did. Evidence, therefore, points to the irrelevance of *absolute* definitions of poverty in determining action.

Politicization seemed to have occurred when poverty actually resulted in additional and perceivable privations being experienced in daily life.

This is when impoverishment becomes "real" in terms of how it is lived and understood as such by the subject. In Gramsci's terms (1998), the struggling middle class who suffered more acute losses developed a more intense awareness of the injustice to which they were subject. Their "good sense" was awakened, subduing their "common sense" so that they questioned hegemonic discourses and adopted political resistance.

Prior Experience of Collective Action

Those with previous experience of collective action were much more likely to have engaged in collective protest following their pauperization during 2002 and in political mobilizations in subsequent years. Their militancy in these protests also tended to be more intense. Those possessing such experience also tended to be more open to all types of collectivist solutions either because their more extensive activist links endowed them with greater awareness that such protest actions were taking place, or gave them the confidence to join them.

Mobilizing Impact of Work

The act of "work" and the workplace itself were identified as processes or sites through which the political mobilization of the struggling middle class occurred. How movements might take advantage of this has been advanced by Scully and Segal (2002). In *Passion with an Umbrella: Grassroots Activists in the Workplace*, they point to the fact that the workplace is a site where people experience injustices firsthand in a nonabstract way and where inequalities based on social identity become salient and contestable. This setting, they argue, therefore, provides the desire to seek some kind of radical response and makes subjects more cognitively "tuned in" to collective opportunities for contentious action. Second, these authors propose that through the workplace, citizens develop an enhanced understanding of how potential resources can be mobilized opportunistically (for instance, booking rooms for meetings, accessing computers and photocopiers to publicize activities etc.). This makes them more confident about promoting collective actions to their colleagues. Recruits to "the movement" can be easily located and mobilized, given that so many people work within the same building or geographical space. Therefore, citizens in the sample who spent more time in the workplace would have been more exposed to mobilizing possibilities in these ways.

Polarized Responses

Impoverishment had a polarizing effect on middle-class citizens in terms of their involvement in political activity. Those in the first group, "the activists" were mobilized into pursuing different actions following their personal descent due to the general climate of economic and political chaos in 2002. The "activists" were more involved in both economic self-help activities (both individual and collective), worked longer hours *and* participated in more collective protest actions. When compared to 2002, between 2003 and 2018 collective action was unsurprisingly less intense, even for the "activists"; however, the polarization persisted with these activists, who were more likely to mobilize during moments of mass protest. Meanwhile, the second group of "non-activists" seem to have been demobilized and demoralized by their experience and consequently neither participated in the protest movement, nor went out of their way to seek additional means of achieving self-help. As they drifted away from political engagement after 2002, those in the latter group tended to adopt comparatively more reactionary or conservative attitudes but were remobilized by causes like Blumberg's anti-crime movement and the 2012–13 wave of protests against the Cristina Kirchner government.

Toward a Theoretical Framework

The conglomeration of results from this research has shed new light on the scant existing literature about how citizens who suffer personal impoverishment and proletarianization from the middle class take decisions about how to confront hardship. Figure 5.1 was designed as a theoretical framework to illustrate the interrelationship between the various different concepts that influence such responses. The ultimate "response" preference is depicted as the inner circle, which is the result of how their biographical characteristics (the second circle that surrounds the response) interact with spaces (shown by the arrows) to engage in any one of the four classifications of action (the four orbiting circles). These "spaces" for action themselves change with time depending on the spaces that open and close for alternative actions (illustrated by the linking "arches"), and with the existing economic and political contexts, which constitute the level of hegemonic control possessed by the dominant class and the fluctuating consent to rule that it manages to secure from the struggling middle class. All the while, responses (and biographical features) are also influenced by capitalism's structures and the middle-class dispositions or *habitus* (the third "outer" circle) that tend them toward individual work-based or entrepreneurial actions as a default response.

Lessons from Argentina

One of the arguments advanced in this book is that the middle class has been a historically important political actor in Argentina and continues to be so. We have seen how middle-class mobilization has

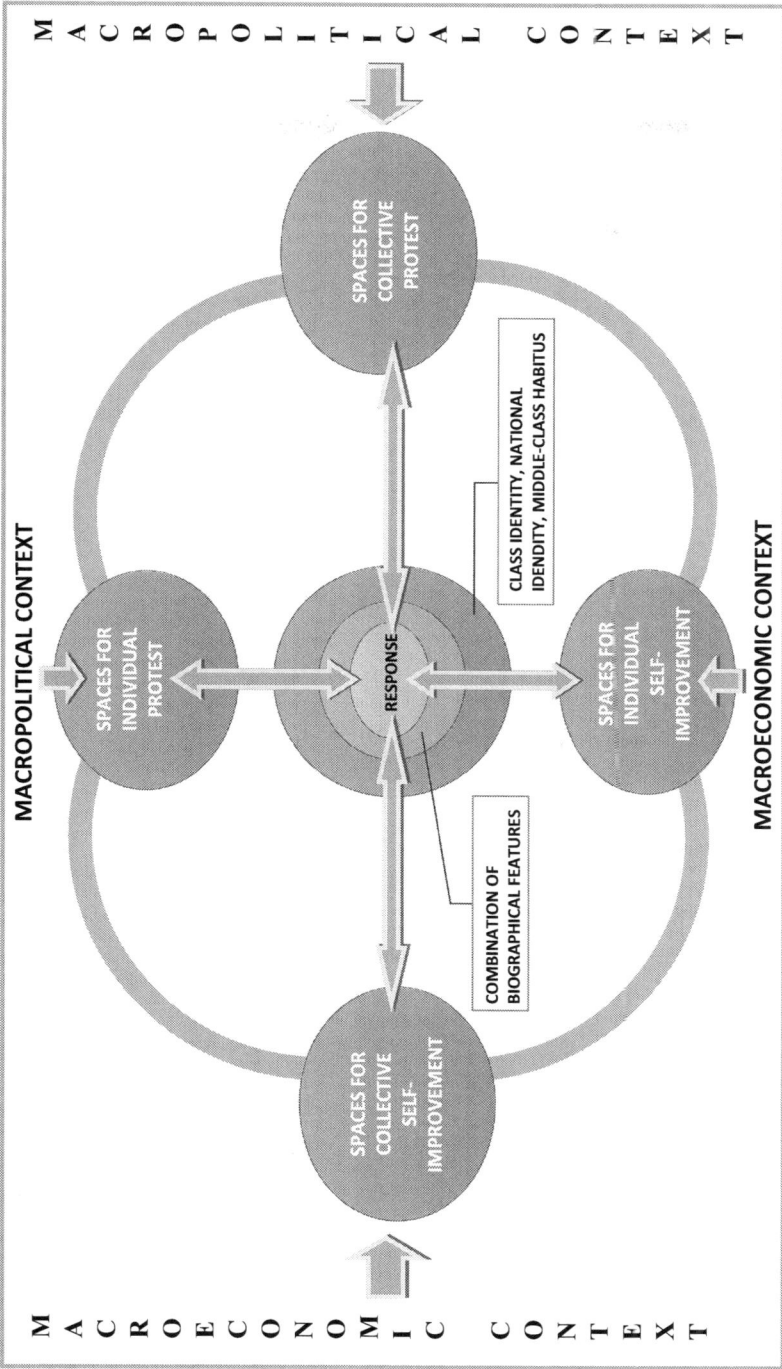

Figure 5.1 Theoretical Framework to Explain Middle-Class Responses to Impoverishment.
Source: Author.

been subject to cycles of contention, with those within it experiencing periods of mobilization and demobilization, including those sectors who have suffered hardship or even proletarianization. They are most likely to transform their responses from economic activities into political demand-making during macroeconomic crises or political turmoil. However, the size and radicalism of the emerging movement on each occasion also depends on the extent to which the ruling class is able to secure consent to govern and secure a hegemonic consensus. Yet, this hegemony does not simply break down on its own, nor does it do so even after an economic and political crisis such as Argentina endured in 2001–02, or for that matter Iceland in 2008–09, Spain or Greece in 2011 and so on. Instead, while such circumstances certainly precipitate objective transformations in power relations, there is no inevitability that impoverished middle-class citizens will revolt against their social conditions either.

On the contrary, these groups are subject to the daily routines and practices that are inherent in capitalism and which reproduce their subordination to the very ideas that support the dominant class (Barker, 2008), while the nature and injustice of their own exploitation is disguised. In this sense, it is unsurprising that as Argentina's economic growth was restored after 2003, the concerns of the new poor shifted away from the goals of direct democracy, political accountability and social transformation toward those that preoccupy the dominant class itself, such as crime and the protection of private property. Here some lessons are offered for the social movements, trade unions, political parties, governments and NGOs based on the findings in this book.

Lessons for Social Movements

In terms of the social movements, how framing processes are set in motion which can be used to further delegitimize and expose the dominant class' authority to rule (Snow *et al.*, 1986), while building counterhegemonic alternatives to replace it requires exploration. It is the movement's ability to capitalize on the correct frames effectively, which will ultimately determine the size of participation in mobilization and its success. The potential of a framing process also depends upon the populations' access to mobilizing vehicles that are available for them to act through. Framing has far greater possibilities for success where permanent rather than temporary mobilizing vehicles exist. Where system-critical framing (McAdam, McCarthy and Zald, 1996) emerges (whereby blame is shifted from the individual to the system), it is unlikely that collective mobilizations for social change will last long if the campaign is limited to a protest movement that can quickly disintegrate once the dominant class enacts defensive strategies to both accommodate and repress it (as happened in Argentina). The movement's mobilizing vehicles must develop mechanisms to increase their permanence, so as to counteract elite attempts to break it down and reestablish political and economic models that reassert their own interests.

In order to foster such collective action, among the struggling middle class collective demands must be framed in a way that (a) prompts them to question the legitimacy of the prevailing economic and political model and the dominant class' authority to rule, (b) provides permanent mobilizing vehicles through which they can organize, (c) may also help stimulate solidarity with those from the working class and structurally poor and (d) is sensitive to the middle-class *habitus* and resonates with their cultural understandings. This way the potential for a politicizing impact is maximized.

Economic grievances require shared meanings and definitions among middle-class citizens to also be applied to their own situations. This is what mobilizes those who are aggrieved about their circumstances to take action. Aside from a collective sense of grievance, they must also feel optimistic enough about their ability to change their circumstances by *acting* collectively (McAdam, McCarthy and Zald, 1996:5). Therefore, the mobilizing mechanisms that are devised here must provide real and regular forums through which such citizens can identify with the injustice to which they are subject, while becoming aware that these grievances are also shared by a large number of others. Writing during the height of the uprisings in Argentina, de Lucía (2002) argued that the movement against the consolidation of the hegemonic order "must also seek to highlight the weakness of reformist projects that are offered to citizens within capitalism" and "should expose the false neutrality of the state whilst revealing its bourgeois character." Mechanisms are proposed here that foster this consciousness.

A Heuristic Approach to Mobilization

Social movements wishing to politicize and engage struggling middle-class citizens in transformative grassroots social movements must take as the starting point the fact that exploited groups experience deprivation and oppression within a concrete setting, not as the end result of large and abstract processes. Therefore, any actions that social movements can use that seek to facilitate the process of politicization must draw attention to the exploitative conditions under which citizens live. They should also highlight the structures and relationships that reproduce these conditions, but which are not observable other than through the particular phenomena or events they produce (Wainwright, 1994:7).

As Piven and Cloward (1977:20) express, it is after all, the daily experience of people that shapes their grievances, establishes the measure of their demands and draws out the targets of their anger. Yet, for the struggling middle class, their experiences of hardship should not merely be understood as temporary incidences of deprivation, but should provide opportunities to (i) discover shared class interests with other subaltern classes and thus establish the foundations of a movement that poses a sustained multisectoral challenge from below and (ii) integrate socially with other dominated classes in society so that solidarity is fostered and the social totality becomes the target of political opposition rather than being fought as atomized struggles. Experience-based learning like this can only result from bringing together struggling middle-class citizens with blue-collar workers, the unemployed and structurally impoverished in regular forums so that they can interact closely with each other and develop relationships and mutual trust. In this environment, fertile ground is created for shared grievances to be identified and a cross-class movement to form. Exploited groups will then be able to combine their fragmented knowledge so that the hidden structures of their oppression are brought within participants' "cognitive reach" (Barker and Cox, 2002).

Another crucial aspect of this is that the types of "oppositional" collective actions and protests that are usually bound to a specific, apparently isolated and "local" experience are transformed into ones that target the social totality. "Local" protests in Argentina include the *piqueteros'* road blockages, which are performed so as to demand improvements in social assistance programs, trade unions' strikes and demonstrations for dignified salaries or labor rights, and cross-class movements encompassing lower-middle-class consumers, self-employed, students, pensioners and other workers like the multisectorial assemblies that emerged from the 2016 *Tarifazo* protests. However, instead, seemingly disparate struggles can be brought together into more widely encompassing and radical counterhegemonic projects through the foundation of an umbrella movement that fosters cross-class collaborations. The Peoples' Assembly Against Austerity (PAAA) in the UK and founded in 2013 is an example of this. While it only had limited short-term success, it paved the way for the rise of Jeremy Corbyn and the resurgence of the Labor Party under a socialist project against neoliberalism and austerity, and which by 2016 had become the largest left-wing party in Europe. In the Laclauian sense, the way that a multisectoral alliance has been constructed in a form of populism that embodies popular traditions of ordinary people's resistance against the powerful will outlast class ideologies as these traditions are the residue of "irreducible historical experience." A similar project to the PAAA, the *Constituyente Social,*[1] was also launched in Argentina in 2008. This brought together a thousand social and community organizations to promote a process of debate and popular organizing. Coordinated via a network of local assemblies, it sought to cultivate a new, multisector political and social vehicle to foster sovereignty, equality and participatory democracy and aid the capacity for self-organization. It declared that it wished to answer the popular refrain from 2001 *que se vayan todos* (get rid of them all) with the response *que venga el pueblo* (the people are coming). The project eventually stalled three years later, but has the local organizing structures in place to be revived in Argentina.

Part of the explanation for the dissolution of the protest movement in Argentina post-2003 was that the middle class lost sight of its initial goals of systemic change and many instead started scapegoating other subaltern sectors for their plight. The increasing postcrisis precariousness and the frustration and tension generated by the state of subordination in which they found themselves led some of those in the struggling middle class to attempt to preserve its threatened social status by drawing a dividing line in society "below" rather than "above" themselves, targeting immigrants, *piqueteros*, the poor, trade unionists and, more recently, those from indigenous communities like the Mapuche People rather than the capitalist class and President Macri's government in whose interests Cambiemos governs.

It is claimed that the history of "identity politics" and organizing around specific individual and collective identities is one that has emerged as a result of the working class' history of defeats and retreats, rather than the postmodernist assertion that it is a natural consequence of changing industrial conditions and a "learned correction" from the totalitarianism of earlier movements (Callinicos, 1988; Barker and Dale, 1998). Therefore, it is unsurprising that the struggling middle class learned the wrong lessons from their own radical movement's defeat in Argentina after 2001–02 either in the sense that as a radical actor, its demands became assimilated, diluted or institutionalized. Others became disgruntled with the National Popular model that emerged from it in the years following 2003. This was true even for those who had once participated in the neighborhood assemblies, *cacerolazos* and street protests alongside movements of the unemployed, workers and shanty town poor. When the carnival of insurgency had died down after 2003 and the focus of daily life returned to the mundane struggle to make ends meet, many of these citizens began to search for who was to blame for their "political defeat" and in doing so turned against their former allies named above.

Class struggle is, therefore, not merely fought *between* classes but also *within* them, because of the practical and theoretical sense that they make out of the concrete situations they find themselves in. Social movements that seek material improvements for the struggling middle class should thus unite their struggles with other sectors while at the same time removing the tensions that are created between them during periods when a surplus army of labor exists in the capitalist economy (and they come to see themselves as enemies in the competition for jobs), while also finding mechanisms to ensure that they attribute their social descent to systemic causes.

Creating and expanding sites of social integration and collective action can help to reverse the fear and distrust that exist between the new and structural poor and between middle and working class. Currently, the main "site of interaction" between them in urban Argentina outside shopping queues or public transport is the *piquetero* roadblock – where citizens lives are disrupted, providing a recipe for tension and atomization, rather than solidarity. *Piquetes* are understood to infringe on the fundamental value of "freedom of movement" in the eyes of the middle class. Positive social interactions, such as those that occurred on the streets during the 2001–02 protests or through the barter clubs, have been frequently replaced by largely negative ones since then. However, trust, solidarity, shared visions for self-improvement can be reconstructed via the promotion of positive "sites of interaction."

Social movements often concerned with mobilizing street protests, should therefore refocus their energies toward promoting regular involvement in collective self-help projects in the solidarity economy like barter clubs, workers cooperatives and community kitchens. Indeed, multisectoral approaches like these are already promoted by autonomist-inspired social movements in Argentina, such as the Darío Santillán Popular Front (FPDS) and the Confederation of Popular Economy Workers (CTEP). Such strategies will broaden the scope of collective action and provide alternatives which demonstrate to participants (through their own practical experience) that these alternatives to individualist, profit-driven activities of the existing economic system are both workable and possible. Autonomous grassroots social movements are also uniquely placed to stimulate interest in these activities among struggling middle-class Argentinians, because as we saw, many in this stratum regard the trade unions or political parties with deep suspicion.

In addition for social movements, the advantage of promoting more low-intensity, day-to-day activities, rather than regularly mobilizing protest, is that it encourages an ongoing form of contact with and among its participants (in this case, the struggling middle class). It also avoids the possibility of "protest fatigue," which happens when protests are held too often on issues that are too familiar (Wilson, 2001:35). Thus, collective self-help or solidarity economy activities can help to overcome protest movements' tendency to be short-lived (Croucher, 1987).

Having said that, most movements would not want to sidelined or replace protests entirely with the solidarity economy. On the contrary, collective self-help activities should be seen as a complement to them, acting as an incubator in which the "good sense" that Gramsci describes is cultivated and where counterhegemonic imaginaries can develop in citizens' minds and increase the effectiveness of protest actions to pressure for change to emerge at a later time. Such actions will provide a base upon which to build and engage non-political participants in the kind of debates that engender longer term politicization, so that protest objectives become more radical, the numbers of participants increases and the movement has a greater chance of securing lasting, social change, especially when a crisis of hegemony presents the opportunity to do so.

As we saw, the workplace can also play a mobilizing role under certain conditions for the struggling middle class. Furthermore, in a society where life projects are increasingly built around consumer choice rather than around work, professional skills or jobs (Bauman, 1998), and in which Argentina's struggling middle class construct their own subjective middle-class identities based upon their capacity for *consumption* rather than *production* (or their labor position with respect to capital), mechanisms must be found to help reformulate the idea that one's class position should be a product of one's place within the realm of the latter. This process would help either encourage an acceptance of their proletarianized, working-class reality or that their class interests lie more closely with the poor than the rich. In doing so, this would break down the barriers that prevent them from building alliances with working-class and unemployed movements.

Mobilizing the Non-Activists: Politicizing the Anti-Politics

While there is no doubt that the scale of collective action during 2002 was widespread and unprecedented among Argentina's struggling middle class, it is important to put this into perspective. Seventy-two percent of those surveyed at the height of the postcrisis cycle of contention in 2002 did not take part in any collective actions whatsoever in the preceding six months. Four in five refrained from taking to the streets in protest. In some ways therefore, the question that is most important of all for progressive social movements that wish to encourage middle-class participation in collective action, is how to reinvigorate the unengaged silent majority of "non-activists." This is no easy task, given that through their alienation they will have lost either their belief or willingness even to try and improve their own lives, let alone those of others, through demand-making or contentious action.

In seeking to achieve their civic engagement, Minujín (2007) calls for cooperation between the state, civil society and the business sector. He argues that the involvement of the struggling middle class in public space should be encouraged by taking advantage of their high cultural values, social "connectedness" and desire for civic participation. He cites placing education at the heart of initiatives to achieve their reintegration into society. He also calls upon governments to implement public policies that encourage:

- The expansion of public space
- Increased citizenship participation in democratic decision-making by promoting citizen observatories and participatory budgeting

- Improved cultural spaces and access to technology, especially for young people
- Provision of high-quality public services
- Broadening social protection
- Tackling discrimination of all kinds
- Assisting microfinance initiatives

However, such policies will ultimately do little to directly reverse some of the problems identified in this book, such as the growing sense of fear and distrust that exists between the new and long-term poor or *la grieta* – Argentina's social divide. Nor would these measures necessarily create a greater sense of solidarity in society. Most importantly, they would do nothing to create counterhegemonic institutions that tackle the root causes of Argentina's social and economic problems. Such measures would also need to be pursued.

Another challenge for social movements seeking the participation of struggling middle-class citizens is to ask, what actions constitute "belonging to" it? The boundaries between movements and the society and culture from which they emerge are indefinite and "fuzzy" (Marwell and Oliver, 1984). Participation can range from more tangible actions, like marching in demonstrations or signing petitions, to less concrete forms of protest. For example, one may instigate a subtle "collective protest" merely through a conversation with a group of friends or work colleagues. Yet, these are the kinds of actions that do not appear in survey data, are difficult to detect in in-depth interviews, nor are they formalized in any way. Nor, indeed, would the participants in them even necessarily understand them to be "political acts."

Research by Zurawicki and Braidot (2005:1107) has, for instance, found that the most common form of resistance among "middle-class Argentinians" during the crisis was actually "virtual" rather than "visible" protest. 36.5% of their sample engaged in some kind of protest communication over the Internet, greatly exceeding the 20% proportion whom we found participated in street demonstrations or neighborhood assemblies. The survey authors cited the "anonymity and convenience" provided by social and electronic media, as well as their "trust in its power" to explain why participation rates in virtual protests were particularly high. If the Internet was a primary mode of protest in the county in 2001, the potential it holds as a protest tool today is innumerably greater, given that Internet access in the country has multiplied tenfold since then (CABASE, 2017). Indeed, social media has played a vital role in protest mobilization and as an initial forum for engagement in the protest movement for "non-activists." It opened a gateway to more contentious forms of street protest during the Arab Spring revolts and the *Indignados* uprisings in Spain (Mason, 2012), as well as during Argentina's own anti-government 8-N (8 November) protest movement in 2012 (*La Nación*, 2012). With this in mind, grassroots social movements should look to further incorporate the Internet and social media into their mobilizing strategies, for example, by establishing interactive discussion forums to cultivate the recognition of shared grievances and awareness about protests and solidarity economy activities. Thus, they would act as forms of virtual mobilizing "spaces" in lieu of the factory or office floor.

"Politics" continues to maintain an awful reputation in Argentina. This was confirmed by the research participants, before, during and after the 2002 crisis. However, Argentinians have a long history of disguising political acts as "apolitical." This is a technique borne of necessity, having lived under repressive military dictatorships for the vast majority of the twentieth century until democracy was restored in 1983. In this way, different protest groups (including the Mothers of the Plaza de Mayo in the late 1970s under the military Junta) have managed to secure broader public support while avoiding the repressive excesses of the state apparatus by framing their movement as non-threatening and apolitical. The Mothers framed their roles as "mothers and wives" who were simply conveying their unbearable grief through the disappearance of their children during the Dirty War (Radcliffe and Westwood, 1993:18). Thus, they ensured that their public protests from 1977 onward – which demanded that those responsible be brought to justice – were broadly tolerated by the ruling military Junta, which found it difficult to credibly categories these women as "internal enemies" or targets of the *National Security Doctrine* Instead they tried to depict them as "crazy women."

Anti-political discourse has been repeatedly used in Argentina by populists, revolutionaries and nationalists, all of whom have strongly criticized representative democracy ever since the 1920s. This includes President Menem in the 1990s, and Néstor Kirchner and Cristina Kirchner post-2003, and Mauricio Macri, all of whom attempted to promote themselves as distant from the political establishment and presented politicians as an obstacle to the country's destined greatness (Armony and Armony, 2005:41).

With reference to Argentina's struggling middle class, as our interviews suggest, "politics" remains synonymous with "corruption" in their minds. They are still highly cynical of politicians and participation in "politics," irrespective of their age, gender or occupation. The only exceptions were those who had prior engagement as political activists, who were not put off by overtly "political" activity. It is for these reasons that movements would need to foster "non-activist" participation in *political* acts, without these actions initially being construed as "political" (which would otherwise deter them). Building their confidence to join collective protests and raising their awareness of their own exploitation will occur simultaneously. As the philosopher Slavoj Žižek (2000) explained, in an age where there has been a "radical de-politicization of the economy," the question is how to foster a politicizing politics. This has to start by taking the particularity of the demands of a certain struggle (those of the middle class, in this instance), but aiming it at something that transcends these *particular* demands so that universalism can emerge.

Fostering the politicization of "non-activists" must be attempted, by nurturing the proliferation of the informal and unconscious political acts mentioned in Chapter 4, so as to set off a series of events and activities that will lead to a "process of engagement" that then precipitate more direct and confrontational acts of collective protest. Transforming subtle, yet seemingly *apolitical* acts, such as dissenting conversations or social media exchanges which complain about one's own personal hardship, into involvement in some kind of collective self-improvement action, with the eventual aim of establishing counterhegemonic social, economic and political projects that are both popular and widely used is a challenge they face.[2]

As earlier attempts to construct counterhegemonic political structures like the assemblies died away and their participation in grassroots resistance dwindled, so did movement participants' belief that it was possible to achieve its aim of a more participatory democracy, where the old politicians would genuinely somehow be replaced. Instead, many developed a dual-consciousness at the time whereby they wished to challenge the system from below, yet at the same time they realized that they were ideologically bound to it. After months of intense struggle, they became disheartened and lost the belief that transformational change was truly possible. In the absence of regular engagement in counterhegemonic forums that confronted the political and economic status quo after 2003, their alternative politics had no platform to sustain itself in the long term, hence the capitulation to supporting Néstor Kirchner's attempts to embody the QSVT and anti-establishment spirit during his presidency. This was understood to be the route capable of providing the greatest possible change within the capitalist system. The middle class returned to their pre-*Argentinazo* understanding of politics as "the practice of the government but the business of the people" (Mazzoni, 2007:189), by delegating responsibility for achieving political change into the hands of reformist representatives (albeit with "new faces") who would instead serve the interests of the domestic bourgeoisie alongside the poor and working class. This need to maintain active citizenship and involvement in the movement is another reason why maintaining the "doing" side of things through collective self-improvement projects in the "now," rather than revert to being a passive agent is so crucial to the restoration of a political challenge from below (Holloway, 2002).

Struggling middle-class Argentinians demonstrated an enduring belief in economic self-reliance. This is because as mentioned, they tend to possess minimalist perceptions of their citizenship, expecting the state to provide little for them in the way of *social* and *economic* benefits but, in contrast demanding that as an entity, the state should guarantee their *political* rights. Returning to our categorization of the struggling middle class as "occasional citizens," encouraging involvement in collective self-help activities (rather than necessarily protest actions) also fits more closely with their values in terms of securing their own economic well-being, without the intervention of the state. Methods of fostering citizen empowerment in the economic sphere must be found so that the link to political action can be reinvigorated and capitulation to Argentina's traditional "delegative democracy" model (O'Donnell, 1994) can be overcome.

Despite their hardship, squeezed middle-class citizens' belief in meritocratic ideals remained high, despite having fallen significantly in the years following the 2002 crisis. Educational achievement, central to the middle-class Argentinian imaginary, also remained the aspiration even if it no longer acts as a guarantee of social mobility. However, in the post-crisis milieu, educational qualifications have assumed more importance as an alternative status symbol and as a safety net against indigence, rather than as a guarantee of actually landing a professional career once skilled work was in much shorter supply. Thus frames which appeal to the injustice of possessing superior education and of working hard, yet not being able to enjoy a corresponding quality of life socially and materially, would be important starting points for movement organizers to use to mobilize those from this social stratum. As Mason (2012) notes with reference to the Arab Spring, and *Indignados* uprisings in Spain and elsewhere, the contradiction between university graduates being promised upward social mobility and prosperity as laid out in the contemporary social contract, yet the reality of their precariousness and downward mobility is what helped fan the flames of revolt, especially among the young.

Second, as mentioned earlier, the middle class in Argentina, and often beyond, understand their citizenship in "political" and not "social" or "economic" terms. In this regard, middle-class citizens are more receptive to justice frames that exploit the low regard they hold for their political leaders rather than social or economic demands like an increase in state welfare or a more redistributive tax system. Mobilizing frames that pertain to the lack of democratic accountability have also been successful, given that "political corruption" remains a prime concern among this sector since 2002. Social movement leaders should make references to the fact that the struggling middle class possess a very high level of education, employment experience and hardworking mentality but they have not reached the status they deserve because their politicians have "let them down." In short, in view of Argentina's potential "national greatness," it must be pragmatically emphasized that they "deserve better," an idea that Donald Trump has seized upon in the USA.

"Equality before the law" is a further value that those in this stratum hold dear. Consequently, proposed frames must challenge the enormous gender disadvantages that women face (in terms of salaries, opportunities for promotion etc.) and which need to be reversed through stricter legislation. New poverty continues to be a feminized phenomenon and age discrimination also continues to be prevalent in the Argentinian

labor market, despite nominal attempts by federal government administrations to legislate against it. In order to enfranchise the middle aged in
the protest movement, appeals should be made to the difficulty of finding
work over the age of 40 and the governments' feeble response to such
discrimination. These appeals should be littered with references to the
prosperous pasts of those in this age group, so as to attempt to make
them question why things cannot be "how they used to be."

Palomino (2005:24) observed that, ultimately, the prospects for the impoverished Argentinian middle class to successfully achieve their desired
outcomes through their collective protests were inherently weak because
of the incongruence between the tactics and demands among different
sections of the broader movement. On the one hand, middle class-led
movements possessed maximalist demands (the replacement of an exhausted political system with direct democracy), but pursued them only
through *minimalist* actions (such as creating the assemblies to set an example "from the bottom up" and establishing micro-projects like soup
kitchens and unemployment centers at community level). Meanwhile, the
structural poor had only *minimalist* demands, like food and jobs, but
employed *maximalist* actions through the *piqueteros'* mass street protests
helped paralyze the production process, which were sometimes violent
and targeted the institutions of power. Had the two movements firstly
cooperated and secondly more extensively coordinated their maximalist
aims *and* actions, the potential they had to achieve the transformative
change the sought during 2001–02 would have been significantly greater.

The research in this book also reveals that young adults are significantly overrepresented among the new poor. As the main "victims" of
new poverty, unemployment and downward intergenerational mobility,
movements and parties have and will no doubt continue to target university campuses. Indeed, Argentina maintains relatively high levels of
university access among the poorest sectors of society, so there is no more
appropriate "incubator" or site of social integration from which to unite
the young-adult children of the new and structural poor.

Lessons for Political Parties and Trade Unions

Trust in political parties of any creed remains low. They seem inadequate
as potential mobilizing vehicles for the struggling middle class, as much
in Argentina as in many other countries we have observed. In Argentina
itself, the Kirchnerist *Frente para la Victoria* were initially able to capture
support from much of the progressive middle class, although they have
since become understood to be too "Peronist" and tainted by corruption
scandals. Meanwhile, the Civic Coalition, Socialists and the Radicals
and PRO to some extent picked up support from those in this stratum in
the 2011 and especially in 2015 elections. Meanwhile, Marxist-Leninist
parties, notably the *Frente de Izquierda y de los Trabajadores* (FIT), have

failed to achieve any electoral breakthrough since 2001 or capitalize on the anti-system and even anti-capitalist sentiment that followed the *Argentinazo* and disenchantment with *Kirchnerismo*. Nor do they appear on the electoral radar for "non-activists" in this stratum, as left-wing parties combined failed to reach even 5% of votes at the August 2015 PASO (first round) elections.[3] Clearly, there was support for PRO and *Cambiemos* during the 2015 election, but it began to disintegrate from 2016 onward. Curiously, the self-defined position of the pauperized middle class on the political spectrum did not change significantly between 1995, 2002 or 2005. Most middle-class Argentinians neither define as "left-wing" or "right-wing."

Podemos and *Ciudadanos* in Spain, Syriza (until the point of taking power in Greece in 2015), Labour in the UK and both the Left-Green Movement and Pirate Party in Iceland and Jean-Luc Mélenchon for La France Insoumise in France were able to capture struggling middle-class votes through presenting themselves as "anti-establishment" electoral options, as was Donald Trump in the USA. Those that have enjoyed greatest success reflected the sentiments expressed by interview participants. They have shed a lot of the dogmatic language used especially by the Left. *Podemos* in Spain have even abandoned the notion of a left-right divide, which as suggested in the previous paragraph, sometimes alienates those who have never seen themselves as "on the left" due to the historical baggage associated with socialism, or how its key principles (greater state interventionism, restrictions on capital accumulation or property etc.) are believed to violate middle-class values of "liberty" and self-sustainability. Nevertheless, both Bernie Sanders (when he stood as US Presidential candidate for the Democrats) and Jeremy Corbyn (Leader of the Labour Party in the UK) explicitly self-define as "socialists," which provides counterevidence in terms of their success in gathering support from significant parts of the middle class.

Political forms of organization have become easy for Peronism and other political forces to penetrate, manipulate and co-opt. Therefore, more impermeable organizational forms, which are embedded in *economic* as opposed to political activity, will have a better chance of withstanding such attempts. It would, after all, be much more difficult for a *puntero* to hold sway over the political decisions made by group of participants in a project that has *economic* goals, because it would involve them having to also become part of their everyday productive practices (unlike those of a political grouping, which meets on a more ad hoc basis).

As both the results of this study and the practical experience of Argentinian politics in recent years have illustrated, to revert back to orthodox and dogmatic mechanisms of trying to politicize the struggling middle class through top-down political parties will probably end in failure. The collective self-improvement form which adopts a double economic *and* politicizing function in order to achieve this may be more fruitful.

Political parties continue to be held in low regard and are seen as vehicles for building individuals' supporter bases while lacking convictions. The generally abysmal reputation that "politics" has, has meant that social movements should consider finding ways of using *economic* forms of collective organization as their mobilizing vehicles for political engagement, *not* the traditional political party structure as such, even though pragmatically they may need to be linked to electoral vehicles.

Faith in the trade unions remains low, with the exception being among those working in specific public-sector professions. This is partly because they have been tainted by the state's corporatist apparatus and the historically contradictory role of the CGT in defending worker rights. The contradiction is that for many struggling middle-class workers, unions are seen as an enemy even though they campaign and often win improvements in labor rights, conditions and salaries that the very citizens who criticize them benefit from. Most of those interviewed were unable to distinguish between the different union confederations or their positions in relation to the state apparatus or degree of independence from political parties. The intensity with which the unions are despised is particularly unique to Argentina, while in most of Europe and North America they remain a potential mobilizing vehicle, despite sometimes being vilified in the corporate media.

Lessons for Governments and NGOs

Governments and NGOs should recognize and take advantage of the extensive human capital that the struggling middle class possess, but which lies dormant or underutilized through such citizens' unemployment or low-skilled jobs (for which they are overqualified). Therefore, they should look to establish cooperatives through which unemployed middle-class citizens teach their professional skills (languages, information technology, business management etc.) to working-class or structurally poor communities who can then utilize these skills themselves to establish or improve their own occupational mobility or social/cooperative enterprises through their involvement in unemployed workers' movements. In this way, this would provide the "altruistic vision" that appeals to struggling middle-class citizens' mindset by supporting the most deprived in society while at the same securing employment themselves. Valuable work experience in teaching capacities will be good for the young, and self-esteem will be restored for such downwardly mobile citizens.

Their salaries should be paid for either by the state or in exchange for services that cooperative members would provide to their unemployed middle-class colleague (babysitting, manual labor etc.) as a form of time bank scheme. This would, therefore, be funded in ways that avoid co-optation by the capitalist state and would help to strengthen those *piquetero*-run autonomist cooperatives, by endowing its members with new capabilities and skills. By fostering cross-class interactions in this way, it will also contribute to reducing the fear and distrust.

Middle-Class Radicalism Globally: Past, Present and Future

This book has provided an in-depth examination of how the struggling middle class in Argentina has responded to pauperization and downward social mobility. We have traced their political mobilization and demobilization over the past three decades and have asked why some join social movements while others refrain from doing so, sometimes in spite of macroeconomic and political crises and their own pauperization.

Further cross-national comparative work that analyzes how the middle class resists underemployment, joblessness or downward mobility is needed, but a brief and provisional attempt was made here. We have identified that politicization is more likely to occur in countries where, on the one hand, the dominant class finds itself losing (neoliberal) hegemonic control and the "consent to rule" from its citizens and, on the other, sufficient political spaces exist for citizens to engage in collective action. Interestingly, the radicalization of a significant part of the middle class has been witnessed not just in countries where there is a strong political culture of middle-class engagement in collective action, like Greece or Spain, but also in those like Iceland and Cyprus, where the middle class has a history of expressing their political dissatisfaction more passively under neoliberalism, and without acting collectively or taking their protests to the streets. In these instances, political radicalization was unexpected and often accompanied by crises of political legitimacy. These protest movements have adopted horizontal organizing, and leadership structures and change has been agitated for outside political party structures, trade unions or formal organizations. They have also adopted many of the strategies and protest methods that were learned precisely from Argentina's middle class revolt. In contrast, in national contexts where wide-scale proletarianization has occurred but where the dominant class has successfully enacted "defensive strategies" of control, resistance has tended to confine itself to the economic realm through self-improvement strategies, such as entrepreneurship, working additional hours or even emigration. Russia and South Africa are examples of this scenario that were analyzed.

Cross-national comparative work is also required because the social, political and economic contexts under which struggling middle-class sectors have both emerged and exist today are vastly distinct in different societies. Further, it must be remembered that new poor mobilization is not inevitably politically "progressive" and may indeed also take a reactionary or even fascist turn. Much of the EU has voted in right-wing conservative governments since the 2008 global crisis, and fascism is on the rise again there and around the world. It has captured support from at least some elements of the proletarianized middle class. Meanwhile, Donald Trump has captured a sizable proportion of these votes on the back of his vehemently nationalist and anti-immigrant rhetoric and those with fascist tendencies like Jair Messias Bolsonaro even became President of Brazil in January 2019. Such cross-national comparisons will help to shed light on the political trajectories and manifestations that different struggling middle class movements might adopt.

Certain universal values that the pauperized middle class possess – such as aspiration, education and hard work – cut across national boundaries and should be borne in mind by social movement coordinators in the mobilizing frames they use to engage them in collective action. However, there are also differences in these values, which must be explored further. For example, we discussed how in Argentina, justice frames should focus on the infringement of democratic citizenship rather than on social and economic rights. Meanwhile in Russia, due to the legacy of state socialism and welfare protection, the opposite is the case. References to loss of social protection and the "right" to a certain standard of living are likely to induce more of a mobilizing impact there than frames that appeal to their "democratic rights" or the demand for immediate political participation. A tradition of top-down government and weak democracy in Russia necessitates a different approach in that country.

Neoliberalism's 2001–02 hegemonic crisis in Argentina swept through the entire spectrum of capitalism's political, judicial, religious and economic institutions. The mobilizing structures that the middle class were involved in were more organic and amorphous, originating in spontaneous and informally organized gatherings, which turned into politically independent civil society associations and solidarity economy activities. Struggling middle class citizens' established and participated in innovative and exciting counterhegemonic projects, such as the neighborhood assemblies, workers' cooperatives, the barter system and mass protest through the *cacerolazos*. The sheer scale of involvement demonstrates that the mass mobilization of the middle class is possible under certain conditions, including those whereby they undergo actions with those in other deprived sectors of society and when they come to develop a shared consciousness as part of an exploited class, albeit temporarily.

However, while the refusal of many neighborhood assemblies and other 2001 movements to negotiate with the state or become institutionalized (Svampa and Corral, 2006) was wise in the sense that it helped them to avoid compromising their counterhegemonic project, such decisions meant they were trapped in a double bind. Without some kind of permanent alternative, noninstitutionalized mobilizing vehicle, it was impossible to maintain the momentum of collective action much beyond 2002. This shortcoming of the movement caused its eventual retreat and led to a return of the status quo – representative democracy (albeit with more accessible channels for democratic participation) and capitalism (in a post-neoliberal, rather than an entirely neoliberal form).

Nearly two decades after the 2001 crisis, Argentina once again finds itself on the precipice of a neoliberal crisis and an economic and social catastrophe. Record indebtedness and IMF-domination have returned, salaries are the second lowest in Latin America, poverty has soared and the cost of living has risen 122% between 2015 and 2018 (Cantamutto, 2018). In many ways, the movement which formed in December 2001 and that demanded ¡*que se vayan todos*! has been defeated. Many in the middle class who became pauperized but politically radicalized at the time had largely retreated back into private responses by 2003. Some have become demoralized, alienated and even more politically cynical since then. High inflation, the collapse of the peso, the stripping back salaries and social security and the removal of subsidies are some of the reasons that account for the ranks of the new poor being swelled very recently under the *Cambiemos* government.

This book has outlined the cycles of protest in which the middle class, as a historically important actor, has participated and often been the protagonist. These movements have oscillated between progressive and reactionary aims and have shown both solidarity with and antagonism to long-term poor and working-class movements. There is no inevitability about the political trajectory of middle-class led movements, instead their character will both be shaped and will itself shape the hegemonic ideas that exist in society at any point in time.

Detailed analysis of middle-class resistance in Argentina was conducted and references that were made to other national contexts which illustrate that their radicalization could potentially occur anywhere where political legitimacy breaks down, although such mobilization is more likely to arise during major economic or political crises. The leaders of many Western nations have certainly become increasingly worried about the possibility of an outbreak of radical, struggling middle-class protest during the next global economic crisis. This would become even more plausible if a significant proportion of the population were to fall victim to the specter of pauperization or proletarianization again, especially in light of the mass uprisings that have shaken several European countries to their foundations since 2008. According to a recent Eurostat report (2016), 24% of the EU's nonpoor population (or 118 million citizens) live in households that are currently at risk of poverty or social exclusion, in addition to the 9% who are already materially deprived (Eurostat, 2018). Meanwhile in the USA, 45 million people live below the poverty line and four out of five US adults struggle with joblessness, near-poverty or reliance on welfare for at least parts of their lives, in a sign of deteriorating economic security and an elusive American dream.

The principal difference in Western Europe or the USA, compared to Argentina, is that civil society and reformist institutions are much more deeply embedded into the political superstructure. Therefore, the hegemony of the dominant class would surely not disintegrate as easily or as quickly as it did in the latter in 2001. The EU is still suffering from the 2008 sovereign debt crisis, but this could deepen at any time.

There are already signs of a loss of faith in the political system among significant proportions of the population in many EU member-states and the prospect of systemic economic collapse has far from disappeared. At the time of writing in February 2018, Paris and several other French cities are burning, following several weeks of huge "yellow vest" protests and rioting led by struggling middle-class citizens who are tired of austerity, precarity, feeling unrepresented politically and who have faced a loss of social status since the 2008 crisis (Smith, 2018). Like in Argentina in 2001, what has fueled such anger was that these people harbored real hope for change in President Emmanuel Macron's election campaign promises, expectations that were soon dashed in the opening months of his mandate. Supported by three-quarters of the population, the revolt was initially sparked by fuel cost hikes which squeezed them further, but its demands then quickly radicalized. As in Argentina, the rebellion has deliberately rejected interference by political parties or institutions and insists on leaderless decision-making amid a cauldron of distrust in the entire political establishment. Here the "yellow vest" has replaced the saucepan as the symbol of resistance, but the extent to which the movement develops a multisectoral character, mechanisms to sustain itself, and develops a political strategy for change remains to be seen. Similar protests are starting to spread to other major European cities in what is becoming the most recent multi-sectoral protest wave, with significant middle-class participation.

How middle-class citizens respond to financial shocks and their personal social descent looks set to become one of the defining issues of the early twenty-first century. We have a lot to learn from Argentina.

Notes

1 www.constituyentesocial.org.ar.
2 In this way, I seek to utilize the *Widerstand* concept – a criterion used by investigators who were keen to promote opposition to the Nazis in Germany. It allows for more or less any expression of a different view from the official position (including those in the cultural realm) to be labeled "opposition."
3 http://elecciones.gob.ar/admin/ckfinder/userfiles/files/P_V__DEFINITIVO% 20x%20Distrito_PASO%202015(3).pdf.

References

Armony, Ariel and Armony, Victor (2005) 'Indictments, Myths, and Citizen Mobilization in Argentina: A Discourse Analysis' *Latin American Politics and Society*, Vol. 47(4), pp. 27–54.
Atzeni, Maurizio (2010) *Workplace Conflict: Mobilization and solidarity in Argentina*. Basingstoke, Palgrave Macmillan.

Barker, Colin (2008) 'Some Thoughts on Marxism and Social Movements' Introduced at *Micro-conference on Marxism and Social Movements*, Manchester, 16th March 2008.

Barker, Colin and Cox, Laurence (2002) '"What have the Romans ever done for us?" Academic and activist forms of movement theorizing' Paper delivered at *'Alternative Futures and Popular Protest' 8th Annual Conference, April 2002*, Manchester Metropolitan University.

Barker, Colin and Dale, Gareth (1998) 'Protest Waves in Western Europe: A critique of "New Social Movement" Theory' *Critical Sociology*, Vol. 24, pp. 65–104.

Bauman, Zygmunt (1998) *Work, Consumerism and the New Urban Poor*, Oxford, Oxford University Press

CABASE (2017) *Estado de Internet en Argentina y la Región*. Buenos Aires, Camara Argentina de Internet.

Callinicos, Alex (1988) *Making History: Agency, Structure and Change in Social Theory*. Cambridge, Polity Press.

Cantamutto, Francisco (2018) '¿Es posible otro 2001–02?' *La Izquierda Diario*, 30th September 2018.

Croucher, Richard (1987) *We Refuse to Starve in Silence: A History of the National Unemployed Workers' Movement, 1920–46*. London, Lawrence & Whishart Ltd.

Elster, John (1986) *An Introduction to Karl Marx*. Cambridge, Cambridge University Press.

Eurostat (2018) 'People at Risk of Poverty or Social Exclusion' *Luxembourg*, 12th October 2018.

Ferree, Myra and Miller, Frederick (1985) 'Mobilization and Meaning: Toward an Integration of Social Psychological and Resource Perspectives on Social Movements' *Sociological Inquiry*, Vol. 55 (1), pp. 38–61.

Hardt, Michael and Negri, Antonio (2004) *Multitude: War and Democracy in the Age of Empire*. New York, Penguin Press.

Holloway, John (2002) *Change the World Without Taking Power*. London, Pluto Press.

Hyman, Richard (1989) *Strikes*. Basingstoke, Palgrave Macmillan.

Kirchner, Néstor (2003) Inaugural Address. Presidencia de la Nación Argentina. May 25th 2003.

La Nación (2012) 'Internet y las redes sociales, protagonistas del 8-N' 8th November 2012.

López-Levy, Marcela (2004) *We are Millions: Neoliberalism and New Forms of Political Action in Argentina*. London, Latin American Bureau.

de Lucía, Daniel (2002) 'La revuelta de diciembre: hipótesis y perspectivas' *Herramienta* 19.

Mansbridge, Jane (2001) 'The Making of Oppositional Consciousness' in J.J. Mansbridge and A. Morris (eds.), *Oppositional Consciousness: The Subjective Roots of Social Protest*. Chicago, IL, University of Chicago Press, pp. 1–19.

Marwell, Gerald and Oliver, Pamela (1984) 'Collective Action Theory and Social Movements Research' in L. Kriesberg (ed.), *Research in Social Movements, Conflict and Change*. Greenwich, CT, Jai Press, pp. 1–27.

Mason, Paul (2012) *Why It's Kicking off Everywhere: The New Global Revolutions*. London, Verso.

Mazzoni, Maria (2007) 'Política y Empobrecimiento' *Revista de la Facultad*, Vol. 13, pp. 185–211, Argentina, Universidad Nacional de Comahue.

McAdam, Doug, McCarthy, John and Zald, Mayer (1996) *Comparative Perspectives on Social Movements: Political Opportunities, Mobilizing Structures and Cultural Framings*. Cambridge, Cambridge University Press.

Minujín Alberto (2007) *Vulnerabilidad y resiliencia de la clase media en América Latina*. New York, The New School.

O'Donnell, Guillermo (1994) 'Delegative Democracy' *Journal of Democracy*, Vol. 5(1), pp. 55–69.

Palomino, Héctor (2005) 'Los sindicatos y los movimientos sociales emergentes del colapso neoliberal en Argentina' in E. Toledo (ed.), *Sindicatos y Nuevos Movimientos Sociales en América Latina*. Buenos Aires, CLACSO, pp. 19–52.

Piven, Frances and Cloward, Richard (1977) *Poor People's Movements: Why They Succeed, How They Fail*. New York, Vintage Books.

Powers, Nancy (1999) 'Coping with Economic Hardship in Argentina: How Material Interests Affect Individuals' Political Interests' *Canadian Journal of Political Science*, Vol. 32, pp. 521–549.

Radcliffe, Sarah and Westwood, Sallie (1993) *Women and Popular Protest in Latin America*. London, Routledge.

Scully, Maureen and Segal, Amy (2002) 'Passion with an Umbrella: Grassroots Activists in the Workplace' *Social Structure and Organizations Revisited*, Vol. 19, pp. 125–168.

Smith, Saphora (2018) 'Who are France's 'Yellow Jacket' Protesters and What Do They Want?' *NBC News*.

Snow, David, Rochford, Burke, Worden, Steven and Benford, Robert (1986) 'Frame alignment processes, micro-mobilization and movement participation', *American Sociological Review* Vol 51 (4), pp. 464–481.

Svampa, Maristella and Corral, Damian (2006) 'Political Mobilization in Neighborhood Assemblies' in E. Epstein and D. Pion-Berlin (eds.), *Broken Promises? The Argentinean Crisis and Argentinean Democracy*. New York, Lexington Books, pp. 117–141.

Tarrow, Sidney (1998) *Power in Movement: Social Movements and Contentious Politics*. Cambridge, Cambridge University Press.

Tilly, Charles (1978) *From Mobilization to Revolution*. Reading, MA, Addison-Wesley Publishing.

——— (1986) *The Contentious French*. Cambridge, MA, Harvard University Press.

Wainwright, Hilary (1994) *Arguments for a New Left: Answering the Free-Market Right*. Oxford, Blackwell Publishing.

Wilson, John K. (2001) *How the Left Can Win Arguments and Influence People*. New York, New York University Press.

Žižek, Slavoj (2000) *The Ticklish Subject: The Absent Centre of Political Ontology*. London, Verso.

Zurawicki, Leon and Braidot, Néstor (2005) 'Consumers during Crisis: Responses from the Middle Class in Argentina' *Journal of Business Research*, Vol. 58 (8), pp. 1100–1109, Elsevier.

Appendix

Background Information of Interview Participants

	Age (2011)	Gender	Locality/Province	Precrisis (2001)	Postcrisis (2011)	Economic Situation in 2011 Compared to 2002	Labor Trajectory (2011)	Speed of Postcrisis Recovery A = Fast B = Medium C = Slow
Agustina	48	Female	Buenos Aires City	Bilingual executive	Shop assistant	Better	Downward	C
Ana	50	Female	Buenos Aires City	Chief executive, clothing company[a]	Personal assistant in religious organization	Better	Downward	C
Brian	37	Male	Rosario, Santa Fe	University student and restaurant manager[b]	Hostel manager	Better	Upward	A
Camila	26	Female	Buenos Aires City	Secondary school student[c]	University student/ works[b]	Better	Neither	B
Carlos	78	Male	Buenos Aires City	Civil engineer	Retired but employed[b]	Worse	Downward	C
Carolina	23	Female	Piedras Blancas, Entre Rios	Secondary student[c]	Private English teacher[a,b]	Better	Neither	B
Cristina	59	Female	Buenos Aires City	Civil servant	Housewife	Same	Neither	C
Daniela	59	Female	Buenos Aires City	Optician	Architect's assistant	Better	Downward	B
Diego	42	Male	Piedras Blancas, Entre Rios	Factory middle-manager	Middle-manager then recently unemployed	Same	Downward	A

Name	Age	Gender	Location					
Federico	26	Male	Buenos Aires City	Secondary school student[c]	University student/teacher[b]	Better	Neither	B
Franco	35	Male	Posadas, Misiones	Biomedical engineer	Ophthalmological salesman	Better	Neither	B
Graciela	50	Female	Buenos Aires City	Formal employee, utility firm	Informal food enterprise[a]	Same	Downward	C
Jorge	36	Male	La Plata, Buenos Aires Province	University student, employed[b]	Laborer[a]	Same	Downward	B
Julieta	86	Female	La Plata, Buenos Aires Province	Civil servant	Retired	Same	Neither	B
Laura	49	Female	Buenos Aires City	State school teacher	Educational consultant[a,b]	Better	Upward	A
Luis	57	Male	Santa Fe City, Santa Fe	Small business owner	Small business owner	Better	Downward	B
Lucía	63	Female	Posadas, Misiones	Primary teacher	Retired	Better	Neither	B
Magalí	36	Female	Posadas, Misiones	University student[c]	Health center receptionist	Better	Downward	B
Marcos	51	Male	Buenos Aires City	Owner, high street chemist[a]	Taxi driver[a]	Better	Neither	C
Martín	50	Male	Piedras Blancas, Entre Rios	Freight manager	Retired	Better	Neither	C
Matías	21	Male	Posadas, Misiones	Secondary school student[c]	University student/works[b]	Better	Upward	B
Micaela	50	Female	Piedras Blancas, Entre Rios	Kiosk owner[a]	Hairdressers[a,b]	Better	Neither	B

(Continued)

	Age (2011)	Gender	Locality/Province	Precrisis (2001)	Postcrisis (2011)	Economic Situation in 2011 Compared to 2002	Labor Trajectory (2011)	Speed of Postcrisis Recovery A = Fast B = Medium C = Slow
Milagros	30	Female	Posadas, Misiones	University student[c]	Private English teacher[a,b]	Better	Downward	C
Nicolás	49	Male	Buenos Aires City	Full-time biology	Insurance salesman[b]	Better	Downward	C
Pablo	58	Male	Piedras Blancas, Entre Rios	Local government manager	Municipal worker	Better	Neither	B
Romina	21	Female	Rosario, Santa Fe	Secondary school student[c]	University student/works[b]	Better	Neither	B
Santiago	60	Male	Buenos Aires City	Architect[a]	Architect[a] (longer hours, and income, less clients)	Same	Neither	B
Vanesa	26	Female	La Plata, Buenos Aires Province	University student[c]	IT worker[b]	Better	Neither	B
Sofia	31	Female	Santa Fe City, Santa Fe	University student[c]	Shop assistant	Same	Neither	C
Victoria	51	Female	Piedras Blancas, ER	Civil servant	Courier[a,b]	Better	Neither	B
Veronica	20	Female	Piedras Blancas, Entre Rios	School student	Nursery teacher	Better	Neither	B

a Self-employed.
b Part-time.
c Child of unemployed professionals.

Index

Printed in Great Britain
by Amazon